P9-DMT-810

"**Poor Richard's Good Advice.** With all great new things comes a proliferation of hucksters and snake-oil salesmen, and the Internet is no exception. The antidote to this swirl of confusion lies in Peter Kent's *Poor Richard's Web Site.* The analogy to Ben Franklin's volume is appropriate: the book is filled with the kind of straightforward information the Founding Father himself would have appreciated."

—Jennifer Buckendorff
amazon.com

"This book is **one of the best I've found for going from zero** Web knowledge to having a site up and functioning."

—Ron Burk
Windows Developers Journal

"We liked the level of rich, high-quality details that went into this publication. You can tell that Kent has poured all of his creative energies into the project. Yet he remained focused enough throughout the book to clearly define in plain English all of the technical information required to create and maintain a Web site. ... **We highly recommend this book.**"

—Peter Cook and Scott Manning
Philadelphia Inquirer

"**Buy This Book!** *Poor Richard's Web Site* won my vote for the most helpful book in Web site management and design ... you will find this book highly valuable. The lessons of just the first three chapters, alone, saved us thousands of dollars and many hours of work."

—David Garvey
The New England Nonprofit Quarterly

"If you follow Kent's common sense approach, your experience as a Web entrepreneur will be less of an ordeal, and **you'll have the best possible shot at actually getting some benefit** from promoting your music on the Web."

—Jim Aiken
Keyboard magazine
KEYBOARD

"This new book makes it possible for ordinary people to set up effective business Web sites without going broke or spending forever online. It's a great read for anyone who wants to build a business site, and it becomes a **part of our recommended library.**"

CMPnet's Techweb
TechWeb The IT Network

"One of the best books about Web site creation is *Poor Richard's Web Site,* by Peter Kent. It's over 400 pages long, and is a very readable soup-to-nuts guide to preparing a site, getting it on the Internet, and advertising it once it's there."

—Christopher Sarson
Mindshare Update, Microsoft's User Group magazine

"Covering all the basics in jargon-free English, he considers what you need to start, where to put your Web site, finding a host, how to pick and register a domain name, creating a site, choosing an editor, adding interaction and taking orders online, distribution lists, and registering your Web site. **Very well written.**"

Library Journal

"Editor's Pick. For the everyday person or business needing a Web site, the first question that arises always seems to be the same: Where do we start? Peter Kent's *Poor Richard's Web Site: Geek-Free, Commonsense Advice On Building a Low-Cost Web Site* may very well be the best answer to that question. … If you're planning on buying only one book about creating a Web site, **Poor Richard's Web Site is the book to buy.**"

—Brian Landel
CIZone.com Books

"We highly recommend that you get a copy of this book, just to see how a complicated subject is presented in a thoroughly understandable manner. … No matter how familiar you are with the Web, we guarantee that you will learn something from this book."

Marketing Technology

"Book of the Month. There was no question this month; Peter Kent's *Poor Richard's Web Site,* **a remarkable book whose subtitle tells it all,** is the undisputed Book of the Month winner. In clear, understandable language, Kent conveys an absolutely incredible amount of information on building and running a Web site."

—Richard Mann
ComputerCredible Magazine

"This book is getting fantastic press reviews and I can see why. Written by best-selling author Peter Kent (he's written over 20 Internet books), it covers all the little details that most Web-creation and HTML books ignore and then some. … In a very easy-to-understand-manner, Kent keeps explaining and explaining and explaining, well, everything … if you're thinking about putting up a Web site yourself or talking to a web hosting company to do it for you, read this book first. … **Wish I'd had it four years ago.**"

—Richard Greene
infoZine

"Kent proves that a computer book can explain technology, can be well-written and can hold a reader's attention for longer than it takes to download your home page ... "Make haste, not waste," to Kent's Web site, to find out more about this **timely and welcome addition to any independent publisher's bookshelf.**"

Publishing for Entrepreneurs

"If you already have a Web site, then you should definitely pay *Poor Richard* a visit. Kent has written the kind of no-nonsense guide to first principles that are especially valuable to people who don't have a lot of time to spend on making their Web site 'just so.' ... even if you don't intend to do your own Web design work, **you will be miles ahead if you get this book and use it as your guide to evaluating your own site.**"

—John Gear
Vancouver Business Journal

"*Poor Richard's Web Site* offers everything needed to build an efficient, attractive, practical Web site and does so in **a jargon-free, user-friendly manner that is rarely so well done.**"

—Jim Cox
The Midwest Book Review

"**We recommend this book.**"

fatbrain.com

"I could not see anything in this book that would be anything but helpful for a new web site owner or a person considering taking the plunge. And I learned a lot from reading it, even after a few years experience. ... All in all, I'd say that if you've already got a Web site, this is a very handy reference for you to add to your collection. If you don't have one, but are considering it, *Poor Richard's Web Site* **is an absolute must.**"

—Paul Myers
The Netrepreneur's Digest/Talkbiz

"If you are looking for a no-nonsense approach to evaluating your options with regard to implementing a Web site, you can't go far wrong with Peter Kent's *Poor Richard's Web Site.* ... Even if you've already created a site, Mr. Kent has number of suggestions that make this book a worthwhile read ... **the potential for increased quality to your site by heeding some of the advice will pay back in the long run.**"

Ed's Internet Book Review

"**In a word, wonderful!** In two words: I'm impressed. Best-selling author Peter Kent delivers all that his subtitle promises, and more."

—Helen Heightsman Gordon, Ed. D.
The Midwest Book Review Internet Bookwatch

"Kent combined just the right elements in his book, which ultimately supplies everyone from the novice to the expert with sound time- and money-saving advice. Kent explains everything in **simple detail so his readers don't have to be computer whizzes to understand the concepts.**"

—Sheila Clark
The Advocate-Messenger, Danville

"Most [Web books] seem to be written in an arcane language few of use understand. Peter Kent has produced **a knowledgeable book that can be followed and understood by non-geeks.**"

Benefits and Compensations Solutions

"It is, in a nutshell, an 'A to Z' compendium of the practical aspects of setting up, maintaining, and promoting a home page ... **Whatever your level of expertise, you will gain valuable information** by reading *Poor Richard's Web Site.*"

—Frank Feldmann
Printing News

"Takes the reader who has toyed with the idea of building a web site on the whole tour from A to Z ... take a clue from the subtitle: *'Geek-Free Commonsense Advice on Building a Low-Cost Web Site.'* If you're like most of us, **this stuff's a real eye-opener.**"

—Jack Teems
Neat Net Tricks

"[A] good source [of information] with **easy step-by-step directions** is Peter Kent's *Poor Richard's Web Site.*"

—Jenna Schnuer
Publisher's Weekly

"Recommendation: If you're thinking of setting up a Web site, buy the book. Chock full of useful information, it'll be **the best return on investment in Web building you'll ever get.**"

—Hilary Lane
Boulder County Business Report

"[helps] **guide you through this step** and others involved in getting a Web site up and running."

—Patrick Marshall
Seattle Times

"The style of the book is friendly and conversational ... **the advice is supremely practical** ... Whether you're thinking of setting up your own site, or you're just interested in the Internet, read this book!"

—Christopher Sarson
The View from Windows (newsletter of the Windows on the Rockies User Group)

Poor Richard's Web Site
Second Edition

*Geek-Free, Commonsense
Advice on Building a
Low-Cost Web Site*

by
Peter Kent

Poor Richard's Web Site:
Geek-Free, Commonsense Advice on Building a Low-Cost Web Site

Copyright © 2000 Peter Kent

All rights reserved. Printed in the United States of America. No part of this book may be used or reproduced in any form or by any method, or stored in an electronic storage system, without prior written permission of the publisher except in the case of brief quotations in critical articles and reviews. Copying any part of this book for any purpose other than your own personal use is a violation of United States copyright law.

SAN#: 299-4550
Top Floor Publishing
P.O. Box 260072
Lakewood, CO 80226

Feedback to the author: feedback@topfloor.com
Sales information: sales@topfloor.com
The Top Floor Publishing Web Site: http://TopFloor.com/
The Poor Richard Web Site: http://PoorRichard.com/book/
Cover design/illustration by Marty Peterson, http://artymarty.com

Library of Congress Catalog Card Number: 99-60718

ISBN: 0-9661032-0-3

This book is sold as is, without warranty of any kind, either express or implied, respecting the contents of this book, including but not limited to implied warranties for the book's quality, performance, merchantability, or fitness for any purpose. Neither the author nor Top Floor Publishing and its dealers and distributors shall be liable to the purchaser or any other person or entity with respect to liability, loss, or damage caused or alleged to have been caused directly or indirectly by this book.

01   00   99   6 5 4 3 2 1

Trademark and service mark terms used in this book are the property of the trademark holders. Use of a term in this book should not be regarded as affecting the validity of any trademark or service mark.

Poor Richard's Web Site
Second Edition

*Geek-Free, Commonsense
Advice on Building a
Low-Cost Web Site*

by
Peter Kent

TOP FLOOR
PUBLISHING

Poor Richard's Web Site:
Geek-Free, Commonsense Advice on Building a Low-Cost Web Site

Copyright © 2000 Peter Kent

All rights reserved. Printed in the United States of America. No part of this book may be used or reproduced in any form or by any method, or stored in an electronic storage system, without prior written permission of the publisher except in the case of brief quotations in critical articles and reviews. Copying any part of this book for any purpose other than your own personal use is a violation of United States copyright law.

SAN#: 299-4550
Top Floor Publishing
P.O. Box 260072
Lakewood, CO 80226

Feedback to the author: feedback@topfloor.com
Sales information: sales@topfloor.com
The Top Floor Publishing Web Site: http://TopFloor.com/
The Poor Richard Web Site: http://PoorRichard.com/book/
Cover design/illustration by Marty Peterson, http://artymarty.com

Library of Congress Catalog Card Number: 99-60718

ISBN: 0-9661032-0-3

This book is sold as is, without warranty of any kind, either express or implied, respecting the contents of this book, including but not limited to implied warranties for the book's quality, performance, merchantability, or fitness for any purpose. Neither the author nor Top Floor Publishing and its dealers and distributors shall be liable to the purchaser or any other person or entity with respect to liability, loss, or damage caused or alleged to have been caused directly or indirectly by this book.

01   00   99   6 5 4 3 2 1

Trademark and service mark terms used in this book are the property of the trademark holders. Use of a term in this book should not be regarded as affecting the validity of any trademark or service mark.

Acknowledgements

Creating a book is more than a one-man job; there are many people working "behind the scenes" to get the book into production. I'd like to thank everyone who worked so hard on *Poor Richard's Web Site*, in particular my Marketing Manager, Melissa Derkacz, who acted as Project Manager on this book; Debbie Remmen for her help in the book layout; Marty Peterson for the great cover he designed; Fred Kloepper for his assistance in making sure the words made sense; Julie Wheeler for proofreading.

I'd also like to thank all the readers of the first edition who gave it such good "word of mouth"; everyone who praised the book to their friends and colleagues, and told them they had to go out and buy it!

For my wife, Debbie.

About the Author

Peter Kent is the author of 40 business and computer books. His work has appeared in a variety of publications, from the *Manchester Guardian* to *Internet World*, *Computerworld* to *Dr. Dobb's Journal*, and his work has been translated into 20 languages. Kent is the Founder and President of Top Floor Publishing, and of BizBlast.com.

Also by Peter Kent

Poor Richard's Internet Marketing and Promotions (with Tara Calishain, Top Floor Publishing)

The CDnow Story: Rags to Riches on the Internet (with Jason Olim and Matthew Olim, Top Floor Publishing)

Making Money in Technical Writing (Macmillan/ARCO)

The Complete Idiot's Guide to the Internet, 6th Edition (Que)

The Official Netscape JavaScript 1.2 Book (with John Kent, Top Floor Publishing)

The Ten Minute Guide to the Internet (Que)

The Best Sex of Your Life (with Dr. Jim White, Barricade)

Discover Windows NT Workstation 4.0 (IDG)

Discover FrontPage 97 (IDG)

Using Netscape Communicator 4 (Que)

The Official Netscape JavaScript Programmer's Reference (with Kent Multer, Ventana)

Career Ideas for Kids Who Like Computers (Facts on File)

Contents at a Glance

Table of Contents

Introduction

Welcome to the Second Edition of *Poor Richard's Web Site*. The Second Edition of what is perhaps the most widely reviewed and praised book in computer-publishing history. Why has this book been so widely reviewed and praised? For two reasons:

1. This book really does live up to the blurb on the front cover. It really does provide geek-free, commonsense advice on building a low-cost Web site. And that kind of advice is pretty hard to find!

2. When I published the first edition of this book I used many of the techniques described in the third section of this book—and in the "sequel," *Poor Richard's Internet Marketing and Promotions*—to promote the Web site related to the book. Those real-world, grassroots Internet promotions helped to push this book in front of reviewers and readers alike. This stuff really does work!

Poor Richard's Web Site describes what is, for many people, the first step into setting up a business or other organization online—the creation of a simple Web site. *Poor Richard's Internet Marketing and Promotions* describes how to bring people to your site—in effect it expands on the third section of this book. And *Poor Richard's E-mail Publishing* (already a best-seller just a week after being published), explains another important step, one that perfectly complements a Web site—publishing e-mail newsletters, bulletins, discussion groups, and so on.

But why *Poor Richard's*? So far none of the authors of this *Poor Richard's* series have been named Richard; nor is the publisher of this series (who is also the first author in this series) called Richard.

In 1732 Benjamin Franklin used the most modern and sophisticated communication system of his time—the printing press—to publish the first edition of *Poor Richard's Almanack*. He distributed his words ("those pithy utterances of worldly wisdom," as the introduction in the 1909 Harvard Classics edition of his autobiography describes them) throughout the English-speaking world ... and beyond.

I named the *Poor Richard's* series in honor of Benjamin Franklin (who, you'll note, also wasn't named Richard ... though he published the *Almanack* under the name Richard Saunders). I liked his concept of down-to-earth, commonsense advice, and I liked his humor. And I liked the fact that there's the word *Poor* in the title! I wanted to convey the idea that you can often achieve something without blowing a lot of money. In particular, I knew it was possible to create a low-cost, yet effective, Web site, contrary to the nonsense that was commonplace in the press.

Ben Franklin used the technology of the time to get his words to the world. *Poor Richard's Web Site* will show you how to use the latest mass communication system of our time—the World Wide Web—to spread your words to the world at large.

Whether you're selling a product, promoting your personal services, or spreading a religious or political idea, the World Wide Web is the ideal forum ... if you know how to use it. Unfortunately the computer press is awash with bad advice about setting up a Web site. Follow some of this advice and your Web site will be expensive, a lot of trouble to build, and ultimately unsuccessful.

There's another way, though, what I regard as a "low-tech" method, a way to build a Web site with minimal expense and trouble and yet still be successful, in some cases more successful than Web sites costing ten or a hundred times more. *Poor Richard's Web Site* explains how to set up a Web site with very little money. There's no need to spend tens of thousands of dollars a year on a Web server, for instance—you can find a Web-hosting service that will cost $20 or $30 a month, or, if your budget is particularly small, you can even find places to host your site for free. (Chapter 4 lists dozens of places to find cheap Web sites.) There's no need to spend $5,000 or $10,000 on "shopping-cart" software; you can find it for free or have someone install it for you for $100 or so (Chapter 13 tells you where to find this software, and how to take orders online using credit cards, checks, 900 numbers, and more). There's no need to spend $1,000 adding a chat group to your Web site; I'll explain how to get someone else to install it for you, and they won't charge you a penny! (Chapters 11 and 12 explain where to get your free chat program and many other useful low-cost or free programs that will make your Web site really sing.)

But there's a lot more to a Web site than, well ... just the Web site. A Web site is *not* a billboard on the information superhighway. A Web site that nobody knows about is a waste of time and money—nobody will "drive by" your billboard and see it; you have to bring people to the site. *Poor Richard's Web Site* explains how to do that, too. Just registering your Web site with the search engines is simply *not* enough!

Benjamin Franklin distributed his words of wisdom so far and wide that they became deeply embedded in the English language. Pick up a copy of *Poor Richard's Almanack* sometime and you may be surprised at how much you've heard before, how many sayings and mottos that seem to be part of the English language originated there. Franklin used modern technology to communicate with individuals throughout the world; not only was *Poor Richard's Almanack* a phenomenal success in the American colonies, but it was translated, and traveled across the Atlantic. One man was able to communicate his thoughts to hundreds of thousands of people in many countries.

Well, you can do the same using the World Wide Web, and a lot more easily and cheaply than Ben Franklin could using the printing press. One person or a small group or business can use the World Wide Web to reach many thousands of people throughout the world. It doesn't have to be expensive and it doesn't have to be difficult. *Poor Richard's Web Site* explains how you can create a Web site that really works but doesn't break your budget.

—Peter Kent

PART I

PREPARATION

Chapter One
==

Do You Really Need a Web Site?

Y ou won't find a chapter heading like this one in many books about the
World Wide Web. There's supposed to be just one answer to the question,
"Do you really need a Web site?" so it's not worth asking. That answer is: *Of
course you need a Web site! Everyone can benefit from one.*

I have a different answer: Maybe you do, maybe you don't. You see, I'm not
convinced that every business needs a Web site. I believe that many businesses
are simply better off without a site. I'll give you an example of a business that
can't benefit from a Web site—and explain why it can't benefit—a little later in
this chapter, and I'll suggest a way that such a business may be able to change
the way it operates and then benefit from a Web site. But before I do that I want
to look at a few good reasons for creating a Web site.

Web Sites—What Are They Good For?

A Web consultant told me about a trick he uses to bring a business meeting to
a standstill. When he meets his new clients and talks about setting up their Web
site, he'll ask: "What do you want to do with the Web site? What's it for?" At
that point the meeting breaks up into a cacophony of voices, all suggesting this
or that or the other. It turns out that most of his clients haven't thought about
this issue. They know they want—need—a Web site; they just haven't
considered why.

Before you set up a Web site, consider what you want to do with it. Set up a
Web site without figuring that out first, and you'll waste a lot of time and
money, and maybe even sour on the whole idea of having a Web site. Plan what
it is you want to do first, then create your site.

By the way, "to make money" simply isn't a good enough answer. *How* do you
want to make money? What are you selling? How will you attract customers?
How will you take orders? How will you ship orders? You may not be able to

answer some of these questions until you've finished reading this book, but you should answer them before you begin your Web site.

Here, then, is a short list of reasons to set up your Web site:

- To get incredibly rich, making huge sales to millions of new customers
- To promote your products, pushing sales in off-Web channels
- To promote an idea, hobby, political movement, religion, or other consuming passion
- To take orders online
- To sell information online
- To distribute information about your company or organization
- To distribute samples
- To provide customer service and technical support
- To meet new customers
- To forge a stronger link between your company and your existing customers
- To provide an internal communications system for your company
- To make shareholders feel more like part of the company
- To make money selling advertising.

This is by no means a comprehensive list—just a few ideas, some common, one or two not so common. Let's examine each of these reasons in turn.

To Get Incredibly Rich

Getting rich is a nice idea, and there are still people suggesting that the Internet is paved with gold. It's not, of course. There are people who have made money on the Internet, but probably fewer than you'd imagine. Unfortunately many Internet books and magazines have declared "successes" of Web sites that have not actually made money. **HotWired**, for instance (a site associated with *Wired* magazine), is often touted as a success

I'm going to be mentioning a lot of URLs—Internet addresses—in this book. You can view a Web page containing all these address links at a Web site associated with this book: http://www. poorrichard.com/. Copy the page to your hard disk and then create a bookmark to the page stored on your hard disk, so it will be easily accessible.

story (see http://www.hotwired.com/). It's one of *the* Internet success stories— except that it doesn't actually make money. Why is it called a success? Generally due to its great popularity. And, of course, its popularity will, to some extent, increase *Wired* subscriptions. (But then, *Wired* magazine doesn't make money, either.) In 1997 *Internet World* ran an article about Internet successes and even stated on the cover that the businesses were making money. The article itself said otherwise. In fact, the article clearly stated that one of the businesses wasn't breaking even and seemed to imply that a couple of the others weren't making money, either. Many of the businesses you see profiled in the press are losing money by the barrel, with very little in the way of revenues yet huge expenses.

On the other hand, there are successful Web sites, sites such as **CDnow** (http://www.cdnow.com/) where you can buy CDs, videos, and video games. CDnow grossed around $6 million in 1996, just two years after being launched by a couple of brothers working in their parents' basement. They made around $16 million in 1997, and somewhere around $50 or $60 million in 1998 … then I stopped counting. Now, that's not to say that CDnow actually makes a profit! But it does have large revenues.

In fact if you're interested in finding companies actually making a profit on the Web, you'll probably have to look for small companies, companies such as Top Floor Publishing, the publisher of this very book. In the first year we sold $30,000 worth of this book online, and pushed over 10,000 buyers into the bookstore. The Web site paid for itself many, many times over.

You see, there are two games being played on the Web. There's the small-business model, in which the business tries to make money right away, or as fast as possible anyway. Then there's the big-business model, in which the business isn't even trying to make money. Amazon.com's Jim Bezos, for instance, has said that if Amazon makes money any time soon, it won't be intentional. (He's also said that they were profitable for a day at one point a year or two ago, but that it was an accident.) CDnow has a significant portion of the online music business (it used to own a third, before Amazon got into the game)—but it won't make money any time soon. Businesses such as these are trying to grab attention, grab "real estate," and grab market share. They're playing long term, hoping to come out on top when this whole Internet commerce

A lot of the advice you'll see in the press about doing business online is what I call "big-business advice." Ask yourself this: How long can you go before your business makes money? A few months? A year or two? A decade? Most of us simply can't play the big-business game. If you can't invest in order to make money "sometime down the road," you're playing the small-business game, so you have to be wary of big-business advice.

thing settles down and stops growing—at which point the market will be immense. They're investing tens or hundreds of millions of dollars now, in order to make billions in a decade or so.

Many small businesses *do* have profitable Web sites. I run into owners of these sites all the time. But If you're going to make money on the Web, you need to know how to promote your Web site. (So you'd better read the rest of this book!) Many of the owners of these successful sites have stumbled upon a system that works; they've found a way to bring customers to their sites partly by luck and partly by being in the right place at the right time. Far more small businesses have stumbled around and *not* found the answer, of course. You *can* sell products on the Web, but the Web is not the ultimate get-rich-quick solution, nor the lazy man's road to riches. Some companies have managed to make money on the Web … but more have failed.

To Push Off-Web Sales

Even if you don't plan to sell much online, you can still use the Internet as a promotional tool. A Web site is just one part of a program in which you promote a product on the Internet. We'll be talking about other components: newsgroups, mailing lists, e-mail, electronic press releases, and so on.

Some writers and publishers have successfully used the Internet to boost sales of books in the real world. For instance, a number of computer-book publishers now make some of their books available online. Anyone can visit the Web site and read part of the book, or even all of it. That's what my publishing company, Top Floor Publishing, does. Visit http://TopFloor.com/ to see information about all our books. It's my experience, and that of various publishers I've spoken with, that this doesn't hurt sales; on the contrary, it helps them. People read part of the book, discover that the book provides the information they need, and so they order it—not always directly from the publisher but perhaps through an online bookstore, or even by calling their local bookstore to order it.

You can promote offline product sales online in a number of ways. Simply providing information about your products and letting people know where this information is available is a promotional tool. But you can take it a step further and provide coupons at your Web site, run contests and free giveaways, set up discussion groups for people using or considering using your products, and so on. Take a look, for instance, at the **Coca-Cola** site (http://www.cocacola.com/). I've got to say I don't like the design of this site. It's corny and poorly structured (I'll explain why in Chapter 10), and I find it confusing; it's trying to be hip and cool at the expense of clarity. But what amazed me was the number of people who are visiting this site and talking with each other about Coca-Cola products,

Coca-Cola memorabilia, trivia, and so on. And anything they say becomes the property of the Coca-Cola company, too.

By the way, Coca-Cola probably spent lots of money on this site, but any small company can run an equivalent site for around $30 to $50 a month. Setting up online discussion groups is quite easy these days, as you'll discover in Chapter 12.

To Promote Your Ideas and Passions

Many people create Web sites without any idea of making money from them. They create them to promote their ideas, their hobbies, or their political or religious beliefs. Web sites can be a great way to meet people with your interests or distribute information about your ideas and beliefs.

To Take Orders Online

You can certainly take orders online. In most cases businesses trying to sell a product should be setting up their Web sites with the idea of promoting the product, pushing offline sales, and taking orders online. If you are promoting the product, doing your best to get the prospective client excited and interested in buying it, you might as well take the order then and there if you can. We'll see later, in Chapter 13, how to do that.

To Sell Information Online

You may want to sell information online. That is, sell access to some kind of data by selling passwords to your Web site. The most common form of "information" being sold in this manner is pornography, so if you want to get an idea of how to sell access to your Web site, spend a little time in the raunchier areas of the Web. You might also take a look at a rather more run-of-the-mill form of data being sold on the Internet, the **Colorado Revised Statutes** (http://crs.aescon.com/). Art Smoot has these law books in electronic form online. It costs $40 to gain access to all the statutes, though you can see samples for free. When you register, you are given a password that lets you get into the site until it expires.

A Quick Word for Publishers

The Internet has attracted many publishers and has led to the creation of new publishing companies, too. It seems to be a natural match. The Internet is an information superhighway, isn't it? So why not sell information on the Internet? But the reality is a little different. While it's true that there's an awful lot of information traveling around on the Internet, the vast majority is free.

At the moment it's very difficult for publishers to sell their wares across the Internet in an electronic form. Many have tried; most have failed. For instance, in 1997 I heard the owner of a new online bookstore, **BookAisle**, talking about the progress of his company. This bookstore sold electronic versions of paper books (it's now changed, or perhaps merged, into **OverDrive Bookworks**: http://www.overdrive.com/), some of which were actually quite well known books that you could find in your local bookstore. The bookstore had scores of titles—over 80, I seem to recall. And all in all they'd sold "hundreds" of books over the previous six months, which is nothing to get excited about.

Why won't people buy information in an electronic form? Well, there are a few problems. The first is that people don't like to read books online. It's uncomfortable and inconvenient. Try Kent's Electronic-Book Bathroom Test: An electronic book is not a real book unless it can be read while sitting on the can. And if you don't like reading on the can, there's always the Couch Test, the Beach Test, the Bus Test, and so on.

Another problem: selling small pieces of information is difficult because the much-vaunted micropayment system does not yet exist. Ideally it should be possible for a publisher to charge someone, say, ten cents to read an article. There is a variety of systems that might allow this sort of micropayment transaction to take place (such as **DigiCash** at http://www.digicash.com/, and **CyberCash** at http://www.cybercash.com/), but there's no standard system, and very few people are using any of these systems.

Now, having said all that, things are about to change. Since I first wrote that in 1997, the electronic-book business has progressed. I don't think anybody's making much money yet, but I do think that we're reaching a stage at which it's worth watching; at Top Floor Publishing we're considering publishing electronic-book versions soon. In 1999 a number of developments occurred that make e-books far closer to reality.

First, there are now several electronic-book readers on the market—book-size boxes with screens on which you can read an electronic book stored within—and large publishers are beginning to publish their works in e-book format. The two important electronic-book readers at present are the **Rocket eBook** (http://www.rocketbook.com/) and the **SoftBook** (http://www.softbook.com/). There are also some standards being set for electronic books; at the time of writing the process wasn't finished, but it's moving along. Also, **fatbrain.com** (http://www.fatbrain.com/) recently launched a system called eMatter which allows anybody to publish material at the fatbrain.com site, and earn royalties. You can publish articles, "whitepapers," lectures, out-of-print books, or whatever. You upload the text, you set the price, and you keep 50 percent of the income.

So things are starting to move in the e-publishing realm, but it remains to be seen how quickly it takes off. The problem remains that most writing is not suitable for viewing on a computer screen, and very few people own electronic-book readers. (My prediction? That we'll see the electronic-book business become something quite substantial sometime between 2004 and 2009. What does "substantial" mean? That's a weasel word that will allow me to say, in the year 2010, that my prediction was right.)

That's not to say that you can't make money by putting information online right now, only that you'd better come up with a better idea than simply selling it directly, or you'd better have the sort of information that people will buy (such as the Colorado Revised Statutes). Here are a couple more ideas:

- **Edmund's Automobile Buyer's Guides** (http://www.edmunds.com/). You can buy the books in stores or view them free online. How does Edmund's make money? It works with Auto-by-Tel; buyers can order cars online, and local dealers will bid for their business. So the local dealers are, in effect, paying to allow buyers to view information for free.
- **ArtToday** (http://www.arttoday.com/) sells clip art online. This is used by professional designers who don't want simply to view the pictures. They make money using this stuff, so they're willing to pay.

In the first case, Edmund's has found someone else to pay, someone who may benefit if visitors to the Web site read the information online—the car dealers. In the second case, ArtToday sells a specialized product: clip art. It's also selling selection—750,000 images—at a competitive price. So it is possible to sell information online. Just don't imagine you can take a paper book, convert it into electronic form, and get rich selling it on the Internet.

Of course all this doesn't mean that publishers can't promote their books online. They most certainly can, as Top Floor Publishing has shown. In fact plenty of publishers have successfully promoted paper books through the Internet. And some have found that placing electronic copies of books online helps to push sales of the paper books. **Macmillan Computer Publishing** (http://www.mcp.com/)—the world's largest publisher of such books—found that when they put books on their Web sites, people often read pieces and then bought the paper copy. They placed scores of complete books online, in fact.

The **National Academy Press** (http://www.nap.edu/) has also placed many books online—reportedly over 1,350—and claims that the electronic versions boost the sales of the paper versions by as much as two to three times earlier levels. Initially they put many of their books online in a scanned format—that is, the pages you see online are pictures of the pages in the paper book, not text Web pages—making it exceedingly slow to load. This is a ridiculous way to put a book online, but maybe there was method in their madness. Reading one of these books is an excruciatingly slow process, like watching molasses flow in a freezer, so if readers find something of interest they'll buy the book if they really want the information. On the other hand, when I checked their site recently, I found that they now have many books in text format, so they load quickly. Presumably this hasn't hurt sales.

MIT Press (http://www-mitpress.mit.edu/) has also placed a few books online, and, I've heard, believes that doing so doubles the sales of the paper versions. That's despite the fact that these books are in text form, so they load quickly. People just don't like reading online, they'd much rather read snippets online and buy the paper if they want the entire book.

To Distribute Information

Many companies use Web sites as a way to distribute information about themselves that they know their users want or need. Now, I've heard it said— indeed I've read it in books giving advice about doing business on the Internet— that a Web site provides the opportunity for you to cut your printing and advertising costs. Set up a Web site and stop sending out catalogs! This is complete nonsense, of course. For the vast majority of businesses this simply isn't possible and won't be for years to come. But a Web site *can* provide another way for your clients and prospective clients to find information about your products and your business. And as you'll learn in this book, you can set up a Web site quite cheaply, so you can at very little cost provide the convenience of near-instant delivery of information to those of your customers who have access to the Internet.

What sort of information should you distribute?

- Your complete product catalog
- Contact information for people who have specific questions
- Job openings
- Technical-support information
- Order status
- Your complete internal telephone directory (if you're really reckless).

You may not make money directly by putting information on your Web site but you may be providing a service that increases efficiency and makes it easier—and quicker—for potential clients to become clients and for clients to get what they need. Rather than having to field a customer-service call, you may also save money by allowing some of your customers to retrieve information online. A classic example of this is the **Federal Express** (http://www.fedex.com/) and **UPS** (http://www.ups.com/) shipping company services. If you want to track a package that you've shipped through one of these services, you have a couple of choices. You can call them, but that will cost them money: they'll pay for the toll-free call and they must pay an employee to talk to you. Or you can go to their Web sites and track the package by entering the number into a form. You get the same information from the same computer that the employee would use to look it up for you, but at a small fraction of the cost to them. FedEx also has a great system that makes it very easy to print shipping documents, especially when you're shipping to someone you've shipped to before: you go to the Web site and log on, then select the person you want to ship to, enter the box-size and -weight information, and click Print. This doesn't save them money, but it's a fantastic little "customer-retention" feature.

Pretty much any company selling software or computer hardware to the public should have a Web site, and most probably do these days (they may not use them very effectively, but that's another chapter). The benefits are tremendous for such companies. Many of their clients are already on the Internet, so by putting this information online they can pander to their clients' need for instant gratification. A client decides he just has to have a new program—he needs a data backup program, for instance. He can go to the company's site right away, read detailed information about what the product will do, and even download a limited-feature version and put it to work immediately. Of course, he can also order the full version right there and then, and have it in his hands the next day.

It's not just the computer business, though. Maybe you publish a teddy bear magazine. Prospective subscribers can connect to your site and read articles from past issues. They can view the most recent issue's table of contents, see a list of upcoming articles ... and yes, subscribe to the magazine.

Oh, and the telephone directory I mentioned. The best example of this I've seen so far was one shown by multimedia and Web consultant William Horton during a presentation he gave to the Boulder Chamber of Commerce. He had found Web pages owned by NASA, with maps showing office locations and a directory of internal telephone extensions. Does the public really need this stuff? As Horton pointed out, it's a great resource for terrorists. Which just goes to show that some information is not appropriate for your Web site.

To Distribute Samples

Commercial software publishers are taking an example from shareware publishers, prompted by the growth of the Internet. *Shareware* is a type of software that uses a form of "try it before you buy it" marketing technique. Shareware publishers literally give away their software. If the software is good it travels far and wide, as people pass it on to their friends and colleagues, shareware "libraries" distribute it, and so on. People who use it and like it—and decide to continue using it—are expected to register the software and pay a fee.

Now many commercial software publishers are playing the same game. Microsoft, for instance, allowed people to download beta copies of Microsoft FrontPage, a Web site creation tool. These beta copies were full-featured but were set to quit functioning on a certain date. Tens of thousands of people downloaded the product. On January 31, 1997, the beta program "timed out," leaving many users with Web sites created using FrontPage, a desire to continue using FrontPage, and no option but to go out and buy it. This system must have worked for Microsoft; they did the same thing with **Microsoft FrontPage 98** (http://www.microsoft.com/frontpage/), and with a variety of other products, too.

It's not just software that can be distributed this way. Anything electronic can be distributed like this, such as clip art, music, video, and so on. As we've seen with the huge boom in MP3 since early 1999.

And the product doesn't have to be electronic. Many publishers put book chapters or entire books online. Magazines have their recent tables of contents and sample articles online. You could even use a Web site to take people's addresses and ship product samples to them. Trying to get a fantastic new shampoo or curry sauce onto the market? Offer free samples.

To Provide Customer Service and Technical Support

Customer service and technical support are a major expense for many companies. Having real live people answer individuals' questions can be very expensive. But most customers' questions have been asked many times before. Wouldn't it be more efficient to answer them once?

Well, you probably won't shut down the technical-support department, but if you can provide a good source of information for your customers and encourage them to use it, you may be able to transfer some of the load from real people to computers. The problem with the technical-support sites that I've seen, however, is that they're often badly designed—making customers do too much digging around for information—and they often don't have all the information you need. I've seen one site that leads you through a series of questions, but if your particular problem is not covered exactly by those questions, you end up getting a completely useless generic answer. There's also no e-mail address to contact a real live human being. And to add insult to injury, they have a series of questions intended to find out how you "enjoyed your technical-support experience," but the questions seem to be designed to elicit only positive responses; I tried to answer the questions honestly, but never did find a question to which I could provide a negative response, or even an area in which I could enter a note explaining why I was irritated with their stupid system. The result, no doubt, was that I ended up in their statistics as a "satisfied technical-support customer."

If you're going to bother doing this at all, do it right. Spend some time and effort figuring out the best way to present the information so the customer can find it quickly. And put on the site all the information you have available. By the way, an interesting example of a support site is the **Microsoft Knowledge Base** (http://support.microsoft.com/support/). This site allows anyone to search the same database that Microsoft's own technical-support staff use to answer call-in questions. It's usually quicker, and sometimes more effective, to use the Knowledge Base yourself. (Once you're into the Knowledge Base area it's fairly easy to use; but Microsoft seems to enjoy having people spend a lot of time at their site ... at least, that's the way it seems. Microsoft has one of the most confusing and complicated sites in the world. But then, it's designed by the same people who designed Windows.)

To Meet New Customers

When you promote your site on the Internet, the intention is to get people to visit you. But a Web site is not a billboard. A billboard doesn't do anything for you, it just carries a message; you can create Web sites like that, but you're wasting an opportunity if you do.

Bring people to your Web site and then meet them. Get their e-mail addresses; as you'll see in Chapters 11 and 12, there are ways to encourage people to divulge their e-mail addresses. You can use those addresses to keep in touch with your new customers, to send out notifications about special offers and information you think they'll find useful at your Web site, and so on. The Web is an interactive medium. Don't use it as a static one.

To Forge Links with Existing Customers

One of the great advantages of the Web is that it allows you to get to know your existing customers—no longer do all your customers have to be faceless statistics. Bring existing customers to your site and ask them what they like about your products. Ask them what they don't like, how they think the product should develop, whether they'd buy the product if you use the multipack bundle you've been considering, whether they like the new packaging.

Give them something in return, too. Discount coupons, the names and addresses of dealers in their area, tips about using your products, promotional tie-ins with other products, and so on.

To Provide an Internal Communications System

The world's getting connected. In Europe, North America, and Australia millions of people have Internet access, many from their laptops. Interest in the Internet is growing rapidly in Latin America, parts of Asia, and elsewhere. As individuals become accustomed to online communications, the manner in which large companies communicate within themselves will change dramatically.

For instance, it's possible for companies to set up their own private Webs, called *intranets*, and use them as corporate communications centers. This can be done using relatively pricey technologies, such as Windows NT/2000's new PPTP (Point-to-Point Tunneling Protocol), which, in effect, creates a private network on top of the World Wide Web. Or it can be done cheaply using the simple technique of making a Web site private. You can do that with Microsoft FrontPage, for instance, a $150 program.

Employees worldwide can reach the Web site from anywhere with a phone link. They can upload and download files, read and leave messages, join online chats with other employees, and read the latest company news. Whether someone is using a laptop in a hotel room in Hong Kong, a PC in a one-man office in Quito, or a Macintosh in a large office in Melbourne, all can reach the Web site and all can be online at the same time.

To Make Shareholders Feel Part of the Company

Many companies provide special services for their shareholders. Own shares in some hotel chains, and you'll get a discount on room rates. Own shares in a ferry company, and ride the ferry at a cut rate. Why not set up a site for your shareholders? It can hold all sorts of useful information. The most recent share price, of course, but also messages from the board of directors, information about special offers for shareholders and how to join the dividend-reinvestment plan, company news, and so on. It had better be well designed and interesting— avoid the typical corporate stodge. It doesn't have to be private, either. If open to the public, it can serve as an ad for your shares and a corporate information source for the public.

To Make Money Selling Advertising

I've left this idea to the last because, for the moment at least, there's very little chance that you'll make money selling advertising. Yes, it can be done, and, in fact, we'll discuss this subject in Chapter 20. But it's very difficult, and the vast majority of the millions of advertising dollars companies are said to be spending on the Internet goes to just a dozen or so companies. Many of the claims are exaggerated anyway; it appears that many estimates are based on published advertising rates, whereas many advertisers are paying greatly discounted rates.

We'll be talking about how to sell advertising and how to buy it, too. But bear in mind that it's very difficult for a small Web site to earn advertising dollars, so don't base your entire plan on it.

Do a Little Research

By now you may have some ideas about what you can do for your company or organization. But I'd suggest you spend a few days cruising around on the World Wide Web. Take a good look at what other people are doing. Follow links to your heart's content—don't rush, just take your time and explore.

Keep notes, because you'll probably come up with ideas as you go. Nobody knows your business better than you do, and once you understand the Web and have seen what other people have done, you'll come up with new ideas of your own.

Not All Companies Need a Web Site

Now, back to the question posed by this chapter's title: Do you really need a Web site? Perhaps not. There are many businesses that really won't benefit from one.

Here's an example. Let's say you own a single shoe store in a small shopping center in a medium-sized town. You want to bring more people into your store so you can sell more shoes. Could you benefit from a Web site? Yes, you could. Would it be cost-effective? Almost certainly not.

The problem is that few people are using the Web to find local services such as these. If I want to buy shoes, what do I do? I go to the nearest shopping mall or shopping center and visit a few stores. I might look in the Yellow Pages, though I probably wouldn't. I might even look in an online version of the Yellow Pages, such as **Yahoo!'s Yellow Pages** (which I use all the time: http://yp. yahoo.com/). But I probably wouldn't. And I certainly wouldn't bother searching for a shoe store's Web site. Now, maybe I'm different. Maybe most people *would* go looking for a shoe store's Web site ... but I don't think so. Am I right? You decide.

So is anyone going to look for your store on the Web? No—or at least, almost nobody. Yes, you might make a sale or two, but the profit won't pay for the cost of the site.

What if I'm a catalog shopper? Might I want to buy shoes through a Web catalog? Yes, I might. But you've told me you just want to bring more people into your store. Now you're talking about a new business. If you want to go into the catalog sales business, then having a Web site might be a very good idea, as long as you promote the site properly, of course.

Here's an example that you may have heard of: **Hot Hot Hot** (http://www.hothothot.com/). This Web site was created by the owners of a hot-sauce shop in Pasadena, California. Their store was one that really couldn't benefit from a Web site. If they'd set up a Web site saying "come visit our store," I'd bet the added business wouldn't have paid the cost of the site. But they did more than that, they started what was, in effect, a new business. They decided to sell their product to people who couldn't come to the store. People can view their product catalog online, order online or by phone, and have it shipped to them.

There are two things to consider here, though. First, Hot Hot Hot had a product that lent itself to being sold by mail order. If you're a hot-sauce aficionado, where else can you find a store with 400 different sauces? Do you know where you can buy Spitfire Red Sauce? In Barbados, sure, but do you have it in your hometown? How about West Indies Creole or Hot as Hell Teralu Pedis? In other words, Hot Hot Hot is a specialty store selling a product with a potential market of millions of people, yet because these people are spread throughout the world, it's hard for them to obtain the product. If you want to buy these sauces, about the only practical way to do so for most people is through Hot Hot Hot. (Another important factor to consider; hot sauce has a very high cost:weight ratio—a high cost compared to a low weight—making shipping practical. Try selling gravel through the mail. ...)

Back to the shoe store. Can you take your run-of-the-mill shoe store, put a catalog online, and sell the product? Almost certainly not. What do you have that I can't get at my local mall, where I can try the shoes on for size? If you want to sell online, you must have a reason for people to buy your product. Here are a few ideas:

- Your product is very hard to find (perhaps you *are* selling shoes, but shoes for disabled people or people with various foot ailments)
- You can sell your product dirt cheap
- You have a huge selection

- You've grouped a class of products together (things for artists, things for parachutists, things for snowboarders)
- You can make it very convenient to buy from you.

These are all different strategies that catalog-sales companies have used in the real, noncyberspace world. If you can't fit one of these categories or find a similar reason for people to buy from you, you won't be able to sell on the Web any more than you would in the real world. In fact the "catalog test" might be a good one to apply to your product before you try to sell online. Ask yourself this: Could I sell this product through a mail-order catalog? If the answer is no, then ask yourself this: Why do I think I can sell this on the Web? I'm not saying that you won't be able to sell on the Web, but you'd better have a really good answer to that question.

A few years ago, before the Internet boom—at a time when most people thought the Internet was some kind of crime syndicate—I tried selling my writing services online. I used CompuServe to post messages looking for companies that needed someone to write technical manuals. Did I get any business? Hell no! Why would anybody use me, somewhere across the country or across the world, when they could find a writer down the road? Later, I tried again, but I took a different tack. This time I offered something that was harder to find: I offered to create Windows Help files for software companies. And this time I found business very quickly, around $20,000 worth with two major companies. What had changed? I'd changed what I was offering from something these companies could find locally, to something that was difficult to find locally, because at that time it was hard to find people who knew how to create Windows Help files. Of course, I still had to convince potential clients that I would do what I promised, but at least I'd gotten far enough to talk with these companies.

Let me tell you what Jason Olim told me. Olim is cofounder of the successful **CDnow** Web site (http://www.cdnow.com/)—we'll look that company later. "There's really no such thing as an Internet business," Jason told me, "only a company doing business on the Internet." Too many people have the idea that the Internet is the path to quick riches, that all you have to do is set up a business on the Internet and away you go. But most of the work will be done off the Internet. So if you want to expand your business into another area using a Web site as a springboard, just remember that you have a lot more to do than simply create and promote a Web site.

Business-Card Web Sites

Before you get the idea that any small local business should save time and money and forget about setting up a Web site, let me explain the concept of the business-card Web site. I must admit that this isn't my idea. I first heard about it from Tom King, host of a U.S. radio show called **CompuTalk** (http://www.CompuTalk.com/). I'm not sure if he used the term "business-card Web site"—he may have—but he was the first person I'd heard describe the concept, which I've elaborated on here.

First, here's the basic idea behind most Web sites. Set up a Web site, register with the search engines, and hope people visit you. You're in cyberspace, so you work on trying to get people in cyberspace to visit you.

The business-card Web site is different in the sense that you don't really care if anyone in cyberspace finds you or not. You don't care too much if you're registered in the search engines, for instance. Instead, the Web site functions like an extended business card, a card you can pass out to people even if you've never met them.

Here's how it works. You set up a simple Web site, perhaps just a single page. The purpose of the site is really to get people to call you; you include all your contact info—business name, phone number, e-mail address, and so on. Then you put the URL to your Web site wherever you can.

For instance, let's say you're a house painter. You put the URL on the sign that you post outside houses you're painting. Of course you want a distinctive URL, something like BostonPainters.com, PaintPaintPaint.com, WePaintQuick.com, or whatever. (By the way, all those URLs are available. With a little imagination, it's still possible to find a distinctive URL that will work on a sign.) You *don't* have to use a domain name that is the same as your company name—the important thing is to pick a memorable and descriptive domain name.

Now, as people drive by your sign, they'll see a phone number (you do put your phone number on your signs, don't you?) and a URL. They won't remember the phone number, but if they see the URL a few times, there's a good chance they'll remember it. They'll be able to reach your site; in effect, you passed out a business card, without either you or the recipient realizing it at the time. Of course the URL can be pasted on everything—the side of your trucks and cars, employee's uniforms, windows … anything you know people will see.

People don't go online to look for a house painter, or a lawn service, or a plumber—they use the Yellow Pages. But if they've seen a memorable URL a few times, they'll remember it and may go to the business-card Web site.

This is a great little system that costs very little—less than a Yellow Pages ad—yet can be very effective. (You could probably create one of these sites for around $3 a week, including the domain-name fee.)

Business-card Web sites can work well for delivery services, carpet-cleaning services, plumbers, house cleaners, kids cutting lawns, milk-delivery services, diaper services, window cleaners ...

Fools and Angels

Here's one little Internet myth that really annoys me: You'd better get onto the Internet quickly, or your competition will be there first. The implication is that your competition, taking advantage of the Internet, will destroy you. The truth may be the opposite. Your competition may waste valuable financial resources on a project that fails or that succeeds only after huge initial losses.

Of course there are businesses that must be on the Internet. Microsoft couldn't ignore it, nor can most computer hardware and software companies. But if you're selling shoes or pet-grooming services, it's a different matter. Here's a little saying that's worth remembering:

Fools rush in where angels fear to tread.

The Internet myth suggests that you're a fool if you don't jump into the Internet right now. But perhaps you're a fool if you do; perhaps you're treading a path that angels quite sensibly avoid. After all, millions of dollars have already been lost on the Internet—do you have to lose your money, too? Plenty of companies have tried the Internet and failed. Some are trying again, some have just given up. Please, please, *please* don't be stampeded into wasting money on the Internet. Do some research, think logically about what you want to do, and plan carefully. *Get online by all means. But do it right!*

"Local" Means "Very Few People"

People in your area use the Internet, don't they? Yes. If you advertise on the Internet, won't locals find you? Well, we're back to my favorite answer: Maybe. There are a few issues here. First, how many people really use the Internet? You've probably heard the figures: 100 million, 150 million, 250 million. I've recently seen a claim that it's around 200M, with over 100M in the U.S. To be honest I don't pay attention to these claims anymore. Several surveys were published in *Internet World* back in December 1996; they ranged from 9M users in the U.S. to 42M. For worldwide use the numbers ranged from 24M to 26M, less than some of the U.S.-only numbers. Clearly many of the numbers are completely offbase.

In 1993, when I began writing *The Complete Idiot's Guide to the Internet,* the number thrown about was 25 million. Most Internet users at the time were in the U.S.—there was very little Internet penetration in the rest of the world. So that would mean almost one American in ten was using the Internet. But most Americans couldn't have told you what the Internet was if you'd used thumbscrews on them. Clearly the number was then wrong. And the numbers now are mostly wrong, too.

I'd like to tell you exactly how many people are using the Internet—even to the nearest 10 or 20 million would be good. But there is no consensus. But let's accept for the moment that there really are over 200M users worldwide, and around perhaps 100M users in the U.S. ... those numbers are as good as any. What I'm absolutely sure of, though, is that there are definitely not 100 million regular, knowledgeable Internet users within the U.S. or even worldwide.

If you want to look at the numbers for yourself, here are a few good places to track down Internet statistics:

EMarketer
http://www.emarketer.com/estats/

Global Internet Statistics
http://www.euromktg.com/globstats/

MIDS Internet Demographics Survey
http://www.mids.org/

Yahoo!—Internet Statistics and Demographics
http://dir.yahoo.com/Computers_and_Internet/Internet/Statistics_and_Demographics/

Yahoo!—Web Statistics and Demographics
http://dir.yahoo.com/Computers_and_Internet/Internet/World_Wide_Web/Statistics_and_Demographics/

Okay, so the number might be this or might be that. But whatever the number is, what does it mean? Here's an example of how Internet-usage numbers are misused. I found this statement on the front of a marketing flyer (yes, a piece of paper) for an Internet mall a few years ago:

The Internet is the world's largest market.

Oh, sorry, I forgot the exclamation mark:

The Internet is the world's largest market!

What does that mean, though? Isn't the U.S. market bigger? The European market? The world soccer-fan market? Well, yes, but the Internet is a single coherent market. At least that's what some might suggest, but of course it's not. The Internet has a lot of computer geeks, and a lot of teddy bear enthusiasts, soccer players, skydivers, quilters, mothers, children, antique-tractor collectors, UFOlogists, astronomers, mystery writers, foot fetishists, Nazis, conservationists, Communists, Peruvian revolutionaries, Shakespearean actors, bodybuilders … The list could go on; well, it does go on, and on, and on. The Internet is not a single market, so even if there really are 200 million people using it, if you approach the Internet as if it were a distinct block of customers, you're going to be badly disappointed. Rather, it's better to consider the Internet as a collection of thousands, many thousands, of niche markets.

And another point to consider. Maybe there really are 200 million users, but what exactly is an Internet user? Someone who uses e-mail now and again to keep in touch with family, friends, and colleagues? Someone who has an Internet connection at home but hasn't used it in a couple of months, or someone who's an Internet Relay Chat fanatic and doesn't care for the World Wide Web? Someone who spends an hour or two online a week, or somebody who's totally connected, on the Web every waking hour? An Internet user may be any of these things. eMarketer Web site reported, early in 1999, that "while nearly 100 million in America have access, that doesn't mean they are getting online with any regularity, or even at all. In fact, of the 98.9 million with access, only 65 percent, or 64 million, get online at least once per month. And only 37 percent, or 36.6 million jump online at least once per week."

Some of these users are of no use to you at all. Some are highly unlikely ever to come to your Web site. So we can reach two conclusions. First, 200 million or not, the actual number of users you can consider your potential customers is much, much smaller. Second, the number of active Internet users in your area is relatively small. You should assume that most people in your area are not using the Internet, and that those who are using it are, in the main, infrequent users.

That's not to say that the Internet cannot be used as a tool for local purposes. Many professional organizations, for instance, have their own Web sites and mailing lists. So a business that wants to market locally to these organizations' members can tie in with them. And businesses looking for the services of these people can find them. But it does mean that setting up a Web site for your local shoe store or dry-cleaning service probably isn't a great idea. (Again, I don't want to be dogmatic about this … maybe a shoe store owner somewhere can think of a good way to exploit a Web site … but it's going to have to be a *really* good idea!)

They Want You to Have a Web Site

I try to write my books from the point of view of a reader's advocate. The point of this book is not to persuade people to get onto the Web, it's to help them make a decision about whether it would be beneficial and, if they decide it is, to help them do so effectively.

Unfortunately other advisors have other interests. There's a lot of pressure on people to get involved in this Internet thing, and many people are in the business of persuading you to set up a Web site, for a variety of reasons. Some will make money if you do. The author of one book about doing business on the Web talks of turning the World Wide Web into a "cash hose." He also explains why you *must* set up your Web site at an Internet mall (a subject we'll discuss in Chapter 3). This author also happens to own an Internet mall. (Disclaimer: I'm now a partial owner in a Web-hosting company. I wasn't when I wrote the first edition of this book, including the words you've just read, but was so disgusted with the state of the business that I decided to get in. I'll explain more in Chapter 4.)

Other writers are so caught up in the excitement of the technology and so blind to economic realities that they think it's obvious that you *must* be on the Web (we'll talk more about the benefits—and drawbacks—of fancy technology in Chapter 9). Writers working for the computer press are often little more than cheerleaders for technology. Yes, I'll admit it, I write for the computer press, though I try to keep my feet on the ground.

For instance, one review I read stated that "the secret to a successful Web site is to create lots of links." Oh, if only it were that easy! Statements to the effect that you must make your Web site "compelling," "cool," or "exciting"— meaning: You need to use all the latest and most expensive multimedia tools—are so common, it's hard not to begin to believe them. Fortunately, they're not true.

A couple of years ago I attended a free talk, hosted by a Web mall, which took place in the real world, in a local hotel. I'd responded to an ad I'd received—a real ad in the mail—telling me that they were going to explain the secret of getting rich on the Internet. This intrigued me—if there's some magic switch that one can flick to gain instant wealth, I'd certainly like to know what it is. It turns out that the secret to getting rich on the Internet is to sell classified ads and Web pages at a Web mall. Not any Web mall, of course, but their Web mall.

One thing the speaker said really sticks in my mind, though. He talked about selling "classified ad" space to local businesses. He explained how one can convince a business to spend $50 to post an ad. The technique is based on convincing the business that there are millions of Internet users and that some are in the business' area, and also appealing to their egos a little: Wouldn't it be nice to be able to say *your* business is on the *Internet!*

What happens when it's time to renew the classified ad? The speaker never actually said "these classified ads don't make their buyers any money." Rather, what he said was that even if the classified ads didn't make their buyers any money, buyers almost always renew because they like the cachet of being able to say they're "on the Internet," and because many businesses regard $50 advertising checks as the sort of expense to be paid without thinking about.

So don't be stampeded onto the Internet by cheerleaders or people who are going to make money from you. Take the advice of these people, and you'll probably end up paying too much and building a Web site that won't do you any good.

Just Remember This ...

Here's something you should remember:

> *The Internet is a giant jobs program for computer geeks.*

That doesn't mean the Internet is not an important tool for many businesses; it definitely is. But when you hear advice, consider where it's coming from. There are probably many more people making a living from providing Internet services than making a living from selling non-Internet products and services on the Internet. What do I mean by Internet services? Internet service providers, Web hosting, Web-site design, Internet-related software, and so on. (If you're unsure of the meaning of some of these terms, you'll find an explanation in Chapter 2.) Oh, and include the Internet writers, people writing books and magazine articles about the Internet, and so on. The Internet has provided a huge boom in the computer-book business with the sales of tens of millions of Internet-related books.

My geek motto is important to consider when you try to sift through the advice you've been given about putting your business on the Web. And it's important to remember the phrase when you consider what your Web site should look like. So you'll see this phrase again later in this book.

So, Do You Need a Web Site?

I hope by now you are ready to make a rational decision about whether or not you need to set up a Web site. Or, at least, to begin the process of research and learning that will bring you to that decision.

Perhaps you're not sure if a Web site can help your business. Perhaps you think it might, but you don't want to invest huge sums in creating a Web site. Well, you don't have to. Web sites can be created very cheaply. An independent businessperson, for instance, can create a nice Web site in spare time and run it for $20 or $30 a month.

Here's a true story: An executive at US West approached a system administrator with the question, "If we give you half a million dollars, could you set up a Web site for us?" (And this was several years ago, when Web sites were in a fairly primitive stage. The system administrator later told me that she tried not to sound too enthusiastic, and, in a serious voice, answered, "Well, I think I probably can.") Many people have inflated ideas of what a Web site should cost, partly thanks to the computer press, who've touted the complicated and expensive technologies over the simple low-cost technologies.

Well, this book is about how to set up your Web site without going broke. Web sites can be cheap, and I'll show you how.

Not Pessimism but Realism

I hope I don't sound too pessimistic about setting up a Web site. In fact I think I'm more optimistic in some ways than many other writers. You see, there's a subliminal message being sent when writers talk about making a Web site "cool" by making it "compelling" and adding Java and JavaScript and every other neat little toy. That message is, "don't bother trying, it's way too expensive, and you just can't compete."

And in fact most people really *can't* compete in that manner, because it's way too expensive. For instance, creating a Java applet is difficult; it will take hundreds of hours for a nonprogrammer to learn enough to create a decent applet, or perhaps thousands of dollars to pay someone to do it. Luckily you don't need to follow this bad advice, you don't need Java, and you don't need "cool." You can, in fact, create a useful Web site at a very low cost. And that's just what this book is all about.

About the URLs

I've mentioned in this book literally hundreds—800 or so, last time I counted—of links to all sorts of useful resources that will help you create and promote your Web site. To save typing all those links, I suggest you visit **the Web site associated with this book** (http://www.poorrichard.com/). You'll find a Web page with all the links sorted according to chapter and alphabetically within each chapter. You can save that page on your hard disk or simply bookmark the page; then you'll be able to go to the sites that I mention in this book with a quick click.

I'll be checking those links periodically so that I can update them as they change—as any group of hundreds of Web links surely will over time. Also, let me quickly explain a simple trick for using links that appear to be broken—a handy little trick you can use whenever you're traveling around the World Wide Web. Let's say, for instance, that you see a URL like this in a magazine:

http://www.thisdomain.com/firstdirect/seconddirect/this.html

Now, you type this URL (or click on the link), and you get a browser error telling you that the requested item has not been found. What can you do? Well, if you typed the link, make sure you typed it correctly; in particular, make sure you used the correct file extension (.html and not .htm in this case). If you did type it correctly, or if you clicked on a link, then it may be that the file has been moved or deleted. What next? Do you just give up?

No, I suggest you work your way up the directory path to see if you find another Web page that might contain information that will help you find the page you're looking for. Remove the filename from the URL in the browser's Location bar and try again:

http://www.thisdomain.com/firstdirect/seconddirect/

Press Enter, and one of three things will happen. Your browser may display a document which is the default document for that directory, or it may display a listing showing all the files in that directory. You can then click on the different .htm and .html files shown in the directory to display them. Or it may display another error, telling you that nothing was found. If so, try moving up to the next directory. Type this:

http://www.thisdomain.com/firstdirect/

Again, you may see a Web page, a directory listing, or an error. If you see an error, move back to the next directory. In this example you'd type the following:

http://www.thisdomain.com/

Now you'll almost always find something, assuming the domain name is correct. You may find a page that indicates where you can find the information you want ... or that the information is no longer present at that server. Using this technique, you can often find the information you need, even if it's been moved to a new location at the Web site.

## Chapter Two

What You Need Before You Start

In this chapter I'll give you an inventory of the things you'll need before you start. If you already have Internet access and have a place to put your Web site, please don't skip this chapter. Many Internet users don't understand the relationship between their Internet service, their e-mail system, and their Web site, and to work efficiently you must know how these three systems hook together.

Here's a quick rundown of what you need to set up your business on the Internet. This is a basic list—the things a small business needs as a minimum to get started.

- A computer
- Hardware connecting the computer to the Internet
- Internet access through an Internet service provider
- A POP e-mail account
- Somewhere to put your Web site
- Basic Internet access software
- Basic Internet knowledge
- Advanced research and marketing software.

We'll take a look at each of these things one by one.

Your Computer

This almost goes without saying: You need a computer. But what sort of computer? I don't want to make any enemies here, but I would advise that you use a Windows 98/NT/2000 PC. Yes, Windows can be extremely frustrating (though I've found Windows 2000 to be a *lot* more stable than Windows 98).

But if you use a Macintosh you will find that your software choices are severely restricted. (I believe the Mac is a wonderful machine, by the way … I don't want to get involved in the Mac-versus-Windows religious war!) Many of the programs we'll look at in this book have Windows versions but no Macintosh versions. In some cases there are no Macintosh equivalents, either, so it's not merely a matter of picking another brand of software. The programs we'll look at can make your work on the Internet and on the World Wide Web much more efficient and effective, so this is no small matter. If you have a Macintosh already and you don't want to spend the money on a new machine—or are unable to do so—that's fine; you can still set up a Web site. But you'll have fewer options to pick from, and a smaller range of tools.

You need a fast computer with lots of RAM (Random Access Memory). RAM is very cheap these days, so don't scrimp. In fact RAM is more important than processor speed. If you buy a new computer, for instance, it's better to buy a slow processor with lots of RAM than a fast processor with too little RAM. How much RAM? If you're using Windows, 32MB is not enough. Just because that's the way many machines are sold doesn't mean it's okay. Windows will not run in 32MB of RAM, so it has to borrow disk space to create "virtual" memory if this is all the RAM you have. And every time it uses the disk instead of real memory, it slows down. You need at least 64MB of RAM, and 96 is better. If you have just a little extra money when you come to choosing your computer, consider increasing the RAM before going for a faster processor.

Windows needs lots of memory to do what it was intended to do—run multiple programs simultaneously. You'll definitely be doing that while promoting your business on the Internet. You'll be running the dial-up software needed to connect to the Internet, a Web browser, perhaps a memory-hogging Web-authoring tool such as FrontPage, a word processor, an e-mail program, and so on. I strongly recommend that you get 96MB of RAM.

Connecting Your Computer to the Internet

The other piece of critical hardware is the line-access hardware. This could be one of these things:

- A telephone-line modem
- A cable modem
- A DSL modem
- An ISDN terminal adapter (often known as an ISDN modem)

- Something horribly expensive and probably unnecessary (T1 and a router)
- Satellite equipment.

Telephone Modems

A modem is used to connect your computer to normal phone lines. It takes the signal from your computer, modulates it—that is, converts the digital computer data into analog phone data—then sends it across the phone lines to the computer you've connected to. When data is sent across the phone lines to your computer, the modem demodulates it—that is, converts it from analog to digital data—and sends it to your computer. The word "modem" is a contraction of modulate/demodulate.

You can buy external modems—boxes that you connect to your computer's serial port, and internal modems—which are the same as external modems except without the box; instead the processor card is installed inside the computer. I recommend that you buy a 56k modem, that is, one that runs at a speed of 56kbps (bits per second, a measure of how fast the modem can send data). That's just theory, though; the modem will actually run more slowly than that (though still faster than other, slower-rated modems). If you want a technical discussion of why this is, take a look at these sites:

3Com/USRobotics
   http://www.3com.com/56k/

The 56k Modem Info Center
   http://www.sirius.com/~rmoss/

56k.com
   http://www.56k.com/

Remember, you can view a Web page containing these links at http://www.poorrichard.com/.

There's been a lot of confusion about these modems, because for two years there were two competing, and noncompatible, systems: 3Com/US Robotic's X2 system and Rockwell/Lucent's K56Flex. There is now a standard, though, known as V.90. In theory, then, all 56k modems should be able to operate with all others. In practice, though, the modem you buy may not yet have the V.90 software, though it's probably upgradeable. Also, many service providers have not yet converted to V.90; they may still be using one or other of the old methods. And in some cases you may find that you have to shop around to find an Internet service provider in your area using *any* kind of 56k modem. Furthermore, you may find that the phone lines in your area don't work properly with 56k modems, so you actually connect at a *much* lower speed, perhaps 28.8kbps.

If you buy a 56k modem, make sure that either it's already V.90 compatible, or it's going to be easy to upgrade (the manufacturer may have placed upgrade software at their Web site). And make sure that you'll be able to use the modem with your service provider.

An Internet service provider (ISP) is a company that provides access to the Internet. Your computer connects to one of the company's computers, allowing your computer to communicate with the Internet. ISPs are often also known as Internet access providers (IAPs).

Cable Modems

You might also be able to connect to the Internet through your local cable TV company ... but chances are, you won't. I'm lucky enough to have a cable modem, and I don't want to gloat ... well alright, I do want to gloat. It's fantastic. It's incredibly fast, so that I now have real trouble using a computer with a telephone-modem connection—it just feels soooo slooow. Unfortunately, though, cable connections are not yet widely available. If you're lucky enough to be in an area in which it is available, jump at the chance. I pay just $40 a month for a permanent connection to the Internet (no need to dial in, you're always connected). I'd been waiting for this kind of connection for five years, ever since the beginning of the Internet "boom." But it's clear that my cable company won't be able to install these things in a hurry; it took two guys three hours to install the equipment ... and it still wasn't working. Then they got another guy in to help, and left about an hour later with the system still out of commission; it wasn't until I spent a couple of hours on the phone with the technical-support people the next day that we finally got the thing up and running.

Cable speeds vary from system to system and time to time, somewhere between 200kbps and 3Mbps (3,000kbps). A few cable systems are only unidirectional; you have to use a phone line at the same time that you are connected through the cable modem. The data coming from the Internet flows along the cable, while information from your computer back to the Internet goes along the telephone line.

So cable is now available, for a few people, in a few areas of North America—call your cable company and find out if you can get it. In most of the rest of the world, cable systems are still not available and probably won't be for some time. For information on cable access, see these sites:

@Home (The largest cable-modem service)
http://www.home.com/

Cable Modem Resources on the Web
http://rpcp.mit.edu/~gingold/cable/

Time Warner Road Runner
http://www.rr.com/

Yahoo!—Cable Modems
http://dir.yahoo.com/computers_and_internet/hardware/peripherals/
cable_modems/

By the way, the $40 I mentioned is the price for home service. If you want to install a cable system in your office, you'll probably be offered the privilege of getting the same exact service at several times the price.

DSL

Finally, DSL (Digital Subscriber Line) has arrived. The phone companies now seem to be serious about installing DSL (they were saying for years that they'd have it ready to install "very soon"). DSL is slower than cable systems, and more expensive. And it's run by the phone companies, which puts me right off them. (Are all the phone companies in North America as bad as US West, I wonder?) But if you simply can't get a cable system, and it doesn't look like you'll have cable any time soon, you might want to get DSL. Problem is, if you can't get cable, there's a good chance you can't get DSL either.

DSL comes in various flavors: HDSL (High-Rate DSL), ADSL (Asymmetric DSL), RADSL (Rate Adaptive DSL), VDSL (Very high data-rate DSL), and so on. These lines range in speed from 128kbps to 700kbps. Rates seem to range from $75 a month to $175 a month. Unlike cable systems, in which you get your line and your service provider in one package (the cable company is also an Internet service provider), with DSL you can choose how to configure it; you can sign up for an all-in-one package, or you might just rent the line from the phone company but connect to a non–phone company Internet service provider.

ISDN

Another option available in many areas, though not all, is to install an ISDN (Integrated Services Digital Network) phone line. In fact, if you can't get DSL, this is the next step down. This is a digital phone line and can carry data much more quickly than an ordinary analog phone line; you can transmit and receive data at either 64kbps or 128kbps, depending on the type of line you select (yes, the faster line is more expensive). In the U.S., ISDN typically costs around $60 to install and $60 to $100 a month to run—more if you use it extensively, because there are per-minute charges. (Note that ISDN prices vary greatly between regions.)

But ISDN often doesn't work well, and in fact the phone companies don't really want to mess with it. They'd much rather install DSL. But as they haven't yet installed the DSL infrastructure in most areas, they can't give everyone DSL, so they have to fall back on ISDN … which they really don't want to mess with. Get the idea? You can buy ISDN, but it may not work well, because they don't care about it. In fact, the unofficial definition of ISDN is: *It Still Doesn't Work*. (At least, that's the U.S. definition; in some other parts of the world ISDN is much more available and reliable.) If you're lucky, ISDN isn't available in your area anyway.

There are other costs associated with ISDN that you should watch out for. Not only will you pay the phone company $60 or more a month to use the line, but you'll also pay for Internet access, perhaps to the phone company or perhaps another ISP. On top of that you'll have to buy an ISDN terminal adapter. (Though often called an ISDN modem, a terminal adapter doesn't actually modulate or demodulate.)

I once had an ISDN line, and a colleague still has one. I found that my ISDN line was sometimes really handy, but most of the time I used my modem line instead because the ISDN line was so unreliable—it kept dropping my Internet connections. My colleague's line, in a different area of the city and a couple of years later, has exactly the same problem. (And why did the phone company have to destroy my neighbor's bush when installing the ISDN line?) If I haven't put you off, or if cable and DSL are not available and you're desperate for something faster, you can find more information about ISDN at your local phone company's Web page, or call them.

Salespeople from ISDN-hardware companies often tout the phenomenal speeds possible through ISDN. If data is compressed, you can actually transmit at several times the 128kbps limit I've mentioned here. Don't be fooled, though. You almost certainly won't be able to go above 128kbps when connecting to the Internet, because most Internet service providers are not set up to compress data.

Satellite Systems

There are other connection options. You can get a satellite connection using **DirecPC from Hughes Network Systems** (http://www.direcpc.com/). This is available in some areas of North America. It'll cost around $430 to $480 to install (around $180 less if you install the equipment yourself), but you'll still need a modem connection, too. It works like this: Your software uses the modem connection to send information out onto the Internet. When you want to display a Web page, for instance, you click on a link in the Web browser, and a message is sent across the modem to the Web site. When the Web site sends the page back, it's grabbed by a computer at the DirecPC operations center, transmitted up into space, picked up by a satellite, and transmitted down to earth, where it's picked up by your satellite dish. Incoming data—the data coming from the satellite—moves at 400kbps; outgoing data (along the phone line) moves at normal modem speeds. You'll pay Hughes around $50 to get 100 hours of service a month. By the way, some other companies plan to offer Internet access via satellite, but for technical reasons can't begin operations until 2002.

T1s and Other Stuff

The phone company can provide you with other neat things, such as 56k lines, T1 lines, fractional T1s, and T3s. These are generally quite expensive and complicated, and more than the average small business really needs. So that's all I'll say about them.

Which Do You Pick?

What should you get? If you can get cable, do so! You may be lucky and not have to pay an installation fee, and you can't beat the $40 to $45 a month it will probably cost you. If you can't get cable, you may want to simply use a fast telephone modem, and for most small companies this is fine. It's relatively cheap, and it will be easy to find an ISP that will work with you. But don't cheap out and buy a low-cost or slow modem. Get a high-quality, fast modem. It'll make a big difference.

If you're willing to spend a bit more (perhaps somewhere between $50 and $200 a month), DSL is the next choice. As for ISDN or satellite ... well, maybe, but think long and hard before you do it.

By the way, if you plan to set up your own Web server—a computer that will hold your Web site—you'll probably need more powerful Internet connections than those I've described here. A telephone modem is really not fast enough; the cable company won't let you set up a server on their system (although it's plenty fast enough), unless you pay a fortune for one of the business accounts; an ISDN connection is too unreliable and not really fast enough; and a satellite system won't work because it only transmits data *to* you, not from you. Instead you'll have to lease from the phone company a very fast and very expensive phone line such as a T1 line (which you'll learn more about in Chapter 4) and install all sorts of expensive hardware (a router) at your computer. However, as you'll learn in Chapter 3, I recommend that you don't set up your own Web server, and I'll explain the difference between a Web server and a Web site later in this chapter.

Internet Access

The next thing you need is a connection to the Internet. The Internet is a giant public network. In order to connect to it, you must connect to a computer that is already connected to the Internet. That's done through what's known as an Internet service provider (ISP). There are more ISPs than you can shake a stick at, ranging from free systems providing very limited service for a few hundred people in a single community, to huge companies providing access for millions of people in many countries. In general the free services won't be of use to you. The majority provide old-style command-line Internet access, and you require the newer graphical-user-interface type of access, what's known as TCP/IP access.

There are essentially three different types of ISP:

- True ISPs
- The online services
- The phone and cable companies.

The true ISPs are companies that are primarily in the business of providing Internet access and associated services—Web-page design, Web hosting, and so on. (We'll be looking at Internet terminology a little later in this chapter, by the way.) These companies range from small local companies with a few hundred subscribers, to national companies with hundreds of thousands. If you already have some form of Internet access, you can track down service providers in your area using **Yahoo!'s Internet Access Provider's** page at http://www.yahoo.com/ Business_and_Economy/Companies/Internet_Services/Access_Providers/ or **The List** at http://thelist.internet.com/. You may be able to get to these pages from a computer at your local library, for instance.

The online services are companies such as CompuServe, America Online (AOL), Prodigy, Microsoft Network, and GEnie. These companies are like private clubs. They provide access to all sorts of services: thousands of discussion groups almost any imaginable subject, chat rooms, news and weather information, and so on. If you want to access these services, you have to join the club. But they also provide Internet access. So if you're a member of the club, you can still get onto the Internet and use the World Wide Web, newsgroups, and other services.

Finally, the phone and cable companies have jumped into the fray. Companies such as Sprint (Sprint Internet Passport), AT&T (AT&T WorldNet), MCI (internetMCI), Time Warner Cable (Road Runner), and TCI (@Home) now provide Internet access throughout North America. Many local phone companies provide Internet access, too. When you buy a cable connection you'll get Internet service thrown in with it. And when you install a DSL or ISDN line, you'll probably be given the option of using the phone company as your Internet service provider.

However, the phone companies often "just don't get it," and although they understand how to connect everything together, they don't really understand what people want to do on the Internet. You'll often get better service from a true ISP than from one of the phone companies.

So which Internet service provider should you use? As I've said before, if you can get cable, do so ... and that answers the question for you. Otherwise, it's a hard question, because it depends on where and when. An ISP that provides good service in one area might be providing lousy service in another, for instance. It may be good today, bad tomorrow.

I'd recommend that you have at least two ways to get onto the Internet, from two separate ISPs. For instance, I have a cable connection and a CompuServe account. When I travel I can use my CompuServe account to connect, wherever I am in the world. And if the cable connection goes down, I can still access using the telephone modem through CompuServe. (Okay, so there are sometimes problems with cable. Like the time that I was beta testing Windows 2000 Server, and without informing me, the operating system automatically turned on certain services—such as DHCP, if you really have to know—so @Home turned off my connection because they thought I was running a network server on their system.)

Before I had cable I used to keep three service providers, because they were all so unreliable I wanted to make sure that I *always* had a way to connect. (with cable, just one backup system is enough.) If everything went well, I used Sprint most of the time. When I had trouble with the Sprint network, I could switch to CompuServe. If things got really bad on both Sprint and CompuServe, I could fall back on my low-cost USA.Net account and pay extra for a few hours if necessary.

Not only does having two or more accounts allow you to get on at all times, but it increases your chances of getting to the Internet sites you want to visit. It's quite feasible for network problems to make it impossible for you to access a particular Web site, for instance, through one Internet service provider, but possible through another service provider.

I'd advise that you talk with other Internet users in your area, check ads in local papers and magazines, and try a few services to find a reliable one. I don't want to recommend any particular service nor denounce any particular service. I've used many, and found that they all have their ups and downs—and none I've tried so far are completely reliable.

Just because a service advertises that it provides unlimited Internet access for $19.95 a month, it doesn't mean it really does so. It may mean "$19.95 for as many hours as you're able to connect, if you can get past the busy signals and if we don't drop you off the system." You may recall that a couple of years ago or so, for instance, 20 state Attorneys General threatened to sue AOL for promising unlimited access but providing only busy signals.

A POP E-mail Account

You need an e-mail account, but you really need a POP e-mail account. POP means Post Office Protocol, and it's the standard e-mail system used on the Internet. While most true Internet service providers and the phone-company Internet service providers will give you a POP account, it's important to understand that the online services generally do not. Rather, they have their own mail systems that were designed before Internet access was important, so they work in a very different manner. If you have a CompuServe or AOL account, for instance, you probably don't have a POP e-mail account. However, note that if you're using an old version of the CompuServe software, it's possible to convert your mail system to POP (you'll find information online if you dig around for it). For some odd reason, though, if you have the very latest software, CompuServe 2000, you *cannot* use POP, at least at the time of writing that was the case.

Why do you need a POP account? Because it's so much more flexible than a non-POP account. Ideally you want your own domain name (which you'll learn all about in Chapter 5) and a POP account. For instance, my domain name is topfloor.com. Because I have my own POP account and my own domain name, I can create as many e-mail addresses as I want: pkent@topfloor.com, info@topfloor.com, sales@topfloor.com, ipn@topfloor.com, whateveriwant@topfloor.com. I can set up addresses for individual employees, for instance.

Furthermore, with a POP e-mail account, you have your choice of e-mail programs. With an online service's own proprietary system, you get whatever software they give you, or, in some cases, you can choose from a limited selection. And these programs are usually not very good. With POP, you have a huge choice, and some really good programs to work with.

Because I have a POP, for instance, I've been able to pick an e-mail program that can filter my messages. That is, it automatically sorts messages into separate folders. When I send a message, a copy is placed in the appropriate folder, and when I receive a message, it's automatically routed to the correct folder. This capability is really essential for anyone serious about doing business on the Internet.

You don't have to get your POP account at the same place you get your Internet access, though. If you wish, you can get a POP account from a completely different company. See, for instance, the **Yahoo! Email Providers** page (http://dir.yahoo.com/ Business_and_Economy/Companies/ Internet_Services/Email_Providers/), where you'll find links to all sorts of e-mail services, and **Web-Quote Central** (http://www.centeroftheweb. com/webquote/), which has lists of all sorts of Internet services, including e-mail providers.

So you can have an account with CompuServe or AOL, for instance, and still have a POP e-mail account somewhere else. How will you access your mail? You'll use CompuServe or AOL to connect to the Internet, then start a POP e-mail program (such as Eudora, Netscape Messenger, AK-Mail, Pegasus, or one of many others). You'll then use this program to connect to your POP account,

*I'm currently using an e-mail program called **Eudora**, which is very good. It's available in a freeware or commercial version for Windows and the Macintosh— though in order to use filters you'll have to get the commercial version:* http://www.eudora.com/. *In the past I've used **AK-Mail**, which is also pretty good. It's a Windows 95/NT shareware program, and you can get it from* http://www.akmail.com/ *or from many shareware libraries. It has some filter features that Eudora doesn't have, but in all Eudora is easier to use. Another very highly rated program is **Pegasus Mail*** (http://www.pegasus.usa.com/), *which is free and available for Windows 3.1 and Windows 95/ NT. See also **Yahoo!'s Electronic Mail** page:* http://dir.yahoo.com/ Computers_and_Internet/Software/ Internet/Electronic_Mail/.

wherever on the Internet that happens to be, and grab your mail. In the same way that you can start a CompuServe or AOL connection, open a Web browser, and connect to a Web site, you can start a CompuServe or AOL connection, open a POP e-mail program, and connect to an e-mail account hosted on a computer out on the Internet.

When you get your POP account, make sure that you can have unlimited e-mail "aliases" within that POP account, that is, unlimited e-mail addresses that will be accepted by that account. Some services may set up the POP account to accept e-mail to only one address: pkent@topfloor.com, for instance. But I want to be able to accept e-mail addressed to pkent@topfloor.com, info@ topfloor. com, sales@topfloor.com, ipn@topfloor.com, whateveriwant@topfloor.com, and so on. So ensure that you're getting the right kind of account before you buy.

Before you run off and buy a POP account, read on. You'll be looking for a place to put your Web site, and most Web-hosting companies will give you a free POP account.

Somewhere to Put Your Web Site

You also need somewhere to put your Web site. I'm going to go into this subject in detail in Chapter 3, but for the moment I want to clear up two misconceptions. The first is that when you get Internet access, you get a Web site with it. Some service providers don't give their members Web space, and even if a service provider does, the Web site probably won't be suitable as a business site. In Chapter 4 you'll learn about the services you need, and you may, in fact, find that your service provider can provide all the required Web services. You're more likely to discover, however, that your ISP cannot provide what you need, or will provide everything for an additional (exorbitant) fee.

The other misconception is that you have to have a Web site with the same company that you get Internet access from; in other words, that if your service provider doesn't provide Web space, you'll have to leave and find one that does. But Internet access and Web space are two completely different things. As with POP accounts, you can set up your Web site on any Web-hosting service anywhere in the world. You can then connect to your ISP, and connect to your Web site across the Internet.

How It All Hooks Together

So you need Internet access, a POP account, and a Web site. This confuses people. Aren't these all much the same thing; don't you get all three at once? No, and no. Let me just clarify how all these hook together.

Internet access merely allows your computer to communicate with the Internet—nothing more, nothing less. It's like your phone service; having your house connected to the phone system allows you to make calls across the system. It doesn't provide friends and a family for you to call—you have to provide them yourself.

Once you have Internet access, you can connect to computers all over the world. Those computers can provide some of the services you're going to need: your POP account and your Web site. You pay a fee to a company somewhere out there on the Internet, it sets up your POP account and provides space for your Web site, and away you go.

Your business may be in Vancouver, Canada. You may be using a large international ISP headquartered in, say, Washington, D.C., in the U.S. You may have your Web site on a computer sitting in London, England. And you may have a POP account in Dublin, Ireland (though practically speaking you're almost certain to have the POP account in the same place you have your Web site).

Geographical location makes little difference (except that you may want to ensure that your ISP has a phone number in your area, or at least a toll-free number you can call). You can use services anywhere in the world. What's more important is how reliable those services are, which is an issue we'll discuss in Chapter 4.

Basic Internet Access Software

Before you can do business on the Internet, you need the software that allows you to move around on the Internet. When you sign up with a service provider, that company will generally provide you with software to get started, though you may want to switch to better programs later. Here's what you need:

- Access software
- An e-mail program
- A World Wide Web browser
- A newsreader
- An FTP program.

Those are the basic tools you need, though as you'll see we'll be adding things as we go along. The access software is the dial-up or network software required to make the connection to the Internet. There are loads of options, but generally an ISP will give you the software you need or tell you how to configure your operating system to make the connection. Windows 95 and Windows NT, for instance, come with built-in dial-up and network software.

You need an e-mail program to send and receive electronic mail. You need a Web browser in order to view pages on the World Wide Web. You need a newsreader to read newsgroup messages. And you need an FTP (File Transfer Protocol) program to upload files to your Web site.

Note that the two major Web browsers, Netscape Navigator and Microsoft Internet Explorer, come bundled with e-mail and newsreader programs. However, in both cases you're better off working with another, more sophisticated program. The bundled programs are fine for getting started, but you need the tools provided by the specialized programs, as you'll see later in the book. Also, most Web browsers, including these two, can work with FTP to some degree. Both Navigator and Internet Explorer allow you to transfer files to your Web site (we'll discuss this in Chapter 6). But you really need a true FTP program to work with file transfers quickly and efficiently.

Which browser should you get? There are literally scores of different browsers available, but only two are popular and only two are up-to-date: **Netscape Navigator** (http://www.netscape.com/) and **Microsoft Internet Explorer** (http://www.microsoft.com/windows/ie/). I suggest you use one of these two. At the time of writing I prefer Internet Explorer ... though when I wrote the first edition of this book I preferred Netscape Navigator, which is part of the Netscape Communicator suite of programs. They keep leapfrogging each other; one's better for a few months, then another version is released, and the other moves ahead. (However, that leapfrogging may be coming to an end, as Netscape loses interest in Navigator, having well and truly lost the "browser war." In fact, it's a good idea to have both of these on your system—when you create your Web site you want to make sure it looks good in both browsers. It's very common to find that something that works perfectly in one browser is completely screwed up in the other.

For Windows users, I'd suggest CuteFTP or WS_FTP, both of which you can find at various shareware libraries. (Personally, I prefer CuteFTP.) For the Macintosh, Fetch is the most popular program, though there are a number of other FTP programs, including several new ones that are getting good reviews: NetFinder, NetBatch, Mirror, and Download Deputy. For a list of shareware libraries see "Where Will You Get the Software?" later in this chapter.

Basic Knowledge

You're going to need two forms of basic knowledge. You need to understand how to work with your computer, and you must understand how to work with the Internet. You'll have to understand how to open compressed files that you've downloaded from the Internet, how to work with your computer's file-management system, how to move around on the World Wide Web, how to work with e-mail, and lots, lots, more.

It's not the purpose of this book to explain these sorts of things. We've got plenty to do once you understand how to get around on the Internet. I suggest that, if you don't already understand the Internet, you read a few good books; you might start with my *Complete Idiot's Guide to the Internet* (Que).

For now, though, in case you are just exploring the idea of setting up a Web site and need to understand some of the basic lingo, here's a mini-glossary with a few basic definitions:

The Internet—A giant computer network connecting millions of computers and millions of people around the world. This is a public network, though many of the computers connected to it are also part of smaller private networks.

The World Wide Web—Contrary to popular misconception, the World Wide Web is not a synonym for the Internet. The World Wide Web is a software system running across the Internet. The Internet is the hardware, the Web is just one type of Internet software. You might think of the Internet as a huge highway system, and the Web as a trucking company moving things hither and thither across these roads. It's not the only company in the business, though; other software systems moving information around on the Internet include e-mail and FTP.

Web browser—This is a program that displays Web pages. If you want to "go onto the Web," "navigate the Web," "surf the Web," or whatever else you might call it, you need a Web browser.

Web server—This term can refer to a couple of things. It's often used to mean the software that manages one or more Web sites. When a Web browser wants to view a Web page, it sends a message to the Web server, which transmits the page back to the browser. The term also often refers to the whole kit and caboodle involved in this process; not just the Web server software, but the computer on which the software is running, too.

Web site—This term generally means a collection of associated Web pages: The Yahoo! Web site, The Library of Congress Web site, and so on. A single Web server may administer multiple Web sites—sometimes a few dozen, sometimes hundreds. One small Web-hosting company told me that its two servers had almost 1,000 Web sites. You will be creating your own Web site—your own collection of pages.

Web page—This is also known as a Web document. A single document stored at a Web site. A single Web browser window generally displays a single Web page at a time, though the window may be split into separate frames with a document in each frame. A Web page is stored in a single computer file with the .htm or .html file extension. (You'll see other file extensions sometimes, generally when a page is created "on the fly" by a program.)

URL—A Web "address." It tells your Web browser exactly where to find a particular file. For instance, http://TopFloor.com/pr/newsltr/ means "Go into the directory named newsltr, which is a subdirectory of pr, at the host computer named TopFloor.com." In this case no filename is included so the Web server will send the default file, probably a file named index.html. Many URLs, though, do specify the filename at the end of the address.

Web host—If you don't have your own Web server (and you probably won't), you can find someone else to "host" your Web site for you. There are companies known as Web-hosting companies, or Web presence providers, which sell space on their Web servers. We'll be learning about these companies in Chapter 3.

Host computer—This simply means a computer connected to the Internet.

Hypertext—A system by which electronically stored documents are linked together. The World Wide Web is the world's largest hypertext system, in which documents are viewed in Web browsers. Links are operated by pointing with the mouse at a picture or underlined text and clicking. Using a link loads the document referenced by the link.

Home page—This has two meanings. Originally it meant the page that a Web browser displays when you start the program or when you use the browser's Home command. Now it frequently means the main page at a Web site.

E-mail—This is short for electronic mail, a system in which messages can be sent across the Internet to an individual mailbox. Messages may take a few minutes to travel across the world, or, when things are getting sluggish, a day or two.

FTP—File Transfer Protocol, one of the early software systems running on the Internet. This system allows you to transfer files between computers on the Internet. Although to a great extent it's been superseded by the World Wide Web (which also allows you to transfer files), there are still many FTP sites around the world. More importantly, when you set up a Web site you'll also get an FTP account, so you can transfer files from your computer to your Web site.

Newsgroup—A form of discussion group. There are tens of thousands of newsgroups around the world, of which over 30,000 are distributed internationally. Think of a subject, and there's probably a newsgroup dedicated to it, which means that whatever you are trying to sell or promote, there's a newsgroup with people who are interested. To read newsgroup messages, you need a program known as a newsreader. These discussion groups are distributed via a system called Usenet, so you'll often see them referred to as Usenet groups.

Mailing list—Another form of discussion group. To read this type of group, though, you'll need nothing more than your e-mail program. There are over 100,000 mailing lists, some private, many public.

There are a few other things you should know about, though you may not actually use these systems:

Archie—This is a system used to search for files at FTP sites.

Gopher—This system was supposed to revolutionize the Internet, taking a complicated command-line system and turning it into a simple menu system. Then came the Web, and Gopher dropped out of the race. But there are still many Gopher sites around, and Web browsers can display them.

Telnet—This system allows you to log onto a computer across the Internet and work on that computer, running programs, searching databases, and so on. Very few Internet users know how to use Telnet or even what it is.

Chat—You type a message and someone else across the Internet— perhaps a whole lot of people—can read it. They can respond immediately, generally with dross. You can respond to the response, perhaps with dross of your own. I can't stand chat; many people love it.

IRC—This stands for Internet Relay Chat, which was the first popular Internet chat system. Dross personified.

VON—Voice On the Net, a way of holding "phone" conversations on the Internet. It consists of a variety of different systems. You'll need a microphone, sound card, VON software, and someone to talk to who has the same setup.

Learn as much as you can about the Internet before you start building your Web site. I won't be explaining too much of the basics in this book!

Advanced Research and Marketing Software

So far we've discussed a basic Internet system, but if you're going to set up and promote a Web site you'll need a variety of programs to help you along the way.

You'll need software to help you create your Web pages, for instance. You may want a program that will help you register your site with the Web search engines, programs that you can use to do research, and so on. We'll discuss these programs as we go along. I'll give URLs to lead you to some of these programs. In some cases you may wish to buy commercial software. There are thousands of different Internet programs, and it's impossible to keep up with all of them. I'll mention programs that I've used, like, or know about, but you may find equivalents that you prefer.

Where Will You Get the Software?

As I mentioned earlier, when you sign up for Internet service, the ISP will provide you with basic software to get you started. Later you'll want more. You'll see ads for Internet software all over the place, of course; in the computer press, in the software catalogs you get in the mail by the dozen, and so on.

You can also find really great software at shareware libraries on the Internet. These sites contain several types of software:

- Public domain—Free software that belongs to nobody. The program author has given away all rights.
- Freeware—This type of software belongs to someone, but the owner is giving away the rights to use it, sometimes in particular circumstances. It's free to individuals, but companies have to pay, for instance.
- Shareware—Take it, use it, if you like it, send money.
- Demoware—Take it, use it, if you like it, send money and they'll send a program that actually works.
- Crippleware—Take it, use it, if you like it, send money and they'll send a program that has all the features enabled.

We'll be talking about all sorts of software in this book. Here are a few addresses of shareware libraries to get you started. I'll be pointing you to particular sites for particular programs as we progress, but if there's ever something you think you need but which I haven't helped you find, check these sites:

Info-Mac HyperArchive ("The Largest Macintosh Software Archive in the World")
http://www.info-mac.org/
http://hyperarchive.lcs.mit.edu/HyperArchive.html

Jumbo! (Programs of all sorts for Windows, UNIX, and the Mac)
http://www.jumbo.com/

Nonags (Windows software)
http://www.nonags.com/

Shareware.com (all types of programs for Windows, UNIX and Macs)
http://www.shareware.com/

Stroud's Consummate Winsock Applications Page (Windows)
http://cws.internet.com/

Tucows: The Ultimate Collection of Winsock Software (Windows, Mac, and OS/2 programs)
http://www.tucows.com/

The Ultimate Macintosh Site
http://www.ultimatemac.com/

Umich Mac Archive
http://www-personal.umich.edu/~sdamask/umich-mirrors/

Winfiles (A large archive of 32-bit Windows software)
http://www.winfiles.com/

Winsite (A huge archive of Windows software)
http://www.winsite.com/

WUGNET
http://www.wugnet.com/

ZDNet Macintosh Software Library
http://www.macdownload.com/
http://www.zdnet.com/mac/download.html

ZDNet Software Library (Windows and Macintosh)
http://www.zdnet.com/swlib/

You can also search for software at Yahoo! and other Web search sites. As you've seen in this chapter, Yahoo! has several useful software categories. I've mentioned the e-mail page, but you can also find pages with information on particular categories, such as these:

To search for Internet software at Yahoo! go straight to the **Internet Software** *page (http://dir.yahoo.com/Computers_ and_Internet/Software/Internet/), select Just This Category from the drop-down list box near the Search button, then type the search term. That way you'll limit the search to useful categories.*

FTP programs
http://dir.yahoo.com/
Computers_and_Internet/
Software/Internet/FTP/

Macintosh programs
http://dir.yahoo.com/Computers_and_Internet/Hardware/Personal_
Computers/Macintosh/Software/Shareware/

Programs for converting word-processing documents to Web (HTML) documents
http://dir.yahoo.com/Computers_and_Internet/Software/Internet/World_
Wide_Web/HTML_Converters/

Usenet newsreaders
http://dir.yahoo.com/Computers_and_Internet/Software/Internet/Usenet/

Who Will Create Your Web Site?

Before we move on, a quick discussion about who should create your Web site. There may be no question about it—for many readers of this book, it's the reader himself who will be creating the Web site. If you have a small, one-person business, then perhaps you plan to become your company's Web-site administrator. It's quite possible to set up a small Web site in your spare time.

If your company's a little bigger, perhaps you plan to delegate the task. I'd advise that you read this book and keep an eye on your Web site, though. Many Web sites are very inefficient, frustrating for users and doing their owners little or no good—a subject we'll discuss in Chapters 9 and 10. You need to take a look at the Web site from the user's point of view to some degree, and make sure it's really doing its job and doing it well. So when you've finished reading this book, pass it on to the administrator.

Even if you own a small or one-person business, you may still want to delegate. You'll find that, although many companies are charging outrageous fees to design and create Web sites, the skills needed to create a decent site are not terribly difficult to learn. You may be able to find a high school or college student willing to learn how to work on the Web at your expense, for instance. Again, you'll need to keep a close eye on the result, but there's no need to spend $50 or $100 per hour to set up and promote a site.

As you'll see in Chapter 6, there are many companies that want to create your Web site for you. Another alternative might be to have one of these companies set up your site; then you can take over and make modifications as required.

## Chapter Three

Where to Put Your Web Site

The next step in your quest for a perfect Web site is to decide where you're going to put it. From the very expensive (thousands of dollars to set up, thousands of dollars to keep running) to the very cheap, there are a variety of options available to you:

- On your own Web server
- On your own Web server at a co-location facility
- At an ISP's personal-page site
- At a free-page Web site
- At a cybermall
- At a Web store
- At an e-commerce service
- At a Web host's site in a subdirectory or subdomain
- At a Web host's site as a virtual domain.

I believe that for most businesses there's really only one choice: the last option. But we'll work our way there; let me explain what each type of Web site is, and why you may or may not want to use it.

Your Own Web Server

I'll start with the most expensive, and, in general, the worst choice. You can set up your own Web server. That means you obtain a computer to run the Web server software, pick an appropriate operating system (generally Windows NT or some flavor of UNIX), pick and install suitable Web-server software (there are lots of options), lease a fast line from your office to the Internet, install a router, and spend lots of time and money maintaining it all. (This method is known as the open-your-wallet method.)

For some reason the computer press seems to push this option, so let me remind you:

The Internet is a giant jobs program for computer geeks.

It's not uncommon for major computer magazines to publish articles about how to set up a Web site that actually discuss how to set up a Web server—a completely different subject—with no mention of how to find someone to host the site for you, a much easier and more cost-efficient thing to do. Having a personal Web server is expensive, complicated, and, I'm glad to say, unnecessary.

Here's a quick guideline that will give you an idea of whether you personally can set up a Web server:

If you don't know what it takes to set up a Web server, don't try it.

Setting up a Web server is a trick that only a certified computer geek should try. Just because you loaded the latest Windows upgrade and installed an internal modem doesn't mean you should try to install a Web server. It'll take you far longer and cost you far more than you realize. Take a look at a book on setting up a Web server and what will you find? Six hundred pages of complicated geek talk.

But what if you have a small company with a computer geek sitting around with nothing much to do? Should you set up a Web server? Probably not, unless you are setting up a large site. It's hard to see how running a Web server can be justified financially when there are much cheaper options available. You'll have a large investment in the equipment and software needed to get everything running, the monthly cost of a very expensive connection to the Internet (perhaps $1,200 a month, perhaps $3,000, perhaps a great deal more, depending on where you are), and the cost of an employee to keep it all running. On the other hand, you can spend from $25 to a few score bucks a month placing your Web site on someone else's Web server, as you'll see near the end of this chapter. Even if your company has the skills to run its own server, if you run the numbers you may find it's just not worthwhile.

So who should set up a Web server? I know people in small companies, even one-person companies, with their own Web servers. Generally these are very geeky people who enjoy this sort of thing. That's fine, as long as they realize it's hard to justify what they're doing from a purely profit-and-loss point of view. It's really a hobby. There are also situations in which very large companies with very large Web sites should set up their own servers.

Perhaps the best reason for setting up your own Web server is if you need—not want, but need—complete control over the site. With your own Web server you have complete control over system security. You can also pick exactly what software you want to run. For instance, you could set up a server running Windows NT Workstation, then run all sorts of fancy software tools for connecting your Web site to a database. On the other hand, you may be able to find a Web-hosting company that uses a Windows NT server and will allow you to use whatever software you need.

Consider an analogy: Does your business use any vehicles? If so, do you employ your own mechanics? There are large businesses that have their own vehicle-maintenance divisions, but for most businesses this is neither necessary nor practical. The same thing goes for Web servers. In general, most small businesses should steer clear of setting up a Web server, regardless of what the computer press might say.

Oh, one more thing. If you plan to set up your own Web server, also consider how you plan to monitor it seven days a week, 24 hours a day. Web servers are not things you just plug in and leave; they require constant supervision.

Your Own Web Server at a Co-location Facility

If you really feel the need for your own server, there is one way to do it relatively cheaply. You can set up your server at a "co-location" facility. Such facilities are in the business of looking after companies' Web servers for them—they have rooms full of computer boxes hooked up to very fast Internet connections. They employ staff to watch over the systems; if your Web server locks up, for instance, they can restart it for you.

Setting up a co-located server might cost you, say, $1,000 for the computer (you don't need to leave a monitor or keyboard, as the co-location facility will probably use a single monitor and keyboard connected to multiple computers through a switch box), and perhaps as little as $200 or $300 a month. Rather than paying for a fast and expensive Internet connection, you'll share it with other companies. Of course you'll still have to set up the software on the computer—or pay the co-location staff to do it for you. Using a co-location service is a good way to go if you have a very busy Web site, but I'd still recommend that most companies start out with a hosting company, and then, if they're lucky enough to build a popular site, move to co-locating. (In fact many hosting companies also sell co-location services.)

An ISP's Personal-Page Site

I'll cover this one next, because it's cheap, and, in many cases, also an awful choice. It may be fine in some situations, depending on what you are trying to sell or promote, but it has significant disadvantages.

First, let me explain what I mean by a personal-page site. Most ISPs and online services allow their users to set up Web pages. Each account comes with a certain amount of disk space which you can fill with your poetry, pictures of your cat, links to your favorite Web sites, and an explanation of why collecting sewer covers is such a great hobby. As a business Web site, this is not so good. If you're on a pocket-money budget, perhaps that's all you can manage. But if you're serious about doing business on the Internet, you need something more, for several reasons.

Take a look at this URL:

http://members.aol.com/acmesewercover/

What's this say to you? I don't want to be rude to America Online members, but this link says to me, and to many other Internet users: "Oh, another AOL user; here today, gone tomorrow." It's hard to take a URL like this seriously, whether it's http://members.aol.com/acmesewercover/, http://ourworld.compuserve. com/homepages/acmesewercover/, or http://www.speedyinternet.net/memberspages/ acmesewercover/; it just doesn't look very professional. You threw up a Web site the quickest and easiest way possible, and it shows. These URLs don't inspire much confidence. (A couple of years ago I heard a market researcher talk about the Internet. He claimed that when his company polled AOL members about their online activities and plans, they found that a huge number, more than 40 percent, said they planned to find another service provider.) Another problem is that some search sites—in particular Yahoo!, which is probably the most important search site out there—won't list your site if it's clearly an ISP site. Why? Because they also believe that these ISP Web sites are "here today, gone tomorrow," and it's a nightmare trying to keep the search-engine listings clean when Web sites keep disappearing.

Yet another reason not to set up this sort of Web site is that ISPs' personal-page sites simply don't have all the services that a business will need to get started and may need later—the ability to take online orders on a secure server or to work with Microsoft FrontPage, perhaps, or the ability to add CGI scripts to your Web pages.

And consider this: What happens when you decide to leave the service? Perhaps your ISP goes out of business or raises the rates. Perhaps it's unreliable or has lousy customer service, or you decide that you really do need a real Web site. All of a sudden you have to change your business' URL. Have you printed business cards, brochures, and letterhead? How many customers already know your URL? Well, they don't anymore!

You need a URL that you can take with you, one that's yours forever—or as long as you're willing to pay a $35-a-year fee to keep it. To do that you need to get your own domain name (see Chapters 5 and 6), and you won't be able to use that domain name at a personal-page site.

A Free-Page Web Site

If your service provider won't give you any Web space, and you're on a tight budget, the next best thing may be space at a free site. This isn't really suitable for most businesses, of course, but if you want to spend nothing, it's hard to beat. The page will cost you ... well, nothing. But you can expect to get little more than what you pay for. In other words, the services that most businesses need at their Web sites won't be available. And you won't own the URL, either.

Still, if you have to set up a Web site even though your budget makes a sixth-grader's allowance look like a king's ransom, it's not hard to find a free site. There are scads of services available that will provide you with space, and many will even provide neat little template tools that help you create pages. These range from the big services, with millions of free Web sites (such as Geocities, Tripod, and Xoom), down to small backwaters on the Internet that have been set up as a hobby. There are sites that put up your Web page for free, then hope that you'll pay them to update the page; sites that provide free space to schools, charities, and other "good causes"; sites for students; sites for actors; sites for artists; and sites for anyone who turns up. Try some of the following links:

Angelfire
> http://www.angelfire.com/

Free Home Page Center
> http://www.freehomepage.com/

The Free Pages Page
> http://starbase.neosoft.com/~peter/freepages.html

Free.com (lists over 120 places providing free Web space)
> http://www.free.com/

Tripod
> http://www.tripod.com/

Xoom
> http://www.xoom.com/

Yahoo!—Free Web Pages
http://dir.yahoo.com/Business_and_Economy/Companies/Internet_Services/
Web_Services/Free_Web_Pages/

Yahoo!—GeoCities (Perhaps the biggest free-space service)
http://www.geocities.com/

A Cybermall

Another type of Web site is one at a cybermall—a shopping mall on the Web. I can't quite get my mind around this concept; it doesn't seem to make a lot of sense. The Internet is supposed to free us from geography, yet here we are bunching businesses together at one site. If you are promoting your business properly, it doesn't have to be at the same Web server as a gazillion other businesses, so what's the point of a mall? You can't stroll through a cybermall; there's no parking, nowhere to eat. And in any case, in cyberspace everything is just a URL away. The mall owners would say that they bring people into the mall, though that's open to debate. It's certain, though, that simply placing a Web store in a mall isn't enough to bring people to you; you'll still need to promote your site elsewhere.

In fact, cybermalls seem to be a thing of the past. In the early days, way back in 1995 and 1996, even some big companies were signing up with cybermalls ... but eventually it dawned on them that it simply didn't make sense. If a company's big enough to draw traffic to a Web site, the last thing they want to do is share it with *other* Web sites! A number of large malls have even gone out of business, and some of the others don't seem to be particularly vibrant business areas!

Still, if you want to check out the malls (it's a great way to find examples of poor Web design, so you can avoid making the same mistakes), take a look at these sites:

Access Market Square (they claim to be the oldest cybermall)
http://www.amsquare.com/

iMall (one of the largest malls)
http://www.imall.com/

ShopInternet
http://shopinternet.ro.com/

Yahoo!—Online Shopping
http://dir.yahoo.com/Business_and_Economy/Companies/Shopping_Centers/
Online_Shopping/Directories/

Do the malls do a good job at bringing you customers? I don't think so. I rarely see an ad on the Web for a cybermall, and even when I searched Yahoo! recently, it took me a few minutes to track them down. If a mall isn't going to bring people to your site, it's up to you to do so. On the other hand, iMall claims huge numbers of "hits" each month for its stores. (What's a hit? That depends on how a Web-server administrator decides to measure activity. A hit may mean a single page being transferred to a Web browser, or it may mean any kind of transfer—a page, an image, an error message, and so on. So a single visit to a site may count as scores of hits.)

Malls also have some of the problems of the personal-page site. You can't take your URL with you if you leave, and the mall may not have all the services you need. And note that at least one mall has a very aggressive campaign to recruit new stores to the mall, holding seminars around the country to show Internet consultants how to convince small businesses that there's money to be made on the Internet. I can't help feeling that, in many cases, this is much better for the mall and the consultant than for the small business.

Having said all that, there is a case in which you may want to use a mall. Let's say you have a product you want to sell, but the last thing in the world you want to do is learn how to put up a Web page. You're willing to promote your product in newsgroups, mailing lists, search engines, and so on, but you don't want to mess with a Web site. It might be worthwhile setting up a mall site, not because you expect the mall to bring you lots of business, but because it will create your Web site for you. All you have to do is promote the product and send people to your site, where, if you're lucky, the mall has set things up so your prospective clients can place orders. Carefully compare costs and quality, though. Even if you want to take this route, read this book and get an idea of what a Web site should be. I've seen some very poorly designed Web pages at cybermalls. Many are very ugly, have text and background patterns that clash atrociously, don't provide contact e-mail addresses, and so on. Don't set up a Web site at a mall because you think you'll get mall traffic. Set one up only if you know the mall will do a good job of creating your Web site at a good price.

Before you sign up with a mall you should try to contact people who have set up stores at that mall, and ask them if it's been worthwhile. Don't just contact one or two—try 30 or 40 to make sure you get a reasonable number of responses.

Wander around the mall a little and look for e-mail addresses. You may be surprised at how many of these "stores" don't display a contact address, but if you find any, copy these e-mail addresses into the Clipboard, then paste them into your e-mail program's Bcc box. Bcc means Blind Carbon Copy. If you e-mail using Bcc, you can send your message to many people at once and everyone will see an individual e-mail message without seeing anyone else's address. That way they are less likely to think: he's contacted 40 people, I'll let someone else respond. (Chapter 2 explains that you need a POP mailbox so you can choose e-mail software with all the features you need.) Note, however, that most mail programs won't let you send a message to the Bcc recipients alone; if that's the case with your program, put your own address in the To: line. Type a simple message asking what the recipients think of working with the mall, whether the mall has brought much traffic to their site, whether they've made any sales, and so on. Then send it off and wait to see what happens.

When I wrote the first edition of this book I e-mailed just 20 stores—not really enough—at one of the big, well-known Internet malls. Here are some of the responses:

- Terrible service ... no value, no support, expensive.
- I get a few leads here and there, but nothing great. From what others say, results are generally so-so.
- I get 200 hits a month, but my products don't sell.
- They don't bring anyone in; they do nothing more than make my store available.
- They're unresponsive and haven't done anything much to get us business.
- Don't do it!
- I've found I can set up Web pages quicker, cheaper, and better than anything the mall has done for us.

That last comment is so true. I did get one positive result, but it turned out that the respondent also sells space at the mall and creates Web sites for people. To be fair, though, this gentleman also pointed out that there's more to running a Web business than simply setting up a site; you must promote it, too. (So what's the point of the mall?) Overall, out of 20 e-mails that I sent out, I received seven responses; six were negative and one was positive.

Now, this wasn't a scientific survey, and I'm not going to swear that these responses are representative of most Internet malls ... but I wouldn't be surprised if they were.

All this doesn't mean that there are no good malls. But if you do find a good mall, it's probably good not because of its "mallness," but because the people running it are providing other important services and helping their stores to market themselves on the Internet—doing the sorts of things you're going to learn about in this book.

How much does it cost to place a Web site at a mall? One mall I looked at is charging a $395 setup fee, plus $50 a month or 5 percent of your sales each month. That's just to get started. Then you'll pay $50 an hour to have someone help you design and set up your site. As you'll see later, you can get a lot more than a few pages for $50 a month by going through a Web-hosting company. And many Web-hosting companies charge a much smaller setup fee, perhaps only $25 to $50.

A Web Store

A Web store is much the same as a Web mall, really, except that instead of acting like a mall, with your Web pages being a single store among many, your Web pages represent a single product or group of products in the store.

Perhaps the best examples of this sort of Web site are the stores selling books, such as the following:

BooksAmerica
　http://www.booksamerica.com/

BookWorld
　http://www.bookworld.com/

BookZone
　http://www.bookzone.com/

ReadersNdex
　http://www.readersndex.com/

SPAN Book Emporium
　http://www.spannet.org/BookEmporium/

(Note that since the first edition of this book, written in 1997, three out of the eight services I originally listed have disappeared, which perhaps says something about the viability of such services.)

This sort of company is harder to track down than a mall. If you do plenty of research (see Chapter 15), you may find such places related to your business, depending on what your business is. The idea behind these companies is that they provide a service for a particular type of consumer—book buyers in the previous examples. If you buy space your product will be displayed and indexed, and if the company is doing the job well, plenty of prospective customers will come to the site. Because this sort of operation is more focused than a cybermall (it's easier to promote a specific product or group of products than simply saying: Hey, come here, we've got everything), I suspect they may do a better job. However, you should still check prices and talk with other companies that have bought space at such a store, and compare with a Web-hosting company. Remember also that you still have some of the problems we've seen earlier. If you decide to leave the store and move elsewhere, you'll lose your URL, for instance. Also, such stores are likely to have a limited number of services available. And if you set up in these stores you end up just one product among many; it's easy for people to miss your product, or to be distracted by a link to someone else's. For instance, in some of these stores all pages contain links that take visitors away, back to the store's main page.

E-commerce Services

There's a new class of service that's become very popular, the e-commerce or shopping-cart site. These sites provide shopping-cart services (which we'll discuss in detail in Chapter 13), but usually little else. Generally they provide a standard shopping-cart system that you can customize, along with a few extra pages, perhaps (or perhaps not). But they don't have all the features that a Web-hosting company provides. Many people combine this type of service with a hosting account; they build their main Web site at a hosting company, and then put their store at an e-commerce service, and link from the main site into the store. So such services are particularly useful if you already have a Web site in one location and have now decided that you need a shopping-cart system.

Some of these services appear to be very much like malls, because it's possible to search throughout all the member stores for products. But that's just an extra feature, it's not primary—these are shopping-cart services, not malls. The following are two popular systems, though I'll mention more in Chapter 13.

MerchandiZer
   http://www.merchandizer.com/
Yahoo! Store
   http://store.yahoo.com/

Now I'm going to plug my own service. At the time of writing some colleagues and I are building an e-commerce system which should be available by the time you read this:

BizBlast.com
   http://BizBlast.com/

A Web-Hosting Company

Okay, now's the time to talk about setting up your own Web site. Forget the malls and stores, forget those silly little personal Web pages; the next type of host allows you to set up a full-blown site of your own. A Web-hosting company, or Web presence provider as they're sometimes known, sells space on its computers. It will give you a directory on a hard disk, and you can place your Web pages there. Such companies have a range of different services that they can provide. For instance, you may get these services, perhaps for an additional fee:

- A POP e-mail account
- E-mail forwarding
- An online ordering system
- Mailing-list software
- Help with design and creation of your Web site
- Help with promoting the Web site.

These are just a few examples; we'll look in more detail in Chapter 4 at the services these companies provide. There are lots of advantages to using the services of a Web-hosting company. You can use your own domain name, so if you have to leave and find another company (or if they go out of business), you can keep your URL. These companies are often cheaper than the malls and stores; their services start at as little as $10 a month, and the range of services available is much larger.

Now, there are essentially five types of service that these companies provide:

- A nonvirtual Web site
- A subdomain
- A virtual Web server (sometimes called full virtual)
- A fake virtual Web server (sometimes called partial virtual or "IP-less")
- A dedicated Web server.

We'll look at each of these in turn.

A Nonvirtual Web Site

A nonvirtual site is a Web site set up without using your own domain; your Web site appears to be part of the Web host's site. That is, your company's URL will start with the Web-hosting company's domain name, and end with your company name. For instance, if your company name is Acme Sewer Covers, your URL might end up being something like:

http://www.bighost.com/acmesewercover/

Of course, if you decide to move your site later, you'll have to get a new URL.

A Subdomain

Some Web-hosting companies can create subdomains for you, so you appear to have your own domain. For instance, you might have this domain name:

http://acmesewercover.bighost.com/

(Strictly speaking this is not a subdomain, it's merely a host computer at the bighost.com domain, but it's generally known in the business as a subdomain.) This looks a lot better than having a directory name after the Web-hosting company's name. It almost looks like you have your own domain name—but you don't. This option has the same problem as most of the other types of Web sites that we've looked at: if you have to find somewhere else to put your Web site, you lose your URL. Up goes the printing bill.

By the way, you can get a free subdomain (http://yourname.dhs.org/) from **DHS (Domain Host Services** at http://www.dhs.org/). They have a little program set up so that wherever your Web site happens to be—even if you have an America Online or CompuServe personal page—people can use the http://yourname.dhs.org/ URL to reach your site.

A Virtual Web Server

In order to set up a virtual Web host, you need to get your own domain name (I'll talk about that in Chapter 5). Your URL will now be http://www.acmesewercover.com/ (or whatever domain name you pick). To the outside world it will appear that you have your own Web server. In fact the Web-hosting company may have dozens, scores, hundreds, perhaps even thousands of different domain names, all pointing to the host's computers and each owned by a different company.

How is this done? It's all really quite simple. When you apply for a domain name, you tell the registration authority where (that is, at which computer) your domain will reside. In fact, you tell the registration authority which nameservers—computers used by your hosting company for routing information in and out of their system—know where your domain resides. Your domain name is then added to the Internet's nameserver system, so that when someone on the Internet wants to go to your Web site, the messages are routed to the correct nameservers.

The Web-hosting company sets up its computers to recognize your domain name, and it "maps" your domain name to a particular IP (Internet Protocol) number, which identifies a host computer containing your Web documents. So now the hosting company's nameservers know which IP number identifies the computer that contains your Web site, and the Internet's nameservers—the computers that Web browsers refer to when trying to track down a domain—know which nameservers to check with when they need to find your domain. (You'll learn more about IP numbers in Chapter 5.)

Now, when a Web browser sends a message saying "Send me the document named index.html from the www.acmesewercover.com Web site, the local nameservers figure out which nameserver is responsible for the domain, then ask that nameserver for the appropriate IP number, so the message can be routed to the correct server. The Web-hosting company's Web server then figures out which directory belongs to that domain, finds the file, and sends it to the browser.

This type of Web site is the best situation for most companies. It's relatively low-cost compared to setting up your own server or buying space at a mall, it's flexible—you can use whatever services you need—and you own the URL so you can take it with you if you have to change companies.

A Fake Virtual Web Server

You may also run across fake virtual Web servers, which are also sometimes referred to as "partial virtual servers" and "IP-less" (pronounced "eye-pee-less") servers. While in the case of a virtual server the Web URL has to be assigned its own IP number, multiple fake virtual Web servers can be assigned to a single IP number. So a large number of different companies, using a variety of different domain names, may all be using the same IP number. In other words, all the domain names—and, therefore, all the URLs—point to exactly the same place.

So what happens when someone types into a browser the domain name used by a fake virtual server? Using a little HTTP trick (HyperText Transfer Protocol is the communication method used by the Web), the Web server can figure out which directory the browser user is looking for. At one time a directory name would be used to identify the particular customer's site (http://www.acmesewercover.com/sewer/, for instance), or perhaps a port number was used (http://www.acmesewercover.com:8010/, for instance). But in most cases these days that's unnecessary, and the server can just figure it all out; you'll use your domain name without a directory name or port number.

There used to be an advantage to a fake virtual account—it's cheaper than a true virtual account. You wouldn't have paid the hosting company quite so much, though you would still have to pay to register your domain name. There were a few disadvantages, though. If you were using a server at which you did have to include a directory name or port number, the address could be confusing. For instance, if someone typed http://www.acmesewercover.com/, forgetting the /sewer/ directory, or the :8010 port number, the URL wouldn't work. The Web server wouldn't know which page the browser user wanted, because the IP number used was the same for dozens, scores, maybe hundreds of other Web sites.

More of a problem was that many older browsers won't work properly with a fake virtual URL. Instead of displaying your main page, the server isn't sure what to display, so it displays a page at which the visitor can click on a link to get to your site. That could be a real nuisance, because users of these older browsers would not be able to go directly to a particular page in your Web site, they'd have to dig their way through the directory structure to get there.

The situation has changed quite a bit in the two years since I wrote the first edition of this book. The primary difference is that now the proportion of users working with one of these old, noncompatible browsers is very, very small. Anyone working with Netscape Navigator 2, Internet Explorer 3, CompuServe 3.0's internal browser, or America Online 3.0's internal browser—or later versions of these programs, of course—won't have any problems. The number of users working with older systems is probably a small fraction of one percent. (And they're used to problems when they're on the Web!)

Because of this I suspect that fake-virtual or IP-less hosting is becoming much more common, to the degree that it's not even always explained to the customer. You probably won't see such a service offered as a separate, lower-cost service, though you may end up with your site being hosted in such a manner anyway.

But there is another problem. You won't get an FTP site that uses your domain name. Web servers and browsers can manage this fake-domain trick, but FTP servers and programs can't, so if you need an FTP site using your own domain name (most small companies probably don't), you'll need a full virtual account. Finally, companies selling fake virtual domains generally have a scaled-down package for fake virtual domains and provide more services when you trade up to a full virtual, so you may find that if you use a fake virtual account you won't get all the services you need.

Fake virtual servers may be adequate if you're on a really tight budget and if you don't need an FTP site using your domain name (you may still get an FTP site that uses a subdirectory of the Web-hosting company's domain name) and don't mind showing a Continue link to the tiny percent or so of users who are working with old browsers. The difference in price isn't huge, though; a fake virtual site may cost $10 a month, while you may be able to find a true virtual site for $20 a month.

In fact you won't find many companies offering this service, and most won't even know what you're talking about if you ask for it, but I'm mentioning it here because you may just run across it or may want to seek it out if you're trying to save every penny you can.

A Dedicated Web Server

The last type of service that a Web-hosting company will provide is the full Web-server service. You'll get not only your own domain name but even your own computer. The Web-hosting company will set aside a computer for you, and you'll have dedicated use of that computer. This service is, of course, much more expensive. For instance, one Web-hosting company I looked at recently charges $500 per month for this service, another charges $295 per month, compared to $20 or perhaps $35 per month for a basic virtual Web host. Still, you may want to use this service if your Web site grows big enough and busy enough to warrant its own computer.

What's the difference between this and the co-location service I mentioned earlier? The only real difference is that with co-location you *own* the server rather than rent it.

Web Hosting Is the Way to Go

It must be obvious by now which method I think is the most suitable in most cases: You should set up a site with your own domain name at a Web-hosting company. (Not any Web-hosting company, of course, but a good one, and we'll discuss how to figure that out in Chapter 4.)

Before we move on, here's a quick summary of why it's such a good idea:

- You don't know anything about running a Web server, and it's complicated stuff—so get someone else to do it.
- It's inefficient for anyone who knows how to run a Web server to do so for just one site—so pay a company that is running scores of sites and gain from economies of scale.
- You'll own your URL; if you move your site, you won't have to reprint all your business stationery, and your customers won't get lost.
- Web-hosting companies have far more services than most malls or personal-page sites.
- Web hosting is generally much cheaper than malls, and much, much cheaper than running your own server.

Disclaimer

Time for a disclaimer. At the time of writing I'm in the process of setting up a hosting company. "Ah," you say, "now I see why he's pushing hosting companies!" All I can say in my defense is that if you go to a library or a used-book store and find the First Edition of *Poor Richard's Web Site*, you'll see that I gave exactly the same advice in that book, two years before I decided to set up a hosting company!

If you'd like to see what services we offer, visit us at http://BizBlast.com/.

Where Now?

Where do you go from here? That depends on what choice you have made.

- You're going to set up your own Web server—If so, you'll have to find more information elsewhere; I don't explain how to set up a Web server in this book. I will explain how to create the Web site itself, though, and promote the site.

- You're going to use a personal-page site—Not a great way to go, but if it's all you can afford, that's fine. Find a service provider that provides Web space, and figure out how and where to put your Web pages. Then carry on reading the book.

- You want to use a cybermall—Spend some time digging around cybermalls and find the best deal. But don't forget to compare prices and services with a Web-hosting company. And even if the mall creates your Web site, you'll still want to read about how to promote the site.

- You want to use a Web store—The same as for cybermalls. Compare prices with Web-hosting companies.

- You're planning to use a nonvirtual site or a subdomain at a Web host—Turn to Chapter 4 to find a Web-hosting company. And consider shelling out just a little more cash to get your own domain name.

- You're going to use a virtual site at a Web host—This is the best choice in most cases: a low-cost way to set up a professional-looking site. Turn to Chapter 4 to find a Web-hosting company.

Which Comes First: the Host or the Domain Name?

It's hard to find a good domain name these days. Domain names are going faster than hot dogs at a ball game, and there's a good chance that the domain name you really want has gone already (acmesewercover.com is still available, though).

In Chapter 5 I'll show you how to find out whether your domain name has gone already. However, you can't buy the domain name until you have least two nameservers to which you can assign the domain name. You can't simply register the name and then assign it to nameservers later.

That leaves you several choices:

- Find a hosting company first, then register the domain name.
- Find someone with a Web server willing to allow you to "borrow" a computer IP number until you find where you really want to put your Web site.
- Register the domain name and "park" it at a free service.
- Pay extra when you register the domain name and park it with the registration authority itself.

We're going to look at tracking down Web hosts (Chapter 4) first, and then I'll explain how to register your domain name (Chapter 5). If you're in a real hurry to reserve a domain name, turn to Chapter 5 and read about the registration services and how you can park the domain name until you're ready to use it.

Chapter Four

Finding a Web Host

It's time to find your Web host. If you're reading this chapter, you've decided not to use the open-your-wallet route—you're not going to set up your own Web server—nor are you going to cheap out and use a free page or personal-page. Rather, you're going to find a Web-hosting company and rent some space.

There's one major problem; there are literally thousands of companies advertising their Web-hosting services, and probably more that provide such services but don't put much effort into promoting them—service providers, for instance, that host Web sites for their subscribers. How are you going to find these companies, and how are you going to choose the right one? Well, that's just what this chapter is all about.

First, a couple of things to consider. What are you going to do about a domain name, and what sort of server do you need?

Are You Getting a Domain Name?

Before you begin, you need to decide whether to get your own domain name so you can have a virtual Web host (http://www.acmesewercover.com/, for instance); whether to use a subdomain of the Web-hosting company's domain name (http://acmesewercover.bighost.com/); or whether to have a nonvirtual site (http://www.bighost.com/acmesewercover/).

In Chapter 5 I'll explain how to get your own domain name. You'll find that many Web-hosting companies will get the domain name for you, but I'd recommend you do it yourself, for several reasons:

- It'll save you a few bucks in most cases
- It's really not hard to do
- If you ever need to transfer your URL to another company, you'll need to know how to do so

- If you allow the Web-hosting company to do it, the name may end up registered in the company's name, making it difficult, if not impossible, to transfer later. (I've seen it happen!)

What Sort of Server Do You Want?

What sort of server do you want? You probably don't know anything about servers, so how on earth are you going to make that decision? I'm not going to get into any terribly complicated technical details. In fact, the choice probably depends on whether you want to use Microsoft FrontPage. Bear with me; we'll be talking about authoring tools in detail in Chapter 8, but you have to make a preliminary decision—whether or not to use Microsoft FrontPage—before you can pick a Web-hosting company.

Microsoft FrontPage is a Web-management and Web-authoring tool. And it's very good. That's not just my opinion (though let me admit my bias: I wrote a book about the product), but it's also the opinion of many others in the business—it consistently gets high ratings in the product reviews.

Now, there's a lot of anti-Microsoft feeling on the Internet. I can understand why, though we're not going to get into that subject here. Many people on the Internet regard recommending a Microsoft product as akin to selling out. So let me just tell you about a statement I saw at one Web-hosting company's site. This company had recently started working with the FrontPage server extensions (more of which in a moment), and placed a statement on the Web site saying, "We don't much like Microsoft, but we've got to say that this is a very good product."

There are lots of different HTML-authoring tools you can work with. Scores. Probably hundreds. We'll talk about your options in Chapter 8. Which should you use? Well, I don't know for sure, but let's say a friend comes to me and asks which program he should use. "I want to set up a Web site quickly," he says, "to be able to manage the site easily—find broken links, set up portions of the Web that are private, and so on. And I want to be able to create forms ... maybe even a discussion group." What would I answer? "Get Microsoft FrontPage." (Unless he's using a Macintosh; unfortunately Microsoft appears to have stopped development of the Mac version of FrontPage about three years ago.)

The decision's up to you (we'll talk more about the pros and cons in Chapter 8). Let's say, then, that after considering your options, you decide you want to use FrontPage. Well, that's where the FrontPage server extensions come into the picture. You see, FrontPage can do a number of neat tricks. For instance, you can create feedback pages: users can type information into a form, click a button, and the information is placed in a file at your Web site. It might be a text file intended for nobody but you, or an HTML page viewable by other Web site users. Using FrontPage you can also build a sophisticated online discussion group. And FrontPage can do all this for you in a matter of minutes or seconds. However, in order for these things to work, your Web site must be managed by a Web server with the FrontPage server extensions installed. You can still use FrontPage without server extensions; you just won't be able to use the more advanced, interactive features.

The server extensions are, in effect, little programs that carry out these special functions. If they're not installed on the server, the FrontPage magic tricks simply won't work. But hundreds of Web-hosting companies have installed the server extensions, with more doing so every day. FrontPage is very popular, and pretty soon the server extensions will be almost everywhere.

FrontPage is not the only system that requires special programs installed at a server—ColdFusion does too, for instance. But FrontPage is the only one of these products that is in common use. Few servers have the ColdFusion programs installed (the servers that do are generally set up for professional Web designers).

Another reason to know which server you want is this: if there's a particular program you want to run in conjunction with your Web site that must be run on the server computer, you need to figure out what operating system that program runs on, and make sure that (a) you find a Web-hosting company that uses that operating system, and (b) you will be able to load the program on the company's server computer. Having said that, most people won't have any particular requirements. (If you do, you know you do. If you can't imagine what those special needs might be, you can forget about them.)

So don't get too hung up on which server to use—with the exception of the FrontPage question, that is. You can't predict the future, so don't try to guess what fancy systems you may need six months or a year down the road. For most small businesses it really won't matter which server is being used. And if, after your Web site grows and you find that you absolutely must move to a different operating system because you just must have the latest toy, you can always switch to another Web-hosting company—as long as you've registered your own domain name, of course.

Starting the Search

The first thing you need to do is to find a few Web-hosting companies to choose from. Spend a little time looking at the following sites.

Budget Web Hosts List
http://www.callihan.com/budget/

budgetweb.com—(A great place to find a low-cost Web host)
http://www.budgetweb.com/budgetweb/

C|Net Web Services
http://webhostlist.internetlist.com/

The Directory
http://www.thedirectory.org/

FindaHost.com
http://www.findahost.com/

Host Find
http://www.hostfind.com/

Host Investigator
http://www.hostinvestigator.com/

HostFinders.com
http://www.hostfinders.com/

HostIndex
http://www.hostindex.com/

HostReview.com
http://hostreview.com/

HostSearch
http://www.hostsearch.com/

ISPcheck
http://www.ispcheck.com/

leasing a server list at budgetweb.com
http://budgetweb.com/hndocs/list.shtml

Microsoft FrontPage Web Presence Providers
http://www.microsoftwpp.com/wppsearch/
http://www.microsoft.com/frontpage/

NerdWorld—Internet Servers Resources
http://www.nerdworld.com/nw1642.html

Top Hosts
http://www.tophosts.com/

WebHosters.com
http://www.webhosters.com/

webhostseek!
http://www.webhostseek.com/

Web-Quote Central
http://www.centeroftheweb.com/webquote/

Had enough? Totally confused by now? There are so many companies vying for your business that it's a little difficult to make a choice. So let's take a look at the things that will affect your choice—the sorts of services you need from a Web-hosting company—and how to compare companies. I'm not going to talk prices here. They change, and there's a wide range of prices anyway. I'll simply mention the different things you should consider.

The Services You Need

Some of the hosting directories listed above provide a great way to start your search. You can use forms to select the services you want; then click on a button and you'll see a list of just those services matching your requirements. For instance, if you have to have a FrontPage-enabled server, click the FrontPage option button, and you'll be shown only services that are set up to work with FrontPage. You can then start going to the hosting companies' Web pages and checking for the services you need.

Most of the following information will be available in the Web-hosting companies' Web pages. For some of it you'll have to e-mail or call and ask. You can use Appendix A to take notes, by the way. This appendix is a checklist of questions you need answered before you sign up. Notice the index numbers to the left of the headings below; these index numbers appear on the lines in the table in Appendix A, so you can quickly refer back here for more information about an option in that table.

So, let's get started. The following services are provided by Web-hosting companies. Some will be important to you, some less so.

#1 Nonvirtual, Virtual, or Fake Virtual?

Most Web-hosting companies will sell both virtual (your own domain name), and nonvirtual Web space. A few also sell subdomains, and a few sell fake virtual (IP-less) domains. The ideal option, as discussed in Chapter 3, is the virtual account. Next comes the fake virtual, then the nonvirtual or subdomain. Well, I suppose the absolute ideal is the dedicated server, but that gets expensive. See Chapter 3 if you don't remember what all these account types are.

#2   Microsoft FrontPage

As discussed earlier, if you want to use all of FrontPage's advanced features, make
sure that the server has the FrontPage server extensions installed. Check the fees
that the service provider wants to charge. They vary from a small setup fee to a
large setup fee and an obscenely large and completely unnecessary monthly fee.
Also, make sure that you're getting a true FrontPage Web site. Some Web-
hosting companies will say "yes, you can use FrontPage," when what they really
mean is that you can create your pages with FrontPage and transfer them to the
site with FrontPage—which you can do with any Web server—but you can't use
the WebBots, the special FrontPage scripts that make FrontPage so powerful.
Get them to specify that the server extensions are installed, not just that you can
"use" FrontPage.

You might also check with the company to see which version of FrontPage it's
set up to use. Many FrontPage features won't work properly unless the latest
server extensions have been installed. For instance, at the time of writing the
latest version is FrontPage 2000, but many companies haven't yet upgraded from
FrontPage 98. (Many companies delay installing the latest server extensions to
give Microsoft time to fix some of the bugs.)

#3   How Much Does It Cost?

If the company doesn't have the server type you want, or if you need FrontPage
and it doesn't have the FrontPage server extensions, there's no point in going
further. If it does have what you need, you should probably take a quick look at
the price next, to make sure it's in the area you want to pay. Most services charge
a setup fee, and then a monthly charge. Some don't have a setup fee, and some
will waive the setup fee if you are transferring an existing Web site and domain
from another location. Even if they don't advertise that they do, if you are
transferring a site it might be worth asking if they will waive the fee.

#4   Minimum Contract and Guarantee?

Some Web-hosting companies want you to pay a year's fee at once, but you
should ask if you can pay for, say, three months. Some simply go month by
month, other's charge by the month and give the first month free—the ideal
situation. Also ask what sort of guarantees they offer; some companies offer 30-
day money-back guarantees, which seems very reasonable to me. And get the
guarantee in writing if you can. Save and print out the Web page that displays
the guarantee.

#5 Disk Space

Your Web site will be limited to a certain amount of disk space, though you can buy more space. Most, even the cheapest services, give at least 10 or 15MB, and you might get as much as 50MB for $25 a month. (Disk space is cheap, and the hosting services know that few people will use all 50MB anyway!) You can actually get quite a lot into a megabyte or two, and a really huge site will need only a few hundred megs.

#6 Hit and Data Transfer Charges

Some companies charge you for the number of hits—the number of times someone transfers one of your pages to his browser. Others charge according to the amount of data transferred out of your Web site. Either way, the busier your site, the more you'll be charged under these pricing schedules. Others have no limit.

Unlimited use may not be so good if it means that all the sites handled by the server are very busy, of course. And in any case, most companies provide a certain minimum data transfer for free, which is usually plenty for most sites. (We'll be discussing how to test the server later.) Consider what you plan to do with your site; if you want to allow people to download software, then data-transfer charges may be a significant consideration, though per-hit charges may not. If the Web-hosting company charges per hit, find out exactly how it defines a hit. Does it mean that a complete page load—text and graphics—is one hit? Or does the company count the transfer of each image within the page as a separate hit? Some services count as a hit only the first loading of a page; if someone loads the page and then reloads it a few moments later, the reload won't be counted. Other services will include both the initial load and reload as separate hits.

#7 Upgrades

If your Web site grows, so will your hosting needs. Check to see how much it'll cost you to add more disk space, transfer more data, create more POP accounts, and so on.

#8 Commercial Use

Some companies don't host commercial Web sites, so if you are setting one up for a business, check the company's policy.

#9   Discounts for Nonprofits

Some companies provide lower rates for charities and other nonprofit organizations.

#10   Domain Registration

Most companies will register your name for you. However, you may be charged an additional fee, and in any case, you should register it yourself for the reasons I mentioned earlier. If you plan to get a domain name that ends in anything other than .com, .net, or .org (one of the regional names, such as .uk, .jp, or .fr, for instance), check to see if the server can work with these domains.

#11   Multiple Domain Names

If you have more than one domain name, you can have them all point to the same Web site. For instance, you might have one domain name for your company and other domain names that you are using to promote specific products. There are different ways to handle this. All the domains can point to the same directory, or you can have separate directories for each domain. Of course, there are different ways to charge, too. You may be allowed two domains for free, perhaps, with an additional fee for extra domains. Or maybe you'll pay an additional fee for all extra domains. Or maybe the company will sell you separate accounts for each domain name, with a discount. For instance, one service told me it charged a $25 setup fee for each additional domain name plus $10 a month if the extra domain names point to separate directories, with no monthly fee if they all point to the same directory. These additional domains are known as "parked" domains, by the way.

Note also that domains that point to a separate directory may be fake virtual Web sites, discussed in Chapter 3. In other words, they may not have their own IP numbers. That's fine for most users: recent versions of most browsers will be forwarded to the correct Web page, even if the URL contains a subdirectory. But a (very) small percentage of users, those people with very old browsers, will end up at your main page—the one set up for your primary domain—and have to dig their way down through your site to get to where they need to go.

Here's one thing to look out for if you are going to have this sort of parked domain; you may find that forms you create in FrontPage won't work properly. This is not an insurmountable problem, but the system administrator may not realize what's happening. Tell the administrator that in order for FrontPage to work properly the FrontPage server must be configured for each domain; if it's only configured for the primary domain, forms in the secondary domains won't work.

#12 POP E-mail Account

As discussed in Chapter 2, hosting companies generally provide e-mail service with the Web site. Sometimes you'll get several POP accounts—POP "boxes"—even though you may need no more than one. Some companies, however, may charge extra for e-mail.

There's often some ambiguity about what you're getting when you're given a POP account, or several POP accounts. Some companies will give you five or six POP accounts for free, but they may limit the manner in which those POP accounts work. Each one may work with only a single e-mail address; one account for info@acmesewercover.com, one for sales@acmesewercover.com, one for joe@acmesewercover.com, and so on.

Ideally, you want the potential to create an unlimited number of e-mail addresses based on your domain name. For instance, let's say you have POP boxes for several employees; for Joe, Susan, Fred, Ann, and John. Mail sent to joe@acmesewercover.com will be placed into Joe's POP box; mail to susan@acmesewercover.com goes into Susan's POP box, and so on. But what about mail that the system doesn't recognize? Messages sent to info@acmesewercover.com, contest@acmesewercover.com, or sales@acmesewercover.com? The system may be set up to bounce these back as undeliverable. But it *should* be set up to send them all to the primary POP box. You can then use a good e-mail program to filter the messages into different folders. In fact, a good mail system should allow you to set up different e-mail addresses to work in different ways, so you can, if you wish, bounce mail back as undeliverable. So discuss this issue and make sure you understand exactly what you're getting; tell the hosting company that you need "unlimited e-mail aliases."

#13 Mail Forwarding

You may also want to make sure the Web-hosting company allows you to set up mail forwarding—automatically defining certain types of incoming e-mail messages to be forwarded somewhere else. For instance, messages to susie@acmesewercover.com could be forwarded to susiesewer@aol.com. You may be able to set up mail forwarding for one or perhaps several mail accounts, and there may be an additional charge for additional forwarding. Also note that some companies make it very easy to set up mail forwarding by providing a simple Web form in which you fill in the name of the account you want to forward and where you want it to go. Other companies make it very awkward to forward mail, expecting you to fool around with various configuration files.

#14 Mail Responders

A mail responder, or autoresponder, is a program that automatically responds to incoming mail. For instance, if someone sends e-mail to info@acmesewercover. com, an informational message can be sent back. These can be very useful, so I recommend that you make sure they are available.

Find out how easy it is to set up the autoresponders. Some companies expect you to understand the intricacies of writing procmail scripts. The company you choose either should have a simple system that allows you to fill in a form to create your autoresponders, or should offer detailed, step-by-step instructions. We'll discuss this issue more in Chapter 14.

By the way, there are several things a good autoresponder should be able to do:

- Quote the incoming message in the autoresponse
- Save the incoming message
- Grab the e-mail address from the incoming message and put it in a text file
- Redirect the message to another address
- Create a log file listing all the incoming messages and time of delivery, and optionally saving a portion of the incoming message.

What are these features for? Well, here's an example. While promoting the first edition of this book I used to give away some free reports and a subscription to my e-mail newsletter (*Poor R ichard's Web Site News* http://PoorRichard.com/ newsltr/). I'd mention an autoresponder address while doing radio interviews, or in articles I wrote for the press. If I'd had a system that could redirect messages, I could have saved a lot of trouble. Redirection means taking the original To: information off the e-mail message, putting a new address on it, and sending it off. (This is *not* the same as forwarding the message; in that case a copy of the message, including the header information, is placed into another message and that new message is sent out.) With a redirect feature I could set up an autoresponder to receive the message, send out the response, then redirect the message to a mailing-list server which could then have subscribed the sender to my newsletter. Instead I had to save incoming messages in a log file, then physically add the subscribers to the newsletter periodically.

What I'm saying, then, is that there's not much chance you'll find an autoresponder system with all these features, so don't get too upset if you can't! (On the other hand, my hosting company, **BizBlast.com**, plans to create just such autoresponders … visit http://BizBlast.com/.)

#15 Mailing-List Server

A mailing-list server allows you to set up a discussion group based on the e-mail system, or to publish an e-mail newsletter. Both these things can be very useful promotional tools; we'll be discussing these systems in Chapter 14. Many companies have mailing-list software available for their clients to use—if so, ask whether there's an additional cost, how many mailing lists you are allowed to have, and how many members per list. However, note that few hosting companies provide mailing-list software that's any good! There are ways to run small lists from your own computer, or you can hire a mailing-list company to do it for you (I'll explain where to find such companies in Chapter 14), so you may never use the hosting company's software anyway.

#16 Shell Account (Telnet Access)

A shell account allows you to log onto the Web site using Telnet, and modify files and directories. This can be useful, and you'll find that most companies provide a shell account. Some don't, though, and this may present problems in a few cases. For instance, if you want to install your own CGI scripts (see Chapter 11), you may need Telnet access so you can get to the scripts and modify their permissions, rename files, and so on. On the other hand, it's sometimes possible to set permissions using an FTP program such as WS_FTP or CuteFTP, if the server is set to allow you to do so (not all servers are). Without the ability to modify settings, you're at the mercy of the Web-hosting company, which will have to make the modifications for you, may charge you to do so, and may take its own sweet time getting around to it. (Having said all that, it's been a couple of years since I've accessed my Web site using Telnet; I generally use Microsoft FrontPage and CuteFTP.) *Now using "FTP Explorer"*

#17 FTP Access

You'll need FTP (File Transfer Protocol) access. This allows you to transfer files to and from your Web site, so virtually all companies provide this service. Some may provide a different way to transfer files, such as using FrontPage. But even if you use FrontPage, it's nice to have FTP access, too. If you plan to use CGI scripts (see Chapter 11), and you don't have Telnet access, ask if the server is set up to allow you to change file permissions using FTP.

#18 Anonymous FTP Site

This is not the same as FTP access to your Web site. Rather, it allows you to set up an FTP site that people can access to download files. You might want to do this if you are distributing software, for instance. While it's possible to transfer files directly from your Web site, it's sometimes handy to have an FTP site, too. People without good Web access can still use the FTP site, and some FTP sites can resume interrupted downloads; that is, if someone tries to transfer a file, gets halfway through, and his ISP or phone company drops the line, he can come back and continue the transfer where he left off—a very handy feature for large downloads.

Incidentally, if you plan to provide files for download, whether at a Web site or an FTP site, make sure they're virus-checked before making them available. You don't want your visitors to catch an infection. And if you allow people to upload files to your site, ensure that these files are virus-checked before you use them.

#19 Secure Server

If you plan to take orders online or transfer sensitive information, you'll need a secure server (you'll often see it referred to as an SSL server, meaning a Secure Sockets Layer server). For instance, credit-card information typed into a form will be encrypted before being sent from the user's Web browser to the server. There may be an additional fee to use the secure server. You don't have to have a secure server to take orders online, but many people won't place orders unless you do. (See Chapter 13.)

Note, by the way, that if you find a Web-hosting company that you really like, but that doesn't have a secure server, you can use a different server to carry out online transactions. I'll explain how that works in Chapter 13, too.

Here's a bit of background about secure servers. In order to set up a secure server, the Web server must have a "certificate" installed. This certificate is generally purchased from VeriSign or Thawte. VeriSign says that a hosting company is not allowed to share its certificate with its clients ... but many hosting companies, perhaps most, do so anyway. (If your hosting company tells you that VeriSign doesn't restrict sharing, well all I can say is that I've discussed this issue with people at the VP level at VeriSign, and they told me that they "reserved the right to sue" companies that shared their certificates.) As for Thawte, it recommends against sharing but allows it nonetheless.

So, this explains why some hosting companies will tell you that if you want a secure server you must buy a certificate (for several hundred dollars a year), yet other companies will provide a secure server at no cost.

#20 Shopping-Cart Software

If you plan to sell products and want to offer users some kind of catalog combined with an order form, you might want to find out if the Web-hosting company has any shopping-cart software already available, and, if so, its capabilities and cost. If not, ask if you can add your own. This requires the use of CGI scripts, so make sure the company allows you to run your own CGI scripts. (It's not easy, though, so I'd recommend against it in most cases.) You can also use a shopping-cart service, and link to it from your Web site. The problem is that the shopping-cart system provided by the hosting company will probably be deficient in a number of ways—it's hard to find a hosting company with all the services you need, *including* a good shopping cart. (I'll explain why, along with all the ins and outs of setting up a shopping cart, in Chapter 13.)

#21 Online Credit-Card and Check Processing

If the company does have a shopping cart available, find out if you can do online credit-card processing. That is, if, when a buyer places an order, the credit card is processed immediately. Without online processing the credit-card information is collected so that you can process it later. Find out how much it's going to cost you, too. Again, see Chapter 13 for details.

#22 Image Maps

This isn't a big deal any longer, but in the interest of a little education I'm leaving it in here. Image maps are pictures in Web pages that contain hotspot links. There are two ways to create these: by adding special code in your Web pages (client-side maps) or by running a special script at the Web server (server-side maps). Any good Web-page creation tool can create client-side maps, and most users have browsers that can work with them. But some older browsers can't, so many Web authors prefer to create server-side image maps. However, not all Web-hosting companies let you do so. This isn't an issue if you use FrontPage at a FrontPage-enabled site, because FrontPage can create both client-side and server-side image maps. And it's not the issue it was two years ago, as very few people are working with browsers that can't deal with client-side image maps.

#23 CGI Scripts

CGI means *Common Gateway Interface*. It's a way to provide interactivity to Web pages, in particular to handle the input from forms. For instance, you can use CGI to take information from a form and send it to your e-mail account. Many Web-hosting companies have libraries of CGI scripts you can use. Some allow you to install your own CGI scripts, but don't provide a library. Others don't allow you to add any CGIs. I recommend that you find a company that at least allows you to add your own. Ideally, it will also have a library of well-documented CGI scripts. Better still, a library of canned scripts that you simply "plug in";

scripts that are set up for their servers already so that it doesn't take much work to install (you'll see what a hassle working with CGI can be later, in Chapter 12).

#24 Server-Side Includes

Here's another feature most people won't need to worry about. A server-side include is the process of embedding a Web document or simple information into another Web document. For instance, the results from a CGI script could be embedded into an HTML page and displayed. Most companies, but not all, will allow includes. You may not find includes necessary, but there are a few useful CGI scripts that require the use of includes.

#25 Database Access

If you want to allow your Web-site visitors access to information from a database, you need to find out whether the Web-hosting company has some kind of database system set up on the server; some have Access or FoxPro, or Microsoft SQL. Quite a few use a public-domain system called mySQL. Also, figure out who's going to handle this. It's not that simple to set up. The Web-hosting company may be able to set it up for you—a number of hosting companies offer this service. If you have the necessary computer skills and plan to set up a database yourself, figure out what system you plan to use and then find a hosting company that will work with it. And, of course, check to see what the additional charge will be to use database interaction.

#26 Java Applets

If you plan to use Java applets or think you may need to in the future, ask if the company allows this capability. Java applets are programs that can be embedded into a Web page. When the Web page transfers, the Java applet transfers, too, and then runs when it gets to the user's computer. Java applets range from the very simple—"hover buttons," for instance, which change color or image when you point at them—to very complicated.

Java applets may also run on the Web server itself. For instance, many order-management systems use Java running behind the scenes on the Web server. If you know that you'll need this sort of thing, then you'd better find out what the hosting company can provide. Not all Web-hosting companies allow the use of Java applets, and most small businesses probably don't need them, though this situation could change as more useful applets become available.

#27 RealAudio Server

RealAudio is a popular streaming audio format. If you want your visitors to listen to sounds played from your Web site in the RealAudio format, the company will need a RealAudio server. Most companies, however, do not need RealAudio. (See Chapter 9.)

#28 Access Reports

Access reports show you information about visitors to your site. You need this information, as it can show you where visitors are coming from, when they arrive, which pages they view, and so on. (See Chapter 21.) Some companies send reports to you automatically via e-mail each day or week. Some create charts to show access information.

#29 Password-Protected Pages

If you need to set up a private area on your Web site, some companies will help you create password-protected areas. This is quite easy to do using Microsoft FrontPage, by the way.

#30 Reselling Web Space

Some companies allow you to set up in business as a Web-hosting company and sell space on their servers. In other words, you can set up your own Web-hosting company—probably not something to be taken lightly. It's a very competitive business, with very high customer-service costs, so don't get into it unless you've really considered the time and expense of running such a business.

#31 Promotional and Design Services

Many companies provide other services, such as design and page creation, as well as registering your site with Web search engines. (See Chapter 16.) If you need these services, remember that you can always buy them elsewhere, so don't base the decision whether to use a Web-hosting company on whether it offers promotion and design. On the other hand, you may run across a hosting company that sells a full package—hosting, design, creation, and promotion— and has created Web sites that you admire. Such packages are often too expensive for individuals, but may be just what a small company needs.

#32 Technical Support

Ask about the type of technical support available. Can you call and talk with someone? And if so, is it a toll-free or local call? This is a significant issue, as you'll almost certainly have to get help at some point. Some Web-hosting services try to handle all their support through e-mail, but too many of them have a very poor response time. You must have some way to talk to someone. Toll-free calls are relatively rare for low-cost Web-hosting companies; you may end up having to use a long-distance number, but that's better than nothing. By the way, some companies will charge you for phone support.

#33 Who Owns the Server?

As you've seen, it's possible for companies to resell Web-hosting space. That means some of the companies you are talking to may not actually run the server. In many cases this won't cause problems, but it means the company doesn't have direct control of the server. If you want the company to do something for you, it may not be able to even if it wants to. Sometimes it's hard to know for sure if a Web-hosting company really does own the server. A utility called Whois—see Chapter 5—can help you find the person registered as being responsible for the server, so you may be able to track down who owns it, but it's probably not worth the time trying.

Why would you want to work with a reseller? Perhaps the company offers an attractive package that includes Web design and creation, promotion, and so on. Working with a reseller is not a problem if the reseller is efficient and reputable, and is working with a good Web-hosting company. But it's worth knowing the situation, so ask. All things being equal, I'd pick the company that owns the servers, but that doesn't mean you can't find a good deal from a reseller.

By the way, one of the hosting directories I mentioned earlier, Budgetweb, categorizes companies into two groups: IPPs (Internet presence providers) and VARs (value-added resellers). IPPs own their own servers; VARs rent space. Judging by the distribution of companies in Budgetweb's categories, most are IPPs; you can use Budgetweb's filtering system to remove all VARs from the list and still have a large list to work with. Incidentally, Alex Chapman, the owner of Budgetweb, told me that "confirming whether a hosting company is an IPP or a VAR" is one of the hardest things he has to do when accepting submissions. He uses a variety of methods to check ownership, and finds that a number of companies are falsely claiming to be IPPs.

#34 How Many Computers?

You might ask how many computers the company uses. It might be a single computer, or a dozen or more. A large investment in hardware probably means the company's in the business for the long haul.

#35 Size of the Company

Call and chat with the company's staff. Ask how many employees it has, and whether they all work full-time. Ask where the Web server—the computer itself—is located. Is it in the company's building, or in a co-location service? Try to get an idea of how big this company is and if it's being run on a shoestring or part-time. A Web-hosting company can be run by a single person working out of a basement, but you probably don't want an account with that type of company. On the other hand, it doesn't require a lot of people to run a Web-hosting company as long as those people are really knowledgeable and experienced.

#36 Connection Speed and Distance to the Backbone

Find out what type of connection the Web server has to the Internet. It's probably a T1 connection (1.5Mbps), though maybe a T3 (45Mbps). Most Web-hosting companies aren't connected directly to the Internet; they're connected through an Internet service provider (ISP)—not the sort of ISP that individuals and most small companies use, but an ISP that specializes in setting up very fast (and expensive) connections. Some large networks have Web-hosting services. For instance, BBN Planet has its own backbone, so Web sites hosted by that company have a very fast connection to the Internet (we'll talk more about backbones in a moment).

Your Web-hosting company should have at least a T1 connection to the ISP and may have multiple connections; ask how many. It may have a T3 connection. Does it matter? Not necessarily; what counts is how much traffic is going over those lines, so a T1 line with little traffic would be a better deal than a T3 line that is maxed out. You don't want a Web-hosting company with, for instance, an ISDN connection; that's simply too slow. Though it is possible to set up a Web-hosting company using ISDN, you probably won't run into companies using ISDN. For reference, the chart below shows relative speeds of the different types of lines:

56k line . . . . 56kbps (kbps=thousand bits per second)
1-channel ISDN 64kbps
2-channel ISDN 128kbps

fractional T1 . . . . Different speeds available:
64kbps,128kbps,
256kbps, 384kbps, 512kbps, 768kbps
T1 . . . . 1.544Mbps (Mbps=million bits per second)
T3 . . . . 44.736Mbps

Now, if you're really picky you could take things a bit further and really get the details. For instance, if the company claims to have a T1 or T3, ask whether that means they're hooked directly to the line, or whether there's an intermediate step. The company may have several Web servers, each hooked to the line through an Ethernet card, for instance, which is much slower than a direct line. So while the company may claim it has a 45Mbps connection to the Internet, it may actually have a 10Mbps connection.

Some Web-hosting companies make exaggerated speed claims. If a company claims it has a T3, consider that a T3 line is very expensive, tens of thousands of dollars a month to lease. A one- or two-person operation working in a basement probably could not afford such a line.

You might also find out how many "jumps" the Web server is from an Internet backbone. For more information about this issue, see "All About the Backbone" below. You could also ask how many connections they have to the backbone. One system administrator told me that her system has two connections, which is useful because some backbones work better going in certain directions than in others. With two connections, data is more likely to get through; if it can't get through on one connection, it can probably get through on the other. And if one line gets cut, your Web site does not go down. (Some small companies have a single T1 line, which means if the phone company or gas company cuts the line—and it's amazing how often they seem to do so—your Web site is out of commission.)

A fast Web site requires these components:

- A fast Web server working well within capacity (that is, not with so much traffic that it can barely keep up)
- A fast connection from the computer to a line (if it's a slow Ethernet card, it doesn't matter how fast the line is)
- A fast line (at least a T1)
- A quick route to a very fast backbone line (that is, not too many hops).

All this has to come together to work properly. Call and talk with the technical staff to get an idea of how their system works.

The speed at which the server can transmit data can be critical in some cases, not quite so important in others. I know of one software company working with a server that can take as long as five or six hours to transmit a 4MB file when it's busy. This should be totally unacceptable to a company that's encouraging customers to download its latest demo or shareware.

#37 Jumps From the Backbone

Okay, I won't tell you *all* about the backbone, but I'll discuss a few issues. A backbone is a data-transmission line that carries very high volumes of Internet traffic—most of the long-distance traffic. Let's use a trucking analogy. A truck has to drive from a factory in City A to a warehouse in City B. The truck uses the minor roads leading from the factory to get onto the slightly larger main roads in City A, then transfers onto the freeway between City A and City B. It drives along the freeway, then, on arriving at City B, gets off the freeway and onto the main roads, then onto the smaller roads leading to the warehouse. The Internet backbone is the equivalent of the freeway. There is only a small number of companies that own Internet backbones: Sprint, MCI, ANSnet, BBN Planet, and a few others. In effect, these companies own the freeways.

Now, say we have two trucks. One starts from a factory in the old part of town, separated from the freeway by old, narrow streets. One starts at a factory at a new business park right next to the freeway. Which truck will get to City B first? The one starting from the old part of town has to make many more "hops" to get to the freeway—the backbone—than the one right next to the freeway. And so it is with Web-hosting companies.

So you should ask the Web-hosting company how many "hops" they are from the backbone. Ideally, you want no more than two or three hops: from the Web-hosting company's Web server to its router, a piece of equipment that connects the computer to the network (first hop); from the router to an Internet service provider (second hop); and from the Internet service provider to the backbone (third hop).

#38 Checking Hops with traceroute

You can, if you wish, check what the Web-hosting company tells you using a program called traceroute. This is a program that sends packets of information out across the Internet, and into the Web-hosting company's system. Each node through which the packets pass responds back to the traceroute program, so you can build a "picture" of the network. (A node is a computer on the network through which messages pass.)

Traceroute measures the RTT (round trip time) for each packet of information to a particular node and back. Sometimes an RTT for a node farther away may actually be less than for a node that's close by. That's perfectly normal, and simply due to changes in network traffic.

You can run traceroute in a variety of ways. Probably the easiest is to use one of the traceroute servers that you'll find on the Web. You can find them through these pages:

Boardwatch traceroute Page
   http://boardwatch.internet.com/traceroute.html

traceroute.org
   http://www.traceroute.org/

Tracert
   http://www.tracert.com/

Yahoo!—Traceroute
   http://dir.yahoo.com/Computers_and_Internet/Communications_and_
   Networking/Software/Networking/Utilities/Traceroute/

You can also use traceroute directly from your computer, using freeware and shareware programs such as the following:

Cyberkit (Windows)
   http://www.ping.be/cyberkit/

NetScanTools (Windows)
   http://www.nwpsw.com/

Network Toolbox (Windows)
   http://www.jriver.com/

WhatRoute (Macintosh)
   http://crash.ihug.co.nz/~bryanc/

Go to one of the traceroute pages and type the domain name of the Web-hosting company that you are considering using: www.gianthost.com, or whatever. Alternatively, you may have an IP (Internet Protocol) number to trace, such as 199.45.153.1. Click the Start button, and the traceroute program begins. You can see an example in Figure 4.1.

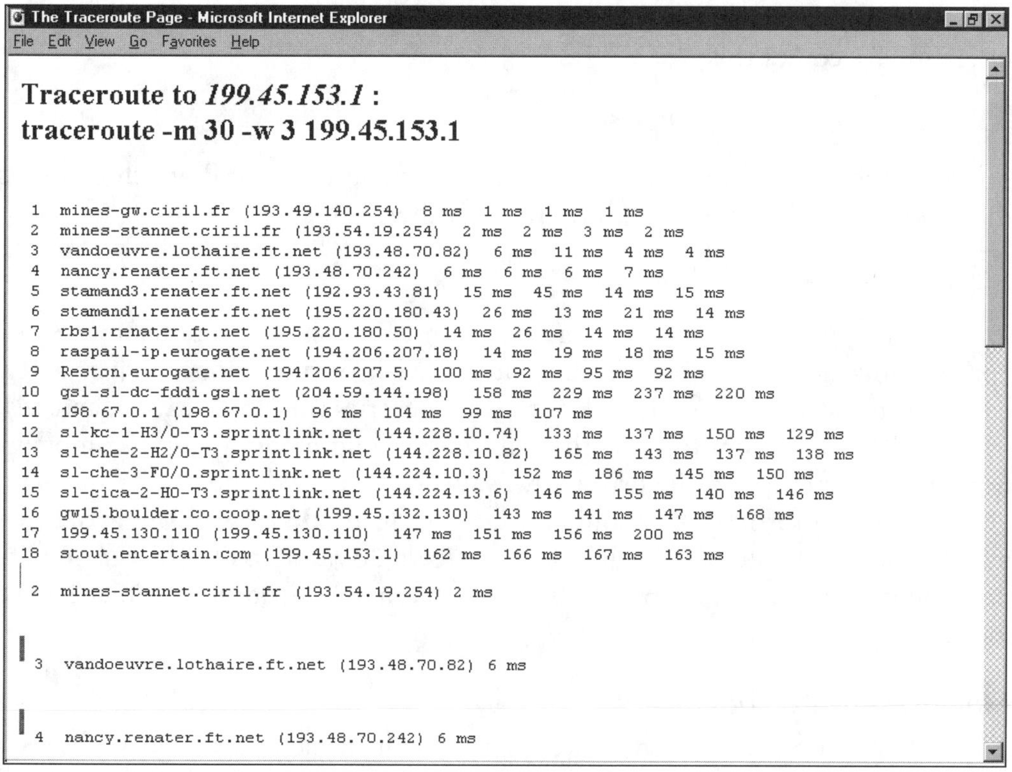

Figure 4.1: Use traceroute to see how information gets to the Web server.

You can see at the top of Figure 4.1 that I'm tracing 199.45.153.1, which is the IP number of a host computer owned by a Web-hosting company at which an acquaintance works. She told me the company has three hops to the backbone, and the traceroute shows the route those hops take. Near the bottom of the screen shown in Figure 4.1 you'll see this:

```
18 stout.entertain.com
```

This is the computer corresponding to the IP number we are tracing (which is not always the same as the IP number shown for that computer, by the way). We're actually using a traceroute server in France, so we are tracing from France across to the U.S. and into Colorado. Right before line 18 in Figure 4.1 you can see this:

```
17 199.45.130.110
```

This is the hop from the Web server to the company's router. Above line 17 in Figure 4.1 comes this:

```
16 gw15.boulder.co.coop.net
```

This is the second hop, from the router to the company's ISP, which connects the company to the Internet. Above line 16, there's this:

```
15 sl-cica-2-HO-T3.sprintlink.net
```

This third hop takes us onto the backbone. This is a computer owned by Sprint. How do I know it's the backbone? Well, Sprint is one of just a few backbone owners. Also, if you look at the other entries (numbers 12, 13, and 14), they're all Sprint computers. So the data is traveling along a single company's network. In effect it's on the private freeway—on the backbone.

For more information about traceroute, read **Boardwatch's article** at http://boardwatch.internet.com/mag/96/dec/bwm38.html and the traceroute documentation at http://infohost.nmt.edu/bin/man?/usr/local/man/man8/traceroute.8.

More traceroute Tricks

There's something else traceroute can do for you: it can show you if there's a sudden drop in speed when the data gets to the Web server. Do a traceroute from a few places around the world, and watch what happens. The number at the end of each line should increase as you go down the traceroute readout. For instance, in Figure 4.2 you can see the graph that the traceroute server has created to show transmission times (not all servers create these graphs). As the data gets farther along the route to the Web, server times go up; the farther the data goes, the longer it takes.

Try from a few locations around the world, and see if there's always a sudden jump in the last number (sometimes shown as RTT—round trip time) when it gets to the Web-server end. That would suggest that the Web-hosting company has a slow connection onto the Internet.

The problem with traceroute, though, is that it's a little tricky to use. You can only really make sense of it if you already know what a traceroute to a good Web site looks like, and even then, a number of factors can make a traceroute look good one moment and not so good a little later, so you really need to use it several times for each site you want to check. You might play with traceroute a little, and see if you've got the patience to use it. If not, concentrate on the following steps.

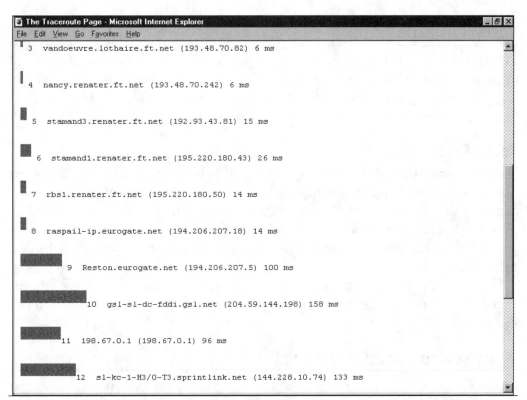

Figure 4.2: This server draws a chart showing transmission times; the longer the line, the slower the transmission.

#39 Ask for References

Here's a method for checking the Web-hosting company that's a little less technical: ask for references. Ideally, ask if it has a Web page pointing to other customer's pages—many companies do—then visit these pages and grab a few e-mail addresses. Send e-mail to these companies; I'd recommend that you mail to at least 30, preferably 40, and ask if they're happy with the service. Ask if they have problems accessing the Web site, whether they've complained about slow connections, if the system administrator is helpful, and so on. If you get a lot of grumpy replies, look for another company.

#40 Look and Feel

Consider the company's "look and feel." Does it explain its services well, or are many questions unanswered? Is its site well designed and easy to work with, or ugly and difficult to get around? Do its Web pages load quickly, or does it seem to take a long time for them to open? Does the service provide Web-form "control panels" to help you set up autoresponders and e-mail forwarding, or do they expect their users to Telnet into their account and fight with UNIX and various other arcane systems? All these things, while perhaps not directly related to the type of service you're likely to get from the company, may in an indirect way give you an idea of how well it treats its customers, and how well its server functions ... and how easy it will be to work with the system.

#41 Real-World Check

Testing is important when picking a new Web host, but when you really get down to it, it's real-world use that matters. So check out the Web sites of the company's other customers. Are they often slower than most Web sites you visit? About the same? Faster? If you find they're slower, visit a few other sites that you've been to before to make sure it's not your connection that's slow for the moment.

If you get the impression that all the Web sites are transmitting back to your system slowly, then you have a problem. Or rather, they have a problem. You can just keep looking.

With Whom Should You Talk?

Most of the work required to run a Web-hosting company doesn't need any great technical knowledge. Sales, marketing, billing, creating Web pages, and so on are all fairly nontechnical tasks these days (yes, even creating Web pages). So there are many nontechnical people in the business, and you may find yourself talking with one of the nontechnical members of the staff. On the other hand, many small Web-hosting companies are run by a very small group of people who do everything from administering the servers to handling billing.

Some of the issues we've looked at are related to technical issues, so I'd advise that you talk with the technical contact, the person who's actually running the server. If you're not sure who this is, you can use Whois to find out (we'll look at Whois in Chapter 5). When you do a Whois search for the Web-hosting company's domain, you'll see the names of people who are registered as the administrative, technical, and billing contacts. It's the technical guy you want.

With the larger hosting companies, of course, you'll have trouble getting past customer support to a really technical person, in which case you'll just have to keep sending the person back to get answers until you're satisfied.

By the way, it's entirely possible that you'll run into a situation in which you simply can't get your questions answered in any reliable way. After receiving a mailing from US West—my local phone company—about its new Web-hosting service, I decided to call and see what was on offer. Unfortunately, the salespeople not only couldn't answer my questions, they didn't even understand them. Later I managed to find someone in the technical-support group that supports the Web-hosting service, but he didn't know the answers, and, again, didn't fully understand them. These were simple questions, too, such as: "Do I get a POP e-mail account with my Web site?" and "Do you have a secure server?" This second question was answered with: "Secure, what do you mean? Why would you need a secure server?" (You'll learn the answer to that in Chapter 13.)

I did, eventually, get the answers I needed. But I was left wondering how well the company would support my site if the technical-support staff understand so little about Internet services.

A Matter of Geography

Geography might be important. If you know that all the people visiting your Web site will be in one geographic location, you might want to look for a Web-hosting company in that area. A Web-hosting company with a fast connection to the backbone in that area will provide faster and more reliable access than a company with a fast connection to the backbone on the other side of the world. It's marginal, though … it's not something I'd rest the decision on.

In general, geography doesn't matter much—assuming that you've asked the right questions about the number of hops to the backbone. You may be in Alberta, Canada, but the Web-hosting company you want to use is in Miami, or Paris, or London. What counts is not so much where the server is, but the sort of service it will give you. And most Web-hosting companies accept credit cards, so you can buy their services regardless of currency differences.

On the other hand, there is another significant geography issue: technical support. Will you be able to get technical support through a toll-free or local phone number? Unfortunately this is often a problem. Web hosting is the sort of business that can be—and is—set up as a part-time business, with all communications done through e-mail. That's good for the Web-hosting company, not always so good for you. You may have to dig around for a while to find a company that has all the services you need—and convenient telephone support.

You Can't Have Everything

It can be tricky to get all the components you need from one company. That's not always a problem, because some of the services I've mentioned here can be obtained elsewhere. While FrontPage and CGI support, for instance, could be critical—if you need them, there's no point getting a Web account at a hosting service that can't provide them—other things shouldn't break the deal. You can get the following services elsewhere if need be:

- Mailing-list servers
- Shopping-cart software
- Online credit-card and check processing
- Promotional and design services.

If You Make a Mistake ...

Remember that even if you make a mistake and end up with a bad Web-hosting company, you can change later (you're going to get your own domain name, right?). On the other hand, you don't want to have to switch. If you set up a simple site, just a few pages with images on them, then it's easy to switch from one hosting company to another. Set up something complicated, with lots of CGI scripts and a shopping-cart system, and it gets more complicated.

But if you follow all these steps carefully and ask all the right questions, you're unlikely to end up with a really bad company, though you might get a mediocre one. Don't rush into selecting a Web-hosting company. Take your time and do it right, and you should end up with the right choice.

One final note. As I mentioned in the last chapter, I've recently started work on setting up a hosting company. The idea is to use what I've learned about the things that small businesses need to work online—and the problems that they run into—to create a hosting service that provides the services these firms really need. (No, I didn't write this book to promote the businesss! In fact I wrote the first edition two years before I began the business, and had the original idea for the book early in 1995.) Take a look and see if we can help you. The company is **BizBlast.com**, and you can reach it at, you guessed it, http://BizBlast.com/.

## Chapter Five

All About Domain Names

In this chapter you're going to learn about domain names: what they are and where to get them. As I've explained in earlier chapters, it's a good idea for your business to have its own domain name. You should be advertising your Web site everywhere. Wherever you put your telephone number, put your Web site's URL: on business cards, business stationery, print, TV, and radio ads, and so on. But if you have to change your Web-hosting company and you don't own your own domain name, you'll have two significant problems. You'll have to get a new domain name, so ...

- All your business cards, stationery, and print, TV, and radio ads will have to be changed.
- All your existing customers will have to be informed of the new URL.
- The existing customers who you are unable to reach will have the old (useless) URL.

If you leave your current Web-hosting company on friendly terms, you'll probably be able to leave a page that "forwards" people onto your new site. If the company's gone out of business or you left under a cloud, you're in trouble.

Furthermore, if you don't have your own domain name—if you are using a subdomain or a "member pages" URL, at least one major search engine probably won't list your site: Yahoo!. All in all, you need your own domain name!

What Are Domain Names?

IP (Internet Protocol) numbers are the basic unit of the Internet address system. An IP number looks something like this:

```
207.25.71.24
```

This number is actually an IP number used by CNN, the well-known news service. So if you want to view the CNN Web site, all you need to do is type this number into your browser, and away you go. (Try it for yourself. Well, okay, it may not work, because CNN may change the number; the number I used in the first edition of this book was changed at some point, so no doubt many readers tried it and it didn't work for them.) But can you remember 207.25.71.24? Or can you remember 204.71.200.245, a number currently used by Yahoo!?

There has to be a better way. And that's where domain names come in. You can remember www.cnn.com, can't you? Or even cnn. In many browsers, all you need to type is cnn and press Enter, and you'll get there (the browser companies changed the way their systems worked in 1998, so you may find that doesn't work in your browser). Most Internet users these days know that the host portion of most URLs starts with www and ends with com (it may end with something other than com, as we'll see later in this chapter, but most domains are .com domains). A name is a lot easier to remember than a number, so the Internet has a system in which names can be associated with numbers—yahoo.com with 205.216.146.42, cnn.com with 205.217.106.20, and so on. That way, users can remember names rather than numbers. The system also allows multiple names to be associated with a single number, so that two or more domain names may point to the same domain number.

www.cnn.com is a host computer at the cnn.com domain. The IP number really refers to cnn.com. The www portion of the URL is often not even required. Try typing cnn.com into your browser, and you'll still get to the CNN site. That's not true of all host names shown in URLs, by the way, but it's fairly common; the CNN server administrator has configured the server to work in this manner.

Here's how it works. When someone types a URL into a browser, the domain name is sent to a nameserver, a computer that holds a directory of domain names. The nameserver looks for the domain name to find the associated IP number. It may not find it; if nobody else has used the name recently, it won't be in the nameserver's cache. (A cache is a store of recently used data.) If it's not in the cache, the nameserver sends a message to another nameserver to get the information.

Once the nameserver has found the IP number, it sends it back to your browser, and that number is used to send a message to the Web server. Note a few things here. First, the protocol used for transmitted data to and fro across the Internet—TCP/IP (Transmission Control Protocol/Internet Protocol)—doesn't recognize domain names. It needs IP numbers, so the nameserver system is used to provide those numbers. Second, the IP number doesn't point directly at a Web site. Rather, it points to a computer that is responsible for that Web site.

Large service providers—the sort of service providers that provide Internet access to smaller service providers and hosting companies—have blocks of millions of IP numbers. When you register a domain name (you'll see how to do that in a moment), you have to tell the registration authority (also known as the registrar) the names and numbers of two domain servers controlled by the Web-hosting company. That company gets an IP number from the service provider and assigns that number to your domain name.

So when someone's browser gets the IP number from a nameserver and uses that number to send a message to your Web site, the message goes to the Web-hosting company's computer, which figures out exactly where (on which computer on which hard disk in which directory) your files are held.

When you get a domain name, the hosting company will probably tell you the IP number that points to your Web site. (However, as I explained in Chapter 4, there are fake-virtual or IP-less accounts that don't assign an IP number to every Web site, but share one number among many sites.) That number may change later, if the hosting company changes things around on their computers or moves to another service provider. For instance, one hosting company I worked with switched from one service provider to Bell Atlantic, because Bell Atlantic could provide them with a very fast connection to an Internet backbone, and very fast access to both the east and west coasts of the U.S. That means I was assigned a new IP number, one that belongs to Bell Atlantic. This is a complicated procedure for the Web-hosting company, because it means that it must maintain two servers for a while: one for the old set of IP numbers, and one for the new set—each server containing a copy of each client's Web site. It takes about a week before the new IP numbers are available from all nameservers worldwide.

Different Flavors of Domain Names

A domain name is structured in a hierarchical system from right to left. Take a look at this simple URL:

http://www.yahoo.com/

This is Yahoo!'s URL; yahoo.com is their domain, and www.yahoo.com is a host computer at that domain. The domain-name hierarchy goes from right to left. In other words, the com piece is the beginning; this is known as the *top-level domain*. Its actual title is the *gTLD*, or *generic Top Level Domain*. The yahoo piece is a subdomain—a second-level domain—of com; and www refers to a host computer at the yahoo.com domain; you can think of this as a subdomain of yahoo.com. You may have noticed other URLs that don't use www. For instance, yp.yahoo.com refers to Yahoo!'s Yellow Pages service; yp might be thought of as a subdomain of yahoo.com. (Some network people would say that strictly speaking www and yp are not subdomains, they're merely aliases for particular server programs, but for our purposes it's fine to think of these as subdomains.)

When a browser looks up a URL, it checks with the nameserver, which finds the IP numbers of the servers that "own" the domain (the authoritative nameservers or domain servers); in this case, the servers that own yahoo.com. The browser can then contact those servers, which know where to find the particular host computer containing the page the browser needs.

Now, your first decision is what sort of top-level domain you want. These are the most common:

.com...........Commercial domains; most for-profit companies have .com domains. This domain is the most popular domain, so popular that all the good domain names seem to have gone (unless you're really creative, as we'll see in a moment). There are plans to create more commercial domains. But then, the plans have been in place for over two years now, and nothing's happened yet.

.org.............Noncommercial organizations and other organizations that don't seem to fit elsewhere; most nonprofit organizations and charities use .org. Note, however, that there's nothing to stop a commercial enterprise from registering an .org domain.

.net ....Used by network-related companies and organizations, such as ISPs.

.edu............Educational institutions; originally intended for all types of educational institutions, now it's limited to "four-year colleges and universities" (that is, degree-granting institutions, which actually may not be four-year colleges in much of the world, but which generally are in the U.S., where this system was devised).

.int.............You may never see one of these; it's for bodies created by international treaty.

These domains are available throughout the world, by the way. If you're in the United Kingdom, for instance, and someone tells you that the .com and .org domains are for U.S. companies, don't be misled. They can be used in *any* country. Many other domains are intended for use in specific organizations, countries, or regions. For instance:

.gov............Restricted to U.S. federal government organizations
.mil............U.S. military organizations
.uk.............United Kingdom
.jp..............Japan
.au.............Australia
.aq.............Antarctica

The domains I've mentioned are recognized by IANA, the Internet Assigned Numbers Authority. There are other domain-name systems in use and some new systems being discussed, but you should use only systems that are recognized by IANA.

While I was writing the first edition of this book, the International Ad Hoc Committee (IAHC) announced its recommendations for new domain names. IAHC was a coalition of various organizations involved in running the Internet (it was dissolved in May 1997 and superseded by the Council of Registrars— CORE).

Because domain names are being assigned at such a phenomenal rate, the committee was charged with devising a new domain-name system. In addition to a variety of procedural changes that we'll be discussing a little later in this chapter, they recommended that a number of new top-level domains should be added:

.firm...........For businesses or firms

.shop..........For businesses offering goods to purchase (you may have seen .store; that was an early recommendation, though it was later replaced with .shop, perhaps because .shop is more widely understood internationally)

.web...........For organizations involved in activities related to the World Wide Web

.arts............For organizations emphasizing cultural and entertainment activities

.rec.............For organizations involved in recreational and entertainment activities

.info...........For entities providing information services

.nom..........For those wanting individual or personal domains

The U.S. government stuck its nose in, and the whole plan fell apart. Over two years after the original proposal the responsibility for managing modifications to the generic top-level domains were assumed by the National Telecommunications and Information Administration (NTIA) and the Internet Corporation for Assigned Names and Numbers (ICANN). At the time of writing it looks very much like there is no set timetable for the introduction of these or any other new generic top-level domain names … but who knows, that could change at any time. If you want to check to see if things have changed, take a look at these sites:

The Generic Top Level Domain Memorandum of Understanding site
http://www.gtld-mou.org/

Internet Corporation for Assigned Names and Numbers (ICANN)
http://www.icann.org/

National Telecommunications and Information Administration (NTIA)
http://www.ntia.doc.gov/ntiahome/domainname/domainhome.htm

More domains may be added soon after these first few; for instance, there may eventually be an .xxx domain, for "adult" Web sites—no, that's not a joke—and .air for airlines and air travel organizations. On the other hand, everyone seems to have forgotten about these things, because getting the basic seven into use has been enough trouble.

For a while many companies were advertising preregistrations for these new domain names; however, note that any company taking preregistrations cannot guarantee that you'll get the domain name you want (it can't even guarantee that the system will ever be put into place). All it can say is that as soon as the "land rush" begins, your application will be submitted.

Most companies and organizations wanting to work on the Internet worldwide will probably get one of the existing three top-level domains: .net, .com, or .org. Many companies outside the U.S. go for country domains, though. That can make sense in some cases, as it identifies the company as doing business in that particular country. But in other cases it's a bad idea. If the company wants to sell its products or services internationally, it's generally better off with a .com domain. And consider the situation of some companies that have registered domain names within a particular country, only to see some other company come along and take the same .com domain! For instance, the faxme.co.uk domain seems to be owned by a British company called Nildram Ltd. Yet there's a faxme.com domain that seems to be owned by someone else, a company called Z P I in Chicago (it's currently unused, but we can guess what sort of service it may turn out to be).

If you are interested in only a particular country, you may want to stick with the specific country top-level domain. For instance, if you run an organization that hosts haggis feasts in Aberdeen, Scotland, and you plan to use a Web site to keep local members informed, you might as well stick with a .uk domain.

For a list of country codes see these pages:

http://www.ics.uci.edu/pub/websoft/wwwstat/country-codes.txt

http://www.rtw.com.au/internet/suffixes.html

Second-Level Domains

A second-level domain is one that is a subdomain of a top-level domain. For instance, the cnn.com domain is a second-level subdomain of the .com top-level domain. You can register a second-level domain of the .com, .org, and .net domains.

Some other top-level domains don't allow registration of second-level domains. Rather, the second-level domains are used to further subdivide the domain system. This is true of many of the country top-level domains. For instance, in the .us domain there's a .co.us domain, a domain for organizations within Colorado. Some countries have a .com subdomain: .com.mx is the Mexican commercial subdomain, for example. Other countries use a .co domain in place of .com. For instance, in the United Kingdom many businesses register under the .co.uk domain. Even third-level domains may be restricted in some countries.

So if you are registering one of the two most popular domains—.com or .org—you'll be able to have a nice short domain name: your chosen name plus the top-level piece. If you register under a country domain, you may find you have to use a longer domain name.

Where Do You Register?

Domain names can be registered in different places, depending on the type of name you want to register. For every first-level domain name there's a *NIC*, a Network Information Center, an organization that controls a database that contains all the information about subdomains within the domain they control. (However, as I'll note in a moment, there are generally other places at which you can register a domain name; you don't have to go directly to the NIC.) The following table should help you track down the registration authorities:

.com, .org, .net, .gov, .edu ....**InterNIC, which Is run by a company called Network Solutions:**
http://www.networksolutions.com/

.us ....**U.S. Domain Registration Services:**
http://www.isi.edu/in-notes/usdnr/

.ca (Canada) ....http://www.cdnnet.ca/

.au (Australia).....................http://www.aunic.net/

.de (Germany).....................http://www.nic.de/

.uk (United Kingdom)..........http://www.nic.uk/

For other countries, try these sites:

Alldomains.com
  http://www.alldomains.com/
UniNet
  http://www.uninett.no/navn/domreg.html

Where, then, do you actually register your domain name? Well, you can go directly to a NIC and register there. But you may not want to. There are three types of places you can register a domain name:

- The NIC
- A registration authority
- A registration service

Registration Authorities

In April of 1999 a new registration system was announced for the .com, .org, and .net domains. At that point five new registration authorities were announced:

- America Online (United States)
- CORE Council of Internet Registrars (global)
- France Telecom/Oleane (France)
- Melbourne IT (Australia)
- Register.com (United States)

After the test period, which was originally planned to last for two months but ended up going on for about five months (at the time of writing the period still hadn't ended), it was planned that these companies would also be able to issue domain names:

- 9NetAvenue (United States)
- A Technology Company (Canada)
- Active ISP (Norway)
- Alldomains.com (United States)
- All West Communications (United States)

- American Domain Name Registry (United States)
- AT&T (United States)
- Domain Direct (Canada)
- DomainRegistry.com (United States)
- eNom, Inc. (United States)
- InfoAvenue (United States)
- InfoNetworks (United Kingdom/United States)
- InfoRamp (United States)
- Interactive Telecom Network (United States)
- Interdomain (Spain)
- Internet Domain Registrars (Canada)
- interQ Incorporated (Japan)
- MS Intergate (United States)
- NameSecure.com (United States)
- Name.Space Inc. (United States)
- NetBenefit (United Kingdom)
- NetNames (United Kingdom)
- Nominalia (Catalonia)
- Port Information System AB (Sweden)
- RCN (United States)
- Telepartner AS (Denmark)
- Verio (United States)
- Virtual Internet (United Kingdom)
- WebTrends (United States)

It seems that this list will grow, so when the test period comes to an end there could be many more. Network Solutions, the company that had, until recently, a monopoly over these domains, will still maintain the central database. The other registration authorities will be able to register names, but they'll have to query the main Network Solutions database to see if the names are available, and to submit the information on new domains to that database. Network Solutions itself can still sell domain names. In return for managing the central database, Network Solutions will earn $9 for every new domain registered by the other authorities; the other authorities feel this is too high, though, so it may be reduced later.

What does this mean to you? At the time of writing, not a great deal. For the moment, prices remain the same, too—$70 for the first two years. But eventually there will be a drop in the price of domain registrations, as the registration authorities start competing against each other. No longer does Network Solutions fix the price—as long as the new authority pays the $9 fee, it can charge as little as it wishes. I suspect, in fact, that registration prices could drop to $9 or below, perhaps even to $0. You may get a free domain registration when you sign up for Web-site hosting, for instance.

Registration Services

Many organizations have been selling domain names for a long time (well, several years, a long time in Internet chronology). Register.com, for instance, has sold over half a million domain names. Previously they would simply pass the information to Network Solutions, Network Solutions would bill the person registering the domain, and Register.com would earn a commission.

So there are many services where you can register a domain name. Unlike the registration authorities, the registration services have no direct link to the Network Solutions database, and no guaranteed access. They simply set up as a convenient way for people to register their domains, and they make money several ways: they earn a commission from a registration authority for every domain registered, they sell domain "parking" services (which I'll explain in a moment), and they may sell advertising or other services. And of course the line between registration authorities and registration services is blurring, as some registration services sign up to become true registration authorities. Indeed the line between a NIC and a registration service is blurring as the NICs get into the business of providing a range of commercial services. Early in 1999 Network Solutions, the company running InterNIC and controlling the main database of .com, .org, and .net domains, revamped its site to compete with the registration services. In addition to the core function of allowing you to register a domain, they now sell domain parking, for instance.

However, there's an important distinction between a registration authority and a registration service. A registration authority has the right to register a particular set of domains (and as far as a I know this whole idea of having multiple registration authorities is, for the moment at least, unique to the .com, .org, and .net domains). But many registration authorities provide "one-stop shopping" for subdomains in multiple top-level domains. For instance, Register.com will help you register a domain name in .com, .org, and .net, but also in .co.uk, .gs, .md, .kz, and so on. And the registration services can often make it easier to register subdomains in some country domains by cutting through the red tape for you.

If you want to find a registration service, try some of these pages:

1 2 3 DomainMe!
  http://www.123domainme.com/

Alldomains.com
  http://www.alldomains.com/

Register.com (Yes, yes, I know, it's also a registration authority)
  http://www.register.com/

Yahoo!—Domain Name Companies
  http://www.yahoo.com/Business_and_Economy/Companies/Internet_
  Services/Domain_Registration/

What Will It Cost?

In order to explain prices, I have to discuss domain parking. As I explained earlier, when you register a domain, you have to "point" the domain to a particular computer. You have to provide IP numbers of domain servers that will be responsible for your domain.

Now, if you've already found a Web-hosting service to work with, you can use their IP numbers. But if you don't yet know where you're going to place your Web site, you'll have to *park* the domain somewhere. In effect, someone is lending you, or renting you, a couple of IP numbers so that the field in the database that's labeled "IP numbers" is filled with something. It's really not a bad deal for the companies renting you the IP numbers, because the IP numbers don't cost them anything, but that's another story.

Pretty much wherever you register your domain name these days, you can park it. The registration services make money by parking your domain for you. You register with them, they charge you $29.95, or $39.95, or something similar, and you get to park the domain at their site for a year or two (parking it for two years costs them no more than parking it for ten minutes, of course). On top of that parking fee you'll pay the domain-registration fee to the NIC, as well. So, for instance, at the time of writing if you register a domain name at Alldomains.com you'll pay $39.95 for the parking, and then you'll pay Network Solutions $70 to register your domain name (that's good for two years, then you'll pay $35 a year).

Some registration services will let you register your domain for free. You'll still have to pay the $70 domain-registration fee, but they won't charge any kind of service fee or parking fee. After all, the IP numbers don't cost them anything, and there's not much work involved in setting up forms. And they can be affiliates of Network Solutions and earn up to 14 percent of your $70 fee. Also, note that the registration authorities may not charge a parking fee. After all, if they're paying Network Solutions just $9 for each domain, and charging $70, they're already making $61. You're not paying a service fee or parking fee, but they're still making money on the deal. (As I mentioned before, though, I think domain-registration fees are going to drop soon, so they may not be making $61 for long.)

Where, then, do you register to get the best price?

- If you've already got a hosting company, register through their forms (many hosting companies are, in effect, registration services—but make sure they don't charge you a service fee for registering your domain), or register at the NIC, or at a registration authority or service that doesn't charge a parking fee or service fee.

- If you don't have a hosting company and need to park the domain, don't register at Network Solutions; you'll have to pay a $49 registration fee—register somewhere that won't charge a parking fee. Register.com, for instance, doesn't charge parking fees.

Picking a Name and Using Whois

Domain names are restricted to 22 characters or less, not including the top-level bit. That is, the piece you are choosing can be up to 22 characters. The name can contain only letters, digits, and dashes, but you can't begin or end the name with a dash. But pick a short name. Make it something easy for your customers to remember. (CDnow.com is easier to remember and spell than Music Boulevard.com, for example.)

The first problem you'll run into when registering a domain is picking a name that you can register. If you plan to get a .com or .org domain, you may find that your first choice is already taken, particularly with the .com domain. You may find your second and third choices have gone, too.

Picking a name can be difficult, but if you're imaginative you can often find something. If you're a painter, how about DenverPainters.com,

You Need .com!

As a general rule, if you can't get the .com domain but you can get the .org or even .net domain ... forget about it. Don't get .net if someone else has .com, because a significant part of your marketing efforts will push people to the .com domain. People assume a Web site is a .com site.

or PaintPaintPaint. com. (They're still available). If you're in the grass-cutting business, how about BostonGrass.com, or GrassGrassGrass.com (there may be some confusion as to what business you're in, of course).

Once you have a name you like, check to see if it's available. You need to use a Whois service with the registration authority you plan to work with. If you are registering a .com or .org domain, go to the **Network Solutions Whois** page (http://www.networksolutions.com/cgi-bin/whois/whois/), or use a Whois form at a registration authority or service. Registration authorities or services generally have Whois forms for the countries for which they're registering domains. Some software programs, such as some of the network programs I listed in Chapter 4, also allow you to search various Whois services.

In Figure 5.1 you can see the result of a Whois search at Network Solutions. I typed netscape.com into the form and pressed Enter, and ended up with the page you can see in the picture. Note that you can search only for second-level domains here. Type the name you want to use, followed by .com, but do not include www. For instance, type acmesewercover.com, not www.acmesewercover.com.

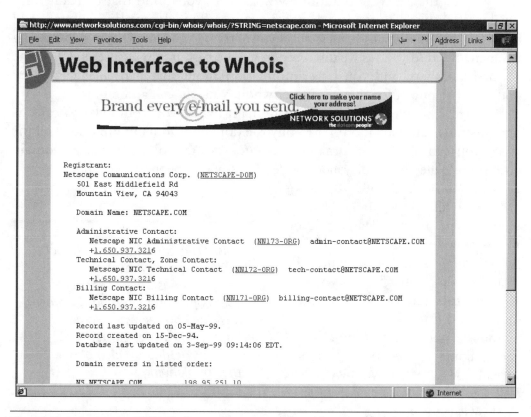

Figure 5.1: I searched Whois for netscape.com, and here's what it found.

Although Whois managed to find the domain name, in effect this figure shows you a "failure"; the name you want has been taken. (Well, you knew netscape.com had been taken, didn't you?) Take a quick look, though, because Whois can provide useful information, especially when you are talking with a Web-hosting company and trying to find out who administers its Web servers (see Chapter 4).

At the top you can see the name of the company or organization that "owns" the domain name (more about ownership in a moment). You can also see the administrative contact—generally the person with ultimate responsibility for the domain, and the technical contact—generally the person running the computer to which the domain is assigned and the person to call with technical questions. You may also see a billing contact the person who pays the bills. Sometimes there's just one contact for all three roles.

Near the bottom you'll see the domain servers—at least two of them, but sometimes more. These are the computers that know exactly where to find your domain and serve as a conduit between the domain and the rest of the Internet.

If you use the Network Solutions Whois form, you'll find that there are links on the IP numbers next to each domain server. This doesn't do you any good while looking up domain names, but if you're trying to verify what a Web-hosting company has told you (as we discussed in Chapter 4), it may be useful. Click one of these numbers, and you'll see information about that particular computer; you'll find a contact for that computer whom you can call and talk to.

If you're desperate for a particular domain name, you could always call the administrative contact and offer to buy the domain. Domains are traded all the time. You can also find domain-name brokers. **Yahoo! even has a Domain Brokerage** page (http://dir.yahoo.com/Business_and_Economy/Companies/Internet_ Services/Domain_Registration/Brokerages/).

You can also do a different type of search. Type a single name without the top-level domain piece. Whois will find all sorts of matches. For instance, see Figure 5.2. I typed the word netscape into the Whois text box and pressed Enter.

You can see that this time Whois found domains owned by Netscape: MYNETSCAPE.COM, HAWAII-VACATION-HOME.NET, SCREAM1.COM, SUNNET SCAPEALLIANCE.NET, etc.

This is a great little research tool for finding out what the competition is up to! Search for your competitor's company name, and you can see what domain names they have registered, perhaps getting an idea of what they're planning next.

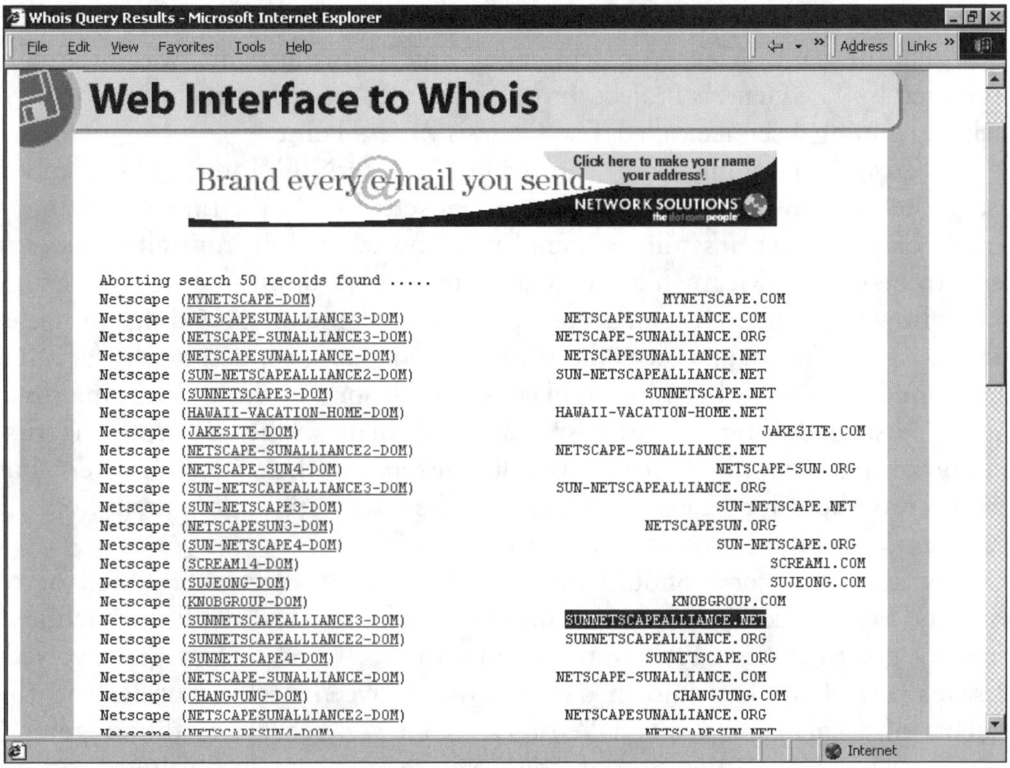

Figure 5.2: This time I searched Whois for netscape instead of netscape.com.

If the domain name you want is taken, you have a couple of options: persuade the owner to sell (call a few large friends to help you persuade him, or call your lawyers), or pick another name. With luck, eventually one of the names you try will return something like this:

No match for "ACMESEWERCOVER.COM."

Great, that's just what you need. Nobody's had the foresight to register acmesewercover.com, so it's all yours. It's time to grab the name.

Domain-Name Ownership

So far throughout this book I've been talking about how you can "own" a domain name. That's really a shorthand term, as domain-name ownership is an issue that has not been resolved. For instance, if you had registered the thegap.com domain name a few years ago, before the major clothing retailer realized what the Internet was and why it needed the domain name, would you own that domain? Maybe, maybe not. This domain name was originally registered by The Genesis Project, Ltd., an Internet service provider in Northern Ireland running a service called The Genesis Access Point.

The Gap (the clothing chain) complained to InterNIC. InterNIC suspended use of the domain name for a week, then reinstated it. At the time of writing, a couple of years later, it's still registered to Genesis, though ironically it doesn't seem to be in use. (Meanwhile The Gap is using gap.com.)

But how about newton.com, a site registered by someone providing computer advice. Apple Computers owns the Newton trademark, so, despite the fact that the name Newton has been in popular use for all sorts of things for some time, Apple persuaded InterNIC to suspend the domain. When I wrote the first edition of this book the domain was still registered to the original "owner," but had been on hold for an extended period. These days it's no longer on hold … but again, for some reason it's not in use either.

How about frys.com? Should that belong to Fry's Electronics, Inc., or to Frenchy Frys, a company that manufactures french fry vending machines? Frenchy got to it first, Fry's wants it, but InterNIC refused to get involved. Perhaps one of the best-known disputes was between Archie Comics and the parents of a small child called Veronica. (Can you see where this is going?) Archie claimed that the use of the veronica.org domain infringed on its trademark for the Veronica character. (You can visit http://www.veronica.org/ and see what two-year-old Veronica supposedly has to say about it all. "We got a demanding letter from the lawyers representing Archie Comic Publications, Inc.," she says. "They claim they own a **trademark** on my first name, Veronica. Now, they want me to surrender my Web domain name. I don't understand …")

But there's more involved. Some companies and organizations may go after you if they feel you are denigrating them in some way. The Church of Scientology, for instance, threatened legal action against the owner of scientology-kills.net.

So you should understand that there's more to owning a domain name than simply registering it. If you have a registered trademark for a product and register a domain name with the same name, you're probably in a strong position. If someone else has a trademark matching your domain name, they may want to take the domain from you. Throw into the mix the fact that many people have registered domain names for speculative purposes—because they plan to sell the names to big companies that will probably want them—and you've got a situation in which many large companies feel justified in throwing their weight around. (These speculators are sometimes known as "cybersquatters.") The latest game is to register domains that comprise the name of a political candidate with the word "sucks" on the end, and then offer to sell the domain to the candidate.

On the other hand, many large companies have the money to buy domain names rather than go through the hassle of litigation, and a number of people have made a great deal of money from selling their domains.

Domains and Trademarks

The whole domain-ownership issue is still unresolved, though there have been a few recent changes that indicate things may be resolved soon. There is no solid legal precedent about this issue, and it's complicated by the fact that the Internet is an international system. Names that are easily recognized as belonging to one company in one country may appear to belong to another elsewhere in the world. It's further complicated by the set of rules established by InterNIC, which are probably indefensible—but it seems likely those rules won't last much longer. (On the other hand, I said the same thing two years ago … in some ways the Internet, contrary to the idea of "Internet time," takes a long time to progress.)

Here's the problem. InterNIC's rules say that if a company holds a national trademark and wants a domain that is identical to its trademark, it can go to InterNIC and demand that the domain be transferred from the original holder to the trademark holder. (The latest domain dispute policy dates back to early in 1998; I seem to recall that before then the policy was a little looser—for example, I don't think it specified that the domain had to be identical.) For instance, there's a British computer-consulting company called Prince plc, which has the prince.com domain. Of course there's a much better known company called The Prince Sports Group, also known as Prince, which makes tennis rackets. The Prince Sports Group wasn't satisfied with princetennis.com, it wanted prince.com, so it demanded that domain, claiming that it had trademarked "Prince," which, of course, it had. So have about 100,000 other companies; trademarks don't stop other companies using a name, they just stop them using it in a similar manner.

InterNIC, following its established rules, told Prince plc that it had several choices; it could give up the domain name, it could prove that it had a trademark, it could post a bond, or it could sign an agreement allowing InterNIC to charge whatever legal expenses it might incur if it didn't give The Prince Sports Group the domain name.

There's a twist in this story, though. The Prince Sports Group sent a letter to Prince plc threatening legal action if it didn't give up the name. Because under trademark law the use of prince.com isn't a trademark infringement, and because in Britain it's unlawful for a trademark owner to make unjustified threats of legal action, Prince plc was able to obtain an injunction and damages against The Prince Sports Group. Since then InterNIC has taken no further action, and the domain remains in use by Prince plc.

There are several problems with InterNIC's regulations. First, they seem to give precedence to U.S. federal trademark holders, even though the Internet is an international system. If you can show a U.S. federal trademark, you can go after a domain held by someone else (on the other hand, domain-name holders can use a foreign trademark as a defense). Second, they are contrary to the spirit of current trademark law, which allows the use of words in different contexts; while another company couldn't sell tennis rackets under the name "Prince," it could sell rhubarb, for instance. The Prince Sports Group claimed that the use of prince.com was a dilution of its trademark. Although it can't claim that the use of the word "prince" dilutes its trademark in most other areas of commerce—witness the 100,000 commercial uses of the word "prince"—InterNIC allowed it to do so in relation to domain names. As a document at the Georgetown University Law Center (which appears to have been removed) said, the regulations "provide no relief to the owner of substantially similar but not identical trademarks, common law trademarks or state registered trademarks. Nor [do they] deal with concurrent uses of the same trademark, or conflicts between U.S. and foreign trademarks."

At one point, InterNIC allowed domain-name defenders to get a trademark within 30 days, leading to a rush for Tunisian trademarks, which apparently can be obtained in a matter of days. InterNIC no longer accepts trademarks obtained after a domain conflict, so that business has dropped off a little.

What, then, should you do to protect your domain name? These regulations could easily change soon, but if you want to be really safe, you should trademark your company or product name, the name from which the domain name is derived. You should make sure that the trademark is identical to the subdomain name (you don't have to include the .com bit, for instance, though that won't hurt), and is issued by the "principal or equivalent registry of any country." A trademark registered with a state, for instance, won't be good enough. You can register a U.S. trademark yourself for $245, though you also need to do a thorough trademark search to make sure your trademark is not in use by anyone else. You may also want to read *Trademark: Legal Care for Your Business and Product Name*, from Nolo Press (see below).

If you'd like to learn more about these problems, and how to get trademarks, try these sites:

Basic Facts About Registering a Trademark, US Patent and Trademark Office

http://www.uspto.gov/web/offices/tac/doc/basic/

International Guide to Trademarks

http://ttdomino.thomson-thomson.com/www/internat-vis.nsf

trademark center (a company that does trademark searches and registrations; a good source of information about trademarks)

http://www.tmcenter.com/

Trademark Express (low-cost trademark searches and registration services)

http://www.tmexpress.com/

Trademark: Legal Care for Your Business and Product Name, Nolo Press

http://www.nolo.com/item/trd.html

Yahoo!—Domain Name Controversies Page

http://dir.yahoo.com/Computers_and_Internet/Internet/Domain_Registration/Domain_Name_Controversies/

Yahoo!—Trademark Services

http://dir.yahoo.com/Business_and_Economy/Companies/Law/Intellectual_Property/Trademarks/Services/

Changes are in the air, though. Late in August of 1999, ICANN, the Internet Corporation for Assigned Names and Numbers, approved a new policy under which arbitration would be used when one company or individual accused another of registering a name in "bad faith" (such as registering a name in order to resell it to a trademark holder). The move is intended to make it cheaper and quicker to resolve disputes (thus making it harder for large companies to pressure small ones or individuals to give up names). The cost, ICANN suggests, will be under $900, to be shared by the two parties.

And a federal judge recently ruled that possessing a trademark does not entitle the owner to a matching domain name. Clue Computing, in Longmont, CO, was using the domain Clue.com. Three years ago Hasbro, the publisher of the game named Clue, decided that it should have the domain name. But U.S. District Judge Douglas Woodlock of Boston rejected Hasbro's claim. He stated that there is no overlap between what Clue Computing and Hasbro do—they're in different businesses. He found that there was little reason for consumers to be confused and think that somehow the Clue.com domain was related to the game Clue. And he also found that Clue Computing was not "cybersquatting," registering a domain in order to sell it to a trademark holder or otherwise benefit from the fact that the name matched another company's trademark. "Holders of a famous mark," he said, "are not automatically entitled to use that mark as their domain name; trademark law does not support such a monopoly." Network Solutions, by the way, almost suspended Clue Computing's domain name in 1996, but were stopped from doing so by a court order. Presumably Network Solutions will now have to reconsider their policies in light of this new precedent.

The World Intellectual Property Organization also has plans for resolving domain-name disputes, as does the U.S. Government. We'll just have to wait and see what comes out of the pot after all these organizations have had a turn at adding to the mix.

Keeping in Control

When you register a trademark with Network Solutions, the domain name gets saved into the database with information about three contacts: an Administrative contact (the person who owns the domain name, or who represents the company that owns the name), a Billing contact (the person who's going to pay the bill), and a Technical contact (generally the person in charge of the servers to which the domain is assigned).

Here's the problem. If you register through a Web-hosting company or a registration service at which you're parking the domain, there's a good chance that the Technical contact will be an employee of that company. That gives the company some control over the domain name. I've heard of cases in which a hosting company has used it's technical-contact position to make it difficult for someone to move a domain away from their servers. It probably doesn't happen often ... but it does happen. If you want to be paranoid, you should register a domain name in a situation in which you can provide all the contact information—Administrative, Billing, and Technical. That way you have full control.

PART II

CREATION

—— —— —— —— —— —— ——

## Chapter Six

Designing Your Web Site

By now you should have your domain name and know where you plan to put your Web site. The next job is to plan the site itself. In this chapter I'll explain what facilities you'll be given by a Web-hosting company, and how to decide where to start.

A Little Bit of Hard-Disk Space

Whether you work with a Web-hosting company, use a personal-page site, or plan to set up your own Web server, your Web site really amounts to a little bit of hard-disk space with some files saved on it. We're not going to be talking about how to set up a server in this book. All you really need to know is that the Web-server software knows where on the hard disk your files are stored and is able to send the files to browsers that request them.

So there are a few things that a Web-hosting company will give you. It will create a directory on a hard disk somewhere, and it should send you this information:

- **An IP number**—As discussed in Chapter 4, there are some cases (fake-virtual or IP-less hosting, or if you're not getting your own domain name) in which you won't get an IP number. But in most cases you will. However, you may find that when you first get your account you are unable to access the Web site using your new domain name; it may take a while for the registration authority to complete the registration procedure, and remember that it takes about a week for the domain name to filter through to the entire Internet. Instead you'll be able to access the site using the IP number your hosting company has given you. For instance, to use FTP you'll be able to type the IP number in place of the domain name.

- **Your account name**—You may have picked this yourself when you applied for a Web site with the Web-hosting company. Anyway, you use this account name to access your Web site "behind the scenes"—to transfer files from your hard disk to the site, for instance.
- **Your password**—Again, you may have defined the password yourself. The password is used in conjunction with the account name to log onto your site behind the scenes.
- **Information about your FTP account**—Almost all Web-hosting companies will give you an FTP (File Transfer Protocol) account. You can use this to transfer files from your computer to the Web site.

Although the Web-hosting company may give you an FTP directory name, you will generally find that when you use an FTP program to connect to your FTP account, the host computer automatically places you in the correct directory, based on your account name. Note, however, that the directory name will look nothing like your Web site's URL. For instance, I have a Web site with the URL http://www.poorrichard.com/. To place files in the directory that this URL points to, I use FTP to transfer them to poorrichard.com/www/topfloor/html/pr/. In other words, the FTP program goes to the poorrichard.com domain, and finds the /pr/ directory, which is in the /www/topfloor/html/ directory path. Remember that in an earlier chapter I explained that the Web server knows where your files are; so it knows that when a Web browser says http://www.poorrichard.com/, the files it wants are in www/topfloor/html/pr.

If you're also getting an e-mail account (you almost certainly are), you should get this information:

- **The POP server name**—This is the domain name of the server that holds your POP (Post Office Protocol) account; that is, where your incoming e-mail messages are stored. You'll enter this information into your e-mail program. This will usually be the same as your domain name if you are setting up a virtual host. For instance, mine is poorrichard.com. That means that for the first week or so, or before the registration is complete, you can't use the domain name to get your e-mail received by your POP account. Of course it also means you won't be receiving any mail, because nobody will be sending you any, so that won't be a problem.
- **The SMTP server name**—This is the domain name of the SMTP (Simple Mail Transfer Protocol) server, a program that transmits mail

out onto the Internet. In other words, it's used for outgoing mail. Again, you'll enter this information into your e-mail program.

- **Your POP account name**—This is the name of the account where your incoming e-mail will be held. This is generally the same as the account name used for your Web site.
- **Your POP password**—This password is used in conjunction with the POP account name. Again, it's probably the same as the Web-site password.

Some Web-hosting companies may provide other things: the URL of a Web page that you can use to make various settings related to your account, such as setting up mail forwarding and autoresponders; the URL of the page where you can see reports related to your Web site's performance (see Chapter 20); information about the Web-authoring tools the company provides, and so on.

So you have the hard-disk space set aside, waiting for your Web pages. You have the information you need to get to that disk space. The next thing to decide is how you are going to create the site.

Creating the Web Site—You or Them?

Someone has to create your Web pages and place them at the Web site. Who's going to do that, and how? You have a few choices:

- **You, using a simple tool provided by the Web-hosting company**— Some Web-hosting companies provide a simple tool you can use to create Web pages, often a program at their site that uses a form to collect information from you and then format a page. However, these systems generally provide very simple pages with little flexibility. If you're in a rush or on a small budget, you may want to use the tool provided, but they're not ideal.
- **You, using HTML**—You might want to learn how to write HTML— HyperText Markup Language. You'll learn the basics of HTML in Chapter 7, though if you want to learn HTML to the degree that you can create really attractive and useful Web pages, you'll have to buy one of those giant HTML tomes that the bookstores are full of these days. It's not a complicated thing to learn, but there's a lot of it, so it takes time to become "fluent," time you may not have available. So one of the following choices may be better for you.
- **You, using a Web-authoring tool**—There are lots of great programs that will help you create Web sites very quickly. We'll be looking at

these in Chapter 8. For most people it's a better idea to use one of these tools than to work with HTML.

- **An employee or contractor**—How valuable is your time? You may find it's more efficient to have an employee or contractor create the Web site for you; you just need to watch over the process and make sure that you get the sort of Web site you want. Creating Web sites is really relatively easy. An enthusiastic and knowledgeable high school or college student can do it in most cases, so you might consider contracting out the work. Many colleges have HTML courses these days, so you can often call and find someone to work for you; take a look at a few samples of his work first, of course.

- **The Web-hosting company**—Many Web-hosting companies provide Web-creation services. These may be a little pricey, however. If you want to get a site up and running quickly, you might let the Web-hosting company do the site for you, but in the long term, it's probably a good idea to hire someone—or pay someone to set up your site and then make minor modifications yourself.

- **Another Web-design and -creation company**—Even if your Web-hosting company also creates Web sites, its services may not be competitive. There are thousands of companies, large and small, creating sites. At the time of writing the **HTML Writers Guild** (http:/www.hwg.org/) had more than 100,000 members. You can find a company—one that you think does a good job at a reasonable price—to create the site for you.

Finding a Web-Design Company

If you're interested in tracking down a company to do some work on your Web site, try these places:

AAAWeb Design List
   http://www.aaadesignlist.com/

C|Net's Ultimate Web Design Directory
   http://webdesignlist.internetlist.com/

Great Artist Registry
   http://www.garegistry.com/

The HTML Writers Guild
   http://www.hwg.org/

Yahoo!—Web Page Designers

http://www.yahoo.com/Business_and_Economy/Companies/Internet_
Services/Web_Services/Designers/

Yahoo!—Web Page Designers— Regional

http://dir.yahoo.com/Business_and_Economy/Companies/Internet_Services/
Web_Services/Designers/Browse_By_Region/

Web-design services range from the low-cost to exorbitant, and the results range from shoddy to wonderful. (And price is no indicator of what you'll end up with!) Make sure you take a close look at samples before you buy, and try to get a solid estimate of how much it's going to cost you. Be wary of hourly rates unless the company's willing to be pretty specific about how much will be produced in how many hours.

Even if you plan to hire someone to do the work for you, you'll need to read some of the next few chapters. You may want to skip Chapters 7 and 8, in which I describe HTML and talk about the different authoring tools available. But you should read the chapters that come after that, because they explain how to avoid many of the mistakes made by Web authors, and how to make sure the Web site does what it should. In fact I suggest that you read these chapters

If you find someone to create your Web site for you, make sure that they have no links from your site to their site; you won't be able to control what they put at their site, even though, thanks to the "created by" link, you will appear to be affiliated with them. Most Web authors want some kind of byline, a link or e-mail address, so visitors to your site can find the person who created it. Allow an e-mail address if you wish, but allowing a link may lead to problems. For instance, one major political institute has a link to the Web designer's Web page ... which contains links to information on how to buy LSD. As this political institute is rather conservative, it's likely that they don't realize where the links from their pages lead!

before you look for someone to create your Web site. Then you'll be able to assess the work that these people have done in the past. Because the mechanics of creating Web pages are really quite simple, there are many barely qualified people working in this business. They may know how to put text on the page, how to add pictures, how to build tables, and so on, but some have the design skills of the average groundhog. I once discovered a wonderful quote in a marketing brochure for a company doing Internet seminars. If my memory serves me, it went something like this: "As a bartender I made minimum wage plus tips; as an Internet Consultant I now make $100 an hour." Do you really want a bartender designing your Web site?

A couple of years ago Peter Flynn, the Academic Computing Manager at the University of Cork, and the administrator of Ireland's first Web server, described the situation in Europe: "We are therefore still in the position which was obtained in the USA three years ago, where anyone with 10 minutes HTML experience and a copy of HTML Crapwriter Deluxe can pass themselves off as a Web guru, because the market is still largely unaware." The only disagreement I had with this comment at the time is that this was not just a European problem; this situation was still common in the U.S.—just look at some of the Web pages in a mall to get an idea of the standards. And today? Perhaps things are a little better, but there are still many people out there who shouldn't be allowed within 100 yards of an HTML-authoring program, and many of them are making money by creating Web sites.

You'll find Web pages with spelling mistakes, Web pages with a text color that clashes with the background (the worst I've seen recently was bright-green text on a dark-green background), pages that load slowly because of the overuse of images—you'll find all sorts of problems, so look carefully.

What's the Purpose of This Web Site?

The next step is to decide what you want the site to do. We discussed options in Chapter 1, but before you begin, you should really figure out a detailed plan concerning what you want to do with the site. You can always make additions later.

Here are a few ideas for what to put at your site:

- **Main page**—Every site has a main page, of course, often called a home page, though I don't much like that term. But you should consider what the main page should do; it should provide links to the rest of your site in an efficient and clear manner. Don't clutter the main page.

- **Discussion group**—You can create discussion groups on your site. Visitors to your site can leave messages, which you or your staff—or other visitors—can answer. For instance, are you promoting your antique-collector's magazine? Why not create a discussion group in which visitors can talk about antiques. If it's lively enough, visitors will return to continue the discussion.

- **Links page**—Many sites have pages with links to related sites. Many authors obviously haven't thought about why they have these links.

There are good reasons and bad reasons; I'll discuss linking out of your site in Chapter 10.

- **Newsletter**—Does your business publish a newsletter as part of your promotion campaign? I mean a real newsletter, a paper one, in the real world? Then why not publish it at your site? If it's useful enough, visitors will come to your site periodically to read it.

- **Sales catalog**—If you're selling a product, you'll probably want to put a sales catalog online.

- **Order form**—Again, if you're selling a product, you'll need an order form of some kind. We'll discuss taking orders in Chapter 13.

- **Technical-support area**—If your company has to provide technical support in the real world, why not try to shift some of it across to the Web and save money. The site should contain all the technical information you have about your products, in an easy-to-get-to format. You might have a discussion group here, too, as a way to answer users' questions. You might also set up a real-time chat area—users can ask technical-support questions and your staff can answer right away (see Chapters 11 and 12). If you're in the software business or produce hardware that uses software drivers, you can have a download area, as well.

- **Customer-support area**—This is very similar to a technical-support area. Set up pages where people can find information about your products, return policies, guarantees, and so on.

- **Feedback page**—Want information about your product? It's easy to set up a feedback page in which people can fill in a form and send you their comments. Use this sort of thing to take customer surveys, find new product ideas, find the strengths and weaknesses in your products, and so on.

I suggest you begin by producing a list of ways in which you can use your Web site. Then go out on the Web and spend some time looking at other Web sites. Look for your competitors' sites and see what they've done. Don't rush; spend some time. Look for what you like about the site, and what you don't like, too. Look for ways in which they could have done things differently; in particular, look at the site from the true visitor's point of view, not from a competitor's point of view. Is the information easy to find, or do they make the visitor jump through hoops to get to it? Can the visitor find a way to contact a real person, or is the Web site floating in cyberspace, detached from the real world? What questions can the visitor not get answered? Is there any way for the visitor to send suggestions and feedback?

Don't restrict yourself to competitors, though. You can often find ideas by looking at a wide range of sites, even noncommercial sites or personal Web pages. If you spend enough time on the Web, you'll get a feel for it and you'll soon understand what things work and what things don't. A couple of days invested in simply surfing the Web may seem unproductive, but they may save you time and trouble down the road.

The Basic Process

Here's the basic process involved in creating and posting a Web page:

1. Create the Web page, either by typing the HTML codes into a text file (see Chapter 7) or by using a Web-authoring tool (see Chapter 8).

2. Save the file on your computer's hard disk.

3. Transfer the file from your computer across the Internet to your Web site. You'll generally use FTP and place the file into the FTP directory given to you by your Web-hosting company, or the Web-authoring program you are using may have a built-in file-transfer utility.

4. Once the page has been saved in the directory at your Web site, it can be viewed by a browser.

This is a fairly simple process (the most complicated part is Step 1, of course), with a few permutations. In some cases, you may have to transfer files to a directory, and the files are then transferred across to your Web site later. This is sometimes the case with personal-page Web sites run by ISPs and online services. In some cases, you can create and edit pages directly on your Web site. Microsoft FrontPage, which we'll look at in Chapter 8, allows you to do this. You open a "web" at your Web site and modify pages there. When you save the pages, they're saved directly to the Web site. However, this is often inconvenient. If you have a modem connection to the Internet, it's slow working like this, so even if you're using FrontPage, you may find it more convenient to create or edit the Web pages on your own computer and then transfer them when finished or modified. (About a year ago I had a cable-modem connection installed, and so I now work in this manner—

Here's a problem people often run into when first setting up Web sites. They transfer their pages without ensuring that the FTP transfer is being done in ASCII mode, so the pages are not displayed correctly. Check your FTP program's documentation to find out how to transfer your HTML files in ASCII mode.

I use FrontPage to connect to the Web site and make changes directly.) Of course, if you're running your own Web server and creating files directly on that server, you're not transferring the files anywhere.

The next major decision for many readers is whether to write HTML directly or to buy a Web-authoring tool. If you've already decided that you want to use a Web-authoring tool, I think it's still a good idea to read the following chapter, in which I explain a little about HTML. You'll get the background you need in order to understand how Web pages work, and this information may be useful later on when you're trying to figure out what exactly can be done with a Web page.

By the way, even if you plan to hire someone to create your Web site for you, you may still want to read Chapter 8. You might want to get someone to create the site and to make major changes, but with a good HTML-editing tool, you can tweak things now and then very quickly, without learning much about Web authoring. For instance, you could write an announcement of important company or organization news and post it immediately, rather than having to wait for the Web author to do it. FrontPage is perfect for this sort of thing, because it allows you to modify the Web pages directly on the Web server, rather than having to change them on your computer and then transfer them.

Chapter Seven

An Introduction to HTML

Basic HTML (HyperText Markup Language) is not complicated—but advanced HTML sometimes is. You can learn how to create a simple Web page in a few minutes. In fact before you get to the end of this chapter, you'll already be able to do that. But in order to do the more complex stuff—creating forms and tables, splitting browser windows into "frames" and placing a separate document into each frame, and so on—you'll need much more information than we can cover in this book. If you go to a bookstore and look at HTML guides, you'll discover that most are several kilos heavier than this book.

Don't despair. Almost everything that can be done by learning HTML can be done with a Web-authoring tool, and we'll be looking at those in Chapter 8. However, it's a good idea to have at least a smattering of HTML knowledge, and that's the purpose of this chapter. As the chapter title states, this is no more than an introduction. If you want to know more, buy a good book, or go to some of the Web sites recommended at the end of the chapter.

Why Learn HTML?

It's a good idea to learn a little HTML, so that when your authoring program screws something up you can figure out what's going on. No authoring program is perfect, and sometimes you may want to edit HTML code directly to fix something. If you understand the basics of HTML you'll be able to use an HTML reference book to figure out a particular situation.

Another reason to learn a little HTML is so that you'll know enough to be able to link from a Web page to a CGI script (see Chapter 11).

HTML Is Not Programming

You may have heard creating Web pages described as "programming HTML." That probably scares a lot of people away from HTML, but don't worry—HTML is not programming. HTML is a page-description language, so it's much, much simpler to learn than programming. You can learn basic HTML in a few minutes and even relatively advanced HTML in a few hours.

HTML coding is used to describe parts of a document page. Open your Web browser and load a Web page, then view the document source. In Netscape Navigator or Internet Explorer you'll generally use the View|Source or View|Page Source command (old versions of these browsers use different commands). If you're using a Windows version of a browser you may be able to right-click on text within a Web page and select View Source, or View Frame Source. (On the Mac you can probably click and hold the button down a moment to see a pop-up menu, and then select View Source.) A window opens and displays the contents of the page—not what you see in the browser window, but what the browser sees when it's trying to figure out what to display in the browser window.

For instance, take a look at Figure 7.1. This shows a fairly simple Web page—the main **White House** page (http://www.whitehouse.gov/).

What you can see in this page comes from several different computer files saved at the White House Web site. First, there's a text file. When you type www.whitehouse.com into your browser and press Enter, the browser sends a message to the Web server asking for the default document at that domain—usually a document named index.html, sometimes default.html, or something similar. This is a plain text file known as the source file. Figure 7.2 shows you what the text file used to create the White House page looks like.

Now, this text file looks nothing like what you see in the browser window, but it contains the instructions that tell the browser what to do. It also tells the browser where to get the pictures that are displayed in the browser window, and where to place them on the file. If you look closely, you'll see references to several .gif files: greeting.gif, flag.gif, and welcome4.gif (there are others that are offscreen in this snapshot of the source file).

These are the files that contain the pictures you can see in Figure 7.1—for instance, greeting.gif is the *Good Afternoon* image at the top of the screen. Flag.gif is, of course, the image used for the flags on either side of the picture of the White House, and welcome4.gif is the big *Welcome to the White House* text. So the browser is actually displaying the result of multiple files in the window: the

Figure 7.1: The main White House Web page.

source text file, which contains the instructions and the text that is to be displayed in the document, and the picture files.

Tag Basics

HTML is based on a simple tag or coding system. Instructions are placed in angled brackets, like this:

```
<TITLE>Welcome To The White House</TITLE>
```

This is the page's title—the text that appears in the browser's title bar when it loads this page. How does the browser know that this is the title text? Because it knows that when it sees the <TITLE> tag, all the following text is the title—until it gets to the </TITLE> tag. Whenever you see </, you know that you're looking at an ending tag. Simple, really.

```
www.whitehouse[1] - Notepad                                              _ 🗗 ✕
File  Edit  Format  Help
<HTML>
<HEAD>
<TITLE>Welcome To The White House</TITLE>

<META http-equiv="PICS-Label" content='(PICS-1.1 "http://www.rsac.org/ratingsv01.html" 1 gen true
<META http-equiv="PICS-Label" content='(PICS-1.1 "http://www.rsac.org/ratingsv01.html" 1 gen true
<META http-equiv="PICS-Label" content='(PICS-1.1 "http://www.rsac.org/ratingsv01.html" 1 gen true
<META http-equiv="PICS-Label" content='(PICS-1.1 "http://www.classify.org/safesurf/" 1 gen true f

</HEAD>

<BODY background="/WH/images/bg.jpg" bgcolor="#FFFFFF" text="#000000" link="#0000BB" alink="#00BB

<CENTER>
<TABLE cellpadding=0 cellspacing=0 border=0>
<TR>
<TD colspan=3 align=CENTER valign=CENTER><img border=0 src="/WH/images/greeting.gif" height=40 wi
</TR>
<TR>

<TD align=CENTER valign=CENTER><img border=0 src="/WH/images/flag.gif" hspace=5 vspace=5 width=10
<TD><img border=0 src="/WH/images/bevel.jpg" hspace=5 vspace=5 align=CENTER height=175 width=300
<TD align=CENTER valign=CENTER><img border=0 src="/WH/images/flag.gif" hspace=5 vspace=5 width=10
</TR>
<TR>

<TD colspan=3 align=CENTER valign=CENTER><img border=0 src="/WH/images/welcome4.gif" hspace=5 vsp
</TR>
</TABLE>
<!-- Banner Begin -->

  <P><B><a href="/WH/New/turkey-relief.html">Turkey Earthquake Disaster Information</a></B>
  <P><A HREF="/WH/New/federal-drought-resources.html"><B>Federal Resources for Drought Informatio

<P><A HREF="/WH/New/html/Medicare/Women/index.html"><B>New Report on the Importance of Medicare t
```

Figure 7.2: The White House Web page's source text file.

HTML uses scores of different tags like this to define what the browser should do with text. For instance:

<B></B> ....Text between these tags is bold text.

<I></I> ....These define italic text.

<FONT SIZE=-1></FONT> ....These tell the browser to make the text a little smaller than normal.

<H1></H1> ....Text between these is Heading Level 1 text.

<H2></H2> ....This is Heading Level 2 text.

By the way, it's important to note that in many cases HTML doesn't explicitly state how the browser should display something. In the case of the <H1></H1> tags, it doesn't tell the browser what the Heading Level 1 text looks like, just that this is Heading Level 1 text. It's up to the browser to decide what that sort of heading should look like. In the early days of the Web a number of browsers actually allowed the user to define exactly how each type of text should appear, though most of the browsers in use today do not.

If you've used WordPerfect, you may be familiar with this sort of tagging. WordPerfect allows you to reveal codes. When you do so, you see special tags that WordPerfect used to format the text.

There are also tags that, rather than modifying text, add features to the page. For instance:

<HR> ....This places a horizontal line across the page.

 ....This creates a line break, moving text down one line but without starting a new paragraph.

<INPUT> ....This tag is used to create elements in a form: buttons, check boxes, option buttons (also known as radio buttons), and so on.

The last tag won't work by itself. Rather, it requires what are known as attributes—special instructions that add detail. For instance, the following tag creates a check box:

```
<INPUT TYPE="CHECKBOX">
```

Many tags have optional attributes that can, if you wish, modify what you've just created. For instance, you could change the <HR> tag like this:

```
<hr color="#FF0000">
```

This is still a horizontal line across the page, but now it's a red line. (The code #FF0000 means red. You could also use <hr color="red">, and most browsers would understand.)

Another important class of tags are those that add the hypertext features—links, for instance. Look back at the White House source document and you'll see this:

```
<a href="/WH/New/turkey-relief.html">Turkey Earthquake
Disaster Information</a>
```

This is a link. Look at Figure 7.1 and you'll notice that near the bottom of the page is some text that says *Turkey Earthquake Disaster Information*. Look at the tags above and you'll see that they enclose this text. And within the first tag you find this: HREF="/WH/New/turkey-relief.html." In other words, this link is pointing at a document called turkey-relief.html, in a directory called /New/, which is itself within a directory called /WH/.

And how about pictures? Look back at the White House source document and you'll find this (you can't see the complete line in the snapshot, so I've filled it in for you:

```
<img border=0 src="/WH/images/greeting.gif" height=40
width=217 hspace=5 vspace=5><br>
```

The <IMG> tag can stand alone—no </IMG> tag is needed at the end. The tag simply says, "get the greeting.gif image file from the /WH/images/ directory." The other attributes define various other characteristics: the height and width of the image, and the horizontal and vertical space to be left between the image and other components—images or text—of the document.

By the way, here's an important characteristic of Web pages that confuses many people. Web browsers ignore line breaks and multiple spaces. Just because you put text a line below the previous line in the source document doesn't mean that's the way it will appear in the browser. Instead you must use a <P> or <BR> tag to tell the browser to move the text down (you can see a <BR> tag after the image tag we just looked at. And if you type lots of blank spaces into a Web page, browsers just ignore them and treat them as if they were really a single space. So source documents often have blank areas that don't show up in the rendered Web page. (*Rendering* is the process the browser goes through when it reads a source file, follows the instructions, and displays the Web page.)

Create Your Own Web Page

If you want to experiment a little—and see just how simple it is to create basic Web pages—open a text editor, such as Notepad in Microsoft Windows, or SimpleText on the Macintosh, and type the following text. (If you prefer not to type all this, you can download it from my Web site at http://www.poorrichard. com/testweb.txt. Save this file as text. Then change the name and add the .htm extension in place of .txt.)

```
<HTML>
<HEAD>
<TITLE>My Very Own Web Page—Replace Text if You
Want</TITLE>
</HEAD>
<BODY>
<H1>Replace This Title with Whatever You Want</H1>
```

```
Put whatever text you want here.<P>
<IMG SRC="http://www.poorrichard.com/images/peter.jpg"
WIDTH="82" HEIGHT="104"><P>
This is another paragraph; use whatever text you want.
<H2>First Subcategory: Replace This with Whatever Title
You Want</H2>
<A HREF="http://www.poorrichard.com/">Poor Richard's Web
Site</A><P>
<A HREF="url_here">Another link: replace this
text</A><P>
<A HREF="url_here">Another link: replace this
text</A><P>
<A HREF="url_here">Another link: replace this
text</A><P>
<A HREF="url_here">Another link: replace this text</A>
<H2>Second Subcategory: Replace This with Whatever
Title You Want</H2>
Put more text and links here.
<H2>Third Subcategory: Replace This with Whatever Title
You Want</H2>
Put more text and links here.
<H2>Fourth Subcategory: Replace This with Whatever
Title You Want</H2>
Put more text and links here.
</BODY>
</HTML>
```

Make sure you reproduce this text exactly as I've shown here. Then save the file. You must save HTML files as plain text files, which is why I suggested you use Notepad or SimpleText. If you use a word processor and save using the word processor's file format, this file won't work as a Web page. (And even if you save in plain-text format, word processors sometimes insert non-text characters such as curly quotes and em dashes, which can confuse a browser.)

That's it, you've created a page with headings, a picture—which will appear on the page as long as you are connected to the Internet when you display the page in your browser—and a link to the Web page associated with this book; again, this link will work if you're connected to the Internet.

Now open the page in your browser to view it. You can see what it looks like in Figure 7.3. If you are using Windows, you can probably just drag the file from Windows Explorer and drop it onto your Web browser. Internet Explorer and

Netscape can both load pages in this manner. Alternatively, use your browser's File|Open or File|Open Page command.

Figure 7.3: Your completed Web page.

There's a Lot More to Learn

If it's that easy, why not create your own pages using a text editor? Why bother with a Web-authoring tool? For three reasons. First, it's easy to make a slip and mess something up. For instance, type <A HREF="http://www.poorichard.com/"> instead of <AHREF="http://www.poor richard.com/">, and you've got a dead link. Web-authoring tools can automate the process and do much of the routine stuff for you, so you're less likely to make mistakes. For this reason almost all HTML authors, even those who like to see their HTML tags, use some kind of authoring tools. (Some HTML tools hide the tags from you and display what the text will look like in the Web page. Others display the tags in all their glory.)

The second reason is that HTML doesn't stay that easy. It can get quite complicated. If you want to create tables and frames, the HTML required gets quite involved. (Did you notice the <TABLE>, <TR>, and <TD> tags in the White House source document? Those are table tags.) Even creating image maps—pictures with multiple links on them, each taking the user to a different document—can be tricky. Why not let an authoring tool do it for you?

Things to Add to HTML

There's more to creating Web sites than just HTML; in order to make these sites interactive, you have to leave HTML and add scripts or programs created some other way. HTML is really limited to defining what happens in the Web page itself. But what if you want to create a discussion group, for instance, or a form that the Web-site users can fill in to send you feedback? You can use HTML to create a form, but the

If you decide to create your own Web pages, you'll have to transfer them to the Web-hosting company's system. You may have to use an FTP program in order to do this, although some hosting companies may provide a special upload program. Here's a tip on how to avoid one of the most common problems with FTP uploads. When you transfer your Web pages to your Web site, make sure you use ASCII transfer. If you use binary transfer, the file that is saved on the host computer will probably have strange text characters embedded into it— generally small black squares— and will not display correctly in a Web browser. This happens when files from a Windows computer, for instance, are transferred to a UNIX computer, and the line-feed characters are not correctly converted. Transferring in ASCII format eliminates this problem.

form won't actually do anything. HTML itself can't do much with a form except create the components—it can't make the components do anything. Instead, you have to add CGI (Common Gateway Interface) scripts, JavaScript scripts, Java programs, or ActiveX programs to make something happen. (We'll examine these below.) HTML is not a programming language, but these other things are, and to use these systems, you need to get into true programming. (Some purists will argue that JavaScript and CGI "programs" are not programs, they're scripts, but the argument is academic; people working with JavaScript and CGI use programming skills to create these scripts.)

There's an easier way to add interactivity to your Web site, though; use an authoring tool. For instance, Microsoft FrontPage can create a complicated discussion group for you in less than five minutes. If you have no programming skills, it would probably take you weeks to learn the skills you need to do this for yourself. Even if you find a ready-made CGI script that can do this for you (see Chapter 12), it'll probably take several hours to install it properly.

Let's take a quick look at the different "add-ons" to HTML:

- **CGI**—Common Gateway Interface scripts were the first form of scripting added to Web pages, and in some ways they're the simplest kind (which doesn't mean they're easy to use). These scripts are saved in a .cgi file that is stored on the Web server. The Web-page forms deliver information to the script, which processes the information in some way. We'll be learning more about these in Chapter 11.

- **JavaScript**—This is another scripting language. There are actually two kinds of JavaScript: client-side—the script is written into the Web page, and server-side—the script is saved on the server. JavaScript can get pretty complicated; it's not something you can pick up in an hour or two. However, you may be able to learn enough to copy JavaScripts from libraries and drop them into your Web pages. We'll look at these in Chapter 11, too.

- **Java**—This is a full-blown programming language. To use it, you need to metamorphose into a programmer. Java programs are compiled into executable program files, which are stored on the server. You can embed Java programs (applets, as they're known) into Web pages quite easily using a special <APPLET> tag; but writing the programs is complicated.

- **ActiveX**—This is Microsoft's answer to Java. Most users these days are working with Internet Explorer, but that still leaves 25 percent who are using Netscape Navigator, which won't work with ActiveX. And again, ActiveX is real programming, not something to be undertaken by nonprogrammers.

- **Other Scripting Languages**—There are a number of other scripting languages, such as **PHP** (http://www.php.net/) and **Miva** (http://www.miva.com/). In both cases you have to be working with a Web server that has had the appropriate programs installed. Both systems are quite popular; PHP is in the public domain, so it's free, while Miva is a commercial product. Both require programming skills.

- **Authoring Tools**—Some authoring tools, in particular Microsoft FrontPage and ColdFusion, can create interactivity through the use of special extensions or drivers installed on the Web server. These scripts are used in conjunction with the authoring tool as a way to provide the benefits of scripts to people who haven't the time, inclination, or ability to write scripts.

Let me say that it's quite possible to create a Web site without ever writing a line of programming code. Much of the programming going on out there on the Web is quite unnecessary. Remember …

The Internet is a giant jobs program for computer geeks.

There are good reasons to use these special tools in some cases, but in general prettying up your Web site is not one of them. Creating order forms, feedback forms, discussion groups, and so on all require some form of programming. But you don't have to be the one doing the programming; you can buy products that create all these things for you in a fraction of the time it would take you to do it yourself. In many cases you can even find free or low-cost products.

We'll be coming back to this issue of adding interactivity to your pages through the use of scripts later, in Chapter 8 (where we discuss authoring tools) and Chapter 11.

Finding More Information

I believe that most people should not be using HTML "raw": if you've got a business to run, your job is not learning Web-page layout. If you really like this geeky stuff, then fine, go ahead and learn HTML. But there are plenty of authoring tools available at a very low cost—free in some cases. Even some of the best tools are in the $100 to $150 range.

If you're determined to learn HTML, buy a good book or visit some of these sites:

HTML Center
   http://www.htmlcenter.com/

HTML Quick Reference (a good start, with useful links)
   http://www.cc.ukans.edu/~acs/docs/other/HTML_quick.shtml

HTML Reference Manual—Sandia National Labs (a great quick reference to most tags and attributes)
   http://www.sandia.gov/sci_compute/html_ref.html

HTML Writers Guild
  http://www.hwg.org/

webreference.com (lots of information and links to more)
  http://www.webreference.com/

Yahoo!—HTML
  http://dir.yahoo.com/Computers_and_Internet/Information_and_
  Documentation/Data_Formats/HTML/

Yahoo!—Page Creation Directories
  http://dir.yahoo.com/Computers_and_Internet/Internet/World_Wide_Web/
  Page_Creation/Web_Directories/

Yahoo!—Page Design and Layout Page
  http://dir.yahoo.com/Arts/Design_Arts/Graphic_Design/Web_Page_Design_
  and_Layout/

If you do decide to learn HTML, though, be prepared to spend a lot of time and effort doing so ... time and effort that might be better spent promoting a Web site that you've created quickly using a good authoring tool.

## Chapter Eight

Choosing an Authoring Tool

You almost certainly need an authoring tool. If you're not creating your own Web pages, the person who is creating them for you needs one. Even if you like working with HTML, you need some kind of tool to speed things up a little. Very few people work with nothing more than a text editor nowadays—not even many of the most experienced HTML freaks.

There are several different types of tools used to create Web pages:

- **Simple HTML Editors**—Simple HTML editors display all the codes, but help you enter them. Instead of typing a code for something, you can click a button, and the editor drops the code in for you. These are like beefed-up text editors.

- **Sophisticated HTML Editors**—A step up from the simple HTML editor is the sophisticated HTML editor, for people who like to see their tags but want to speed up the process of creating pages. These editors have a plethora of tools to enter the codes more quickly. Many expert HTML authors use this sort of tool.

- **WYSIWYG HTML Editors**—WYSIWYG means *What You See Is What You Get*. In other words, while creating your pages, you can see, more or less, what a user would see while viewing the page in the Web browser. You don't see the HTML tags. This is like working with a word processor and for nonexperts is much easier than using a simple or even sophisticated HTML editor.

- **HTML Converters**—There are a number of programs used for converting files into Web pages; converting them from various word-processing and desktop-publishing formats, for instance. This is very handy for companies that have a lot of paper documents that they'd like to convert and put on the Web. You generally use a converter in conjunction with a good HTML editor, because converters do little more than convert.

- **Hybrids**—There are, of course, hybrid programs that seem to sit astride two or more of these categories. For instance, there are programs that allow you to create Web pages from within your word processor, enabling you to quickly convert word-processing documents to Web pages and add images, links, and so on. And WYSIWYG editors such as FrontPage generally allow you to view the HTML code and modify it directly, though they generally won't provide tools to drop tags in for you (that is, you can modify the tags directly, but in order to get the program to automate tag creation you'll switch back to WYSIWYG mode).

HTML programs are available over a wide range of prices; there are freeware, shareware, and commercial versions available. You can see an example of a sophisticated HTML editor in Figure 8.1. This is **HotDog Professional** (http://www.sausage.com/), one of the most popular editors on the Web. The large pane within the HotDog window is where you create your Web pages. HotDog puts

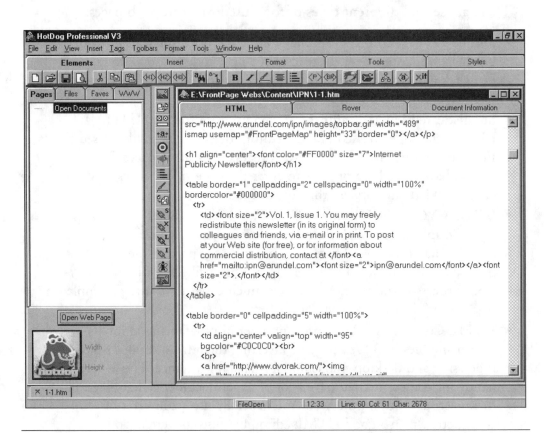

Figure 8.1: Here's where you create Web pages in HotDog.

most of the tags into the document for you—when you click buttons on the toolbar, HotDog either adds tags or opens a dialog box asking for more information so it can do so. The main problem with this program is that you can't see what the Web page looks like while you're creating it.

HotDog does have a window in which you can view the Web page; you can see it in Figure 8.2. But you can't actually work in this window, so

The people at Sausage Software, the publisher of HotDog, realize that there are different needs for people in different situations. They've recently released HotDog PageWiz, a WYSIWYG tool, and HotDog Junior, a wizard-type program designed for young kids (6 and up).

in order to see what's going on, you have to keep switching back and forth between views.

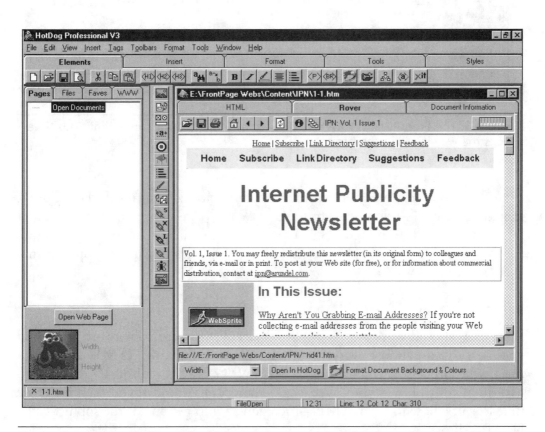

Figure 8.2: HotDog's "Rover" window shows you what the document looks like.

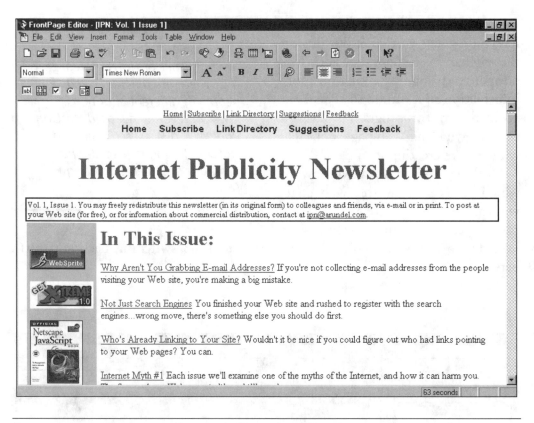

Figure 8.3: The FrontPage WYSIWYG editor, showing the same document. This time it looks the way it will in the browser.

HotDog is a great program with lots of sophisticated features. In fact, I use it sometimes. But it's not as easy to use as a WYSIWYG program. Take a look at the FrontPage Editor in Figure 8.3. This is the same document you saw in Figure 8.1, but this time it looks the way it will—more or less—when it's opened in a Web browser.

Which Do You Need?

Most users should work with a WYSIWYG HTML editor. There are now good ones that can do almost everything that can be done with HTML. If you can use a word processor, you can use a WYSIWYG HTML editor. If you want to have total control over your Web pages—and don't mind spending a lot more time learning how to use HTML—then you should get one of the sophisticated HTML editors.

But be careful about taking the advice of knowledgeable Web authors. Remember that in the computer business there's a tendency for people to believe that everyone needs geek knowledge: it doesn't matter how long it will take you to learn HTML, you should do it. I recently heard it said, for instance, that anybody who doesn't know how to write a Java program—see Chapter 7—can't be regarded as educated. And that means everyone: doctors, lawyers, truck drivers ... So take the advice of geeks with a pinch of salt. If you are more interested in the ends (the creation of your Web site) than the means (learning HTML), then a WYSIWYG editor is for you.

But which one in particular? As you probably realize by now, my preference is for **Microsoft FrontPage** (http://www.microsoft.com/frontpage/), but you'd better believe I've gotten a lot of criticism for that choice. Ask me which is the best word processor, and I could give you a choice of several, but there are a few good reasons why FrontPage is the choice for HTML. I'll come back to that in a moment.

For a sophisticated HTML editor, I sometimes use HotDog, a program that has a wide following. There are many choices available, however. Here are a few of the more prominent choices and where you can find more information about them. Note, by the way, that almost all of these products are available in demo form, so you can download them and try them before you buy.

WYSIWYG Programs for the Nonexpert

Carouselle (Windows 95/98/2000/NT)
    http://www.ist.ca/

Claris HomePage (Macintosh, Windows 95/98/2000/NT)
    http://www.claris.com/products/homepage3.html

CorelW EB.DESIGNER (Windows 3.1/95/98/2000/NT)
    http://www.corel.com/corelweb/webdesigner/

HomeSite (Windows 95/98/2000/NT)
    http://www.coldfusion.com/

HotDog PageW iz (Windows 95/98/2000/NT)
    http://www.sausage.com/

Internet Creator (Windows 95/NT)
    http://www.formaninteractive.com/

Microsoft FrontPage (Macintosh—but the Mac version isn't very good—
    Windows 95/95/98/2000/NT)
    http://www.microsoft.com/frontpage/

Symantec Visual Page (Macintosh, Windows 95/98/2000/NT)
http://www.symantec.com/vpage/

WebExpress (Windows 3.1/95/98/2000/NT)
http://www.mvd.com/

Sophisticated HTML Editors

Note that some of these products also include WYSIWYG modes, but nonetheless their fairly sophisticated products designed for experts.

BBEdit (Macintosh)
http://www.barebones.com/products/bbedit/bbedit.html

ColdFusion (Very popular with professional designers: Windows 95/98/2000/NT)
http://www.coldfusion.com/

Dreamweaver (Windows 3.1/95/98/2000/NT)
http://www.macromedia.com/software/dreamweaver/

HotDog Pro (95/98/2000/NT)
http://www.sausage.com/

HotMetal Pro (Originally a sophisticated HTML editor, it's now also a WYSIWYG editor. Windows 95/98/2000/NT)
http://www.softquad.com/

HTMLed (Windows 3.1, 95/98/2000/NT)
http://www.ist.ca/

NetObjects Fusion (Windows 95/98/2000/NT)
http://www.netobjects.com/

PageMill (Macintosh, Windows 95/98/2000/NT)
http://www.adobe.com/prodindex/pagemill/main.html

More Products

There's no shortage of HTML-authoring tools. You can also find programs at the software libraries I mentioned in Chapter 2. With so many choices, it can be hard to find the best for you. You might take a look at a few of the following sites that have product reviews:

C|Net
http://www.cnet.com/

CMP NetGuide
   http://www.netguide.com/

Internet World Daily
   http://www.internetworld.com/

Techweb WebTools
   http://www.webtools.com/

ZDNet
   http://www.zdnet.com/

And don't forget Yahoo! for links to more products:

Yahoo!—HTML Converters
   http://dir.yahoo.com/Computers_and_Internet/Software/Internet/World_
   Wide_Web/HTML_Converters/

Yahoo!—HTML Editors
   http://dir.yahoo.com/Computers_and_Internet/Software/Internet/World_
   Wide_Web/HTML_Editors/

An Editor's Tools

What should an HTML editor do for you? A good program should offer a variety of functions, such as the following:

- **Format paragraphs using the standard HTML paragraph formats**—Normal, the various Headings, Address, and so on.
- **Format text**—Bold, italic, underlined, colored, different sizes, and so on.
- **Create lists**—Bulleted and numbered lists.
- **Create links**—You highlight text and click a button, and a box pops up displaying a list of files—select a file or enter a URL.
- **Insert images**—You click a button and a dialog box opens allowing you to select the image you want to insert.
- **Create tables and forms**—Use buttons and dialog boxes to format these complicated things for you.
- **Create framesets**—These are complicated, too, so the editor should be able to do most of the work.

In each case, the editor should be entering the tags for you. If you want to create a form, for instance, you shouldn't have to type all the different tags; you should be able to specify the information in a dialog box, and the editor should create the tags for you. If you're using a WYSIWYG editor, you won't even see the tags. It will be just like working with a word processor.

Why FrontPage?

No, I'm not paid to recommend Microsoft FrontPage, and although some time ago I wrote a book about the product (FrontPage 97), recommending it here isn't going to sell any copies of that out-of-print book. In fact, I feel a little uneasy about recommending a single product in a book such as this.

However, my role in writing this book is one of advisor. In effect, you, the reader, are paying me to give my advice—I'm a consultant. You're not paying me to be unbiased, you're paying me to tell you the best way to do something. And I'm assuming the advice you are looking for is how to set up a Web site without breaking your budget.

If you've decided that you need a WYSIWYG editor, and if you are going to set up your Web site at a Web-hosting company, then the clear choice, at the time of writing, at least, is Microsoft FrontPage. That's the advice I'd give my friends—indeed I already have. That's the advice I'm giving here, and here's why. FrontPage is much more than a simple HTML-editing tool. It will do the things I've talked about, but it also has a few Web-site management tools:

FrontPage for the Macintosh

I wouldn't recommend FrontPage for the Macintosh. Microsoft did begin a FrontPage line for the Mac, but it stopped work on it after the very first version. It's old, and so it doesn't have many of the features of the Windows versions.

- **Find bad links**—It can test your Web site and tell you where your links are broken; that is, where you have links that no longer point to Web pages.
- **Show you a site picture**—It can display an overview of your Web site, in which you can see where documents link together.
- **Systemwide spelling, find, and replace**—You can spell-check all the pages in your Web site at the same time. You can also search the entire Web site for a word, or even do a sitewide search and replace.

FrontPage is not the only program to have those sorts of tools, but what really sets FrontPage apart is the ability to add interactivity to your site and to automate a variety of processes. It can do these things for you:

- **Create forms** that take information submitted by a visitor to your site and place that information in a text file—you can import the text file into a database program—or e-mail the information to you.

- **Take information from forms and place it into Web pages** that are visible to other visitors—you can create a Guest Book or Comments page with this information.

- **Create a discussion group**—people can leave messages or respond to other people's messages.

- **Set up portions of your Web site as registration areas**—people can register when they first arrive, then use their "account names" in discussion groups.

- **Set up private areas** of the Web site that are accessible only to the people you've given permission.

- **Create a search page** so visitors can enter keywords and search your Web site for information.

- **Include text** from one Web page in another, a simple way to create headers and footers that you can modify quickly.

Doing these things takes just a few minutes once you're familiar with the program. Just answer a few questions or make a few modifications, and you have the pages ready and waiting for use. FrontPage is not a free program—you can pick it up for around $100 if you shop carefully—but you can save so much time using this product that for most people the cost is a great investment.

If for some reason you decide not to use FrontPage, you can still add various interactive features to your Web site, but it'll be more complicated and take longer. In Chapters 11 and 12 we'll look at CGI scripts that you can copy to your Web site and then customize. (Even if you use FrontPage you may want to use CGI scripts to add functions that FrontPage can't currently create.) Take a look at the examples in Chapter 12, and you'll see that setting up CGIs is no cakewalk. What might take five minutes in FrontPage might take several hours—or more—using CGI.

FrontPage has a number of other important features, though features you may find in other authoring tools. The ability to create tables and frames, for instance, using fairly simple tools that do most of the work for you. It has a large clip-art library, which includes a link to an even larger library of clip art at the Microsoft Web site; a tool that takes a large image, creates a thumbnail image, and links the thumbnail to the large image; a quick way to add navigation bars to all your pages; and plenty more.

Why Not FrontPage?

Is FrontPage the perfect authoring tool? No, absolutely not. There are reasons why you might not want to use FrontPage; in fact I have one Web site at which I don't use FrontPage.

If you need total control over the HTML tags, you're better off with a product such as HotDog that allows you access to the HTML tags. FrontPage does allow some control over HTML tags, but it also has the habit of reformatting things. For instance, I have a Web site that contains examples of **JavaScript scripts** (http://www.topfloor.com/javascript/). I don't use FrontPage for this site because it shifts lines and spacing in the source code in ways I don't like. So when I try to show the code I've used in a particular JavaScript, FrontPage may add blank spaces where I don't want them and shift text down onto the next line where I don't want it. (However, note that the recently released FrontPage 2000 is much better about this, fooling around with code far less than earlier versions.)

On the other hand, at my **Poor Richard's Web Site** (http://www.poorrichard. com/) I do use FrontPage. Why? Because it does everything I need it to do in this case. That site doesn't require me to control every single space in the source code, so FrontPage is fine, just as it is for the majority of small organizations and businesses creating Web pages.

Of course, another reason for not using FrontPage is that you have to pay for it. If you're on a tiny budget, you may want to try a shareware or freeware program. On the other hand, FrontPage is currently available for around $100 through many mail-order companies, and the time savings it can provide will, in most cases, more than make up for the money you spend.

Also, there are a number of bugs in FrontPage that are very irritating ... you have to figure out ways around them. But then, after 18 years in the software business I've yet to see a bug-less software program!

Will FrontPage Remain Front-Runner?

I said earlier that FrontPage is the clear choice "at the time of writing, at least." However, I doubt that this situation will change soon, for an important reason. You see, in order to do its magic Microsoft FrontPage has to use the server extensions. These extensions must be installed on the Web server—without them FrontPage is no more than a good Web-authoring tool, not a great one.

Luckily for Microsoft, many Web-hosting companies, and undoubtedly many companies setting up intranets, are installing these server extensions. A couple of years ago, when I wrote the first edition of this book, there were almost 450 Web-hosting companies listed at the Microsoft site as FrontPage-enabled—that is, almost 450 companies with the server extensions installed on their Web servers. The list is too big to count now, but as FrontPage server extensions have become a standard feature at most hosting companies, there are probably now thousands of hosting companies to choose from. (Microsoft calls these companies WPPs: Web presence providers. See the list of **FrontPage Providers** at http://www.microsoftwpp.com/wppsearch/.)

Now, for another product to challenge FrontPage, it has to be able to produce the same sort of interactivity that FrontPage does. The easiest way to do that would be to create another set of server extensions. But it's too late, FrontPage got there first, and it seems unlikely that another company will be able to convince a significant portion of Web-hosting companies to switch to a different set of server extensions, at least in the short term. There are other ways to add this sort of interactivity—with JavaScript or CGI scripts, for instance—but these other schemes all have a number of drawbacks and lack the simplicity of the server-extension scheme. I suspect that we'll see FrontPage leading the pack for quite a while.

Your Nose, Bill Gates' Face

There's a definite anti-Microsoft bias these days. Many believe that you shouldn't buy FrontPage, because buying Microsoft products is selling out. They may not tell you this—they may simply say that there are much better Web-authoring tools. And in some ways they may be right.

If you are setting up a Web site on your own server, or on your company's server (see Chapter 3 for a discussion of the different places to put a Web site), you can pick whatever tool you want. Just be sure to find one that, like FrontPage, provides tools that help you create form interaction.

If you plan to set up your Web site at a Web-hosting company, though, you have only one good option: FrontPage. Hundreds of Web-hosting companies are set up to work with FrontPage, and that's something that can't be said about any other authoring tool.

Of course, if you don't need these interactive features, you may be better off with a product such as HomeSite or HotDog PageWiz. And you may try FrontPage and simply not like it for some reason. Since I recommended FrontPage in the first edition of this book I've received e-mail from people complaining, saying that FrontPage is no good. On the other hand, I've received more feedback from people telling me they were glad that I recommended the product, and that they've had a lot of success with it.

So, if you're going to work with a hosting company, before you decide against FrontPage you should think about why you are doing so. If you decide to avoid FrontPage because it's a Microsoft product, do so with the understanding that you'll spend much more time and effort creating a decent site. Don't cut off your nose to spite Bill Gates' face!

The Next Step

Before you can move on, you need to pick your authoring tool, assuming, of course, that you are going to create the site yourself rather than have someone else do it for you. Pick carefully; you're going to be spending a lot of time with this program.

I'm not going to explain how to work with your Web tool. There are a couple of hundred options, and each works differently. I suggest you find a good one and start creating your Web pages right away. You can learn as you go. It's also a good idea, as these products can be fairly complex, to find a book about your product and read the whole thing carefully. In the following chapters I'll be talking a bit about Web-site design, but I'm going to assume that you understand how to use your HTML editor.

## Chapter Nine

Creating an Effective Web Site

There's more to creating a great Web site than taking your paper documents and throwing them online. Working in hypertext takes a little more thought and planning. By its very nature, hypertext works differently from paper documents; it's more of an active media, with readers choosing from a virtually unlimited range of directions. Furthermore, you have a number of choices and techniques available that are not available on paper: Should you link to other people's Web sites? How many routes through your own Web site should you provide? How many pictures should you use, at the risk of irritating people by providing slow downloads?

In this chapter we're going to begin by looking at a few major issues in a design overview. In the following chapter we'll get a little closer and discuss some very specific design issues.

Two Schools of Thought

There are a couple of schools of thought about what makes an effective Web site. Here's what the first school seems to consider the essence of perfection in the world of the Web:

- Web sites must be "cool."
- You need lots of pictures.
- Adding sound to your site can help make it more interesting.
- Adding animation to your site makes it more exciting.
- Your site must be in a state of constant change or people won't come back.

What do these people think the Web is? An entertainment system? Certainly many of them do believe that, and, of course, parts of the Web are just that. If you're MTV or Nickelodeon, maybe you do need to have all these things: pictures, animation, sounds, constant change. But there's no rule that says every Web site must be "cool."

Let's get back to the real world for an example. When I ship a package via FedEx or UPS, I can call the company to come and pick up the package. Now, when someone from FedEx or UPS comes to the door, do I expect a song and dance? Do I demand poetry or a joke? Of course not. So why do I need these things when I arrive at a Web site? In most cases I don't.

I've said it a few times before, but I just have to say it again:

The Internet is a giant jobs program for computer geeks.

Why are so many people telling you that your Web site must be cool? Because creating a cool Web site is really a lot of fun. I've used many of the tools required to do this sort of thing, and if you're of a geek frame of mind (as I freely admit I am now and then), this stuff really is entertaining. Hell, it's better than working! You get to express your artistic tendencies a little, even if a little is just how artistic you happen to be. You get to play with pretty pictures and the programs that create them, fool around with all sorts of neat software, connect a microphone to your computer and pretend to be a radio announcer, tweak this and tweak that. Playing with computers can really be fun—after all, why would I be writing this book rather than getting a real job?

Let me give you an example. A couple of years ago I watched a presentation given in Las Vegas at the National Association of Broadcasters convention. A young man (a Webmaster, as he called himself) who worked for a television station in California was showing his Web site, and at one point he played some video of the funeral of David Packard of Hewlett-Packard. He'd put the video at his Web site for visitors to view. His explanation? "Now people all over the world can feel like they were there."

If I'd had the opportunity to talk with him, I would have asked two questions. First: So what? And second: How does this make money for your television station? Someone in Japan, for instance, could view this video; how nice. But does it help the company posting the video on the Web? Not at all.

Your Web site doesn't necessarily need "cool." Here's the other school of thought:

- Web sites should be useful.
- Web sites should be designed with a real purpose in mind, and the designers should make sure they fulfill that purpose.
- Web sites should work quickly—not keep your visitors waiting.

- Web sites should be structured in such a manner that visitors can find what they need quickly and without fuss.

So here's another of my little mottos to live by (or at least, to build Web sites by):

Forget cool, think useful.

Am I saying there's no place on the Internet for pictures, sounds, animations, and all the other neat stuff? No, of course not. A few pictures here and there really can help a Web site. Consider the purpose of the site. If that purpose includes entertaining people, then by all means add a little cool to the site. If not, don't worry about cool and think about how to make the site useful.

A couple of sites I mention as good examples are the **UPS** (http://www.ups. com/) and **FedEx** (http://www.fedex.com/) sites. Are these sites cool? No, not particularly, though they're reasonably attractive. Are they useful? They are, and they get a lot of traffic. How many people visit the UPS or FedEx sites and think, "I'm not coming back here, this site's not cool enough"? Not many, I'll bet.

Here's what Edward Tufte said about this issue in an interview in the *Computer Literacy Bookshop's New Book Bulletin* (Computer Literacy is now known as FatBrain.com). Tufte was named by *The Utne Reader* as one of "100 Visionaries Who Could Change Your Life," so presumably he knows something worth hearing. While talking about poorly designed sites, he pointed out that the

allocation of space on the screen tends to reflect the distribution of political power controlling the site. Programmers have a great deal of control, so there are lots of fancy tricks employed ... designers control a great deal, so there are elaborate page navigation systems, and elaborate buttons to click on. The result is that content winds up with only a tiny share of the screen, often only 20–30 percent of the bandwidth! ... For Web pages, bare bones design is the way to go.

It's those same programmers and designers telling you that you need "cool," that you need form over substance. It's simply not true; it's an idea that is not based on any sound business principle. And if you want proof, take a look at the **CDnow** Web site (http://www.cdnow.com/). This business was launched in 1994 by two brothers in their early twenties. They began the business in their parents' basement and in 1996 grossed $6 million. In 1997 they'll probably gross $16 million. By the summer of 1998 they owned 33 percent of the online music business, more than MCI, Blockbuster, and Tower Records put together. When you visit their site, you'll find that the main page loads quickly, because there are no huge pictures, no animations, and no sounds. CDnow limits itself to a few bright buttons and navigation bars, and some album art (CDnow sells music CDs). That's not to say CDnow eschews all multimedia—it has 250,000 music clips. But it does limit itself to using multimedia for a purpose, not simply for effect.

Ask Yourself These Questions

If you are considering adding something fancy to your site, there are a couple of questions you should ask yourself. Before you add video, some strange file format that requires a special browser viewer or plug-in, sounds, animations, or anything else out of the ordinary, answer these questions:

*A year after I wrote the first edition of this book I wrote **The CDnow Story: Rags to Riches on the Internet** with Jason and Matthew Olim, the founders of CDnow; you can find information about the book at* http://Top Floor.com/cdnow/. *About a year after that CDnow merged with Music Boulevard, their largest rival, and reportedly one of the pre-merger discussions related to the background color of the new Web site! Music Boulevard favored a "cool" black background, despite the fact that it was hard to read. CDnow favored a clean layout with a white background. CDnow won the argument, and you'll find that their Web site still has that easy-to-read white background.*

1. How does this benefit the visitor?
2. How does this benefit me or my organization?

At the National Association of Broadcasters conference I was chatting with someone who manages a Web site and was planning to add video to his site. I'd just stated during my presentation that video on the Web was mostly a gimmick (this early in 1997, by the way), and though this gentleman didn't quite disagree with my answer, he had another perspective. Sometimes, he suggested, it's necessary for people to adopt a technology before it's economical, without regard to any kind of financial payback. That's the way that technology progresses. I agree with him. I think the people who have become what's known as "early adopters," those people who just have to use the newest gadget as soon as it's available, price be damned, are an important factor in the development of various technologies, from VCRs to DAT, from squeezable cheese tubes to electric cars.

But that doesn't mean you have to be an early adopter. That doesn't mean you have to waste your money, or the money of your organization, using something—

such as video on your Web site—that's going to bring no benefit at all to you, your organization, or, in most cases, your Web site's visitors.

So consider the following two questions before trying anything unusual. Will it benefit the visitor in some way? (If not, why bother?) And will it help you achieve your aims? (Sorry, "building a cool Web site" is not a valid aim unless this is just a hobby). If you are doing something that does not in some way achieve one of these goals, then you're probably doing something that doesn't need to be done.

Remember this:

> *A lot's changed in the last couple of years, and I believe video is becoming more viable. However, consider that even late in 1999 perhaps only 2 percent of all Internet users in North America have fast cable or DSL connections to the Internet. Video can be useful in some cases, but it's still not something that most users are going to want to see as a regular part of a Web site.*

The number one complaint by World Wide Web users is slow page loading, not lack of video.

Multimedia and Plug-Ins—More Trouble Than They're Worth?

It's not just video that's the problem, it's all sorts of multimedia formats. Imagine for a moment that you've gone shopping—not on the Web, but in the real world. You arrive at a store, and see a big sign:

> *If you want to view our products, please go five doors down the street and get the special rose-tinted glasses (available for free). Then fit the glasses properly; they're a little awkward to fit, so it'll take a few minutes. Then return to our store to see just how cool we are!*

How many customers will this store lose? This is a real nuisance. You arrive at a Web site and you see a message telling you that to really benefit from the site you need to download the new ShockSnapViewer browser plug-in. So you go to the Snap Incorporated site and download the plug-in—that may take 20 or 30 minutes, of course. You then install it—another 10 or 15 minutes. Then you return to the Web site, fully prepared … and you see a picture of two pigs dancing. Very nice, but was it worth it?

There are sites that really need these fancy plug-ins. If you are running a Web site related to multimedia, video, or music—or dancing pigs—your visitors may not mind getting the latest plug-in or viewer so they can benefit from your site. But in most cases, plug-ins and viewers are simply not necessary, and they're often a symptom of a Web author with too much time on his hands.

Think about the formats that your visitors can view; in most cases that means text, .HTML, .GIF, and .JPEG images, and a few sound formats (.WAV, .AU, .AIF, and .SND). If you want to use some other format, think carefully about why. Yes, it might be nice to provide Word for Windows files, for instance, and there's even a Word viewer freely available from Microsoft. But do you really want to force all the non-Word users to go to Microsoft and download the viewer before they can view your information? And definitely don't provide PostScript document files unless you are sure that your visitors have a PostScript viewer—such people are probably UNIX users or very geeky in some other way. PostScript is a nuisance for most users, as good viewers are few and far between. The vast majority of Web sites need RealAudio, they don't need Shockwave, and they don't need VRML. A heading in *Internet World* a couple of years ago asked: "*Who's Making Money Besides the Companies that Sell Streaming Audio and Video Products?*" The related article says, "the answer may not surprise you; hardly anyone."

Sound's a Problem

Even sound can be a real problem. The two major browsers recognize different tags for embedding sound, and Netscape Navigator in particular has a number of bugs that make playing sound at your Web site (specifically .WAV files, I believe) a bit of a nuisance. If you add sounds, you can't be sure that they'll play in all your visitors' browsers.

By the way, you'll save yourself a lot of trouble if you remember this simple statement:

The Internet is not a multimedia system.

Contrary to all the nonsense we've been fed by the press over the past few years, the Internet is not a true multimedia system. In fact, many of its problems stem from the idea that somehow it is, and that people seem determined to prove that it is—by adding video, animations, sound, and more. The Internet won't be a multimedia system for some time, not until most users are working with fast connections to the Internet, and that won't be until sometime early in the next century—perhaps even somewhere around the middle of the first decade. (I haven't touched this previous sentence, which I originally wrote in the first edition of this book. As I write this second edition we're almost in the next century, and it's quite clear that what I wrote is completely correct. It won't be until the middle of the first decade that half or more North American users are working with fast Internet connections, and it will be a few years more before the rest catch up.)

How can the Internet be called a multimedia system when data is transferred at rates designed for transferring text? How can the Internet be regarded as a multimedia system when, compared to television, video games, movies, and computer multimedia CD-ROMs, it moves at the speed of a drunk turtle?

A couple of years ago, I was asked to submit a list of Web sites using sounds to a legal firm which was preparing for a lawsuit and needed to document the ways in which sound was being used on the Internet. I was surprised at just how few Web pages use sound—probably a fraction of one percent. A tiny fraction of the Web works with sound, and an even tinier fraction uses animation and video. The Web is overwhelmingly text, with a few static images thrown in for good measure.

Don't Be Too Clever

There are all sorts of neat little things you can do with HTML, but I'd advise that you don't try to be too clever. Here's the problem: each browser works a little differently, and while most HTML features work with most browsers, there is a significant number of features that only work—or only work well—on specific browsers. The two main browsers, the browsers used by 99 percent of all users, are Netscape Navigator and Microsoft Internet Explorer. Both browsers have features that other browsers do not and that require particular HTML tags that are nonstandard. For instance, Internet Explorer has a feature called a marquee, which is a line of scrolling text, and another feature, a watermark, which is a static background image—if you scroll the page, the text scrolls over the image. Explorer is the only browser that can view these features, though they're fairly harmless in other browsers;

Microsoft Won

It's clear that Microsoft won the browser war. While most users in 1996, perhaps over 90 percent, worked with Netscape Navigator, today Internet Explorer is used by around 60 percent to 76 percent of all Web surfers, depending on whose statistics you believe.

other browsers simply display a marquee as static text and a watermark as a normal scrolling background.

Now, these advanced features are often very nice and very useful, but you have to consider whether visitors to your site will be using browsers that work with these features. You need to know not only which browser most visitors will be using, but also which version of the browser they're likely to be using. New browsers introduce new versions, but that doesn't mean that all users are working with the latest browsers. Many will be stuck back in an earlier version.

The following Web sites publish statistics that will give you an idea of the current browser distribution.

BrowserWatch
http://browserwatch.iworld.com/stats.html

EWS Browser Statistics
http://www.cen.uiuc.edu/bstats/latest.html

Hawaii Webmasters Sources of Up-to-Date Browser & Server Stats
http://www.connect.hawaii.com/hc/webmasters/current.browser.stats.html

IPT Browser Statistics Page
http://www.ipt.com/agent.htm

NightFlight
http://www.nightflight.com/htdocs/browsercounter.html

StatMarket
http://www.statmarket.com/

Yahoo!—Browser Usage Statistics
http://dir.yahoo.com/Computers_and_Internet/Software/Internet/World_Wide_Web/Browsers/Browser_Usage_Statistics/

You've undoubtedly seen those little signs: "Best Viewed with Netscape Navigator" or "Best Viewed with Internet Explorer." There may be, in some cases, very good reasons to build a Web site that uses advanced features, but in general, putting up a sign telling someone to go away and install a different browser is a little rude and very foolish, like a store that makes you change your shoes before you enter.

Here's my advice:

In the Web-design world, stay a couple of steps behind.

Unless you have a good reason for trying to prove just how technologically advanced you are, avoid the headaches that come from using the really fancy Web features. Note also that you can check to see which browsers your users are working with by reviewing your server's log files; see Chapter 21 for more information.

You might bear this in mind:

There are always more people using the previous version of a browser than the current version!

That means there will always be more people using the previous set of HTML features and JavaScript features, for instance, than the most up-to-date set.

Two Versions of Your Web Site?

Some Web authors create two versions of their Web sites, one for advanced browsers and one for earlier browsers. This is a great way for them to spend more time doing what they love most—creating Web sites. Or a great way to bill their clients more.

In general, though, I don't think it's particularly worthwhile or necessary to create two Web sites. You should try to create a single site that doesn't use too many advanced features, so that virtually everyone can view it. There are still people using early Web browsers that won't work with tables, and that's a real problem, because tables are very useful. But there aren't many nontable browsers in use, and in any case, the people using them know they have a problem and must be used to dealing with the problem by now. The same goes for frames. Early browsers couldn't work with frames, but there aren't so many nonframes browsers left.

Real-World Metaphors Are Dangerous

Here's another technique that should be employed with great care: the use of "real-world metaphors." This is an idea that was at one time much touted in the world of computer user-interface design, but thanks to a variety of failures that have highlighted its weaknesses, you don't hear about it quite so often these days.

The idea is that by making a computer look like something people are used to in the real world, the computer becomes easier to use. The basic principle is sound. Using a trash-can icon on the computer to indicate somewhere you can "dump" files you don't want is a reasonable idea, and probably does help people learn to use the computer. Using folder icons to denote directories on a hard disk is fine, too, as is using document icons to indicate individual files. The system falls apart, though, when it's taken too far and the entire design of the user interface—or, more to the point, the Web site—is molded by some cute real-world metaphor.

You've probably seen computer "desktops" that look like, well, desktops. There's a desk. There's a drawer; maybe you store files in the drawer, I'm not exactly sure. There's a light switch; that's probably to close down the program … maybe. There's a trash can on the floor; well, we know what that's for. There's a writing pad; that's used to start the word processor. There's a picture on the wall; use that to start the paint program. All very cute, but it puts a layer of fuzz between the user and the job the user is trying to accomplish. And it's not necessary. People aren't stupid. They don't need a real-world metaphor to use a computer or a Web site.

What would we have ended up with if the designer of the first Yellow Pages decided to use a real-world metaphor? Instead of an index and listings, maybe the book could be organized like a street, with buildings on each side of the street—that's where you could put the listings for each business. And you could have different pictures for different sections—you'd have a garage on the side of the street for auto mechanics, a burning building for the fire department, and a fight on the street outside a building that houses the telephone numbers of the local bars—all very silly, and all very unnecessary.

Yet you'll sometimes run into Web sites built around a metaphor. Typically it's the cybermalls that do this—but then, you know what I think of the concept of cybermalls (or you do if you read Chapter 3).

You can see an example of a real-world metaphor in Figure 9.1. There are several links on this, but the links could have been displayed in a fraction of the download time using text or a much simpler image. Instead, visitors using a 14,400bps modem have to wait 17 seconds just to be shown a cutesy little lobby. In fact, this is the second page presented to visitors; the first is the outside of the building, and Doctor HTML told me that it'll take a 14,400bps modem a whopping 63 seconds to load. (Who's Doctor HTML? The doctor analyzes Web sites and provides useful information about them, including how quickly a Web page is likely to load. We'll talk about this later in this chapter, but if you can't wait you can find **Doctor HTML** at http://www2.imagiware.com/RxHTML/).

Why waste visitors' time? Why not provide a fast-loading starting point and allow the visitor to decide whether or not to waste time with large graphics.

In fact, the designer of this Web site has provided two options, high-bandwidth and low-bandwidth options. High-bandwidth means a site that uses a lot of graphics and is slow; low-bandwidth means fewer images and faster downloads. But why not show these options first, rather than making the visitor wait well over a minute to see the lobby?

This example is no longer in use. The company removed it sometime after the first edition of this book was published, but it seemed like such a good example

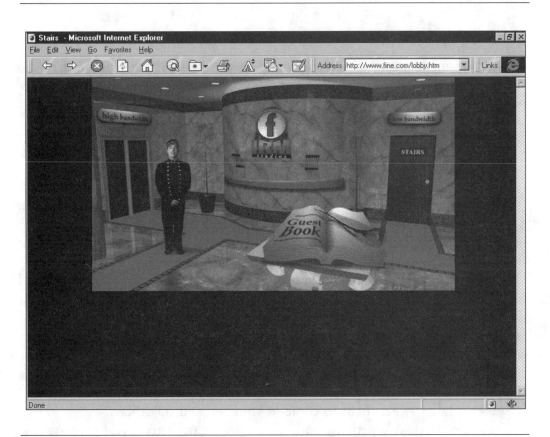

Figure 9.1: Does this lobby really do any good? There are faster ways to get people into your site.

I thought I'd use it again. There's another example I'd like to use, but can't remember where I saw it. It was a Web mall that actually had parking spaces ...

By the way, if you're hiring someone to design and create your Web site for you, be a little wary of a suggestion that you need two Web sites, a high-bandwidth and a low-bandwidth version. A good designer should be able to design something that looks attractive, fulfills its purpose and is a low-bandwidth version. There again, it's more fun—and, from the designer's perspective, more profitable—to create two versions.

As with any rule, the one against the use of real-world metaphors can be broken if you really know what you're doing, and if breaking the rule is appropriate. For instance, a museum might want to duplicate its own lobby online. Generally speaking, though, real-world metaphors are too cutesy to be anything but irritating.

Lead Your Visitors

I know I've made a number of comments in this book about making the Web site easier for the visitor, but after all, it is your Web site, so you have to consider two conflicting needs:

- You are trying to achieve something by bringing people to your Web site.
- The visitors are trying to achieve something by visiting your Web site.

The perfect Web site, from your point of view, is the one that satisfies both desires: you get what you want, your visitors get what they want. Everyone's happy. Of course, this is a circular dynamic. If your visitors' needs are not met, they won't come back, so your needs won't be met.

So when creating a Web site, you must consider what you want to get and what you can give to people in order to get them to visit your site and use it in the way you want. For instance, you're planning to set up a site that attracts a lot of visitors so you can sell advertising. (You probably won't make a lot of money selling advertising, but we'll discuss that issue in Chapter 20.) Your aims are simple: get lots of people to your site as often as possible and for as long a duration as possible. The site will focus on giving something to your visitors—whatever it takes to get them to come to your site and stay there.

On the other hand, perhaps your aim is to set up a technical-support site, where customers can get information about your products so they're less likely to call your technical-support staff. In this case, you really want to get your customers in and out as quickly as possible—for your sake and theirs. Yours, because it's less stress on the Web server, and theirs, because they're trying to get a job done and not waste time on the Web.

Or maybe you're selling something. You want to get your prospective clients to your site and sell them whatever it is you have. But sometimes in cases like this you run into conflict. You have to bring them to your site somehow—perhaps you offer them information or a discussion with other people who have similar interests, or a freebie of some kind—but while they're at your site, you don't want them just to take, you want them to give, as well.

So consider also how you are going to lead your visitors. They've come to get something from your site, but you want to make sure your needs are met, too. I've said you should make things easy for them, and that's where the conflict lies; if it's too easy for them, they'll go directly to what they want, take it, and leave. Instead, you need to lead them to where you want them. So, for instance, you don't take them straight to a page where they can take part in a discussion group.

First you lead them through another page containing information that you want them to see about a product or service you are trying to sell. You don't take someone straight to a download page for demo software, you take them through a page that explains what's so great about the full version of the software. Now, you don't want to make this process obnoxious. Make it too difficult, and you'll drive away your visitors. And don't make it hard to navigate your site, either. Try to find a balance somewhere.

Make It Easy to Move Around

Think about the way your site is structured. You might even use an old technology—pencil and paper—and sketch out how your site will be structured. If you're using a program that can display a Web-site map, you'll be able to view how everything fits together as you go along, too. Make sure that the site's structure is logical and that visitors can find the information they need without digging through dozens of pages. You'll also want to remember the point that I've just made—that you may have reasons to lead your visitors through certain parts of your Web site. While allowing for your needs, make the site as easy to move around in as possible.

And don't forget to provide a way out of every page. Yes, every browser has a Back command, but what if people arrive at a page directly, using a URL they've received from friends or colleagues? A page without any links back into your site is a page that's isolated in cyberspace. At the very least, create links back to the page from which you have linked the current one.

Here's a very simple piece of advice that can be the difference between a great Web site and a terrible one:

> *Think of the really obvious items visitors want to find, then make sure they can find them easily.*

If you were a visitor to your site, what would you want to know? What the product is that you're selling, for instance, what features the product has, how much it costs, where and how to order it, how to contact someone with questions, and so on. This is all so obvious it seems ridiculous that people could forget it, but spend some time on the Web and you'll see that they really do. You shouldn't.

Find the Web Awards

I've already suggested that you travel around on the Web looking for examples of good Web sites. You can also get more specific help. You could, for instance, view Web sites that are rated highly by various review services on the Web. Try these sites to reach the rating and award sites:

Best of the Web
http://www.botw.org/

PC Magazine's Top 100
http://www.zdnet.com/pcmag/special/web100/

Project Cool
http://www.projectcool.com/sightings/

USA Today Hot Sites
http://www.usatoday.com/life/cyber/ch.htm

Web 500
http://www.web500.com/categories/Links/links.htm

Yahoo!—Best of the Web
http://dir.yahoo.com/Computers_and_Internet/Internet/World_Wide_Web/Best_of_the_Web/

Yahoo!—What's New
http://www.yahoo.com/picks/

Unfortunately, viewing top-rated sites is not always a good way to find good sites. These sites are often rated on a "cool" scale, so many sites are listed because they're heavy on graphics or multimedia.

Find Lousy Sites

Another form of example is the lousy Web site; take a look at some really bad sites, decide what you don't like about them, and promise yourself not to make the same mistakes. One of the best ways to find lousy sites is to visit the cybermalls (see Chapter 3). You'll find all sorts of amateurish rubbish with the following kinds of faults:

- They don't tell you what they want you to do
- They don't have e-mail addresses
- They use horrible colors
- They use ugly backgrounds
- They use ridiculous text and background contrast, making their text unreadable
- They contain spelling and grammar mistakes.

But some of these Web sites are really horrible. When I say a site is horrible, I don't mean it's not pretty—that it's not a work of art. I'm no graphic artist myself (my wife says I'm color-challenged), but some of these sites are so bad, they're hard to read. Tiny blue text on a mottled gray background pattern can be quite

Here's one mistake that drives me nuts. Sites that tell you to do something—"visit our press center"—for instance, but don't provide a link so you can do as they suggest.

irritating. Wood-grain backgrounds are pretty nasty whatever sort of text you put on top of them. Enormous dark-blue text (so big that in VGA mode you can only see six or seven words across the page) on a light-blue speckled background is just plain stupid. Who's designing these things?

Another way to find awful Web sites is by looking at one of the indexes of bad sites:

The Useless Pages
> http://www.go2net.com/internet/useless/

Web Pages That Suck Daily Sucker
> http://www.webpagesthatsuck.com/sucker.html

Yahoo!—Not Really the Best
> http://dir.yahoo.com/Computers_and_Internet/Internet/World_Wide_Web/
> Best_of_the_Web/Not_Really_the_Best/

Get Some Design Advice

I want to tell you about two really useful sites. The first is **Web Pages That Suck: Learn Good Design by Looking at Bad Design**, by Vincent Flanders (http://www.webpagesthatsuck.com/). I think this is important because it's such a wonderful way to learn about lousy Web-site design. And once you've learned lousy Web-site design, you can avoid it. (The site was eventually turned into a book, by the way, published by SYBEX.)

It will take a few hours to go through this entire site—it had 52 individual topics last time I checked—but it will be well worth it. Find out what's wrong with black backgrounds, the problems with those little flickering animations you see so often (GIF89a files), why Kai Power Tools can be a nuisance, how shadows can be ugly, all about pretentiousness, and plenty more. If you ever need a license to publish a Web site, I hope they make everyone work their way through *Web Pages That Suck* first.

Another very handy little site is the **Doctor HTML** site (http://www2. imagiware.com/RxHTML/). All you need to do is enter a Web page's URL—your Web page or one you are interested in learning about—make a few selections, and Doctor HTML will analyze the page. It will tell you how large the image files are, how long they'll take to transfer, whether you've made mistakes in your HTML tags and whether there are broken links, and will check for spelling mistakes. It will even suggest ways in which you can improve your tags to make the page work better.

We'll be consulting Doctor HTML a few times in the following chapter, but bear in mind that the download times calculated by Doctor HTML may be optimistic. They assume a reasonable connection to the Internet, but if the Internet's having a busy day, the visitor is connecting through a slow ISP, or the Web site itself is busy, the times stated by the good doctor may be underestimates.

Test Your Site

Don't forget to test your Web site, whether you create it or someone else does it for you. If you create it, take a rest from the site for a day or two, and then connect to the site across the Web and use it as a real visitor might. Try to put yourself in that visitor's frame of mind: what is the visitor coming to your site for? And then again, what do you want the visitor to do? Also test in different video resolutions (at least in VGA—that is, 640×480—and in 800×600), and using different browsers (at least the latest and immediately previous versions of Netscape Navigator and Internet Explorer).

If you are using frames at your site, you might want to check your Web site with a nonframes browser, too. However, the vast majority of Web users now have browsers that do handle frames: Internet Explorer 3 and Netscape Navigator 3 and later handle frames well. Netscape 2 handles frames, but with problems. And the latest America Online and CompuServe browsers work with frames, too. So there aren't that many people using browsers that don't handle frames, and it's actually getting hard to track down a Windows or Macintosh browser that is in wide use and doesn't use frames.

Don't forget to also test for broken links, links that you've added to your pages that no longer work. This is something you should do periodically, because Web sites come and go; you may link to a site today, and that site could disappear tomorrow. Many HTML-authoring programs have utilities that will check all your links for you. Try to remember to do it once every few weeks.

Change Your Video Mode

What size video screen are most people using? No, it's not 17 inches, it's 15 inches or less. Sure, many new computers these days come with 17-inch screens, but that's fairly recent. Most people didn't run out and buy a machine last week, so they're still using relatively small monitors: 14- or 15-inch monitors.

So what video mode are these people using? Perhaps 800×600, but in many cases VGA (640×480 pixels); have you tried using a higher resolution on one of these small screens? It's almost impossible.

Nonetheless, many Web authors are working with large screens and high video resolutions, and never think about changing video mode to see what the page looks like. How do I know this? Because I've seen too many sites that are almost unusable in VGA mode. You must test your Web site in VGA mode, even if you keep your computer set in a higher resolution. You may be surprised at how ugly things look all of a sudden when you squeeze your pages down into 640×480 pixels.

Get Off That Fast Connection

Here's another major problem with Web authors. All too often they're sitting in their offices with fast network connections to the Web site. The site may actually be in the next room, and the author is connected across an internal network. Or maybe it's out on the Web, but the connection to the Internet is with an ISDN or even T1 line. And these days many people are getting cable or DSL connections in their homes, and forgetting that not everyone else is so lucky.

Most Internet users are not on fast connections; they connect through telephone-line modems. How many members does America Online have? Eighteen million last time I heard. Add in all those CompuServe, Prodigy, GEnie users—millions more. Then the tens of thousands of small service providers, millions more.

Most people are still using modems; millions, perhaps most, are still working at speeds of 28.8kbps or less. These are the people for whom most Web authors should be creating sites. If your Web site is not being used exclusively by people using fast connections, make sure you don't get carried away and create a fast-connection site.

Finish Before You Publicize

In Chapter 16 you'll see how to begin publicizing your Web site, but it's a good idea not to get started too soon. Don't set up a sparse main page, then immediately begin publicizing the site. Instead, make sure you've got something worth visiting. Otherwise people will visit your site and leave immediately, perhaps never to return.

Web sites are never completely finished, though. There's always something to add or something to tweak, so don't feel that your site must be completely perfect before you begin getting the word out. You may want a few "Coming Soon" signs here and there, and perhaps links to pages that explain a new feature you'll be adding soon. If you plan to add some features that you believe people will really want to see, it's a good idea to let them know you'll be adding those features soon. If it's a major feature, you may even want to add a feedback form (see Chapter 12) to collect people's e-mail addresses so you can let them know when you've added the feature.

## Chapter Ten

More Tips For Effective Web Sites

In Chapter 9 I provided an overview of the Web-site creation process. I'd strongly recommend that you visit Web Pages That Suck and some of the other advice sites I mentioned in that chapter to get more detail. However, in this chapter I'm quickly going to cover a few key issues that can help you make your Web site work.

Always Use an index.html File

Web servers are set up to transmit default files if a browser requests a URL without a filename. For instance, if you type http://TopFloor.com/ into your browser and press Enter, which file will the server send to your browser? After all, you haven't specified a file.

Well, the server will probably send a file named index.html (ask your server administrator what filename is configured as the default; it's usually index.html but is occasionally something else, such as index.htm or default.html). So it's a good idea to have an index.html file in every directory at your Web site. If you don't have one, what happens when the user requests a URL without a filename? The server can't send a file, because it can't find index.html, so it does one of two things: It may send the directory information, so the user can see a list of all the files saved in that directory—which is something you may not want to happen. Or it may send an error message saying that it can't find the requested file.

You never know how your URLs will get mangled as they're passed around on the Web. You may include a filename at the end of a URL when you give it to people, but the filename may disappear as it passes between people. Make sure the main page in each directory is the index.html file, and visitors will still be able to find their way around your site.

Fix the Basic Structure

Plan the basic structure of the Web site, then try to stick with it. If you keep shuffling things around, you're likely to end up with broken links within the site, though a good authoring program will automatically update links when you rename or move a file. You may also confuse visitors, who may have bookmarked a page earlier and now find that the page has gone.

If you have to move something within your own site, put a page redirecting people to the new one. However, good planning can help you avoid most changes.

Provide Different Ways to Find Things

You are already providing links to the Web pages within your Web site, but there are a few other things you can do to help your visitors find their way around:

- **Provide a Table of Contents or index.** Consider creating a page that contains links to all the pages in your site, organized in a Table of Contents format, as an alphabetical index, or perhaps both. Microsoft FrontPage and some other products have tools to help you do this very quickly.
- **Add a search engine.** Users can type in a keyword and see a list of all matching pages. FrontPage also helps you create a search page very quickly.
- **Provide a site map.** Some companies provide an actual image, a map of the site (create it using just two colors, so it's not too big in download terms). Others provide a text-based system that is similar to a table of contents (see **BookZone's sitemap**, for instance: http://www.bookzone.com/services/sitemap.html).
- **Provide navigation bars.** These are the button bars that you often see at Web sites. You can create navigation bars using plain text, too, and if you want an image (button) navigation bar you should consider having a text navigation bar as well, as it will load quicker than the images and be available even if a visitor has images turned off. Think carefully about the links on your navigation bar. Consider the visitors' needs, and include links that they'll find useful: *Home, Search Page, Contact Us, Index,* and so on.

Make Sure Page Titles Make Sense

Every page can—and should—have a title. Make sure these titles make sense and will help visitors find their way around your site. Remember, the page titles will turn up in the visitor's browser's history list, in the bookmark list if the visitor sets a bookmark, and in an index page if you use an automatic indexing tool. Meaningless or ambiguous page titles—*Page 3, More Info, Download,* and so on—make it harder for users to find their way around or return to a page they find useful. Page titles also turn up in Web search engines such as AltaVista, another reason to use a logical and understandable title.

You may want to start each page title with a short version of your Web site's name or a description of the particular area in which the page is found. For instance, *Acmesewer, Inc. Download Page* rather than just *Download Page.*

Don't Overwhelm the Visitor

Don't clutter your pages with too much stuff. Try to make each page clear, with a few obvious routes the visitor can take. This is especially important if you're trying to lead the visitor somewhere, of course. Too many links will confuse, as I'll discuss in a moment. Breaking the information down into more manageable pieces and splitting those pieces off into different pages will make it more manageable. Here's an example of a really awful Web site, the **ICQ** site: http://www.icq.com/. I picked this example because, although I've long thought that this site was a mess, a colleague recently mentioned it in a discussion about cluttered sites. The funny thing is that it contains probably a third less text on it now than it did a year or so ago.

The idea of hypertext is to allow people to follow routes they find useful, so there's no need to throw everything at them at once. Rather, allow them to make choices early in the process. On the other hand, this can be overdone, in the same way that so many voice-mail systems seem to do these days. You know the sort: you have to go through five or ten menus before arriving at where you want to be. Allow the user to choose a route, but try to keep the Web site fairly "shallow"—that is, the user should not have to dig down through too many levels.

Quick, Not Cool—Speed Up Access by Reducing Images

The single most common complaint by World Wide Web users is that using the Web is too slow—Web pages take too long to load. People don't want huge pictures and video and all that fancy stuff on Web sites, they want the Web site to load quickly. That's not to say pictures have no place on the Web, but they should serve a purpose, and the size of the image should be commensurate with the purpose being served. In other words, don't use a large image for a trivial reason.

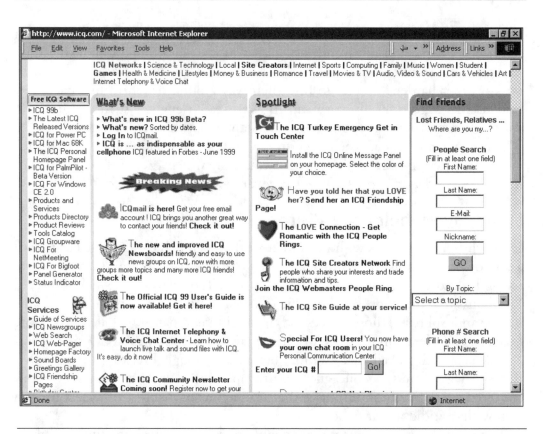

Figure 10.1: The ICQ site is one of the most confusing and cluttered Websites I've ever seen (which didn't stop AOL buying ICQ for $400M, though). The page is actually three times the length of what we've shown here.

It's quite possible to create attractive Web sites with pages that load quickly. You don't have to use huge images in order to make a Web site look good and work well. Let me give you a couple of examples: the **FedEx** (http://www.fedex.com/) and **UPS** (http://www.ups.com/) sites. What I like about these sites is that they both serve a real purpose, and serve it well. And they're both in exactly the same business—shipping packages. However, the FedEx site loads much more quickly than the UPS site. Now, I'm not saying the UPS site is bad, just that it could be better. The FedEx site seems to load more quickly than the UPS site, and it appears to be because UPS is using relatively large images for some reason.

Now, I analyzed the text and images on the main pages of these two sites using **Doctor HTML** (http://www2.imagiware.com/RxHTML/—see Chapter 9 for more information). And sure enough, UPS's images are bigger. Here's what Doctor HTML told me:

The UPS site:

- The text and HTML commands of the document take up 12.4k.
- The total number of bytes in images found on the UPS Web page is 59.8k.
- The total number of bytes transferred while loading the page is 72.2k.
- This will take approximately 41.1 seconds to load over a 14.4kbps modem.

Now for the FedEx site:

- The text and HTML commands of the document take up 10.3k.
- The total number of bytes in images found on the Fedex Web page is 31.9k.
- The total number of bytes transferred while loading the page is 42.2k.
- This will take approximately 24 seconds to load over a 14.4kbps modem.

So what's the doctor's diagnosis mean? For some reason UPS' images are almost twice the size of FedEx's. And UPS is making visitors wait almost twice the time that FedEx makes its visitors wait. Why? Perhaps because UPS' designers are trying too hard to be cool. Actually UPS' site really isn't so bad, it's just not as good as FedEx's, from a speed point of view. There are many sites on the Web that are far worse—sites that make you wait and wait for the images to appear on the page.

So what can you do to avoid forcing people to wait? One thing is to strip pictures out of the pages altogether, then see what you can do with text formatting to spruce the page up a little; most browsers will display colored text, text of varying sizes, text aligned in different ways, and so on. And the majority of users—well over 98 percent—are

I noticed that since the first edition of this book these two sites have switched places (the UPS site used to be much quicker than the FedEx site), with the UPS site more than tripling the size of the images transferred and the FedEx site reducing the amount by a third. (I can only conclude that UPS read the book, while FedEx didn't.) And the amount of text went up considerably—The UPS site increased the amount of "text and HTML commands" by around 15 or 16 times, and the FedEx site increased by about two and a half times.

working with browsers that can display tables, too, so you can use tables to format text.

Once you've done what you can with text, add a few pictures back in, but not many. Keep an eye on the combined size of the images: keep it under 30k per page, if you can. And consider using some of the following techniques.

Test With Lynx

Computer-book author Ray Lischner has pointed out that some people using the Web are incapable of seeing images in Web pages: "Some of my friends are blind," he explained in an Internet mailing list:

They can browse the Web, but only if the Web pages have text equivalents for their graphics. All too often, I have seen image maps with no textual equivalents, so these sites are effectively closed to the visually impaired. What I find helpful in designing pages is to turn off images completely, and see if the Web pages still make sense. Or run Lynx to browse your pages.

Blind Internet users can use special software to translate the text on Web pages into speech; but if all a page has is graphics, there's nothing to translate, of course. Lynx is a text-only browser that was popular for a while in the early days of the Web, and is still used by people who don't have TCP/IP connections to the Internet or who want very, very fast Web access—or who are blind. Lynx is not a point-and-click program, either; links are shown using numbers in brackets ([1], [2], [3], and so on), and users select links by typing the numbers.

You can see how Lynx views your Web pages by using Lynx directly—ask your service provider for information—or by using a "gateway" Web page such as the **Salt Lake Community College's Lynx** page (http://sol.slcc.edu/webguide/lynxit.html). By the way, if you're particularly concerned with the issue of making your Web pages accessible to the disabled, see the **Designing an Accessible World—Web Sites** page (http://www.trace.wisc.edu/world/web/), and **Bobby**, a system designed to test for "accessibility to people with disabilities": http://www.cast.org/bobby/.

Don't Be So Proud of Your Logo

You arrive at a Web site and wait for the page to download. And wait. And wait. Finally, the page finishes, and you realize that all you've got is a logo and a "welcome to our Web site" message. Now you've got to click on the logo to enter the site—and probably wait while some other huge image loads.

Sorry, but I don't feel very welcome! This is like making me wait at your front door for a while so I can admire your beautiful house. Well, you know what? I'm not impressed. A variation on this theme is the site that makes me wait while it displays its logo *and* all the "cool Web site" awards that it's won. Again, very irritating.

Add Text Links near the Top

Web authors often use image maps—you click on the picture to get to another document. The problem with image maps is that you're often forcing people to wait while the thing loads, even though all they want to do is pick a link and move further into your site.

You've probably noticed that many sites use both image maps and corresponding groups of text links; for every hotspot on the image map, there's a text link that takes the visitor to the same place. These are very useful, and you can increase their utility with one simple step: Place them near the top of the page. Visitors will see those links very quickly, and can move on to the next page right away without waiting for the image map to finish downloading. That saves them time, makes your site appear faster than it really is, and saves your Web server work, too.

Include ALT Text

When you add an image to a page, include the ALT text. The ALT attribute in the HTML <IMG> tag is used to provide alternative text that a browser can display in place of the image. This text will appear in the page if the user has turned off the display of images, or if the user is working with a nongraphics browser, as a few hundred thousand users still do. In many users' browsers—those working with Internet Explorer 3 or Netscape Navigator 4—the text message also appears if the user lets the mouse pointer rest on the image for a couple of seconds. Also note that some browsers allow the user to replace missing images selectively. That is, the user can work with images turned off, but when he needs a specific image, can load just that image. The ALT text can help the user identify which image he needs.

So use the ALT text and make it meaningful—*Company Logo*, *Image Map*, *Site Map*, and so on.

Use Height and Width Tags

The <IMG> tag has optional HEIGHT= and WIDTH= attributes. These tell the browser how large an image is, so the browser knows exactly where to place the image and adjacent text, even before it's received the image. This is important, because it speeds up the page layout; the user will be able to read the page's text even if the images are not there yet. So don't forget to use the HEIGHT= and

WIDTH= attributes whenever you use images. Some HTML editors, such as FrontPage, can automatically add these attributes for you. Or open the images in a graphics program and look for an image information dialog box somewhere, then add the attributes to the tags by hand.

Interlace Images

Another technique for making a Web page appear to load more quickly is to use interlaced images. These are a form of GIF image that is loaded into the page in layers. You've probably seen these images in action. When the image first loads, it's fuzzy, but it gradually comes into focus as the other layers of the image are transferred to the browser.

Using interlaced images is one of those little psychological tricks that don't actually speed up the loading of the Web page but that may seem to do so. The user has something to see a little earlier than with noninterlaced images and in some cases may even be able to identify enough of the image to distinguish probable hotspots on image maps.

Reuse Images

Once an image has transferred to the visitor's computer, it's placed into the browser's cache. This is an area of memory or hard-disk space that is used to store files that the browser thinks it may need again soon. So if you use an image on the first page at your Web site, and then again on another page that the visitor is likely to view a little later, that image will load very quickly from the cache rather than having to be retrieved from the server.

Reusing images, then, allows you to create an attractive Web site with very little data transfer. Don't transfer 30k or 40k of images for every page; reuse images, and you might be able to transfer 5k or 10k per page. Because images are reloaded from the cache, you can use a single image over and over again throughout your site with no significant slowdown in the speed at which browsers load those pages. You might want to use the same background image throughout the site, or your company logo in the corner of every page. Standardize one image for bullet lists, back arrows, horizontal lines, and so on, and you'll not only create a common look for all your pages but will add a little visual variety with minimal data transfer.

Use Several Small Images Instead of Lots of Biggies

By scattering a number of small images around a page instead of transferring a single large picture, you can add visual variety at a low download cost. You can even reuse images several times on the same page in some cases. The total number of bytes used by these smaller images can be much less than that of one large image and still look attractive. And again, when you use an image multiple times in a page it has to be transferred across the Internet only once, providing more bang for the metaphorical buck.

Use Fewer Colors

Reducing the number of colors in your images does two things. It reduces the image size, and it makes the image clearer to more people. Many users are still working with their video modes set to 16 colors (basic VGA is a 16-color mode). If your images are using 256 colors or even more, those images will look grainy to people working with a video mode set to 16 colors, so if possible stick to the basic 16 colors of the VGA palette. How can you be sure which color is part of the basic 16-color palette? Set your computer to VGA mode, then start your graphics program. Colors that are solid colors are part of the palette. Colors that are dithered—created by mixing dots of various colors—are not. A good designer can design something attractive with 16 colors. There's no law of art that says images using more colors are intrinsically more attractive.

Now, having said all that, perhaps I'm being a little compulsive. You may want to simply work with what's known as the "browser-safe" palette. Most computers these days will display 256 colors. The browser-safe palette has 216 colors. Why only 216 colors, if these computers display 256 colors? Because different computers display a *different* set of 256 colors—the 216 in the browser-safe palette are the 216 that are common to all systems. If you're interested, there's a good article on this subject called **Consistent Color on ALL browsers—10 easy steps** at Netscape: http://www.netscapeworld.com/common/nw.color.html. Now, these colors will display well on virtually all browsers on monitors that can display 256 or more colors. And on VGA monitors, they won't look great, but they'll probably look okay. (However, check your site in VGA mode just to make sure.)

By the way, I recently found a fantastic little color picker, the 216-Color **Webmaster's Color Laboratory** at the VisiBone site: http://www.visibone.com/colorlab/. If you're trying to pick colors for your Web site—for page and table-cell backgrounds, and for text colors—you can use this site to pick colors that work well with Web browsers. When you pick colors, the Color Laboratory does several things. It ...

- Displays the colors you pick next to each other, so you can see how well they match (up to eight colors at one time).

- Places text onto each color swatch, using all the other colors you've selected, so you can see how well a background color and a text color work together.
- Gives you the HTML hexadecimal code for every color, so you can enter the color into your Web pages.

Use Thumbnails

If your site really requires lots of images—you're running an art museum, selling clip art, or showcasing your own artwork—you still don't have to throw them at visitors. Don't fill every page with huge images. Instead, use a few thumbnail images here and there and link from the thumbnails to the full-sized images. Or warn users before they enter an area of your Web site that loading times are going to slow down because you're going to present large images.

Oh, and when I say use a thumbnail, use a real one, not a fake one. Many people simply change the HEIGHT= and WIDTH= attributes in the image tags to place an image into the page at a very small size. But the full image still has to transfer when you do this, so you're not saving any download time! A real thumbnail is a small file created from a larger one; many graphics programs can do this for you.

Don't Put Text in Graphics

Take a look at Figure 10.2. (I found this at the **World Travel Net** site, though I'm not sure that the site is still up and running: http://www.world-travel-net.co. uk/country/usa_hom.htm.) This page loads very slowly. This may be operating off of a slow server, because the images aren't absolutely huge: Doctor HTML tells me that it has 49.4k of image files. But the Web author could improve things a little here by cutting down on the use of images. Notice that much of the page is text—but all the text on this page is in the images; there's no real text transferred. Does that huge UNITED STATES OF AMERICA banner have to be a picture, for instance? How about BOOK NOW! and WORLD COUNTRY GUIDE. Couldn't it be text, which will transfer very quickly? Yes, of course it could.

If You're Not an Artist, Don't Pretend You Are

Some of us are artistically challenged. If that classification includes you, don't try to be an artist and design something really flashy. Leave it up to the professionals or limit yourself to designs that you're fairly sure you can manage. In particular, be careful when modifying text and background colors or when using background patterns.

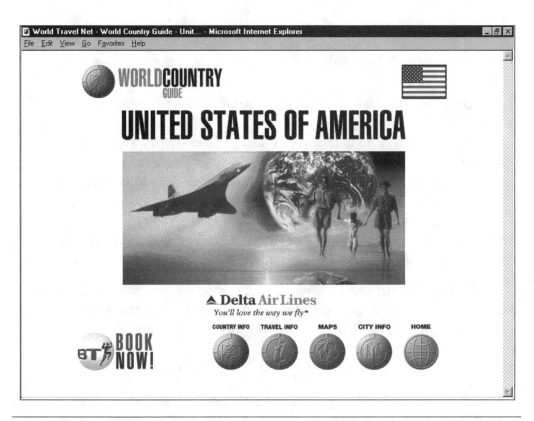

Figure 10.2: Why put text in images when real text transfers so much more quickly?

Have you heard the phrase "Kidnap-note desktop publishing"? It refers to the ugly effect created when one of us artistically challenged computer users gets hold of a desktop-publishing program and a collection of fonts. You've got the fonts, so, well—why not use them? In fact, why not use them all on one page? The effect is ugly, but in our enjoyment of the power provided by modern computing, we don't seem to notice.

The same thing is happening with Web pages. It's just so easy to add a background image. So easy to change text colors, so easy to modify the background color, so easy to drop pictures in here and there and everywhere else. The effect can be quite disgusting. The problem is that we have the power to make all these changes, but not necessarily the artistic sensibility to do it in a way that creates a visually pleasing document. All too often we come up with something that looks like a scene from *Beavis and Butthead Teach Web Design*.

I've seen all sorts of nasty combinations, such as these:

- Pages with dark-blue link text on dark-purple backgrounds—almost unreadable
- Light-purple clicked-link text on dark-purple backgrounds—even more unreadable
- Bright-green text on a dark-green background—what were they thinking?
- Text that crosses from a white background area onto a background area containing a complicated image—the text seems to merge into the image, making it very hard to read
- Incredibly bright and ugly backgrounds that overwhelm the page— distracting all attention from the text.

Incidentally, it's not just at "amateur" sites that you see bad combinations of colors and patterns, but even on sites run by multimillion-dollar companies. As for background patterns, here are a couple of rules of thumb:

Wood-grain backgrounds are always ugly.

Ninety-nine percent of backgrounds found in image libraries are too gaudy for use by anyone but high school kids.

Think carefully about your color and background combinations, and make sure you're not creating some kind of monster. Remember, the color and pattern combinations should work with your message, not submerge the message. In particular, make sure the contrast is sufficient to allow people to read your pages. That may seem obvious, but it's apparently not so obvious to thousands of Web authors.

Cute Can Confuse

Cute's very nice, but does it hide your message? For instance, take a look at Figure 10.3. This is a page I found at the **Coca-Cola** Web site (http://www. cocacola.com/). What do all these icons mean? The six at the top are bad enough. What are *Tour de Jour, Mind Candy, Bits O' History, Curvy Canvas, Netalogue,* and *E-cards*? *Netalogue* is probably a catalog where you can buy Coca-Cola stuff. *Bits O' History* is probably the museum, or something. *Curvy Canvas*? I've no idea. (By the way, Coca-Cola was kind enough to keep this site almost exactly

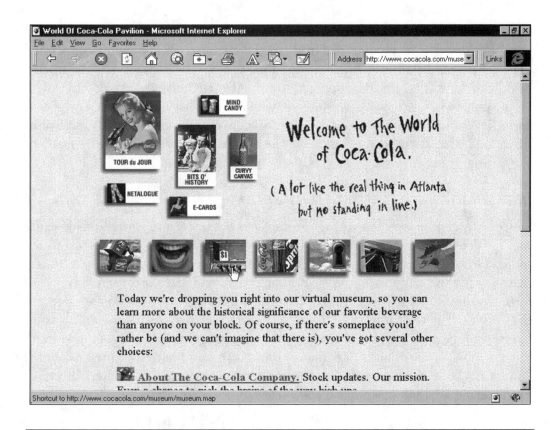

Figure 10.3: Do you know what these icons mean? No, nor do I.

the same so I didn't have to bother resnapping the image two years after the first edition.)

But the really bad bits are the pictures on the icon bar: someone carrying a crate of coke, a mouth, a cash register, a Coke bottle, a keyhole, something I thought was a toilet cistern at first but is probably really a turnstile, and a rooster, I think. What is all this? I don't know, and I'll bet that unless you spend time at this site, you don't either. But I'm not going to spend enough time to find out.

Cute is okay, I suppose, as long as it doesn't interfere with understanding and the visitor's ability to move around your Web site.

Spell It Out

This is, to some degree, the flip side of "Cute Can Confuse." Make it easy for your visitors to find what they are looking for. Use straightforward and understandable language that anyone can understand. For instance, a small publisher decided to change the link titled Masthead after people complained that they couldn't find information about how to contact the company. Masthead might seem obvious to some visitors, though even some who understand what the word masthead means ("the listing in a newspaper or periodical of information about its staff, operation, and circulation") might not figure out what it's used for here. Use *Contact Information, Contact Us Here,* or something quite obvious.

Longs Links are Better Than Short

Short links can be very confusing. Some Web designers use short links because they're nice and tidy. You can line them up and they don't take up too much room. Or you can create image links, in which every link is placed on a button that's exactly the same size. Looks very nice. Unfortunately this is an example of form triumphing over function, because short links are often confusing. Because the designer has to "force" the link into a particular size, it may be ambiguous. It seems to me common sense that a link that is long enough to explain what it's for has to be better than a link that is limited in size for design reasons, but if you don't believe me, read the study of the subject at the **User Interface Engineering** site: http://world.std.com/~uieweb/bookexpt.htm.

Be Careful with Links

Not so long ago, every Web site seemed to be a links site; you'd arrive at a Web page and be presented with links to other Web sites. One computer-magazine review of a Web-authoring tool stated that the secret to a "successful" Web site is adding lots of links. Complete nonsense, of course.

Links are a double-edged sword. You might add links as a service to your visitors, but remember that links take people away from you. Imagine setting up a shop in a mall or on Main Street. When visitors walk into your store, they're presented with a list of great things they can do somewhere else; there's a park just down the road, great food a couple of stores down, and by the way, if you want to view a movie, there are five running right now just across the street. A stupid way to do business, isn't it? So why do so many Web sites operate on the "Welcome to our Web site, now leave" system?

The World Wide Web is a hypertext system, and one of the great features touted by the early proponents of hypertext was that everything would be linked together; if the reader finds something interesting in one document, he can jump to another document that will provide more information. The idea was, for some hypertext advocates, a sort of limitless linking of information—

whatever related information you needed, you'd be able to find. Unfortunately, in the real world of the Web that's not always such a good idea.

You could put a link on virtually every word in a document if you really wished, but it would be horribly confusing. Still, I've seen people try to do this. For instance, imagine the following sentence in a document from a company selling hardware for IBM PCs: "Our widget board fits IBM-compatible PCs to dramatically improve the speed at which your JPEG images display during editing, and to serve coffee whenever you need it." You could have a link on the word widget across to the International Association of Widget Manufacturers' Widget Description page, a link on IBM to http://www.ibm.com/, of course, a link on JPEG to the JPEG Playground Web site, then a link on coffee to the Coffee Talk's Lists and Links site. Very nice—using all the capabilities of hypertext to allow users to leave your site for several different reasons.

The problem is not just that you risk sending your visitors elsewhere, but that a page stuffed full of links is confusing. Remember, you're trying to lead your visitors where you want them to go or at least make it easy for them to find what they are looking for. Put too many links on a page, and you'll prompt the question: "What do they want me to do next?"

Think about the purpose of links. They're there for a few reasons. They're there to assist the visitor in moving around in your site, and they're there for you to lead the visitor in a particular direction. Of course those are generally internal links, links within your Web site. However, links may also be there as a service to your visitors, though only to the extent that they serve your purpose, of course, as we discussed in the previous chapter.

So we come to the question of link pages, or meta-indexes, as they're sometimes known. Should you provide a list of links leading away from your site, as a service to your visitors? Well, maybe. Many sites use such links as the draw that brings visitors to the site in the first place. The search engines, for instance, are based on this principle. Why do visitors come to the search engines and directories? So they can use links to leave again as soon as possible. Many Web sites provide lists of links as ways to attract people, and that's a valid use of such links. But if your site does this, you still want to make sure visitors who come just for the links see something else that attracts the eye; you want to make sure your main message—the product or idea you are trying to promote—gets noticed by the visitors. So on the links pages make sure you have prominent links back into your site.

If you're not using your list of links to bring people to your site, think carefully about whether you should bother having external links at all. They'll act as a conduit taking people away from your site, and as they're not bringing people into your site ... what's the point?

When you add a link, think about why you are adding it and what purpose it serves. If it doesn't serve a purpose, remove it. And here's a quick tip for including links and making sure that people don't leave your site when they use them. Set up the links so that the referenced page is displayed in a new window. That is, they'll still have the window open showing them your Web site, and the newly loaded page will be in a different window. To do that, add the target="windowname" attribute to the link, like this:

```
<a href="http://www.poorrichard.com/"
target="Window1">Click Here</a>
```

This makes the visitor's browser open a new window, and places the http://www.poorrichard.com document in that window. The new window will even have an "internal" name, Window1 (internal in the sense that the visitor won't see this name, but the browser knows the name). So if the user then clicks on a different link, a link targeting Window1, the new page is loaded into that window.

If you have a huge list of links, and want them all to load into a window named Window1, you don't need to add the target attribute to all your links. Instead you can use something called the <BASE> tag. Place this at the top of your Web page, before the <BODY> tag, and enter something like this:

```
<base href="Window1">
```

Now all links on that page will open their referenced documents into Window1. For those few links that you don't want to act in this manner—links that take the visitor to other pages at your site, for instance—use this target attribute inside the link:

```
TARGET="_top"
```

Tell Your Visitor What to Do

If I had a dollar for every time I've visited a Web site, read a little, and then thought "what am I supposed to do next," I wouldn't be writing this book, I'd be managing my investments. A lot of Web sites really are set up like the proverbial billboard, as if they're ads that people glance at as they drive by. But a Web site can be much more, so it should be much more—otherwise you're just wasting good electrons.

Have you asked your visitors to do something? Not just sign a guest book—that's a little lame, really; why should they bother? No, have you asked them for their e-mail addresses so you can inform them the next time you release a new or revised product, so you can send them special offers, so you can send them your free mailing list?

Have you asked your visitors to place an order? A maxim in sales is that you must ask for the order—don't just hope that the sales prospect will buy from you. So if you're selling something at your site, have you asked the visitor for the sale? Have you led the visitor to a sales form? Have you reminded the visitor of the benefits of your product, reminded the visitor of your great guarantee? Don't believe what people have been saying for the last year or two—that the Internet changes everything. It doesn't. It's a new tool, but basic human nature remains the same; you have to ask for the sale or ask for action in the real world, and you have to do the same on the Web.

Create a Footer

Consider using a footer at the bottom of each page. The footer can include copyright information and a contact e-mail address, for instance. You might even want to include your URL in the page footer and on your contact-information page (more of which below). It may seem obvious, but it could be a handy reminder to visitors of how to find you again, and is also useful if the page is printed using a browser that doesn't automatically print the page's URL; most do, but some don't.

Microsoft FrontPage, by the way, allows you to create a single footer file, then automatically include that file at the bottom of every page. Then if you have to change any information, you only have to change it once. Few other products provide a feature like this, though it's possible to do it using a more complicated method known as server includes.

Don't Forget Contact Information

Have you provided contact information so that a visitor can get his questions answered? At the very least you should have an e-mail address, and ideally you should also include a phone number and mail address. I'm amazed at the number of Web sites that provide no way to contact the site owner, except perhaps a Webmaster's e-mail address. Don't use Webmaster addresses, by the way—include addresses of people or departments with real, recognizable, sensible titles: *sales, information, customer service*, and so on. And don't hide this contact information away; make it easy to find.

Including a telephone number can be very important. Some surveys have shown that a significant proportion—perhaps 70 percent—of sales made at a Web site are not really made in cyberspace at all, they're made when the visitor calls a telephone number. If you have a sales number, include it on the Web site, or you may lose sales.

It's the World Wide Web, Stupid!

Remember, it's the World Wide Web—not the U.S. Web, not the North American Web, not the First World Web, but the World Wide Web. Think about the people you want to talk to, and how important it is to have a site that's understandable to people from places other than the country or region in which you live.

Now, I'm not talking about language here, though some companies may want or need to set up multiple Web sites. (In fact, the Internet has given English, already the world's most important language, an enormous boost.) I'm talking attitude. If you want your information to be available to people of all nations and regions, keep that in mind and think about how your words may be misinterpreted or how they may paint a picture you don't intend.

Netscape recently had the following link at their Web site: "Enter now to win a week-long Caribbean cruise." Not a bad idea—I'd like a Caribbean cruise, I thought. I clicked on the link and discovered that it goes to the AmericaOne page; all you need to do is to make a donation to "Help the U.S. win back the America's Cup," and you could win a cruise. The problem with this is that it might be mildly irritating to many of this Web site's visitors. It shows a very provincial attitude. Here's a company doing business worldwide, but acting as if it's doing business locally. Yes, this was on the English-language Web site—they have others in different languages—but that means they get visitors from the United Kingdom, Canada, Australia, South Africa, Hong Kong, Singapore, India, Sri Lanka, New Zealand, as well as all the speakers of languages that don't have Netscape Web sites.

Another example: I once ran across a Microsoft Network Web site that reviewed Web soap operas. The Microsoft Network is an international network, and Microsoft is, of course, very much an international company. The author of this particular Web page seemed to be stuck in the rut of narrow-minded provincialism, though, criticizing one Web soap opera for using British, instead of American, spelling.

Of course that raises an important issue. How far should you go to cater to foreign audiences? Should British Web sites "internationalize" by using American spellings? No, no more than American Web sites should use British spellings. Most people accept and understand certain national and regional differences, but it's up to you to consider who your audience is, and to create the Web site appropriately. Some specifics:

- If you create a feedback or registration form, consider that different nations format addresses and telephone numbers differently. Design your forms so that they'll accept different types of information.

- Most of the world uses the metric system. If you want to do business with other nations and have to describe products using measurements, consider using kilos instead of pounds, meters instead of yards, or use both systems.

- Include information for shipping products overseas. If you sell books, for instance, why limit your sales to one nation? Include shipping charges for different regions around the world. (As you'll see in Chapter 13, that's easier said than done, as most shopping-cart systems don't make shipping overseas easy.)

- Include specific billing information. If you accept checks, you might want to specify that you accept only checks drawn on U.S. banks if that's the case. Accepting credit cards helps, of course, as Visa, MasterCard, and American Express are international systems.

- Specify the currency. It's possible to set up a Web site that is not identifiably "in" any particular country. So if you state that a product is 30 dollars, do you mean U.S. dollars or Australian dollars? Or Canadian, Bahamian, Belizian, Fijian, Hong Kong, or Zimbabwe dollars?

- Consider what to do if you get orders in foreign languages, or perhaps specify on the order form the languages that you can handle.

If you're interested in having your Web pages translated, you can often find translators at local colleges—or look on the Web. Try **Yahoo!'s Translation Services** page, where you can find scores of translation services and even services that specialize in translating Web sites (http://www.yahoo.com/Business_and_Economy/Companies/Communications_and_Media_Services/Translation_Services/). There are also a number of software translation services on the Web, in which you can enter text or a URL pointing to a Web site, and the program will translate it for you. *These systems do not work!* Sure, some of the words—okay, most of the words—will be translated correctly. Consider this e-mail machine-translated from German, talking about the German edition of *Poor Richard's Web Site*:

Dear Mr. Kent, I reads even with large interest its book "the ABC of the own web page". Probably best which I read until today. I am beginner since ca.2Wochen.Vieleicht can you times my web page look at themselves and you judge. Unfortunately I do not have anybody me times for problems help or which I for advice to ask kann.So I must make everything independent beibringen.Ich am even thereby me and do not think the one-own homepage to be very helpful can nevertheless I white simply as I mean homepage into the search machines enter in such a way that it can I from you assistance expect it me also found much would make happy. My PAGE is in the address: http://xxx.xxxxxx.xxxxxx.de I thanks you in vorraus and hopes you writes also in the future still many as good books as which before me is situated. With being pleased DL greeting ...

If that translation's okay with you, then go ahead and use the translation services.

Forget the Visit Counter

You know those little visit counters you see on so many pages? The ones that say, "You're the umpteenth visitor since whenever"? Well, forget it. They're just another bit of cute clutter that your page can do without, and they're very cliché, too. Worse, they're often bad advertising. Now and then you'll run across counters showing that the site has had a few dozen or a couple of hundred visitors. It's almost as if the Web designer is saying, "Hey, come visit us! Nobody else does, and we could do with the attention!"

Spell-Check and Edit

Don't forget to run your spell checker and have someone edit your site. With more than one or two spelling mistakes, your site's going to start to look amateurish—more than one or two grammar mistakes, and people are going to stop taking you seriously.

You could use an electronic grammar checker; many word processors have these now. I wouldn't bother, though—the grammar checkers are a little stupid, finding mistakes where none exist and trying to make your writing conform to some kind of cookie-cutter writing style. See if you can find a real person to check the text for you.

What About "Click Here" Links?

I've seen writers advise that you should never use a "click here" link, that is, a link that says something like this: "If you want more information, click here."

Personally I don't fully agree with this advice. I'd modify it to say that "click here" links are generally not necessary—people know that they're supposed to click on links to operate them—but that they can be useful in some cases. I'd also say that if all or most of your links are "click here" links, your site will look a little amateurish.

It's generally not necessary to say "click here" because what the visitor is supposed to do is, in most cases, obvious. For instance, you may have a bulleted list, with several entries: *More Information*, *Tell Us What You Think*, *Useful Links*, and so on. Each line can be a link, and visitors will realize what's going on. On the other hand, there are occasions when you do want to spell out what you want the user to do, and simply placing a link on a word just isn't enough or perhaps sounds strange. For instance, if you want people to send you feedback, you might say, "If you want to tell us what you think of this site, click here," with the link on the *click here* portion. To me that sounds fine, and certainly better than a link in the middle of the paragraph that says merely, "You can tell us what you think of this site." Sometimes adding the phrase "click here" allows you to mix both text and hypertext in a manner that makes sense.

Also note that some experts in Internet advertising claim that the words "click here" actually increase the rate of clicks. So don't assume that "click here" is a horrible faux pas; on occasion it may make a lot of sense.

Be Careful with Frames

Frames are panels that open in browser windows at some Web sites. You've seen them, I'm sure. You arrive at a Web site, and all of a sudden your browser window splits into two or more pieces, each piece containing a different document.

Frames are a double-edged sword. They can be very useful in some cases, a complete nuisance in others. There are a few issues to consider when using frames. First, a lot of people hate them, probably because they're so often misused—and partly because Netscape Navigator 2, the first frames-capable browser, often crashed when displaying frames. So unless you feel frames are really serving a purpose, avoid them.

And how are they misused? Well, many authors use too many frames. Personally I believe that in most situations two frames is the maximum, because many Web users are working in VGA mode—640 pixels wide by 480 pixels high. If you just have to use frames, check them in VGA mode and see how little room you have in each document. I've heard of sites using nine frames, which is completely ridiculous. I've seen many using four, which is very awkward in VGA.

Another problem is the way in which authors configure their frames. It's possible to set a frame to be scrollable or nonscrollable. Many authors create their frames in a high-resolution mode and set them as nonscrollable, not realizing that in VGA mode, parts of the documents are offscreen. Visitors working in VGA mode cannot see the entire document, and, because the frames are nonscrollable, can't even scroll down and view the rest.

So, to sum up, if you don't need frames, don't use them. If you do, use them sensibly and test in VGA mode.

The Final Rule

Before we move on, one final rule:

All rules can be broken, but you'd better really know what you're doing.

As in most areas of life, rules are made to be broken. However, it takes real skill to break rules and get away with it. If you don't have a good reason to break a rule, and if you are not sure you can do so without creating an ugly, irritating, or useless site, then don't bother trying.

Read through your Web pages periodically. You'll often find things you wrote earlier that are no longer applicable.

Get Some Help—Design Books and Templates

Why not get a little help? Many Web-authoring programs provide templates you can use. Simply load the template, modify the text and graphics, and you have a finished Web page. There are also a number of good books on design. I'd recommend *Home Page Improvement*, by my friend Elisabeth Parker (IDG Books, ISBN:0-76453-083-6; http://www.byteit.com/HPIWeb/), though it's out of print at the moment (perhaps back in print sometime). This provides lots of tips for using colors, laying out pages using frames and tables, working with graphics, and so on. It's all aimed at the nonprofessional—unlike many other design books that are clearly intended for someone who's willing to spend a lot of time working on design, the sort of books that discuss complicated procedures using expensive art programs. *Home Page Improvement* provides simple, low-cost things you can do to spiff up your pages.

Be very careful, though. Consider what your primary goal is. Is it to design a really cool Web site, or is it to promote your products, services, or ideas? Playing with Web design is a lot of fun, so the danger is that you'll be distracted from your main purpose. There are thousands of cool little tools to help you with your site, thousands of things you can do to make your site look great. But the time you spend on these things is time that could be used to promote the site, so use these tools and techniques judiciously, and try not to get carried away.

You may also find books with CDs containing Web-page templates. One I used that you may find useful is the *Web Design Templates Source Book*, by Lisa Schmeiser (New Riders, ISBN:1-56205-754-5; http://merchant.superlibrary.com:8000/catalog/mcp/PRODUCT/PAGE/15620/bud/1562057545.html). This contains almost 500 templates, for a variety of different purposes. Just view them in your Web browser, and when you find the one you need, copy it from the CD to your authoring program, then modify it to suit your site. Such templates are a fantastic resource for the design-challenged, among whom I count myself!

## Chapter Eleven

Web Sites Are Two-Way Streets— Adding Interaction

A long time ago I saw an ad in a local paper from a Web-design company. "Build your own billboard on the World Wide Web," it said. You've probably heard this bit of nonsense, haven't you, about how a Web site is like a billboard? Well, it's not, and it's a good thing it's not. A Web site can't work like a billboard, because people won't see it unless you bring them to the site (a subject we'll discuss in Chapters 16 to 21). A real billboard can be seen by people as they just happen to drive or walk by, but the Web doesn't work like that.

But not only is a Web site not like a billboard, it's foolish to try to make one work like a billboard. I see these all the time—Web sites that just sit there. You read them, they tell you a little about a product, perhaps, and then you leave because there's nothing else to do. That's a lousy way to build a Web site, because a Web site can do so much more.

Web Sites Should Do More

A Web site should engage the visitor in some kind of interaction to draw the visitor in. A Web site should be used to make the visitor take some kind of action that furthers the purpose of the Web site. I'm not talking about some useless but cute little game, I'm not talking about unnecessary JavaScript or ActiveX controls, I'm talking about things like this:

- **A form in which the user can register for something**—A free newsletter, information updates about your products, free "stuff" sent directly to them periodically.

- **A discussion group**—In which visitors can talk with your staff or with other Web-site visitors. By discussion group I mean a newsgroup-type system, in which visitors can read other people's messages, post their own, and return later to see if there have been any responses.

- **A chat group**—In which visitors can chat in real time with your staff or other visitors. By chat group I mean a system in which a user types a message, and someone else can view and respond to the message almost immediately. These are ideal for technical-support groups, periodic "lectures," celebrity chats, and just plain chats between visitors interested in your products.

- **Feedback forms**—Used to gather information from users. Carry out surveys to find out what your customers want—what they want from your Web site and what they want from your products. Find out what they like about your products and what they don't like. Gather testimonials that you can use in your marketing materials, ask them about your competitors and how your products compare, find out more about your customer's interests, demographic profiles and geographic locations, and so on.

- **Hold contests and give away free products**—A great way to attract people to your Web site and to gather e-mail addresses that you can use for product announcements later.

- **Announce new products**—And ask visitors to fill in a form so you can inform them when the products are available. You might sweeten the offer a little by giving a special discount to customers on your mailing list.

- **Find product reviewers**—Writers and journalists have a very high rate of Internet use, so many of the people you need to contact to promote your product already have Internet access. Once you've brought them to your Web site, you can get them to apply for a review product or press kit by filling out a Web form.

- **Set up a classified-ads page**—Where visitors can post information about products they have to sell, or read other posts. This could serve the same purpose as a links page, another service that attracts visitors to your site.

- **Allow people to add links**—If you use a links page (a meta-index) as a way of attracting people to your site, why not allow people to add their own links? For instance, if you are setting up *The World's Greatest Emu Farming Web Site*, you can have links to all the emu sites on the

Web (right now that's an easy job, but who knows what the future holds). Visitors who know of emu sites you haven't listed can fill in a form to add their own. You might have a separate Visitor's Links page.

Use your imagination and spend some time on the Web seeing what other people are doing, and I'm sure you can come up with other ideas.

Here are some real-life examples, from my own experience. Just recently I set up a form at which people could sign up to win a copy of *Poor Richard's E-mail Publishing*, the third book in this *Poor Richard's* series. It's written by Chris Pirillo, the publisher of a newsletter called *Lockergnome*, which goes to around 150,000 people every day. Chris announced the drawing in his newsletter, and over 5,700 came to the form to enter the contest. Over the three days of the contest we sold thousands of dollars worth of books, and we signed up around 3,800 new subscribers for my own newsletter, **Poor Richard's Web Site News** (http://PoorRichard.com/newsltr/). In fact I'd added a couple of Yes/No option buttons on the contest entry form, so the entrants could decide whether they wanted to sign up for the newsletter.

I've used forms for lots of contests, in fact. I also have forms at my site, on various pages, where people can subscribe to my newsletter. I've used response forms as simple order forms, too (a subject we'll look at in Chapter 13). I've set up discussion groups, though to be honest I've never really followed through with them … I've got enough things to do without finding time to run a discussion group as well!

Creating Forms on Your Web Pages

There's a problem with all this talk of interaction: it's not necessarily easy to create. In order to make a Web page interactive, you have to create forms. That part is easy—there's a set of HTML tags designed for form creation, such as <input type="text"> (a simple text box), <input type="checkbox"> (a check box), and <input type="radio"> (a radio or option button). The problem is that HTML itself can't really do much with forms. It can't provide true interaction—all it can do is send the contents of the form somewhere else, so that a program can manipulate the form contents in some way. In other words, in order to make a Web site interactive, you must add some kind of program, such as the following:

- A **CGI** (Common Gateway Interface) script, the first type of program used to add interactivity to Web pages
- A **CGI-like system** such as PHP or Miva

- **JavaScript**, a relatively simple scripting language that will run in Internet Explorer and Netscape Navigator
- **JScript**, Microsoft's answer to JavaScript; it contains some JavaScript commands plus a few other commands not present in JavaScript
- **Java**, a full-blown—that is, complicated—programming language used to create programs that can run in a Web browser or at the Web server
- **ActiveX**, Microsoft's answer to Java; it runs in Internet Explorer but not, at the time of writing, in Netscape Navigator
- A special scripting language used by an **HTML-authoring product** of some kind, such as Microsoft FrontPage
- A **utility service** at another Web site.

Which of these should you use? Well, in some cases your Web-hosting company will already have some templates ready to use, CGI scripts that they've configured for use on their server. You may find that your hosting company has made it very easy for you to quickly modify a script to make it work in your site ... and you may not.

So let's say your hosting company *hasn't* provided such easy-to-use scripts. What next? The easiest systems, from the list we just looked at, are the last two, utility services and products such as Microsoft FrontPage. (Well, I say "such as," but practically speaking it's just FrontPage, because only FrontPage has its "server extensions" installed on thousands of Web-hosting companies' servers.) Some people may also want to try to use CGI scripts to create the sorts of interaction that a utility service or their authoring product cannot create.

If you use FrontPage or some other kind of product with built-in scripting, you won't have to do any programming. You'll have to learn the authoring program's form-creation tools—and learn them well—but the program will do all the scripting for you. For instance, if you want to create a discussion group, Microsoft FrontPage can do it for you in a few minutes. Discussion groups are quite complicated examples of Web-site interaction. You have to have a page with a form where a visitor can type a message. The message title, once submitted by a visitor to your site, must be added to a list of messages that other visitors can view. This list should be organized in threads so you can quickly see messages that are responses to earlier messages. Readers must be able to view the message texts and respond to them.

All this is quite tricky to create; it might take a programmer a few days to put a simple discussion group together from scratch. You can buy discussion-group programs ready-made for between $50 and $400, or you can use a product such as FrontPage that will create a group for you in a few minutes. If you don't use FrontPage, you can also use a freeware discussion-group program (I'll talk more about discussion groups below).

Even if you have FrontPage or a similar tool, it won't do everything for you. There may be things you want to do that it can't help you with, such as set up chat groups or shopping-cart systems. You can still use ready-made CGI scripts, though. There are many free and low-cost scripts available on the Web (I'll explain where to find these below), so you can modify them to make them fit your site.

What about JavaScript, JScript, Java and ActiveX? All are complicated. In order to use these, you need to be a programmer. You may be able to find scripts you can use, though they will probably be fairly simple and of not much use. If you are prepared to spend a lot of time learning JavaScript or JScript, or you don't mind paying someone else, you can create relatively sophisticated programs (for an example, see my **JavaScript Area Code Application** at http://TopFloor. com/javascript1.2/19-1.htm). If you are prepared to spend a huge amount of time to learn Java or ActiveX or a great deal of money paying a programmer, you can get very sophisticated systems. Many large Web sites, for instance, use Java working in the background to take orders.

However, if you're creating your Web site on a modest budget, you'll probably want to avoid these things and stick with the utility services, Microsoft FrontPage, and CGI scripts. They're low-cost and relatively easy to work with. (Note that I say *relatively* easy; while the first two are easy, fooling around with CGI scripts can be very frustrating, but it's still much easier than JavaScript or Java programming.) And the scripts you'll be using have no compatibility problems, either. A CGI script or FrontPage script will work with any Web browser that can display forms. That's not the case with JavaScript and JScript—these scripting languages have serious compatibility problems: a script that works well in one browser might not work at all in another browser. (For an example of what I mean, take a look at the **JavaScript Weirdness** page at http://nctweb.com/articles/javascript_limitations.html). This applies to Java and ActiveX, too—although Java works, in theory, in most users' browsers these days, that doesn't mean it works well, and ActiveX is limited to less than seventy-five percent of all users' browsers at present.

Utility Services

Perhaps the easiest way to create forms and interactivity at your Web site is through the use of a utility service. There are a number of services around the Web that allow you to set up forms at your site and direct the output to programs running on their Web servers.

When you send data to the program. For instance, take a look at this code:

```
<form action="http://www.bravenet.com/emailfwd/
senddata.asp" method="POST">
<INPUT type=hidden name=userid value=ce211fg2202>
<INPUT type=hidden name=webpage value=Submission_Review>
```

The <form> tag tells the Web browser what to do when the user clicks on a Submit button. In this case it's being told to send information from the form to http://www.bravenet.com/emailfwd/senddata.asp. The bravenet.com site is a utility service, and senddata.asp is a program running at that site. You'll also notice that the next line is a hidden form field, called userid. This sends an ID number (in this case ce211fg2202) to the program, identifying this information as coming from your Web site. There's also another hidden field, one that identifies the Web page.

So as you can see, you can place a form on your Web site, but run it on another site. What type of forms and services can you use? These sorts of things:

- Address books (that can be shared by friends and colleagues)
- Autoresponders
- Cartoons (they change periodically)
- Chat rooms
- Classified ads
- Countdown timers
- E-mail forms (forms that e-mail the information to you)
- Forums (message boards)
- Free For All links (pages that allow visitors to your site to add links)
- Greeting cards
- Guest books
- Hit counters and site statistics
- Mailing lists (for newsletters and discussion groups)
- Navigation tools (such as drop-down list boxes or buttons that act as links)
- Random links (the page the visitor is sent to when clicking on the link is picked randomly)
- Referral tools (so visitors can let their friends and colleagues know about your site)

- Search utilities
- Web "polls" (visitors can vote at your site).

I won't go into detail about how to set these things up. You'll need to know a little HTML, though not a lot. And each service functions differently. Here are a few places to find such services:

1-2-3 Web Tools
 http://www.freeguestbooks.com/

agum Network
 http://www.agum.com/utilities.htm

Beseen
 http://www.beseen.com/

BigInfo.Net (a list of around 50 free-utility services)
 http://www.biginfo.net/pages/FreeServices/

BoingDragon's Lair
 http://boingdragon.com/

Bravenet
 http://www.bravenet.com/

CGI Free
 http://www.cgi-free.com/

CGI-Resource Index (lists over 460 utilities!)
 http://www.cgi-resources.com/Programs_and_Scripts/Remotely_Hosted/

Homestead
 http://www.homestead.com/

i-DEPTH
 http://www.i-depth.com/

Inside the Web (free message boards)
 http://www.insidetheweb.com/

Komy.Net
 http://www.komy.net/

TheFreeSite.com
 http://www.thefreesite.com/freejava.htm

ToolZone
 http://www.toolzone.com/

ukibi (an online address book)
 http://www.ukibi.com/

Finding CGI Scripts

Utility services are often the simplest way to get a form into place and functioning. But if you can't find quite what you need, you might want to work with CGIs. There are hundreds of useful scripts that you can use for free. Ask your Web-hosting company. Many provide libraries of useful CGI scripts, and the great advantage to using one of these is that it probably won't require much modification to set it up and you may be able to get help. The CGI script will probably already be installed on the server, saving you the trouble and disk space. Second, look through some of the following sites:

CGI City
http://www.cgicity.com/

The CGI Collection
http://www.itm.com/cgicollection/

CGI Now
http://www.cgi-now.com/cgi-now/

CGI Resources (large CGI site)
http://www.cgi-resources.com/
http://cgi.resourceindex.com/

CGI101.com
http://www.cgi101.com/

Dale Bewley's Perl Scripts and Links (a huge list of CGI resource sites)
http://www.bewley.net/perl/

Extropia (public-domain scripts, or pay for support)
http://www.extropia.com/products.html

Freescripts
http://www.freescripts.com/

GetFreeScripts
http://www.getfreescripts.com/

Matt's Script Archive (a very well-known CGI site)
http://www.worldwidemart.com/scripts/

PerlCrawler (a search engine that helps you find CGI resources)
http://perlsearch.hypermart.net/

Q&D Software Development (has a special program for creating Web forms)
http://www.q-d.com/

The Scripts Home
http://www.virtualcenter.com/scripts2/

Yahoo!—CGI Page
http://dir.yahoo.com/Computers_and_Internet/Internet/World_Wide_Web/
CGI___Common_Gateway_Interface/

Yahoo!—Web Software Companies
http://dir.yahoo.com/Business_and_Economy/Companies/Computers/
Software/Internet/World_Wide_Web/

If you are looking for CGI scripts, there's an important consideration you mustn't forget: you can use only CGI scripts that are designed to work in the operating system on which your Web server is running. For instance, if your Web-hosting company is using a Windows NT Web server or a Macintosh Web server, you won't be able to use CGI scripts that were designed for UNIX. That's another advantage of using scripts provided by your Web-hosting company, of course: they'll be scripts designed to work with that company's Web server. However, this isn't usually a major problem—most scripts will run on UNIX servers, so unless you are working with an NT or Macintosh server, most of the scripts you run across will work. CGI scripts are text files. You simply copy them to your computer and make any changes that are required in a text editor. Then you copy them to the Web server, making sure that you set your FTP program to do an ASCII transfer. That's the theory, anyway;

Because CGI scripts are generally designed to run on UNIX computers, you may find them stored in .tar files at the CGI libraries. A .tar file is a "tape archive" file, a file that contains multiple files "wrapped up" inside. Many decompression utilities—such as WinZip—can open .tar files. To extract the files from within a .tar file that's sitting on a UNIX system, use Telnet to go to the directory and type tar -xvf filename.tar, *then press Enter.*

with some sophisticated scripts it can be quite tricky to get them set up correctly if you're not used to working with CGIs. Don't worry, though; I'll explain how you may be able to get them installed for a small sum.

Here are a few ideas for the sorts of things you can do with free CGI scripts. I found these at some of the sites mentioned earlier; they're not all designed for interaction with users—some do things that don't require input from the visitors—but you may find some of the noninteraction scripts useful nonetheless.

Matt's Script Archive

- Guestbook—Visitors can sign a page at your site.
- Free For All Links—Visitors can add links to a link-directory page.
- WWWBoard—A discussion group.
- Simple Search—Visitors can enter keywords to search your Web pages.
- Counter—A visit counter, using an image to show how many people have been to your site—as I mentioned in Chapter 10, you should probably forget this one.
- TextCounter—A text-based visit counter.
- FormMail—A popular script for mailing the contents of a form to any e-mail addresses you specify.
- Random Image Displayer—Displays an image or background from a collection, choosing at random.
- SSI Random Image Display—The same as the previous script, but this one also includes links and text. SSI means, in the world of CGI, server-side includes, an issue discussed in Chapter 4. An SSI script won't work unless your Web server allows server-side includes.
- Random Link Generator—Visitors click to go to a Web page selected at random. For example, you could use this to send people to a link chosen from your link directory.
- Random Text—Displays inside the Web page a portion of a text file chosen at random. You could use this to display a quote of the day or tip of the day, for instance.
- TextClock—Displays the time and date.
- Animation—Creates simple animations, though, as pointed out at this site, you can create GIF89a animations more simply.
- Countdown—Displays the time until a particular event or date occurs. You could use this as a reminder of some upcoming event you are planning, such as a product release or competition deadline.
- Credit Card Verifier—Checks credit-card numbers entered into a form to make sure they are in the correct format.
- Book 'em Dan-o—Logs visits to your site: the time, the domain the visitor is coming from, and the browser being used. (See Chapter 21 for a discussion of tracking activity at your site.)

The CGI Collection

This site has lots of useful scripts similar to ones I've mentioned already. It also has the following:

- Frame-Chat—Another Web-based chat program. Users can select from multiple chat rooms.
- PickMail—Search a list of people to find their e-mail addresses. This might be handy for a professional organization; visitors could search for a member they wanted to send e-mail to.
- Poll It—Visitors can take part in a poll.
- UDLoad—Allows visitors to upload files to your Web site. A shareware library could use this to allow visitors to submit software. Works only with browsers that allow software uploads, though most recent ones do.
- BookMark—Uses your Netscape bookmarks to create a Web page, placing each subfolder on a separate page; a quick way to create a set of links pages.
- Redirect—Visitors can use buttons, rather than links, to select another Web page.
- Internet Phonebook—Visitors can view and modify the contents of a phone book. This can be used for other purposes, too: modify the script to work as any kind of simple database. Visitors can use this script to submit e-mail addresses and URLs.
- Dir-It—Creates a set of Web pages based on the structure and contents of a directory. Visitors can then move around by viewing directory contents as links and text files.

Dale Bewley's Perl Scripts and Links

This is a very useful site with links to scores of mailing lists, discussion groups and CGI libraries, and some interesting scripts, such as the following:

- SlideShow—Produce a self-scrolling slide show displaying one page at a time
- Survey—Visitors can submit answers to surveys
- hform—Visitors can create their own Web pages at your site.

Another interesting script I found is **LW Gate,** a WWW Mailing List Gateway (http://www.netspace.org/users/dwb/lwgate.html). This script can be used to help visitors to your site subscribe to mailing lists and view mailing-list archives.

You can often run into problems working with scripts you find on the Web. They're often written by programmers who are far more interested in creating scripts than explaining how they work. These programmers write instructions that are often intelligible only to other programmers—it's strange, but whatever real-world language they speak, programmers can make themselves understood by other programmers but not necessarily by real people. So unfortunately you may find yourself spending a lot of time figuring out how the scripts work.

If you're willing to hire someone to customize a script for you, take a look at the **CGI Resources Programmer's Page** (http://www.cgi-resources.com/Programmers/) or the **CGI Collection Programmer's Page** (http://www.itm.com/cgicollection/index. cgi?page=10). Some of the other CGI sites probably have links to programmer listings, too. Some companies selling commercial CGI scripts include installation with the price or install for an extra fee. These guys know their scripts so well that they can install them very quickly; I've seen companies advertising installation of scripts for as little as $45. You may also find that your Web-hosting company will install CGIs for you—even CGIs that it doesn't have in its library. (The smaller hosting companies may do this; the larger ones are unlikely to.) It will probably charge around $50 an hour, but installing a simple CGI may take less than an hour.

Finally, be flexible when working with CGI scripts. A script that has been designed for one purpose can often be used to serve another. For instance, if you're using FrontPage, you have a way to create a discussion group very quickly. You don't, however, have a tool for creating a classified-ad page. However, you can modify a discussion group and set it up as a classified-ad page. Simply create a discussion group, setting it up as a group without threaded messages. Then people can send messages but can't reply to other people's messages. Each message will stand as an independent ad, not part of a "thread."

Here's another example. Above I mentioned the Internet Phonebook CGI script. This allows a visitor to enter his name, e-mail address, and Web-page URL. Visitors can also search the database for other people's entries. But there's nothing to say that the three fields have to be name, e-mail address, and URL. You could modify the script to allow people to enter their favorite links, for example: the three fields could be Web-page title, comments, and URL.

JavaScripts

Another way to add certain types of interactivity to your Web site is through the use of JavaScripts. Although working with JavaScript is far more complicated than CGIs, you may run into people selling JavaScript utilities that carry out some kind of function you want to add to your site; or you can simply borrow

JavaScripts from other sites (just open the Web page's source and copy the script). The major problem with JavaScript is that many browsers won't work with it. Well, actually, the two major problems with JavaScript are that many browsers won't work with it, and even the ones that do often don't work with it very well. One statistics site I looked at recently indicated that 10 percent of all users are working with browsers that won't run JavaScript—either the browser is simply incapable of running the scripts, or the user has turned off the feature. Personally I wouldn't trust JavaScript to do much at my sites (and I've written three books about JavaScript). I don't mind using it for little things that don't matter much if they don't work, but I wouldn't trust something important to it.

I use them now and then to open secondary windows. Of course you can do that with plain old HTML, as we saw in Chapter 10. But the problem with that is you have no control over what the window looks like. With JavaScript you can control the size and position of the window, and various other attributes. Here's how you'd do it. First, you'd drop the following script into the top of your Web page:

```
<SCRIPT LANGUAGE='JavaScript' </p>
<!--
// launch function

function launch() {
var win1= 
.open("","newwindow","width=600,height=400,screenY=200,sc
reenX=200,resizable=yes,toolbar=no,status=no,menubar=no,
scrollbars=yes");
    win1.focus()
}
//-->
</script>
```

This creates a *function*—which is, in effect, a little program waiting to be run—called launch(). Then you create a link like this:

```
<a href="store/six.htm" onclick="launch()"
target="newwindow">Your link text goes here</a>
```

When the visitor clicks on this link, it runs the launch() function (see the onclick attribute) and puts the six.htm document into the window called newwindow. And what, exactly, does the window look like? Well, you'll see from the launch()

function that it creates a window that is 600 pixels by 400, and that is positioned 200 pixels down from the top and 200 pixels across from the left, that is resizable, that doesn't have a toolbar, statusbar, or menu bar, and that does have scrollbars.

Without going into an explanation of why and how, the bit in the script that says win1.focus() does something else pretty handy; it ensures that if you're loading the document into a window that's already open, focus changes to that window. That is, rather than loading a window that is out of site, the window is brought into site.

All in all it's a useful little JavaScript, making the launching of secondary windows work much more smoothly. And if the person using the page is one of the 10 percent that doesn't have a JavaScript browser? Well, the link still works, it still opens a secondary window in the normal way.

This is a fairly simple JavaScript. They can get very complicated. If you want to learn JavaScript, read *The Official Netscape JavaScript Book* (Top Floor Publishing: http://TopFloor.com/javascript/), written by myself and my brother. We wrote this book for nonprogrammers, and it's received a great deal of praise (in a sense it's a programming primer using JavaScript as the example programming language).

And Other Stuff

You may also run across a variety of other CGI-like systems, such as the following:

Aestiva HTML/OS
   http://www.htmlos.com/
   http://www.aestiva.com/

Miva
   http://www.miva.com/

PHP (a public-domain scripting system, also fairly popular)
   http://www.php.net/

These other systems are similar to CGI scripts. They comprise a program that runs on the server; then Web authors can write scripts that use the program. In some cases the script is actually written inside the Web page, rather than in a separate file sitting on the server (Miva, for instance, works in that manner). The only reason I'm mentioning these other systems is that you may run across them; some Web-hosting companies have them installed on their servers. The average user will probably never use them, though.

Chapter Twelve

Interaction Examples

In Chapter 11 you had an overview of adding interaction to your Web site. In this chapter I want to discuss three particular situations—grabbing information from your visitors, discussion groups, and chat groups. I'll also show you an example, the Free For All Links CGI script.

Visitors Are Prospects—Grabbing Information

People visiting your site are, in general, business prospects. Why would they be there otherwise? If you are selling something, they're prospective clients. If you are running a professional organization's Web site, they're potential members or people who might hire your members. If you're selling advertising by keeping people at your site, they're potential repeat visitors.

One way or another, most visitors—all but people who've stumbled across your site by accident—are valuable to you, so it's a shame to allow people to visit your site and then wander off without providing you with some way to contact them. You should at least make some kind of effort to add these visitors to your mailing lists—both e-mail and snail-mail.

Now, I'm not talking about some furtive trick for stealing e-mail addresses. All I'm talking about is asking visitors to your Web site if you can add them to your e-mail list. Contact information is valuable, yet thousands of businesses are throwing away potential contacts. All it takes is a simple Web form, and you can start creating an e-mail mailing list right away, as soon as the next person views your site. But how do you get people to fill in the form? What's in it for them?

If you've managed to get users to your Web site, there's a very good chance that they're interested in your product. So why not offer them something more, something to entice them to give you their e-mail addresses? Here are a few ideas:

- Tell them you'll keep them up to date with your product's new releases by sending a periodic message informing them of changes.
- Give them a free subscription to a newsletter. Distributing an electronic newsletter is cheap and easy, so why not create one? You can include news about your industry, tips about working with your products, techniques employed by other users, and so on. Make the newsletter truly useful, though, and not simply an extended ad for your products. (We'll look at electronic newsletters in Chapter 14.)
- If you're selling software of some kind, or something that can be distributed in electronic form, you might combine the offer of a periodic message or newsletter with a freebie—the Web page containing the freebie is accessed after the user fills in the form, of course. If you're selling clip art, offer to give your visitors a few free samples; if you're selling programs, give them a free utility. You can give away music if you're in the music business, short stories or chapters from your books if you are a publisher, and so on.
- When you allow people to download a demo or shareware program from your site, make them fill in a form first. If you are worried about scaring people off and getting fewer downloads, structure the form to be nonthreatening. Ask users to fill it in so you can let them know when you update the program, but state that if the user prefers, he can just leave the form empty and click the Submit button.

It's surprising how many Web sites allow users to download software without grabbing contact information first. Don't make it a nuisance; don't force users to fill in a long and complicated form—make it quick and easy, and people will give you their e-mail addresses. You'll never get everyone's e-mail address, of course, but you will get many. At least make some kind of attempt to grab e-mail addresses. They're valuable and they're there for the taking.

There are basically two ways to grab information from a form. You can set up a form that sends the information to you via e-mail, or a form that saves the information in a file. Some scripts will even do both at the same time. The information in the file can then be imported into a database program. As you'll see in Chapter 14, it's very easy to set up a system that grabs information from incoming e-mail and drops it into a file that controls a mailing list, so you can build a mailing list with very little direct interaction on your part.

Consider what you want the form to do. If you merely want to grab people's names and e-mail addresses, all you need is to create fields for those items. You might also have a Comments field. In most cases, people won't fill in the Comments field, but this field can be a good way to get testimonials. For instance, while promoting my book, *Making Money in Technical Writing* (http://TopFloor.com/techwr/), I had a form that people could submit in order to win a free copy of the book. A number of people had read the first edition of the book and made some very nice comments about it. I then used these in a testimonial page at that Web site. On the other hand, if you have a Comments field it means you have to actually read the messages now and then, which you may not want to bother with.

If you're using Microsoft FrontPage you can very quickly create forms that will save information in a text file. If you're working with the very latest FrontPage, you can also create forms that will send e-mail messages to you.

Another popular way to send e-mail messages from a form is by using FormMail. If you'd like to see an example of how to set up **FormMail** to work at your Web site, see http://PoorRichard.com/examples/cgimail.htm.

Creating Discussion Groups

Many Web sites use discussion groups (also known as a bulletin boards, message boards, and sometimes a Web forum) as a way for people to discuss your products or simply as a service to people—a way to attract them to your Web site. For instance, setting up a discussion group for people interested in emus is one way to make your emu-lovers' site stand out. A discussion group can be part of an overall package that makes a site popular with a certain group of people, just one more element that attracts people to your site and keeps them coming back. You can even set up several groups for different purposes; once you've set up one, it's quite easy to set up another.

Here's another way to use a discussion group. Set up a week-long discussion with a celebrity or well-known person in your field. Your emu site might invite a successful emu farmer, a music site might invite a musician, a company selling software might invite the author of a book about their software, and so on. For one week, or however long this person is willing to take part, people can visit your site to pose questions and read the celebrity's responses.

There are a number of ways to create discussion groups. FrontPage has a wizard that helps you build one. If you're not using FrontPage, you might use a utility service to set one up—there are a number of places that will allow you to build discussion groups at their sites, and link into them from your own so that it appears to be part of your site. Here are a few such services:

CGI-Resource Index List of Remotely Hosted Programs and Scripts
http://www.cgi-resources.com/Programs_and_Scripts/Remotely_Hosted/

Cybersites
http://www.cybersites.com/

Delphi
http://www.delphi.com/

eCircles.com
http://www.ecircles.com/

EdGateway
http://edgateway.net/

eVine
http://www.evine.com/

Excite Communities
http://www.excite.com/communities/

FriendFactory
http://www.friendfactory.com/

interClubs
http://interclubs.com/

JointPlanning
http://www.jointplanning.com/

Lycos Clubs
http://clubs.lycos.com/

Network54
http://network54.com/

Yahoo! Clubs
http://clubs.yahoo.com/

There are now so many of these free services, it hardly makes sense to install your own software. (So why *would* you want to install your own software, then? Perhaps if you wanted full integration into your site—these services won't look exactly the way you want them to—or perhaps if you want more advanced features.) If you really feel the need to install something at your site, there are a number of freeware CGI scripts that will run discussion groups. Or you can buy a commercial CGI script. You can find CGI scripts, some commercial and some for free, at the following sites:

BBMatic BBS for the Web
   http://www.GetCruising.com/crypt/
Comment Line Webware
   http://www.eclipse.net/~mainstek/snet/softinfo.shtml
Emaze Forums ($295 and up)
   http://www.emaze.com/
HyperNews (freeware, reportedly quite easy to set up)
   http://www.hypernews.org/
ichat Message Boards ($800 and up)
   http://www.ichat.com/
Know-It TalkTrak ($129)
   http://www.know-it.com/talkTrak.htm
Post-on-the-Fly Conference ($495)
   http://www.homecom.com/
WebBBS (freeware, or $300 includes documentation and support)
   http://www.extropia.com/products.html
WebForum
   http://www.virtualcenter.com/scripts2/
WWW Board (freeware)
   http://www.worldwidemart.com/scripts/wwwboard.shtml
Xpound! ($1,195 and up)
   http://www.xpound.com/

Chat Groups

A chat group provides real-time discussions. Rather than leaving a message and coming back later to see if anyone has responded—which is the way discussion groups work—with chat groups you type a message and see an instant response from other chat-group members.

Chat groups can be useful in a couple of ways. Again, they're a way to add a service for visitors to encourage them to return. Whatever your company or organization is involved in, you can set up chat groups in which people interested in that subject can chat with other visitors. I don't much like chat groups, and I know many others don't, either. But there are obviously many Internet users who do like them—chat groups are very popular on the online services, and on the Internet itself there's Internet Relay Chat and a variety of Web-based chat groups, too. Evidently some people enjoy holding conversations by typing. Furthermore, some Web analysts claim that adding chat groups to Web sites can dramatically increase the number of times people visit your site and the amount of time they spend at your site once they get there. Chat groups, in combination with discussion groups, are a way to create a sense of community at your site. As *Fortune* magazine put it, "A bicycling Web site that offers nothing but products and articles about tours is little more than a catalogue; add chat, and it becomes a meeting place, the digital equivalent of the neighborhood bike shop."

But another way to use a chat system is to allow people to communicate with you or your staff directly. Some software companies now use chat groups for their customers to "talk" to technical support. This is a slow way to communicate, but it may be useful, in particular for companies that have many users overseas, where making phone calls would be prohibitively expensive.

You could also use chat groups as a way to transmit lectures or celebrity appearances. Many online services do this. At a specified time people go to the chat group and "listen" to someone talk. The visitors can post questions that the lecturer or celebrity can answer. If you want to try this, you should probably make sure you have software that provides you, or a chat moderator, some way to control the questions being posed by visitors. Chat groups can get quite chaotic when everyone's "talking" at once. One way to control such a lecture or celebrity appearance would be to lock the chat group so that only two or three people could send messages to the group. Anyone who wants to pose questions could send the question in an e-mail message beforehand. Or you could have two chat groups. Some of the chat-group products allow you to set up multiple chat "rooms." One room could be used to pose questions, while the actual lecture or celebrity appearance would be run in the other room. A moderator, one of the people allowed to send messages to the main chat room, would pick questions from one and submit them to the other.

If you're interested in setting up a chat group at your Web site, see some of the products in the list below. You'll want to look for features such as the ability to have multiple chat rooms and private chat rooms, the ability to send private messages, the ability to prevent users from certain domains joining in so you can block troublemakers, the ability to allow people to "listen in" to a chat room but not to send messages to the room (a feature that's very useful for lectures and celebrity chats), and so on. The fancier systems also have "avatars"—group members can be represented by little pictures—and other advanced features. (Personally I find these avatars to be little more than a gimmick, and they can be very distracting.)

You can get a free chat room set up for you, if you wish. A number of the services that provide free discussion groups, which I listed earlier, also provide free chat groups, so check with them. There are some other services dedicated to chat, so their systems may well be of a higher standard. TalkCity, for instance, allows you to set up a chat group using their servers but linked to your site, so the chat group appears to users to be at your site. You get a free chat room, and the company gets some advertising space.

Chat Script and Chat Script Pro
http://www.freescripts.com/

eAuditorium and C.U. Chat
http://www.netdive.com/

ichat ($495 and up)
http://www.ichat.com/

SuperChat ($25)
http://www.superscripts.com/scripts/superchat.html

TalkCity (free room at their site)
http://www.talkcity.com/

ToolZone (free service)
http://www.toolzone.com/

WebChat (public domain, or pay for support)
http://www.extropia.com/products.html

WWW Chat (freeware)
http://www.virtualcenter.com/scripts2/

Common Gateway Interface

Should You Use CGIs?

Things have changed a lot in the last two years, since the first edition of this book. Things that were quite complicated to do two years ago are much easier, because there are sites that will provide what you need for free, in an easy-to-set-up format. As you've seen in this chapter and the previous, there are utility sites that allow you to create forms, chat rooms, discussion groups, and plenty more, without the hassle of learning how to work with CGI scripts.

And the fact is, using CGI scripts can be complicated. Should you use them? Well, let's discuss that issue for a moment (and then I'll show you an example so you can make up your mind). A CGI script is a little program that runs on a Web server and interfaces with Web pages. Information is sent from an HTML form to a CGI script at the server. The script processes the information and sends some kind of response back to the Web browser. CGI scripts are very useful things. But, as with everything in life, there's a cost involved. While many excellent CGI scripts are available at no cost, or for a very low cost, the problem is that scripts are often quite difficult to install. I believe that many people should not touch CGI scripts ... at least until they've learned certain skills.

In order to work with CGI scripts you must understand a variety of basic concepts and skills. You must ...

- Understand how to use Telnet and FTP
- Understand how to move around in the directory tree at your Web server
- Know some basic UNIX commands so you can create directories and change file and directory permissions
- Be comfortable fooling around in scripts. You need to be able to understand a little bit of programming gobbledygook; that's not to say you need to be a programmer (though it helps), but you must be able to read and understand, to some degree, what the script is doing.

If you think learning to work with a word processor or Web-authoring tool was a major achievement ... you shouldn't be fooling around with CGI scripts. On the other hand, if you believe you can pick up most computer skills with a little effort, and perhaps have created program macros before, you may be able to install CGI scripts.

However, there's one more problem. Beyond the fact that CGI scripts require certain technical skills, they're also very hard to work with because the documentation is generally absolutely awful. The documents explaining how to install scripts are usually written *by* programmers and *for* programmers; they're close to indecipherable for normal people.

A Little CGI Background

Before we look at a CGI, let's get a little background information. First, how does a Web browser know how to send information from a form to a script? The action attribute of the <form> tag tells the browser where the script can be found. Here's an example:

```
<form method="POST" action="https://www.bigbiz.com/
topfloor/cgi-bin/send_mail.pl">
```

This tells the browser to take the information from the form and to send it to a script called send_mail.pl, which can be found at https://www.bigbiz.com/Top Floor/cgi-bin/ (note, by the way, that this is an https server rather than a mere http server; it is a secure Web server, so the data is sent to the script in an encrypted form). View the source of a form you find on the Web, look for the <form> tag, and you'll see that it refers to some kind of script. Of course now and then you'll see a different sort of form, one that doesn't send the form contents to a CGI. The form may be using another form of scripting, such as FrontPage server extensions. Below, for instance, is a reference to a FrontPage script (in this case not only is the script defined by the action attribute, but additional information is provided within the <!—webbot> tag):

```
<form method="POST" action="—WEBBOT-SELF—"><!—webbot
bot="SaveResults" startspan u-file="guestlog.htm"
s format="HTML/DL"s-label-fields="TRUE" s-builtin-
fields s-form-fields —>
```

Now, in order to use CGI scripts you have three steps to complete. You must install the CGI script at the Web server, create a form, and enter the action attribute information into the <form> tag to specify the CGI script's location. You can copy scripts from CGI libraries onto your computer, modify them to work on your Web server, then transfer them to the server. Modifying a script varies from very easy to horribly complicated. (As discussed in Chapter 11, you may want to pay someone—it sometimes costs as little as $50—to install the script for you.)

There are a number of important points you should understand about working with CGI scripts taken from CGI libraries:

- Check to see the condition of use for the script. Some scripts are free as long as you retain the author's copyright information in the script, and, perhaps, on the page using the script. Some are shareware, and some are in the public domain.

- In order to set up your CGI script, you need to understand how to use FTP—to transfer the files to your Web server—and perhaps Telnet—to log onto your Web site and modify permissions. Using FTP is quite easy, Telnet is not as easy. You may be able to use your FTP program to make all the changes. You can certainly use the FTP program to move, copy, and rename your files, and on some servers, with some FTP programs, you can also modify permissions. Otherwise you'll have to understand enough about the server's operating system (probably UNIX) to allow you to set permissions.

- Before starting, talk with the server administrator. You must know whether to call the script file scriptname.pl or scriptname.cgi (it depends on how the server's set up). If you've downloaded a .cgi (Common

Gateway Interface) script, you can simply rename it to a .pl (Perl) file if that's what your server requires. You should also ask the administrator where you should put the file. (Generally it will be in a cgi-bin directory.)

- Some servers, such as servers running the Microsoft FrontPage server extensions, may not normally allow scripts to use the POST form of data submission. Ask your server administrator if the account has been modified to allow POST.

- The CGI library may store the scripts in a variety of file formats: in plain-text format viewable from your browser (you can just save the file from the browser), in .zip files (a compressed format used on IBM-compatible PCs), or in .tar files (UNIX tape archive files). If you are working with a PC, you can use a program such as WinZip to open both .zip and .tar files. On the Macintosh you can use a program such as DropStuff with Expander Enhancer. (See Chapter 2 for information on tracking down software.)

- You'll probably be transferring scripts from somewhere on the Web to your computer, and then onto the Web server. When you transfer to the server, you'll almost certainly be transferring using an FTP program; if you are transferring script files, make sure you use an ASCII transfer, not binary. Binary transfers from PCs to most servers mess up the line feeds in text files (CGI scripts are saved in text files). If you're transferring a .zip or .tar file, use binary.

- You'll probably need to set the permissions on the CGI script file. If you don't, the script simply won't work. Look at the file when saved on the server; you should see -rwxr-xr-x after the filename in a file listing. To change permissions you'll have to log onto the server, generally using Telnet, change to the directory holding the script, type chmod 755 filename.cgi, and press Enter. (Replace filename.cgi with the actual filename, of course.) This modifies the file to allow anyone to execute—to run—the file. Or check to see if you can use your FTP program to set permissions. Some programs allow you to do so, as long as the server is set up to allow it, too.

- Many scripts require that you modify the permissions of a Web page, too, because the script has to write text to that Web page. If so, you'll have to change permissions for that file as well, probably using chmod 777 filename.htm. Again, you may be able to use FTP to change permissions.

- I'm not sure about recent versions of Microsoft FrontPage, but early versions (certainly FP97) limit your ability to modify the permissions of files created by FrontPage itself. That doesn't matter as far as the script file goes because FrontPage doesn't create that file, but if you have to change permissions for a Web page you'll have to create the Web page and save it outside the FrontPage web. You can still use FrontPage Editor to create it, but save the file separately, outside the web, then transfer it to your Web site using FTP, placing it in a directory that FrontPage did not create.

- Microsoft FrontPage may also restrict permissions to the cgi-bin directory. Certainly at one point (I'm not sure about the more recent versions), it didn't let you POST to CGI scripts you've placed in the cgi-bin directory. There's a file called .htaccess in your root directory that controls access to all your directories, and this is probably set to stop posting to scripts. So make a copy of the .htaccess file—make sure you do an ASCII transfer from your Web site to your computer—and find the following:

```
<Limit POST PUT DELETE>
order deny,allow
deny from all
</Limit>
```

Change it to show this:

```
<Limit POST PUT DELETE>
order deny,allow
deny from all
allow from all
</Limit>
```

Copy this into your cgi-bin directory—again, make sure you do an ASCII transfer. Before using this procedure, though, check with the Web server administrator to make sure it's appropriate on his server.

- The first line of a Perl script must begin with something like this:

```
#!/usr/local/bin/perl
```

This tells the script where to find the Perl binary, the program that runs the script, so what should appear on the first line of the script depends on where that is stored on your Web server. It quite likely is at /usr/local/bin/perl, but to make sure, get to the UNIX prompt (use Telnet), then type which perl and press Enter. You'll be shown the path that you must enter on the first line of the script. Make sure you precede the path with the #! symbols.

- Most script libraries have links to sites where you can see examples at work. Take a look at these, and carefully read any other documentation available.
- You can customize scripts and the pages that refer to them, but don't customize the script until you've got it working at your site. Make the minimum changes necessary to install the script at your site, then make customization changes one by one, testing each time.

Okay, I know I've lost some of you already! If all this sounds too complicated to you, you may find it more efficient to pay someone to install the CGI for you. If you're still with me, let's see a real-life example.

A CGI Example—Free For All Links

We're going to use the *Free For All* script to allow visitors to add their links to a page at your site. Why bother? Well, if you use a links page as a way to attract visitors to your site, this script could be a useful addition, a way for your links page to grow with minimal work on your part—of course now and again you'll need to check the pages that have been added. Your visitors will help you build your list, and you can periodically transfer appropriate links from your Free For All page to your main links page. You can see an example of the form created by this script in Figure 12.1.

Now, the following may all seem quite complicated. Actually it's not so bad, if you follow along carefully, step by step. If you've ever created

By the way, there is one problem with such Free For All links lists. People often add completely unrelated links, under the misguided impression that links to their sites on a totally inappropriate page, are better than not having links to their sites on that page. Of course you never know who might see a link and follow it, but this idea that links should be strewn willy-nilly across the Internet is based on a false premise: that there really is such a thing as a free link. There isn't. At the very least one has to spend time placing the link, time that might be better spent placing the link somewhere more appropriate!

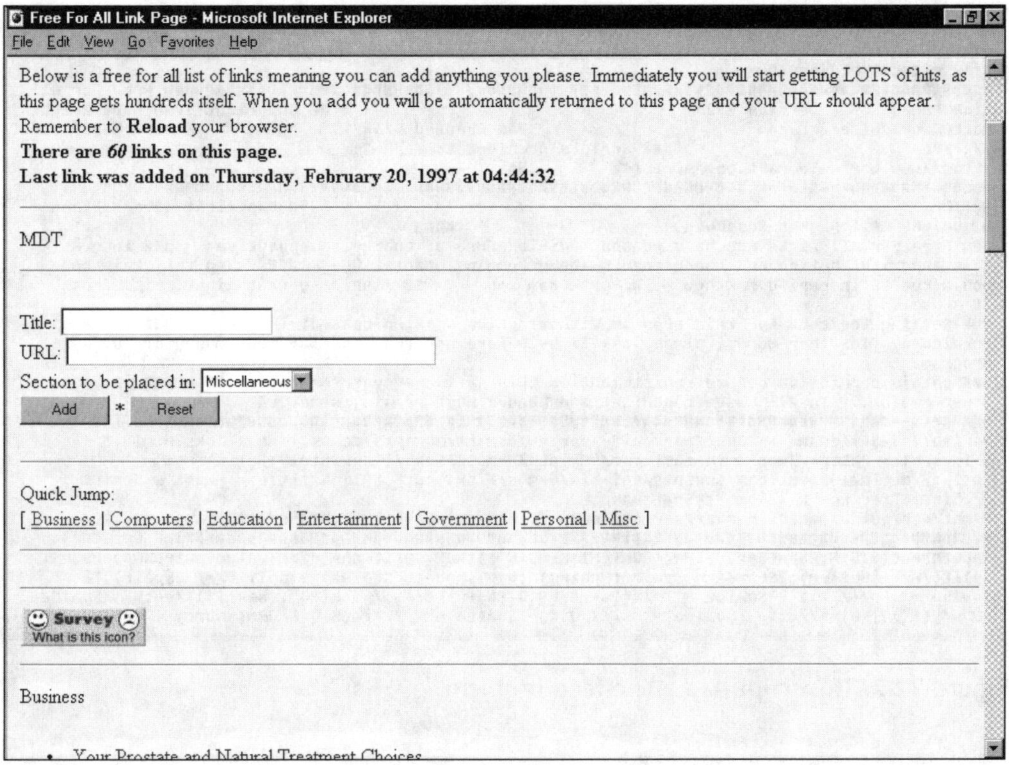

Figure 12.1: The Free For All script is called from this form.

macros for your word processor or spreadsheet, you can probably do this. On the other hand, if creating macros for your word processor or spreadsheet is something you'd never consider doing ... then perhaps setting up this CGI script—and most other CGI scripts—is not something you should do. Take a look at what's involved, and decide for yourself.

Here's the procedure I followed. I began by downloading **Free For All Links** from Matt's CGI Archive (http://www.worldwidemart.com/scripts/). There were three files: the script file (links.pl), the Web page containing the form that calls the script (addlink.htm), and a file containing instructions (readme.txt). I downloaded these files in a single .zip compressed file (they're available in several formats).

When I extracted the files from the .zip file and viewed them, I found that they had line-feed problems. In Figure 12.2 you can see that the text in the script file has little black squares, and all the text is run together. Instead of moving text down a line, the line-feed character being used simply places a black square in the text. This is a common problem when transferring files between DOS or

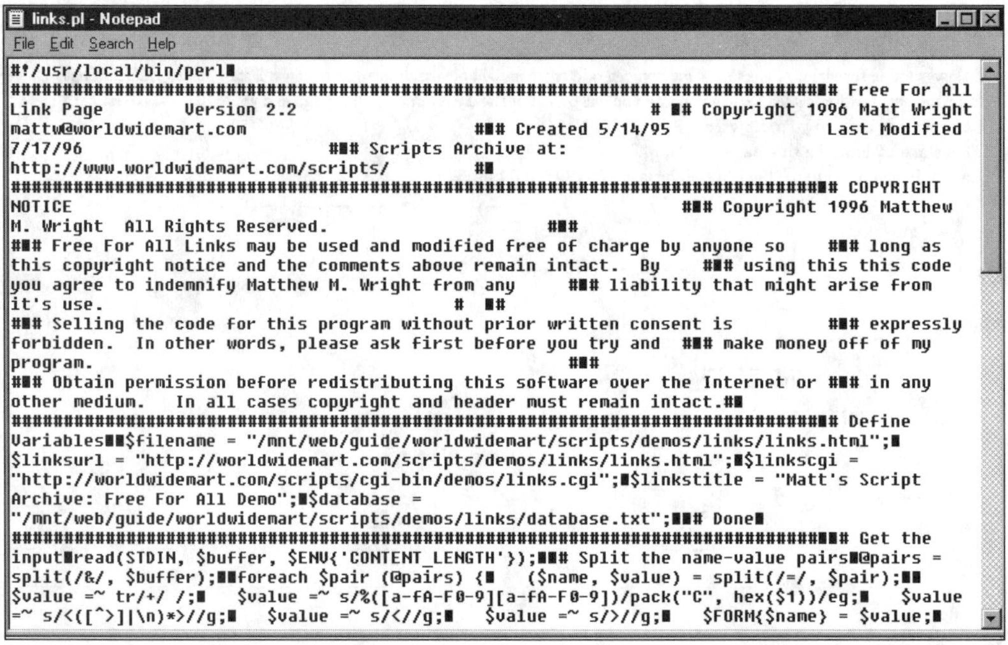

Figure 12.2: This script had a line-feed problem.

Windows and other operating systems. You can fix this problem quite easily, though. I opened the files in Word for Windows, then saved the files again—they must be saved as text files, not as word-processing files. This replaced the bad line feeds with correct ones. You'll probably be able to do this with most word processors. If necessary, you can open the file in a text editor, highlight each black square in turn, and replace the square by pressing Enter.

Next I renamed the script. When I got the script it was called links.pl, but the Web server administering my site works only with .cgi, so I renamed it links.cgi.

I then transferred the file to the directory specified by the server administrator; this is normally a directory called cgi-bin. In this case, due to an idiosyncrasy with the FrontPage server extensions, the server administrator told me to put it in a different directory. As discussed earlier in this chapter, there is a way to get around the FrontPage problem by placing an .htaccess file in the cgi-bin directory.

Next I had to set permissions for the files. I set the script permission using the chmod 755 command in Telnet. There are two ways to set file permissions. If your FTP server is set up to allow it, you can use your FTP program to set permissions, and this is probably the most convenient way to do it. If the FTP server doesn't allow this, though, you'll have to Telnet to your Web site and use this command:

```
chmod 755 links.cgi
```

As specified in the documentation that came with the script, I also changed the Web page (addlink.htm) permissions using the following command:

```
chmod 777 addlink.htm
```

In the Web page itself I had to modify the <form> tag to specify the location of the script file. The tag was initially the following:

```
<form method="POST" action="http://your.host.xxx/
cgi-bin/links.pl">
```

I had to change it to the following:

```
<form method="POST" action="http://www.poorrichard.com/
cgi-bin/links.cgi">
```

In the script file I had to modify several lines. The following were in the original:

```
# Define Variables
$filename = "/mnt/web/guide/worldwidemart/scripts/demos/
links/links.html";
$linksurl = "http://worldwidemart.com/scripts/demos/
links/links.html";
$linkscgi = "http://worldwidemart.com/scripts/cgi-
bin/demos/links.cgi";
$linkstitle = "Matt's Script Archive: Free For All
Demo";
$database = "/mnt/web/guide/worldwidemart/scripts/demos/
links/database.txt";
# Done
```

I had to change the lines to the following:

```
# Define Variables
$filename = "/www/topfloor/html/pr/examples/addlink/
addlink.htm";
$linksurl = "http://www.poorrichard.com/examples/
addlink/addlink.htm";
$linkscgi = "http://www.poorrichard.com/cgi-
bin/links.cgi";
$linkstitle = "Poor Richard's Marketing List ->
```

```
Directory—Add Links";$database =
"/www/topfloor/html/pr/examples/addlink/links.txt";
# Done
```

These lines tell the script where the page that it's writing to is stored, where the script file itself is stored, the title of the page it's writing to, and the name of a text file in which the script can save a list of all the links written to the page. That text file can be used by other scripts, such as a random-link generator.

That's all it took to modify the script and make it work on my site, though it took a long time to do all this—thanks to some mistakes I made, I ran around in circles for quite a while. Also, I wanted to modify the script more. It had link categories that didn't work for my purposes—the script allows people to choose a category under which to enter a new link—so I changed them. In order to change categories, I had to do the following:

1. For each category, I had to add an entry to the list box on the Web page, as follows:

   ```
   <option value="Mail">Mailing Lists and Newsgroups
   </option>
   ```

   The value= text is important; this is the text I'm going to use to identify this selection to the script.

2. For each category, I created a heading in the file, then added an HTML note tag—the <!-- --> tag. The script searches for these notes when trying to figure out where to add the link. For instance:

   ```
   <!--Mail-->
   ```

3. In the script, I found the following text:

   ```
   %sections = ("busi","Business","comp","Computers",
   "educ","Education","ente","Entertainment","gove",
   "Government","pers","Personal","misc",
   "Miscellaneous");
   ```

   These are the categories used in the original script. For instance:

   ```
   "busi","Business",
   ```

   busi is the name in the HTML note, Business is the name returned by the list box in the Web page. The original Web page didn't use the value= attribute in the list box, so the form returns the name of the selected entry in the list box.

4. I replaced this text with my own categories, as follows:

```
%sections = ("Advice","Advice","Mail","Mail","Demo",
"Demo","Recip","Recip","Direct","Direct","Adv","Adv",
"What","What","Domain","Domain","Find","Find","Web",
"Web","Set","Set","Finding","Finding","Soft","Soft",
"Other","Other");
```

I've used the same names for both the first and second positions. For instance:

```
"Advice","Advice",
```

I did this because I used the same name for both the value= attribute in the list box and in the HTML note tag.

I made a few cosmetic changes, too. I put the form at the bottom of the page, for instance, and changed its look. I added some of my own text, too.

So, how does this all work? When the user enters information into the form and clicks on the Add button, the contents of the form are sent to the script. The script looks for the text returned from the list box—from the value= attribute— such as Adv or What. It then uses this to figure out where to place the title and URL submitted by the user; it searches the Web page for the matching HTML note, and places the link below that note.

You can see my completed form in Figure 12.3, and see it in action at the **Poor Richard's** Web site (http://PoorRichard.com/examples/addlink.htm) in the examples area of the Web site.

Well, that's the short explanation. Thanks to a few mistyped words here and there, this all took quite a while. Setting up these scripts can really be a hassle and take a long time, perhaps several hours. In fact, if you're a computing neophyte, I'd recommend that you don't even try. Consider the value of your time, and pay someone to do it for you. What may cost $50, might take you five or ten hours—or much, much, more—to do for yourself.

On the other hand, if you're used to fiddling around with computers and don't mind fooling around with scripts of various kinds, you may want to do it yourself. You'll find that it gets easier—the more scripts you customize, the simpler the process will become.

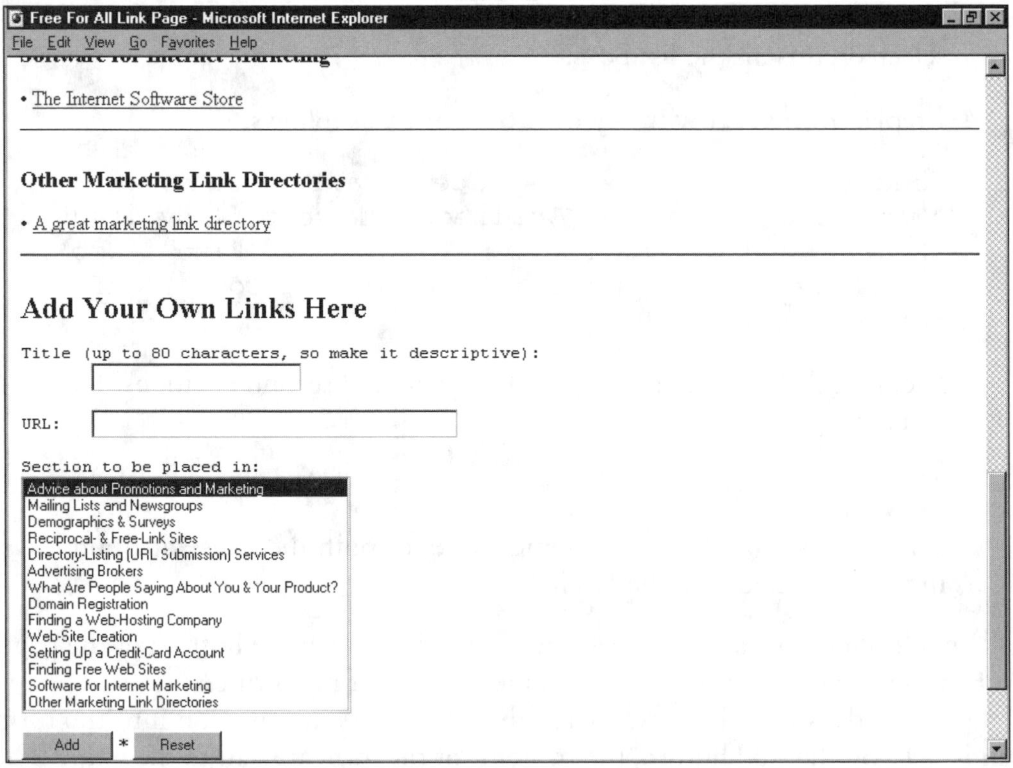

Figure 12.3: I've modified the script to use different categories, and I've given the form a different look, too.

Troubleshooting Your Script

Remember to test your CGI scripts thoroughly. Try everything the script can do; all it takes is one misspelled word, and part of the script may be broken. If you just can't get the script to work at all, check the following items:

- Did you use the correct script file extension (.cgi or .pl)?
- Did you put the script in the correct place?
- Have you changed file permissions correctly, for both the script file and any other files that it works with? To test, view the file directory using FTP. You should see something like this:

```
-rwxr-xr-x   1 pkent    nobody        6719 ->
Feb 19 17:24 links.cgi
```

The information at the start of the line shows the permissions; there should be three x characters to show that anyone can execute (run) the program. If it's a Web page that the script wants to write to, you should see -rwxrwxrwx instead.

- Do you have a correct #!/usr/local/bin/perl path on the first line of the script file?
- Did you clear out the DOS line feeds if transferring from a PC? You must make sure that your FTP program is transferring the files in ASCII mode.
- Try running the script from the command line in UNIX or even from the Location box in your browser. Simply type the URL that points to the script and press Enter. You should get some kind of response, depending on what the script has been designed to do in such a situation; you might see a title page, with a link back to the script author's Web page, or perhaps an error message telling you that the script didn't get the information it needs. If you can't run it from there—if you get a message from the server telling you that you don't have permission, or that it can't find the script—then the script won't run from within your form, either.

- Have you referred to the correct script location within the Web page that calls the script?
- Does the script refer to the correct file locations?
- If you can't get anything to work, try renaming the file nph-scriptname.cgi, then run the script. You may see error messages that help you figure out what is going on.

What's the single most likely problem with your script? Something typed incorrectly. A word misspelled, a missing ; or }, an additional colon ... it doesn't take much to screw up a CGI script! The other major problem is with improperly set file permissions. Also watch for an improperly typed URL in the <form> tag's action attribute.

Following are a few error messages you may run into when trying to use the form in your Web browser:

```
Forbidden - You don't have permission to access
/ipn/cgi-bin/links.cgi on this server.
```

The permissions of the files may not be set correctly, or the script file may be in the wrong location.

```
Server Error - The server encountered an internal error
or misconfiguration and was unable to complete your
request.
```

This is probably due to a script error, although it says server error. You may not have set the #!/usr/local/bin/perl line, for instance, or perhaps the script file has bad line-feed characters.

```
Method not implemented - POST to /ipn/cgi-bin/links.
pl not supported.
```

This may be a problem with the location or the filename, or perhaps the server is not set up correctly to accept POST submissions.

Ask Your Visitors to Do Something

The whole purpose of CGI scripts is to allow visitors to your site to interact with the site. Not just to visit, look around, and leave, but to do something. So before we move on, a little reminder:

Don't wait for visitors to do something—ask them to take some action.

There's a basic maxim in sales: Ask the prospect for the sale. You don't wait for the prospect to mull it over, you ask the prospect to buy. This is a principle little understood by many people doing business on the Web. As the owner of a successful Web business told me: "People in love with the Internet are jumping in with both feet, but although they understand the technology well, they don't understand business and they don't understand entrepreneurship." I'm amazed at the number of business Web sites that are created by people who don't understand this basic principle of sales: Ask for the sale.

The principle applies to whatever you want the person to do at your Web site. You want a journalist to review your product? Then ask journalists to visit your press page, and ask them to contact you for a review copy. You want people to give you their e-mail addresses? Then ask them to fill in a form and give you their e-mail addresses. You want someone to download your software demo? Ask them to do so. You don't make all these things available and hope that somehow people will find them. You direct them, you lead them, you take them to the part of the site you want them to visit, then ask them to take action—and you can use CGIs to help you do that.

Chapter Thirteen

Taking Orders Online

If you are trying to sell something from your Web site, you'll have to spend a little time figuring out how to do so—and perhaps a little money setting up an ordering system, though it can be done surprisingly cheaply (though it's very hard to find a *good* system). There are a variety of ways to take orders from your Web site, and several different forms of money you can accept. Some you'll definitely want to use, others you may not want to bother with. They include the following:

- Through snail-mail (that is, through the Post Office)
- Through a telephone number—a toll call or 800 number
- Through a fax number
- Through a simple Web form
- Through e-mail
- Through a sophisticated "shopping-cart" system
- Using 900-number systems (to pay for Web-site access only).

There are also several types of money you can accept:

- Using a credit-card number
- Using checks
- Using a digital-cash system.

Let's examine each of these possibilities in turn.

Mail and the Phone

Don't think that just because you are working on the Internet you can forget the real world. Significant numbers of orders initiated through a Web site are completed using an offline method. For quite a while around 15 percent or so of all orders placed at my publishing company were by phone, fax, or mail, though the percentage has dropped quite a bit over the last year or so.

Sometimes people order offline because many companies make it hard to order through their Web sites. They provide incomplete product information and even incomplete ordering information. Or perhaps the information is there, but the Web site is structured in such a manner that it's hard to find. And some sites simply don't provide any method for online ordering, though in general they're the sort of sites that don't do much business. I've also run into sites at which the online ordering system simply didn't work properly, so I was forced to pick up the phone.

But even if you do a good job at your Web site, and make sure that all the information a buyer is likely to need is at your Web site, you'll still find customers who want to order by telephone for several reasons, as follows:

- They have unusual questions about your products that you couldn't possibly have foreseen, so they need to talk to someone.
- They've been scared away from placing orders online by all the talk of credit-card fraud (more of which later in this chapter).
- They simply prefer to talk to a real person when placing an order.
- They want to make sure the order has really been taken—that someone has seen the order and it's not just floating around in cyberspace.

For these and other reasons, you should provide enough information for a visitor to your site to order offline. Provide a phone number—use your company's toll-free phone number if you have one, of course. Provide a full mailing address, too—people overseas who don't want to order online may not want to make an international phone call, either.

Also, remember to include full ordering details. Tell your buyers exactly how much the product costs, what discounts are available, and full shipping information. Don't forget to include shipping information for overseas buyers, too. Remember, this is an international forum, so there's no need to limit your sales to one country. It's an immediate-gratification forum, too. Many Internet users have become accustomed to getting what they want right away, so provide information about express or overnight deliveries.

When you provide instructions for sending mail orders, why not provide a form that the buyer can print? Create a page that looks just like an order form in a newspaper or magazine, and tell the buyer to use his browser's Print command to print it out. The buyer will get all the instructions he needs to make the order, in an easy-to-use format, and you'll receive orders with all the required information. When you create such a form, make sure you test it to ensure that it looks okay when printed. You'll probably need to use fairly short lines of text aligned on the left side of the page, and perhaps use the <pre></pre> tags to format the page so all the text lines up properly.

It's essential that you make it as easy as possible for the client to complete the order online. There's a myth that online ordering provides a cheap and simple way for companies to take orders. In fact, the experience of many companies shows that online ordering often fails. Online ordering often requires a lot of offline assistance and is far more expensive than is implied by the hype we've all heard. You'll probably never be able to take 100 percent of your orders online without human intervention, but the more information you provide to your customers, and the better designed your system is, the less intervention will be required.

> *Remember that whatever method a user employs to order from you, you should always get his e-mail address. Even if he's ordering by phone or snail-mail, ask for his e-mail address. You'll want to add all your clients to an e-mail mailing list.*

Fax

Many businesses accept orders via their fax machines. If you want to do this, make sure your fax machine is connected at all times, and provide an order form at your Web site that people can print out and fill in.

Better still, use one of the online fax services—then you don't have to worry about the machine running out of paper or ink, or jamming (I've had a lot of bad luck with fax machines). A number of these services are free, in fact—you'll get a fax number, and any faxes sent to that number will be e-mailed to you. My company uses such a system, eFax, and it really does work very well. (Another advantage: wherever I am in the world, I can get my faxes via e-mail.)

David Strom's Internet Fax Technologies List
http://www.strom.com/places/faxtable.html

eFax
> http://www.efax.com/

Fax4Free
> http://www.fax4free.com/

FaxMe
> http://www.faxme.co.uk/

Jfax
> http://www.jfax.com/

uReach
> http://www.ureach.com/

E-mail

In the first edition of this book I said that you should provide an e-mail order address. I think it's far less important now … but you should still include an e-mail address at which you can be contacted with questions. You must include an e-mail address, even if you include a phone number. Many businesses are selling products that can be sold overseas. If you're selling books, music, or software, for instance, there's no reason to limit your sales to one country. The world really is getting smaller, and people on the other side of the world may be willing to place orders. I've sold my books in Iceland, South Africa, Chile, and Japan, for instance. However, they may not be prepared to make a phone call that may double the price of the product. So include an e-mail address—better still, include several e-mail addresses: one where they can send orders, one where they can send requests for more information, another for customer support, and so on. We'll talk more about working with e-mail in Chapter 14.

By the way, include e-mail addresses in a couple of ways. You can create mailto: tags in your Web pages. These are special links that, when clicked, open the visitor's e-mail program. But they won't work for all visitors, depending on the browsers they're working with and how they have their browsers configured. And in any case, many of us find them a nuisance because they always seem to open up some stupid Microsoft mail program, never mind how many times we set up our mail program to intercept mailto:. So make sure the e-mail address itself is visible on the page. In other words, don't just create a mailto: link that says *Order Here*. Create a mailto: link that says something like *Order Here: sales@ acmesewercover.com*, so people can actually read your e-mail address.

You can also create forms that buyers can use for e-mail submissions, just as you did for mail submissions. Tell the user to copy the form to the e-mail program or save the form as text and import it to the program, and then fill out the form by adding text in the appropriate spaces. However, few people are willing to place orders by e-mail, and it's been a long time since I've seen a company even trying to take e-mail orders.

Simple Web Form   ASK AT NET

In Chapters 11 and 12 we discussed adding interactive components to your Web site. You can create simple forms using your Web-authoring program's scripting system or CGI scripts, and use those forms as sales forms. It's a fairly simple matter to use a CGI script to set up a form and have the information saved on the Web server. It's a little more complicated, but not much, to set up the form so that it works with a secure server, so that when the customer submits the form, the credit-card information—and everything else on the form—is encrypted; that is, it's transmitted in a form that is perfectly safe.

For the first few months after publication of *Poor Richard's Web Site*, we used a simple Web form—a "dumb" form, as I like to call it—to take orders. It worked fine. The main problem was that many buyers said "if you're writing a book about how to set up online, you ought to have a form that calculates the total based on shipping and tax." Well, this was back in 1997, when relatively few stores had any kind of shopping cart, but a few months later we took the plunge and installed a shopping-cart system. The dumb order form really did work reasonably well, and I think that for many small businesses it still might suffice. It's much easier to install than a shopping-cart system, and you can actually do it for free. If you'd like to see an example of such an order form, and an explanation of how to set it up so that it works in secure mode, visit my Web site: http://PoorRichard.com/examples/shop.htm.

A Shopping Cart

If you're serious about selling products online, you really need a shopping-cart system. (*Shopping cart* is the term commonly used to mean the system of forms employed to take orders at a Web site.) It should be simple to do this, but at the time of writing it's really not quite so simple, especially if you want a full-featured system.

Well, you may have seen a few products advertised, perhaps in software catalogs. You may have heard claims like these:

Just install the program on your computer, create your Web site, and then transfer the site to the Internet quickly and easily with the automatic upload feature.

Or how about these "system requirements" stated on a product box:

- MS Windows 95, or Windows NT 4 or higher
- Internet connection.

Sounds simple. Buy the packaged software, install it on your computer, create your site, and publish it to the Web. Unfortunately many software publishers are exaggerating how easy it is, and Web-site owners are buying products that they discover they can't use, or can use only if they move their Web sites to a hosting company that supports the software they've just bought. Furthermore, the vast majority of shopping-cart systems are mere toys, deficient in important features, as I'll explain a little later.

First, some background. As we saw in earlier chapters, HTML cannot make a form actually *do* anything. In order to get the form to do something, you need a special program running on the server. That program might be a CGI (Common Gateway Interface) script, or it could be some other kind of program. But one way or another, something has to be running on the Web server.

> ### Disclaimer!
>
> *At the time of writing my hosting company, **BizBlast.com**, was in the process of negotiating an arrangement with a major software distributor to sell a shopping-cart system in the office-supply and computer stores. And the same product will be available at our Web site. See http://BizBlast.com/ for more information.*

When a site has a shopping-cart system, the buyer sees a series of forms. When the user enters information in those forms, and submits the forms, the data is taken by the program on the server, and manipulated—sales tax, shipping costs, totals, and so on are calculated. Then the information is sent back to the user's browser. So when you buy a product that will create a shopping-cart system, there are two important questions to be answered:

a: How does this product create the program required to handle the forms data?

and, more importantly:

b: Will the program run on the Web server I'm using?

Here's an example. Foreman Interactive sells a product called Internet Creator, and that product can set up an online store. At Foreman Interactive's Web site you'll learn that:

E-mail ordering, shopping basket management and searching capabilities are just some of the features included in Internet Creator's E-Commerce Edition.

You'll also learn that the system requirements are a Windows PC, 10MB hard-disk space, and 8MB RAM. After reading the blurb, you might be ready to buy. And in fact you can navigate from the main page, through the promotional text, and into an order form, without discovering that the only way to set up a store with this product is to sign up for service SiteAmerica (Foreman Interactive's partner Web-hosting company). If you already have a Web site, and don't want to move it, this program won't work for you (or rather, it will allow you to build Web pages, but the shopping cart won't work unless you host with SiteAmerica).

This program is not alone; there are other products that claim you can quickly set up a shopping-cart system … until you look closely at the small print (if you can find it).

Picking a shopping-cart system is not easy. There are basically four ways to set up a system:

1. Buy the software and install it on your own server.
2. Buy the software and install it on your hosting company's server.
3. Sign up with a Web-hosting company that has shopping-cart software available.
4. Sign up with a shopping-cart service; the shopping-cart software runs on their server, linked to from your Web site.

As we noted before, option 1 is out of question for most small businesses—it's way too complicated and expensive. So you're left with the other three options. Before you buy a product, you have to be sure you know what you are getting into. Internet Creator, for instance, really falls into category 3; although you can create Web pages with this program for use on any server, if you want to use it to create an online store, you'll have to sign up with a certain hosting company.

When you go looking for shopping-cart software, make sure you ask the following questions; don't rely on the company's product blurbs or declared system requirements:

- How does the system create the program that runs the forms? Does it require special extensions at the server, does it install CGIs, or does it require a particular server?

- Can I use this at any hosting company, or do I have to work with a particular company or choose from a list of companies? (Some products are set up to work at a few dozen companies.)
- If I can use it with any hosting company, which types of Web servers will it run on? (Make sure it's compatible with the one you or your hosting company uses.)
- Who will install the program on the server? (It's not a simple task to install these programs, so at the very least you need good technical support available.)

Let's look a little closer at the three options applicable to most small businesses.

Install Software on Your Hosting Company's Server

There are many products that you can install on your host's server. These are generally products that use CGI scripts running on the server, so you must make sure that you're allowed to use CGIs on your server, that the ones you are buying are compatible with the server, and that you're sure that either you are capable of installing them or you can find someone to install them for you. These things can be *very* tricky, but some software companies will install the products for you.

Such programs vary widely in cost. There are actually freeware programs available, but they're generally difficult to set up; perhaps you can hire a consultant to install them for you. Prices go up into the many thousands of dollars.

Use a Hosting Company with Shopping-Cart Software Available

Perhaps the simplest thing is to sign up with a Web-hosting company that already has shopping-cart software available for use. At least you know it's already installed on the server, so should be relatively easy to get running ... well, perhaps. Just because your hosting company chose it doesn't mean it is easy to use or has all the features you need. Check it out carefully. (We'll discuss features in a moment.)

Use a Shopping-Cart Service

There are a number of companies that will host your shopping cart. They are not necessarily Web-hosting companies—they may not be interested in hosting your entire site—but they will run the shopping-cart system, with your products, on their server.

In other words, you can have your Web site at one location, and the shopping cart at another, and link from one to the other. Most customers won't even realize that they've jumped from one site to another during the order process.

The advantages? You may find a Web-hosting company you really like, with the exception of its shopping-cart system; you can keep your Web site where it is, and pick and choose between shopping-cart services. They're usually relatively easy to set up (*relatively* easy we said, not easy!). It's someone else's responsibility to keep the thing going. (If you install your own system, by contrast, you'll have to worry about maintenance.) And they can be quite affordable. But they're often rather weak systems, lacking important features.

Picking a Shopping Cart

At the time of writing choosing a shopping-cart system is a real exercise in compromise. There's no perfect solution. You'll be juggling features, price, and ease of installation. Here, to help just a little, are a few things to watch for when picking a shopping-cart system:

- Will the program be able to handle as many categories and products as you need?
- Does the program allow the buyer to add products, to a basket, then continue shopping and add more products?
- Can you import items? If you have a lot of products you really need to be able to import a list. If you only have a small number of products, you can enter them by typing in the information.
- Can a buyer leave, come back later, and continue shopping where he left off? (This is a nice feature, though not essential.)
- Can buyers search for products? (This is not important if you have a small number of products.)
- Will the program allow you to add fields? For instance, you may want to add a check box that allows buyers to sign up for a free newsletter, or a "where did you hear about this product" drop-down list box. (Of course, this information must then be included in the order information provided to you by the program.)
- How does the program calculate state sales tax? You should be able to specify sales tax for particular states—ideally for particular ZIP codes. But some programs don't calculate sales tax well. (For instance, if the user types *Colorado* instead of *CO*, the sales tax may not be calculated.)
- Does it allow you to specify all the shipping methods and rates you want to use? Some programs provide little flexibility, or even don't allow the customer to choose a shipping method at all but only tack on a set shipping price. (A ridiculous situation when you consider that

the Internet is an international forum.) This is perhaps the most serious and common problem related to shopping-cart systems.

- Will the program verify that credit-card numbers and e-mail addresses were entered in the correct format?

- How does the program provide confirmation to the user? It should display a confirmation page, but it should also send an e-mail message.

- Will the program e-mail a message to you letting you know that an order's been taken?

- Does the system require that buyers register before making a purchase? (It probably shouldn't, but some do.)

- How is the order information delivered to you? It should be easy to import into a database, so you need a text-file format (comma- or tab-delimited text) or a database format. Some systems deliver in an e-mail message, which is usually inconvenient. (How do you get it into a mailing-label or credit-card processing program?)

- Try entering information in many different ways—foreign phone numbers and provinces, different country names, and so on. Does the program handle different situations well, or does it give error messages?

- Do you like the overall "look and feel" of the product? Is it confusing, or simple to use? Does it make your customers "jump through hoops," or is it quick and easy?

Don't rush out right now and find a system, though; read the rest of this chapter first. Before you buy, you need to decide how you want to process payments. You can get a shopping-cart system to send you the information, and you can then process the transactions offline, or you can process transactions online. As you'll see later in this chapter, you can process not only credit cards but even checks online. Whichever method you choose, you'd better make sure both these components—the shopping-cart system and the transaction processing—will work together.

Online Transaction Processing

When I wrote the first edition of this book, back in 1997, setting up online transaction processing was quite complicated. These days it's built into most of the shopping-cart products you'll see.

By *online transaction processing* I mean that when you take an order, the credit card is processed immediately. The buyer chooses his products, enters billing, shipping, and credit-card information, clicks on a button, and the information is sent across the Internet to the credit-card network right away. Within a few seconds a response comes back authorizing or declining the transaction.

With *offline transaction processing*, the information from the buyer is merely collected and saved for later processing. Once a day or so the merchant retrieves the information and processes it using a terminal or perhaps even a credit-card processing program.

There are a number of companies, such as AuthorizeNet and CyberCash, that have built gateways between the Internet and the credit-card networks. Shopping-cart software companies then build an interface between their shopping-cart systems and the gateway so that the merchants using their shopping carts can have online transaction processing.

Why doesn't everyone use online transaction processing? The cost and hassle.

- To use one of these gateways you'll have to pay a sign-up charge, perhaps $100, and a monthly fee, maybe $20 or $30.
- There may be per-transaction fees, too.
- If you already have a credit-card merchant account, you may discover that you can't use it with the gateway, so you have to apply for another one. Even if you *can* use it, you'll probably still pay a fee to have your existing account processed—to make sure it will work with the gateway and to configure the gateway for the new account.

By the way, most of these online transaction services also provide a Web interface for you to process credit cards; that is, a form in which you can enter sales information by hand. If you sell a product offline, you can then process the product by hand—you simply go to the Web form, type all the information in, and submit it.

900 Numbers

In North America you can use 900 numbers—telephone numbers in the 900 "area" code—to sell access to your Web site. (You can't sell products using this method, because Federal regulations don't allow it.) These 900 numbers are telephone numbers that charge the caller an amount defined by the person setting up the number. They're often used by sex-chat lines, and on the Internet they're often used by the pornographic Web sites as a payment method.

Here's how it works: You provide the 900 number as one of the payment methods at your Web site. If someone wants to use the number to pay, he simply calls the number, writes down a password, then returns to your site and uses that password to enter the Web site. The charge will appear on the customer's phone bill later.

You may have to dig around a little to find the right service. Some have caps on the amount you can charge. For instance, last time I checked MCI had a $5-per-minute, $35-per-call maximum, though reportedly you can get a waiver to allow you to take as much as $50. I've heard of other caps as high as $59.95. Remember also that there is a variety of fees associated with the call, so you may have to adjust your pricing accordingly. Those fees can be quite high, as much as 25 percent to 34 percent, but you can find lower rates—The Internet Billing Company charges 20 percent, for example, so shop around. Unfortunately, the fees are so high that the use of 900 numbers for doing business on the Web is probably limited to a few very specific areas. Also, getting your money can take a long time. Some services don't pay for the first 60 to 90 days, and after that initial waiting period you may get paid once a month. Other services promise payment within 30 days. The company may also hold a portion of the money to cover "chargebacks."

Check these places for more information about 900 numbers:

Future Fone Web Source900
   http://www.futurephone.com/
ibill Web900 (takes a cut of 20 percent; this site seems the most coherent and understandable of the lot, so start here)
   http://www.ibill.com/
Saturn Communications
   http://www.900income.com/
Yahoo!—1-900 Services Page
   http://dir.yahoo.com/Business_and_Economy/Companies/Telecommunications/
   Phone_Services/1_900_Service/

Money, Money, Money

What type of money should you accept? There are actually several options: credit cards, checks, and digital cash. You must accept the first, you may want to accept the second, and as for the third … I'd be in no hurry to use it.

Credit Cards

We've heard a lot of talk about new electronic forms of money that will be developed for use on the Internet, but there's an electronic form of money that's been with us for years: credit cards. You provide a number, and the transaction is processed electronically. It's tried and true. There's no new and untested technology required to work with it, and the really great thing is that most

Internet users have credit cards, so they're ready to do business. Furthermore, there are a number of international credit cards: Visa, MasterCard, and American Express are used throughout the world.

That's the good news. Now for the bad. Credit-card orders are processed electronically across special networks that have been set up for the purpose—there's a small number of these networks, half a dozen to a dozen, I believe. In order to take credit-card orders you'll have to have a "merchant account" with one of these credit-card networks. The credit-card networks charge a small application fee, somewhere around $35. But they don't charge you, they charge what are known as "merchant service providers" (MSPs), companies that sell credit-card merchant accounts. The MSPs will charge you anywhere from $300 to $3,000 for the privilege of applying for an account. In some cases they'll include software or a hardware terminal, but even if they do, the real value of these products is pretty low.

This whole business is a real scam, though I believe it's probably coming to an end soon—for reasons I'm not going to elaborate on here I believe the Internet is going to force prices down, and force many of the MSPs out of business.

Many MSPs talk in terms of "leases," when in fact they are simply processing paperwork and not even providing you with any hardware or software. For instance, if you buy access to an online transaction-processing service, you'll pay a monthly fee to use that service. But you may also pay the MSP a monthly "lease" payment. What are you leasing? The MSP may tell you that you're leasing the transaction-processing software, and the Web form I told you about that allows you to enter transactions by hand, but in fact that's already included in the monthly fee for the transaction-processing service. So what's the lease payment for? It's to pay for the MSP to process your paperwork (on average they can do two or three customers an hour), and to pay the network's $35 application fee.

My dictionary defines "lease" as "a contract by which one conveys real estate, equipment, or facilities for a specified term and for a specified rent." But in fact with a credit-card merchant account the lease you're paying is often really nothing more than a processing fee. Rather than tell you the paperwork processing fee is $2,400—which would be pretty hard to swallow—the MSP tells you it's a lease that you have to pay over 48 months for $50 a month.

Another example: in some cases you will pay a large lease payment, perhaps over several years, for software that costs $350 or so on the open market. You might get a merchant account and along with that account get a copy of PCAuthorize. Your "lease" maybe $2,000. But PCAuthorize—which is one of the best PC-based credit-card processing programs—can be bought directly from

Tellan Software: http://www.tellan.com/. Late in 1997 I paid $358 for my copy. They don't sell the product online, and don't even post the prices online, but if you call them you can purchase over the phone. So what did you pay $2,000 for? For the MSP to process your paperwork, to pay the network's $35 application fee, and to send you a software program with a retail price under $400.

So these lease payments are generally not true lease payments, you're simply paying for the MSP to submit your application to the credit-card network. The merchant service provider may tell you that you're also paying for customer service—this may be true, maybe not. Many merchant service providers do not provide customer service, they merely sign up merchants for the credit-card networks, which then provide customer service (and probably charge a small monthly fee for it).

So how do you find a merchant account? Ah, that depends on how you plan to process transactions. If you want to do online transaction processing, the procedure goes like this:

1. Pick the shopping-cart system you want to work with (making sure, of course, that it can be used for online transaction processing).
2. Find out who sells merchant accounts that can be used with the transaction-processing "gateway" the shopping-cart system is set up to use (in some cases you may be given just one company to go to).
3. If you have a number of companies to choose from, call one by one and shop carefully for the right price. (I'll tell you what to ask in a moment.)

If you are going to process all your orders offline, you have much more choice; you can shop for a merchant account anywhere. Here's the best place to get a merchant account; through some kind of association that has an agreement with a credit-card network to sell accounts to its members. What an MSP may sell for $2,000, you may be able to get for just $25 through your association. For instance, **Costco** provides its Executive members with a very low-cost plan—just $25 to sign up, and no monthly fee: http://www.costco.com/. **Sams Club** also has a merchant-account program for their business members, though I don't know the costs: http://www.samsclub.com/. If you're in the publishing business (or want to be just so that you can get credit-card merchant accounts!), I know that **PMA** (http://www.pma-online.org/) and **SPAN** http://www.spannet.org/ both have merchant-account programs, but I'm sure many other business and industry organizations do, too, so look around.

If you can't find a merchant account through one of these sources, you should really shop very carefully. I've found some companies selling merchant accounts for between $300 and $500, others that you'll end up paying thousands. Here are a few things to ask:

1. What is the setup fee?
2. What is the monthly statement fee?
3. Is there a monthly minimum charge?
4. If so, is the statement fee applied against the minimum?
5. What's the discount rate (the percentage that is taken from each order)?
6. What's the transaction fee (the flat rate per order, perhaps 25¢ 35¢)?
7. Are there any other charges we haven't discussed?

If you're using online transaction processing, there are some more questions:

8. What's the gateway fee?
9. Is there a gateway transaction fee?

If you haven't found an association that will provide you with a credit-card merchant account … try again. If you still can't find one, I suggest you start at the **Yahoo!—Merchant Services** page: http://dir.yahoo.com/Business_and_ Economy/Companies/Financial_Services/Transaction_Clearing/Credit_Card_Merchant_ Services/.

Can You Avoid Credit Cards?

Quite simply, No. It really doesn't make a lot of sense to try to take orders on the Web if you are not going to accept credit cards, though you may run into companies trying to do this. I've seen one small software company in Europe taking orders in checks drawn on a German bank or in cash—no credit cards. I wonder how much money they're losing. Taking credit cards allows you to accept orders from outside your country, and it also allows you to do business with people who simply won't do business with you if you don't take credit cards. Accepting cards provides a degree of comfort for some buyers; they feel that you must be a real business and that if you don't deliver—remember, this is a blind transaction, a purchase across cyberspace with people they've never seen—they'll have the credit-card company on their side and be able to cancel the charge. In most cases you really do need to work with credit cards if you're selling something online. (Okay, so there are always exceptions, such as if you're selling antique cars or works of art—maybe you can work with checks. But in most cases, you'll need to accept credit cards.)

Checks

You can accept checks online in more ways than one. Sure, you can provide buyers with your mailing address and have them send you a check, but you can also use something that's often known as *checks by phone* or *phone checks*. With this service you can accept checks over the phone, by e-mail, through a form at your Web site, or by fax. All you need is the information from the check, not the check itself.

How can you deposit a check without a signature? Well, you have to put something on the signature line, but you can put SIGNATURE NOT REQUIRED, or the buyer can authorize you to sign the check. In effect you are creating a bank draft. It's perfectly legal and it's been done for years. The difference is that now it's being done by small businesses. The process is regulated by the Federal Trade Commission, which stipulates that either the buyer must verbally authorize the transaction, or a notice of the transaction—a copy of the check—must be sent to the buyer.

There are software programs that are available for as little as $99 to print these checks. You simply type in the information provided by the buyer, print the check, and deposit the check at your bank—you need this software in order to create checks that are machine-readable. Or you can use a service that will process the transaction online; you fill in the information in the program, and that information is transmitted to the service. The service may verify the check information by ensuring that the user has included all the required and valid information and by searching a database of bad-check writers. Then it prints a bank draft and sends it to you. Some services even have a check-guarantee service; for an additional fee the payment from the buyer is guaranteed, so if the check bounces, the service has to collect, not you.

These check-processing services charge a transaction fee—perhaps as much as $1.50 a transaction, or sometimes a percentage—and generally charge a sign-up fee, too. Some services provide you with an Internet form that you can use for your customers to fill in, and process the transaction on a secure server. However, note that many of these services work only with U.S. checks; you'll have to look a little harder to find services that will process non-U.S. checks.

There aren't many shopping-cart programs that are set up to process checks, but some of the gateways I mentioned earlier, such as AuthorizeNet, can also do check transactions. Right now I think you'll find check transactions a hassle, but we may see them being added to more shopping carts at some point.

You can find information about processing checks at these Web sites:

Automated Check Transfers ACT
http://members.tripod.com/~conjelko/

CFI Group
http://www.dfw.net/~jedwards/

Online-Check Systems
http://www.onlinecheck.com/

PhoneChex
http://www.phonechex.com/

Quick-Checks
http://www.quick-checks.com/

Redi-Check
http://www.redi-check.com/

USA Check
http://www.valleynet.net/~usaweb/usachek.htm

Yahoo!—Check Services
http://www.yahoo.com/Business_and_Economy/Companies/Financial_
Services/Transaction_Clearing/Check_Services/

Digital Cash

You've probably heard of various digital-cash systems—methods for transferring money between people on the Internet. These are not checks—the money's not drawn on a bank—nor credit transactions—the money is not drawn from a credit account. These are actual "cash" transactions, using a form of digital cash.

Unfortunately their time has not yet arrived. These systems are available today and have been in use for several years. But there are still problems to be dealt with, perhaps the most important of which, from the merchant's perspective, is that very few Internet users are working with these systems. I believe that at present you simply don't need to use digital-cash systems. That situation may change, though I don't expect it to do so for several years.

The idea behind a digital-cash system is that a user can fill up a wallet—a special program running on his computer—and then spend money from it. The wallet is filled with digital money by "buying" the money at a bank, just as with real money. When a buyer makes a purchase, a special number is used; the number is given to the merchant, who gives it to the bank and receives real money in return. At the same time the buyer's wallet loses the amount that he's just spent.

Since the first edition of this book, digital cash seems to have gone into decline. A major player, First Virtual, is no longer around; another major player, DigiCash, sold out to eCash; and CyberCash, at one time *the* big player in this game, has gotten so deep into the credit-card processing business that they seem to have forgotten about the digital-cash business.

So right now, forget about digital cash. But long term, we need some sort of digital-cash system. Many people are eagerly awaiting a digital-cash standard that is widely accepted. Many writers, for instance, would love to be able to charge Web-site visitors five or ten cents to view information or commentary, but such small transactions are currently impractical. And these digital-cash systems still have significant problems. For instance, as publisher Tim O'Reilly pointed out to me, a fully anonymous cash system is not what people want in many cases. Sure, they may want a simple and untraceable way to pay. But they sometimes need a receipt, too, so they can return the product for a refund if it's faulty. Digital-cash systems that promise anonymity don't have a way to provide a receipt. So if you buy software or information using digital cash, transfer it to your computer, and discover that the file is damaged and unusable, you may have no way to prove that you bought the product in the first place and so no way to get a refund or replacement. This is just one of many problems that digital cash has to resolve.

Digital Equipment's Millicent program would allow buyers to spend as little as one tenth of a cent, the smallest transaction possible by any form of digital money. For instance, a writer could charge 5 cents for someone to read an article at his Web site—or even a cent or less—or a company could charge someone 50 cents for a week's access to its site. The Millicent "wallet" can even be set up to automatically pay certain charges. For instance, a user could set up a threshold of two cents. If a page costs a cent, or two cents, the wallet will automatically pay. If the page costs more than two cents, the wallet will ask the user for confirmation first.

With tiny transactions like these it's possible to sell all sorts of information and software, with relatively little sales resistance; who cares about a cent, or five cents? The problem with this system? How many people do *you* know using it? It's a Catch-22; until ordinary people start using these systems, merchants aren't interested, and until merchants are using it, ordinary people won't.

Following are a few Web sites you can visit for more digital-cash information:

CyberCash
  http://www.cybercash.com/
eCash
  http://www.ecashtechnologies.com/

Millicent
> http://www.millicent.digital.com/

Mondex (this company makes smart cash cards)
> http://www.mondexusa.com/

NetBill
> http://www.netbill.com/

Yahoo!—Digital Money
> http://dir.yahoo.com/Business_and_Economy/Companies/Financial_Services/
> Transaction_Clearing/Digital_Money/

Using a Secure Server

A secure server is a Web server that is able to encrypt communications from the server to the browser and accept encrypted communications back from the browser. This is done using a complicated system called public-key encryption. All you really need to know is that if a browser user is viewing a Web page that is administered in secure mode, information sent from the browser is encrypted—garbled—in such a manner that only the Web server administering the page is able to decrypt the information. The server can then save the decrypted information in a file on its hard disk, where you can access it.

This is important to you because it's important to many Internet users. Many people simply won't use their credit cards online, though resistance to doing so is dropping. But many of those who will use them online will use them only at a secure server. So if you use a secure server, you increase the chance that people will buy from you. You'll probably be transferring the saved information back to your computer using an unencrypted FTP session, however, which just shows that public perception is often more important than reality. However, you can transfer this data by setting up a Web page at your hosting company's secure server, and including a link to the file you want to transfer, so the file will transfer securely.

How do you get a secure server, then? If you're using a shopping-cart system set up by your hosting company, or by a shopping-cart service company, none of this is a problem; the secure server will be set up for you. You'll probably get to share the company's server "certificate," too—in order to set up secure forms the server has to have a certificate. In most cases the companies are not legally entitled to share the certificate, but they do it anyway (most companies are using VeriSign certificates, and VeriSign expressly forbids the sharing of certificates). Some companies tell their merchants that they must buy their own certificate if they want a store, and they're half right (because VeriSign says they mustn't share), but half wrong (because Thawte sells certificates and allows sharing, and in any case VeriSign doesn't currently enforce the regulation). You can find **VeriSign** at http://www.verisign.com/, and **Thawte** at http://www.thawte.com/.

In some cases—if you're installing your own shopping-cart software at your Web site, or a dumb form—you may need to know a little more about setting up form security. Many Web-hosting companies have secure servers, as we discussed in Chapter 4, so you may be able to use your host company's. The cost of using the server may be included in your Web-site fees, though some companies split off this service and charge extra. Even though a server is a secure server, this doesn't mean that all the pages at that site will be secure—it can be set up to make some pages secure and others not.

*You may not be able to use forms created with Microsoft FrontPage at a secure server. If the system administrator has not configured the secure server with the FrontPage servers extensions— and there's a good chance he hasn't—then the form won't work. You can use another form handler, though, such as the Form to File example script at this book's Web site (see this page at the **Poor Richard's** Web site: http://PoorRichard.com/examples/ shop.htm).*

Using the hosting company's secure server is really very easy. For instance, when you use http://TopFloor.com/, you are actually taken to a directory on a hosting company's server that can also be addressed in this manner: https://www.bigbiz.com/topfloor/. So let's say I want to put an order form in that directory and link to it from another page at my site. I can link to the form in the normal way—for instance, I can simply create a link with the filename order.htm—or I can link to the form through the hosting company's secure server, like this: https://www.bigbiz.com/topfloor/order. htm (that's an example, not a working form). If I use the first type of link, the form is not secure. If I use the second type of link, the form is secure.

Fulfillment Services

The Internet has prompted the creation of many new businesses. For instance, many writers and programmers have seen a way to promote their writing online. If they do so successfully, they quickly run into a serious problem—fulfillment; in other words, handling the process of packing the product that has been ordered and shipping it out. This is a time-consuming and costly procedure, and many people who regard their time as very valuable end up spending way too much of it licking stamps and going to the post office. With software, many products can be delivered online, of course, though often it's still necessary to deliver manuals or CD-ROMs.

There's another way: use a fulfillment service, one that ships products according to your instructions. You can even find fulfillment services that will handle orders that come in over the phone—you are going to put a phone number at your site, aren't you? You can even use a fulfillment service to fill orders in other countries. For instance, if you are in Britain or France, you may want to sell your products in the U.S. Rather than shipping individual orders across the Atlantic, you may find it more efficient to ship large quantities of your products periodically to a U.S. fulfillment service, and have that service ship individual orders. You'll be able to accept orders in cyberspace in U.S. funds and ship directly to U.S. consumers, yet have no direct business presence in the U.S.

You can find local fulfillment services in your local Yellow Pages. Directories of publisher's resources are good places to look, too, because so many publishers use fulfillment services to ship their books. Or try the following places:

Bookmasters
http://www.bookmasters.com/

NetShip
http://www.netship.com/

Yahoo!—British Fulfillment Services
http://dir.yahoo.com/Regional/Countries/United_Kingdom/Business_and_
Economy/Companies/Marketing/Fulfillment_Services/

Yahoo!—Canadian Fulfillment Services
http://www.yahoo.com/Regional/Countries/Canada/Business_and_Economy/
Companies/Marketing/Fulfillment_Services/

Yahoo!—Fulfillment Services
http://dir.yahoo.com/Business_and_Economy/Companies/Marketing/
Fulfillment_Services/

Here are a few things to consider when looking for a fulfillment service:

- Do they have staff who can take orders by phone 24 hours a day, or do they just ship products to lists of people that you send to them? (Many fulfillment companies ship, but do not process orders.)
- Do they have their own toll-free lines, or do you have to provide your own line?
- Do you have to provide your own credit-card merchant account, or are they willing to process credit cards for you?

- Can they accept orders by fax and mail?
- Can you e-mail orders to them?
- What are their charges? Make sure you understand every little charge, as you'll probably be charged for every "touch" (that is, every little process involved in taking the order and shipping the product).

Online Transactions—Are They Safe?

Yes.

Okay, perhaps that's not quite enough of an explanation.

One of the big questions in many people's minds is whether, if they provide their credit-card numbers, the information can be stolen. Online transactions are safe—very safe. The credit-card companies consider them safer than real-world credit-card transactions. That doesn't mean that online credit-card fraud is not possible—it clearly is. But it's less likely than in the real world; only a tiny fraction of the billion dollars of annual credit-card fraud is carried out online.

Why is it safer? It's a simple matter of numbers and abilities. It's much harder to steal a credit-card number online than in the real world. There are all sorts of real-world strategies for stealing credit-card numbers, from getting a job at a convenience store to rifling through the convenience store's trash, from looking over people's shoulders in supermarkets to calling them on the phone and offering a deal they just can't refuse. Very few people know how to steal credit-card numbers online; millions know how to do it offline.

Also, there are ways to make ordering online safer still. If you set up an order form at a secure Web server, you can have data transmitted from the buyer's browser back to the Web server in an encrypted form. Anyone listening in on communications between the server and browser won't be able to read those communications, and so won't be able to steal any credit-card numbers. Don't worry about all the talk of how such encryption can be cracked. If you are sending national security secrets across the Web, you should be worried. If you are carrying out credit-card transactions, you shouldn't.

Having said all that, it's true that however secure such transactions are, many people won't make online transactions because they believe they are not secure. It's still the number one reason cited by people who won't buy online. So you still need to provide a way for people to order products offline. Cover all your bases; allow them to order by mail, by phone, and by fax.

Chapter Fourteen

Working With E-mail

You've learned by now how to set up your Web site, but you haven't finished yet. Before I explain how to promote your site there's another setup issue: you need to set up your e-mail. Now, that might sound like a simple thing, but there's perhaps more to it than meets the eye, and an effective Web site—one that is not a mere billboard but that is designed to work interactively with its visitors—cannot work alone.

In this chapter we'll be looking at the following issues:

- Why you need your own domain name
- Using autoresponders
- Using autoforwarding
- Collecting e-mail addresses
- E-mail newsletters
- Mailing-list discussion groups.

You Need Your Own Domain Name

If you have your own domain name, you can play all sorts of fancy tricks with e-mail by creating as many e-mail accounts as you want, then managing each account separately. Here's why. When an e-mail message is being transferred across the Internet, the text that appears to the left of the @ sign is pretty much irrelevant. For instance, if you send an e-mail message to theboss@acmesewer cover.com, the message will be sent to the acmesewercover.com domain. None of the computers transferring the message to acmesewercover.com know or care whether there's an account at that domain called theboss; they'll transfer the file and let the computer administering the domain figure out what to do with the message.

Now, when the message gets to the mail server handling this domain, one of several things may happen. The mail server may look at the message, notice that there is a POP (Post Office Protocol) box of the same name, and drop the message into that box. (A POP "box" is really a text file—every time a new message is dropped into the box, it's really just appended to the end of the text file.)

The mail server may look at the message, decide that there is no such account as theboss, and send the message back to the person who mailed it. Or it may notice that it's been given special instructions for this address—it may have been told to delete all messages to that address, or perhaps forward messages to another address. Finally, it may do something that has a lot of implications for us. It may have been told that one of the POP boxes is a sort of default or primary box, and that if it sees any message it's not sure how to handle—there's no matching POP box and it has no other instructions—it should drop it into the primary box. In which case the person responsible for that box can figure out what to do with it. That's a very useful situation: a POP box that will receive messages sent to all and any e-mail accounts at your domain. Why all and any? Because then you can create as many e-mail addresses as you want:

- sales@acmesewercover.com
- info@acmesewercover.com
- sewernews@acmesewercover.com
- theboss@acmesewercover.com
- susan@acmesewercover.com
- whateveryouwant@acmesewercover.com.

What do I mean by "create" an e-mail address? Well, if your e-mail system is set up to drop unrecognized messages into the primary POP box, when you *tell* someone to use a particular e-mail address, you've just "created" that address. Forget about e-mail addresses you've used before—when you signed up with AOL, or a small local ISP, you were given an e-mail address, and they set it up on their system so that you could receive e-mail at that address. This is different, you're no longer limited to just one address, you can have thousands if your mail system is set up correctly.

You'll probably do two things with e-mail addresses. First, you'll have a small number for which you set up POP boxes. All mail to fred@acmesewercover.com, for instance, can be dropped into a POP box, and only Fred will grab e-mail from the box. You might have one box for each of your employees. (So now you're playing the role of the ISP, handing out e-mail addresses.)

The other kind of e-mail address is the one you want to go to the primary POP box. You might use lots of different addresses, and they all go into the primary POP box. For instance, let's say you're setting up a form at your Web site that will be used to collect e-mail addresses to which you can mail a newsletter once a month or so. You want to be able to take the e-mail addresses submitted from that form and automatically drop them into a mailing list (I'll show you how to do that later in this chapter). So you tell the CGI script handling the form to send an e-mail message to newssubscribe@acmesewercover.com. That's it—you've just created an e-mail address. The mere act of telling someone a new e-mail address or putting it into a CGI script is, in effect, creating the address. As soon as the first visitor fills out the form and clicks the submit button, the CGI script will send the message to newssubscribe@acmesewercover.com, and the mail system will drop it into your primary POP box. You can then use your e-mail program's filters to act on the message in some way, as we'll see later.

So, as we discussed in Chapter 2, make sure you get the right kind of POP account. Make sure the Web-hosting company or e-mail company sets up the account so that unrecognized e-mail is *not* returned to the sender—it should be dropped into the primary POP box.

Using Autoresponders

An autoresponder—also known as a mail responder—is an e-mail program that … well … automatically responds. When a message arrives that's addressed to the account being monitored by the autoresponder program, the program immediately returns an e-mail message.

You've probably seen info@ e-mail addresses. These are often autoresponder addresses. For instance, acmesewercover.com might set up the info@acmesewercover.com address. Anyone mailing to that address will automatically get a message about the company.

The autoresponder I've just described is sometimes known as a *one-to-one autoresponder*. There's another form, known as a *server autoresponder*. In this case the program looks at the contents of the Subject: line or the Body of the incoming message, and decides what to send out according to what it finds there. So, for instance, Acme Sewer Covers might have a single autoresponder address—info@acmesewercover.com—and users could type something in the Subject: line to determine what they receive. For instance, Large Covers in the Subject: line would retrieve information on large sewer-hole covers, Small Covers would retrieve information on small covers, Contest would get information about the contest for tickets to visit Vienna's world-famous sewer system, and so on. (You probably won't be using one of these systems, though; by far the most common type of autoresponders are the one-to-one responders.)

If you are using a Web-hosting company, you probably already have autoresponders available—most hosting companies provide them. There are a number of features a really good autoresponder should have, as follows:

- You should be able to define the From: e-mail address and name, and the Subject: line of the outgoing message (or choose to use the same Subject: line as the incoming message). Virtually all autoresponders can do this.
- You should be able to quote the incoming message in the outgoing response.
- You should be able to create a log file showing you the name and e-mail address from every incoming message, along with the date of receipt and the first few characters of the incoming message.
- You should be able to forward the message to another e-mail address, so you can save a copy of every incoming message, or perhaps send the message to a mailing-list server to subscribe the sender.

You'll have trouble finding an autoresponder with these features, though. The last is particularly useful, though extremely rare. I could have used this feature when I was doing my radio "tour" promoting the first edition of this book. On the air I would give the Web site's URL, and mention my autoresponder so that listeners could get several free articles I had written and subscribe to my newsletter at the same time. The last feature would have allowed me to automate the whole process, but instead I had to add them to the newsletter mailing list by hand.

Setting Up an Autoresponder

Your Web-hosting company or POP company should have a system you can use to set up autoresponders (remember, this was one of the issues covered in Chapter 4). This may be easy to install or it may be downright awkward. With luck, your Web-hosting company has a nice, simple-to-use system that helps you quickly configure an autoresponder—they should have some kind of form you fill in on a Web page. Unfortunately some Web-hosting companies are not quite so enlightened; they don't provide autoresponder forms. Rather, they expect you to fool around with mail-processing scripts. One system used by a number of Web-hosting companies is procmail. Unfortunately procmail can be complicated to work with, and it's also very poorly documented, so if the Web-hosting company doesn't provide more information about the program, you'll probably find procmail very difficult to work with. Well, okay, you might find it next to impossible. Another common system is sendmail, but that's even more complicated, and I have no intention of explaining it!

In the first edition of this book I spent several pages explaining exactly how to use procmail. That was 1997, and things were a little different then. I think most hosting companies probably have forms now, so I've pulled that section from this book. But just in case *you* run into a situation in which you have to use procmail, I've posted the information at my Web site:

Procmail Instructions: http://PoorRichard.com/examples/procmail.htm

But if your hosting company, in the year 2000, still isn't providing a nice, easy-to-use e-mail setup page, maybe you need another hosting company!

Using Your E-mail "Client"

You may have heard your e-mail program referred to as an e-mail "client." That's a geek word for *program*; I generally avoid the term, but sometimes it's handy. If I said e-mail program I might be referring to the e-mail POP server, for example. What I want to talk about right now, though, is the program you use, the client program, to read your e-mail.

You can, if you wish, set up autoresponses to be sent from your e-mail program. For instance, let's say you are using **AK-Mail** (http://www.akmail.com/), **Pegasus** (http://www.pegasus.usa.com/), or **Eudora Pro** (http://www.eudora.com/). These programs allow you to filter incoming mail. I'm not going to explain how to do that—each program works differently, and in any case, you may be using another program. Read the documentation that comes with your e-mail program and play with filters for a while, and you'll find that you can tell the program what to do when it receives certain messages. You can see an example of an AK-Mail filter screen in Figure 14.1.

For instance, you could set up a filter to look at the To: line of every incoming message. If the filter saw the word info on the To: line, it could send out an e-mail message taken from a file called info.txt. If it saw the word newproduct on the To: line, it could send out the newproduct.txt file, and so on.

You can also set up filters to look at the Subject: line. People wanting information could send all messages to info@acmesewercover.com, then put on the Subject: line a word describing what they want. If the filter sees Large Covers in the Subject: line, it sends the text from the large.txt file; if it sees Small Covers, it sends text from the small.txt file, and so on.

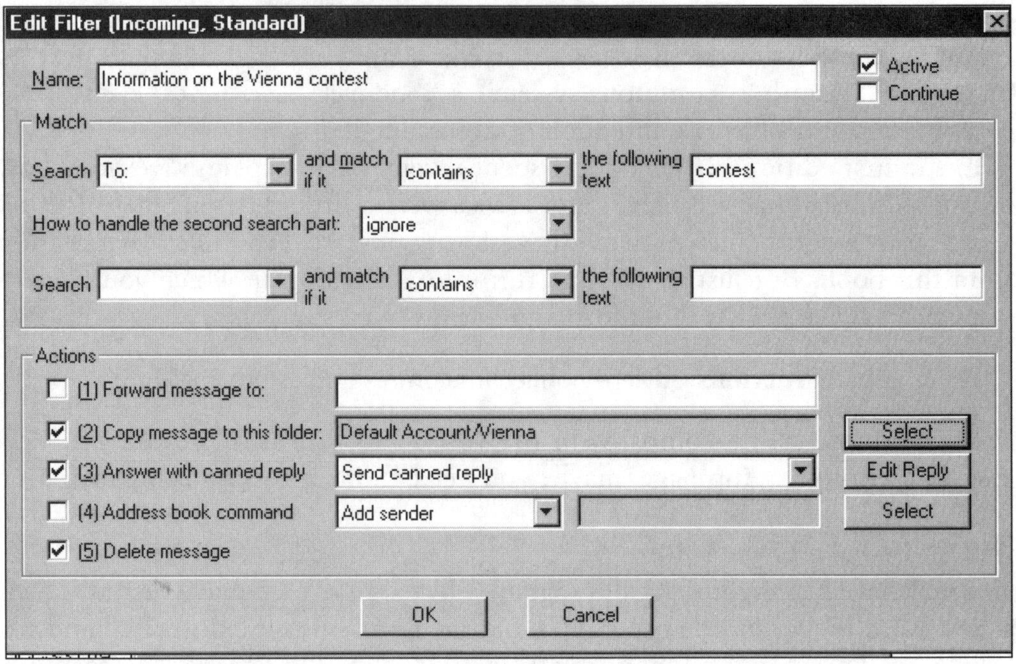

Figure 14.1: Here's where you set up filters in AK-Mail.

The limitation with this method may or may not be serious, depending on how you work. The problem is that autoresponses are not sent until your e-mail program receives the incoming message, processes the message, and sends the response. So if you log onto the Internet only once or twice a week, this method may not be suitable. If you log on and stay on all day, and have your e-mail program check for mail every 10 minutes, then it will probably be fine. Of course, autoresponses won't be sent if you log off when you stop work each day. But it's fairly easy to set up an e-mail program to log onto the Internet automatically, grab your incoming mail, and log off again, so you can set up a computer to do this every half hour, even during the night.

Autoresponder Services

Another way to set up autoresponders is to use an autoresponder service. As with everything else on the Internet, there are services, both free and paid, that you can work with. Some of them have advanced autoresponse features. For instance, I've see *sequential autoresponders* that engage the sender in a sort of "conversation" in which an interested sender can request and receive more information in a series of steps; *list-building autoresponders* that respond and then add the person to a mailing list (as I described earlier); *follow-up autoresponders*, which send a series of responses spread out over several days or weeks, and so on. Some of these services also provide reports showing you the number of messages you've received.

Autoresponder service may cost as little as $50 or $60 a year, maybe less if you can find a free service (see Chapter 11 for a list of free-utility sites). Since the first edition of this book, though, most of the autoresponder companies seem to have disappeared, so there's a bit less choice now.

Here's an example of a real-life use of an autoresponder. When the publisher of The Official Netscape JavaScript 1.2 Book *let the "Online Companion" Web site disappear, there were many complaints from readers. So I set up the Online Companion at my own Web site and tried to post the URL at the book's page at Amazon.com. But Amazon.com has banned the placing of URLs in reviews (they don't want people leaving their site). Instead I set up an autoresponder and mentioned that in a review— now readers needing to find the Online Companion can simply e-mail* JavaScriptOLC@TopFloor.com *to find out where it is.*

Autoresponders.com
http://www.autoResponders.com/

DataBack Systems
http://www.databack.com/

Hartley's
http://www.hartley.on.ca/

InfoBack.Net
http://www.infoback.net/

Using Autoforwarding

Another service you may want to use is autoforwarding. This is not really a marketing tool so much as a convenience. Autoforwarding simply allows you to set up your mail account at the Web-hosting company to send all the mail received to another place. This may be useful, though it's not as big a deal as it's sometimes made out to be. It appears to be a big deal because many Internet users, even people setting up Web sites, still haven't quite understood the concept that the company that provides you with Internet access doesn't have to be the same one that provides you with e-mail service, as we discussed in Chapter 2. They have a service provider or online service, they've always got their e-mail there, so now they want all the e-mail forwarded to that account.

Still, it may be useful, especially if you have several employees and you want to forward their mail to their individual accounts, or if you want to forward mail to someone who's watching the site for you while you're on vacation.

Autoforwarding may be set up using some kind of form provided for you at the Web site, or you may have to edit the .domains file. ... No, I'm not getting into that. Again, your hosting company should have provided you with a forms-based system that you can use to forward e-mail. This is almost a new century, and if you have to be messing around with the .domains file, you probably need another hosting company. If you want to see the **.domains description** that was in the first edition, go to http://PoorRichard.com/examples/domains.htm.

Distributing Information via E-mail

There's more to working with e-mail than just setting up autoresponders and mail forwarding. How about using the mail system to communicate with your clients and potential clients? How about sending out newsletters, announcing products, and even creating mailing lists in which people can get involved in discussions related to your area of interest? These things can be done quite easily and cheaply. I have a mailing list that goes to 35,000 people every couple of weeks (and it's growing by 1,100 to 2,000 every couple of weeks, too). I have friends that mail to 150,000 or 160,000 people every day! In fact there's money to be made in the e-mail publishing business—one e-mail publisher I know, who works by himself out of his home, was recently offered $1M for his publication ... and he turned it down, because it wasn't enough.

By the way, Top Floor Publishing recently published a book on this very subject. The rest of this chapter is an overview, in effect. If you want to go into real detail, read *Poor Richard's E-mail Publishing* (http://PoorRichard.com/email/), by Chris Pirillo. Chris publishes *Lockergnome*, which goes to around 150,000 subscribers six times a week.

Collecting E-mail Addresses

As I've mentioned before, you should be collecting e-mail addresses—of people who visit your Web site, of people who contact you, and of people mailing to your autoresponders. How can you grab these addresses? Well, there's a variety of ways. At the Web site, you can use the following techniques to grab addresses entered into a form:

- Use a form that places the e-mail addresses into a text file
- Use a script that sends the e-mail addresses to you, then grab the addresses from the e-mail using one of the following methods

With incoming e-mail you can do these things:

- Filter the mail, placing the e-mail addresses into an address book
- Copy addresses from messages to the address book with a menu command
- Save addresses from messages directed at your autoresponders into a log file.

Let's consider each issue in turn.

Use a Form to Create a Text File

As we discussed in Chapter 12, you can create forms that save information in a text file. You can then transfer this text file back to your computer and open it in a text editor or a database program. Microsoft FrontPage can create such forms very quickly, or you can use a CGI script to do so, or perhaps one of the free-utility services listed in Chapter 11. (I haven't seen one of these services that saves the form response in a text file, but there might be one out there.)

If you save the information in the correct format, importing into a database program is very simple. For instance, FrontPage allows you to specify how to separate the data stored in each entry (each form submission). You can select *Text Database Using Comma as a Separator*, *Text Database Using Tab as a Separator*, or *Text Database Using Space as a Separator*. There are CGI scripts that can do the same sort of things.

Database programs can import text files formatted in various ways, so you should take a look at your database program and see which import format is best, then set up the form to save the data in that format. Why do you need a database program? Because then you can quickly import text from your forms and export it in any way you wish. For instance, perhaps the form collected a first name, last name, e-mail address, and comments. If you want to use this in a mailing list, you need only the first three items; the format you need those items in depends on the e-mail program you are using. For instance, your mail program may require something like this:

```
first_name, last_name <e-mail address>
```

Other e-mail programs may require different formats for you to import the text into an address book (we'll get to that below). A database program will allow you to create a text file in most formats, or in a format that can be quickly modified in a word processor. Furthermore, you may want to use the information as part of a more sophisticated customer database, not just for handling e-mail mailings. The information you import into your database program can be the core of that customer database.

Use a Script to Send E-mail

As you saw in Chapters 11 and 12, you can use a CGI script to capture text from a form and send it as e-mail to whatever address you want; or, again, one of the free-utility services. You may want to do this if you don't have a busy site so it's no big deal to handle the few incoming messages you receive directly, rather than needing to load them into a text file and then import them into a database. You may also want to use this method if people are using a form to submit their e-mail addresses to join a mailing list, as we'll see below.

Filter the Mail into an Address Book

It may be possible for you to load e-mail addresses from incoming messages directly into an address book. I know of two e-mail programs that can do this: **AK-Mail** (http://www.akmail.com/) and **Pegasus** (http://www.pegasus.usa.com/). The major programs (Eudora, Outlook, and Netscape Messenger), as far as I know, still can't do this.

We discussed filtering systems earlier, when I showed you how to set up a simple autoresponder. You can use these filters in AK-Mail and Pegasus to grab an e-mail address from an incoming message, then drop it into an address book (or distribution list, as it's called in Pegasus). For instance, take a look at Figure 14.2. This is the box in which filters are set up in Pegasus Mail for Windows, and it's fairly straightforward; I've

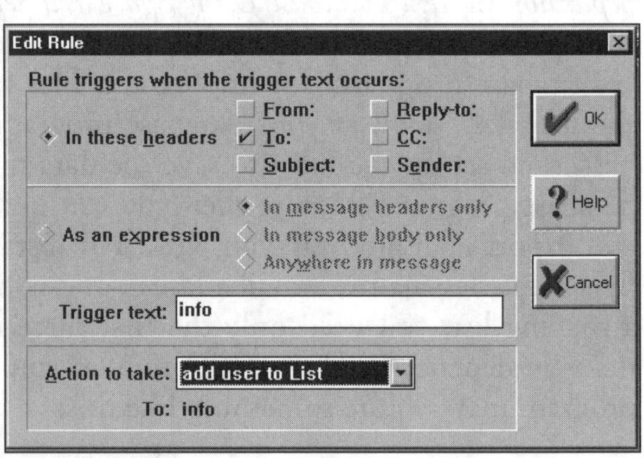

Figure 14.2: Setting up a filter in Pegasus Mail for Windows.

selected In These Headers and the To: check box to tell Pegasus to take a look at the address in the To: line. In the Trigger Text text box I've told it to look for the word info. And in the Action to Take drop-down list box I've selected Add User to List. When I did so, a box opened in which I could create or select a distribution list; I created one called info.

So what happens when someone sends e-mail to info@acmesewercover.com if you've set up a filter in this manner? The address is taken and placed into the info distribution list.

Copy Addresses with a Menu Command

If you can't filter e-mail directly into an address book—and few e-mail programs let you do so—there's generally another way to add the address. Most e-mail programs have a command that will take the selected message's e-mail address and place it into an address book; in other words, although most programs can't add the addresses to the address book automatically, you can use a menu command to do so manually. For instance, in Eudora Pro you can select a message and then select Special|Make Address Book Entry. You can even select multiple addresses, then select Special|Make Address Book Entry, then enter the name of an existing mailing list. You'll be given the option of replacing the list or adding the addresses to the list.

Save Addresses in Autoresponder Log Files

If you have access to a decent autoresponder system, you should be able to set it up to place the names and addresses of people sending you messages into a text file, as I mentioned earlier. You'll end up with a log file containing a list, perhaps something like this:

```
Mon Nov 11 10:47:09 EST 1997 : Robin Hood
<robin@sherwood.com> :
Tue Dec 10 03:27:07 EST 1997 : George Washington
<georgew@whitehouse.gov> :
```

This log file can be transferred from the server to your computer, and the addresses imported into an address book.

Working with Mailing Lists

Now that you've got a list of e-mail addresses, what do you do with it? The first thing is to get the list into a mailing program in some way. You want to place it in the program as a single list, so you can create one message that will be sent to all the addresses on the list at the same time. If you've been filtering messages directly into a distribution list or address book, you've already got them there. Or if you've been using some kind of Add to Address Book menu command to add messages one by one, you've got them there too. If you have a list of addresses in a text file, though, whether created by an autoresponder or a Web form, you'll have to import them somehow.

For instance, if you are using AK-Mail, there's a *Create From Address List* command. You have to create a text file with the addresses in this format:

```
Andreas Kinzler <akinzler@akmail.com>
Peter Kent <pkent@topfloor.com>
```

You can use a database program to export the list separated by spaces, then add the <> brackets in a word processor—you can use the word processor's search-and-replace feature to add these fairly quickly. Make sure you save the list as ASCII text. Then open the Address Book window and select Book|Create From Address List to import all the addresses. If you're using Eudora Pro 3.0, you can simply select a list of e-mail addresses from a text file, copy them to the Clipboard, then paste them into the Address Book window. Each program's a little different, so check the documentation of the program you're working with.

You may also be able to find programs designed especially to work with a database program, pulling addresses out of the database as needed. For instance, take a look at **Arial Software's Sign-Up** (http://www.arialsoftware.com/). This program will take incoming e-mail messages or data from a Web form and place the contact information into a database.

Distributing Newsletters and Other Information

You can use your mailing list in a variety of ways, such as the following:

- To distribute newsletters and other forms of information to clients, potential clients, and employees. The newsletter is often used as a promotional tool in the real world—outside cyberspace—so there's no reason you can't use it on the Internet. The big difference is that on the Internet it costs next to nothing to distribute.
- To announce new products and modifications to existing products.
- To announce special offers such as discounts or bundling deals.
- To let people know when you've added an important new feature to your Web site. But think about what you are announcing; are you telling them something they really want to know, or simply something you think is cool?

- To announce a special event of some kind—a celebrity chat or visit to your discussion group (see Chapter 12), for instance.
- To ask for feedback on your products.
- To ask people who've downloaded software from your site why they haven't registered it—if they're not using it, why not, what features are missing, what didn't they like?
- To ask for product testers.

There must be thousands of ways to use an e-mail list. Don't overdo it, though. Don't mail too often, and if anyone asks to be removed from the list, do so immediately. If people have given you their e-mail addresses, there's nothing wrong with using them, as long as you do it in a sensible manner. (We'll be discussing spam later in this chapter.)

Consider placing a note at the top or bottom of the message explaining how the user can get off the list. One way is to have them mail to an e-mail address that is filtered to remove the incoming address from a distribution list or address book—the opposite of the situation we've just discussed.

Unfortunately different programs handle the Bcc: line differently. Some will place the address from the Bcc: line onto the recipient's To: line. Others display the Bcc: address on a Bcc: line, and display the original To: line, as well. Experiment to see how your program works—mail to a few friends and to yourself.

How do you mail to all these people? It's important to get this right, or you'll upset a lot of recipients. You see, most mail programs allow you to mail to an address book, a distribution list, or an "alias" or "nickname" that contains multiple addresses. But if you simply enter the address-book or distribution-list name into the To: text box and send the message, you've just committed a faux pas; everyone who receives the message will see everyone else's e-mail address in the To: line—well, it's no longer a To: line so much as a To: *page* if you have a big list. I've received e-mail messages containing literally hundreds of addresses in the To: line.

Instead, you must use the Bcc: line. The Bcc: line is the Blind Carbon Copy line. It means that everyone on the list gets a copy of the message, but nobody can see who else got a message. Although you place the address-book or distribution-list name on the Bcc: line, when a recipient views the message he'll see his address on the To: line, and won't see the addresses of any other recipients, on any line.

Some e-mail programs won't let you mail to just the Bcc: line; you must have an address in the To: line, as well. So you can put your address on the To: line, then the address-book or distribution-list name on the Bcc: line.

There are a few programs designed for sending out large numbers of e-mail messages at once, as you would be doing with newsletters or bulletins. These programs mail only individual To: copies—that is, everyone on your list gets an individual To: copy. You'll never see more than one address on the To: line—so if you're scared of making a slip and accidentally mailing with a list of addresses on the To: line, use a program like that. And whatever you do, don't use the Cc: line; this is as bad as using the To: line, because all recipients will see the other recipients' addresses on the Cc: line.

Some of these programs even provide merge functions; in other words, you can take information from a contact record and merge it into the message. Instead of saying "Dear Recipient," you can say "Dear John," for instance. Try these programs:

It's a good idea to set up your mail program so that the Cc: line is not normally visible. Turn on the Bcc: line so it's always there. Not all programs will let you do this, but some will.

If you leave the Cc: line visible, believe me, one day you will send a couple of hundred messages on the Cc: line—yes, I've done it. If you're very lucky, people won't be too mad at you.

Campaign (a very capable program, but hard to use)
   http://www.arialsoftware.com/

eMerge (For the Mac—$175)
   http://www.galleon.com/

InfoPress Email-On-Demand ($995)
   http://www.castelle.com/

NetMailer (Very buggy!)
   http://www.alphasoftware.com/

WorldMerge (Very easy to use; a good little program!)
   http://www.coloradosoft.com/

WW Mail ($39.95)
   http://wizardware.com/

By the way, before anyone writes to me complaining that I'm encouraging spam—the mailing of large numbers of unsolicited e-mail messages, which we'll discuss later in this chapter—I just want to say that I'm not. Of course there are many programs out there for mailing spam, but that doesn't mean that some of the functions of these programs can't also be useful for more legitimate purposes, such as sending newsletters. Remember, the telephone may be used to call Gran, or for telemarketing. There are also mail programs that not only send out messages, but also can extract e-mail addresses from newsgroups and online-service directories; I've chosen not to include these, because there are good merge programs that don't have these functions, and I believe that such functions are a real nuisance.

If you're sending out huge numbers of e-mail messages at once, you may need to use a mailing-list program or service, which we'll discuss in a moment.

Setting Up Mailing-List Discussion Groups

There's another meaning for the term *mailing list*. I've already used the term to mean a collection of e-mail addresses to which you can mail

When you mention a URL in an e-mail message, always place the URL on a separate line, or at least with a space immediately before or after the URL. Don't enclose a URL in parentheses or angled brackets.

Rather than this: (http://www.url.com/)

or this: <http://www.url.com/>

Simply do this: http://www.url.com/

Don't place a period at the end of the URL, either. The problem with placing characters before or after URLs is that some e-mail programs choke on them. When the user clicks on the URL to open his browser, the program may send the character at the end of the URL to the browser, causing a browser error that many users won't be able to figure out. Different e-mail programs choke on different characters, so the safest thing is always to begin and end a URL with a space.

a message with a single operation: one message, multiple recipients. But the term also refers to a discussion group based on the e-mail system. Send a message to the discussion group's e-mail address, and a message is sent to everyone who's a member, so everyone can take part in or listen in on (*lurk*, as it's known) a discussion as e-mail messages fly to and fro.

There are really three types of mailing list. We've just discussed the *announcements-only* list—it's used to send messages out, with no incoming messages; newsletters are an announcements-only list. Then there are *moderated discussion groups*—these are true discussion groups with two-way traffic, but they also have a moderator, someone who has the right to reject messages if he feels those messages are inappropriate or abusive. Messages go to the moderator, who checks them, then forwards them to the list. This may be seen as a form of censorship, but there's an awful lot of noise in Internet discussion groups, and a well-moderated group can be a Godsend. Finally, there are *unmoderated discussion groups*. Incoming messages go directly to the mailing list without being vetted by anyone first.

Mailing lists can be a very useful promotional tool. A company can set up a mailing list related to its field of business, and then carefully use the list for promotional means. I don't mean to say a company should do anything unethical or obnoxious in the manner in which it uses the mailing list. But the mere fact that it is hosting the list is often good advertising. And if there's always a company employee listening in and making comments, it's a good way to get an audience for your company, keep a thumb on your industry's pulse, and so on. You might even use the list for occasional advertising messages, as some mailing lists do. As long as it's clear to new members that the list is used for this purpose, and as long as the advertising messages are not too frequent or too obnoxious, it seems that there's no problem with this, and members of a useful group will accept it.

How can you set up a mailing list? Well, you can begin very easily, with your e-mail program. When you start out, you'll probably have few members anyway, so an e-mail program could handle the traffic. However, it's a good idea to set up your computer and e-mail program to check your mail every 10 or 20 minutes throughout the day and night, or the delay in messages reaching the group could prove to be an irritation to many members.

You can set up your filters so that when a message arrives addressed to the group, it's automatically forwarded to a particular address book or distribution list; in other words, it's forwarded to everyone on the list—simple.

You can also set up the program to accept automatic subscriptions and cancellations—to do that you'll have to use an e-mail program, such as AK-Mail or Pegasus, that can filter addresses into and out of address books or distribution lists. You could, for instance, set up an address to accept subscriptions and cancellations—sewernewssub@acmesewercover.com, for instance. You can then set the filters so that when a message arrives with the word Subscribe in the Subject: line, the address from the incoming message is automatically added to the discussion group's address book. When a message arrives with the word

Unsubscribe in the Subject: line, the address is automatically removed from the address book. As an example, see Figure 14.3, where you can see the filter in AK-Mail that is used for removing an address from an address book.

Then set up another e-mail address—sewernews@acmesewercover.com—to be used for the mailing list itself. That is, people would mail to sewernewssub to subscribe and unsubscribe, and sewernews to take part in the mailing-list discussion.

Mailing-List Services

If your mailing-list discussion group—or your newsletter, for that matter—grows very large, you may eventually need a more powerful mailing-list system. As usual, you have several options. You can use the software provided by your Web-hosting company, if any; you can find software for yourself and install it in the directories at your Web site, if your hosting company will let you do so; you can install mailing-list software on your own computer (it's available for PCs and Macintoshes); or you can find a service to run the mailing list for you. These programs and services are good for handling newsletters and announcements, not just mailing lists—even if the flow is just one way, if you're mailing out enough messages at one time, you may want to consider using a special mailing-list program or service.

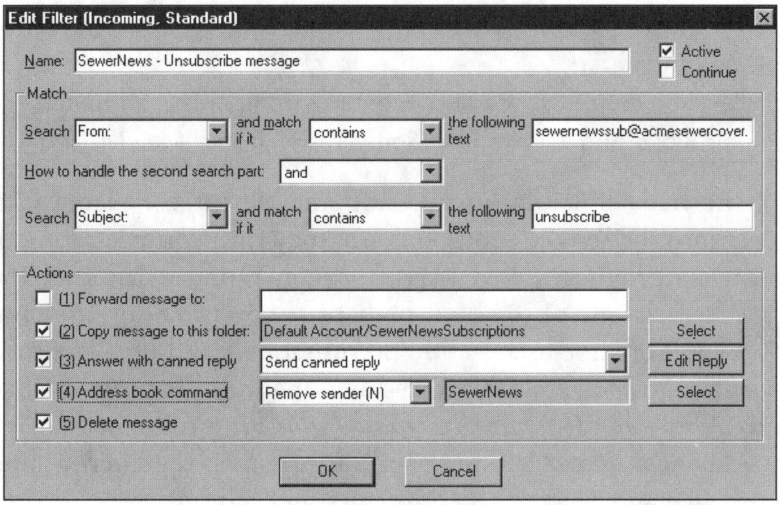

Figure 14.3: Here's how to set an Unsubscribe filter in AK-Mail.

While you can run a small mailing list on a computer connected to a dial-up line, if a list gets too big, you've got problems. Remember, every message sent to the list has to be sent to everyone on the list. So if you have 1,000 members on your mailing list and you are getting 30 messages a day—not an unusual number—you have to send out 30,000 messages a day. How long will it take you to send those out over a modem?

In fact, if you have a big list, your Web-hosting company may not want to host the list. You may be forced to go to a mailing-list host. That's not necessarily a problem, as rates are often quite reasonable. Or free, of course … after all, this is the Internet. Here are a few free services you can look into:

CoolList
   http//www.coollist.com/

EGroups
   http://www.egroups.com/

ListBot
   http://www.listbot.com/

OneList
   http://www.onelist.com/

Topica
   http://www.topica.com/

Web Site Post Office (W SPO)
   http://www.websitepostoffice.com/

Yahoo!—Mailing Lists
   http://dir.yahoo.com/Business_and_Economy/Companies/Computers/
   Communications_and_Networking/Software/Electronic_Mail/Mailing_Lists/

Some of the free services are really not suitable for very large lists, though; when you get into the tens of thousands you may find you need something more powerful. I use a program called **Lyris**, through **Dundee Internet** (http://www.dundee.net/). Lyris is one of the best, perhaps *the* best mailing-list program, and quite a few owners of large lists—100,000 subscribers and up—use this program.

If you want to investigate the professional mailing-list programs, take a look at **Appendix A in** *Poor R ichard's E-mail Publishing* You can find it online, at http://PoorRichard.com/email/. Chris Pirillo has put together a huge list of services, both free and paid, with comments on each one.

Spam, Spam, Spam, Spam ...

If you're a Monty Python fan, you may recall the Spam sketch, in which a customer at a café discovers that there's little on the menu that doesn't include Spam: "... egg and Spam; egg bacon and Spam; egg bacon sausage and Spam; Spam bacon sausage and Spam; Spam egg Spam Spam bacon and Spam; Spam sausage Spam Spam bacon Spam tomato and Spam. ..." The sketch includes a group of Vikings singing a song, the most memorable chorus of which is:

> *Spam, Spam, Spam, Spam*
> *Spam, Spam, Spam, Spam*

What's that got to do with the Internet? Well, the Internet was created and nurtured by the sort of people who watch Monty Python. So it's no surprise that when someone was looking around for a succinct term for a message that is sent to scores of Internet newsgroups at once—over, and over, and over again—he came up with the term spam. There are other theories for the origin of the term. One theory is that it's named after the concept of throwing a brick of Spam at a rotating fan blade. And, as pointed out to me by a colleague, "anyone who was a member of the U.S. military can tell you Spam was ubiquitous, largely unwanted, tasteless, and you got it whether you wanted it or not—all characteristics shared commonly with junk e-mail."

The term spam has changed a little. It's now commonly used to mean any kind of unwanted electronic message that is sent in large quantities. This can include messages sent to newsgroups, to mailing-list discussion groups, or to personal e-mail addresses. The purists may disagree and say that spam refers only to newsgroup messages, but then, the purists are no longer running the Internet.

I must admit, spam is very tempting—Internet spam, that is, not necessarily the meat. You can buy low-cost electronic mailing lists and programs that will suck e-mail addresses out of newsgroups, CompuServe and America Online directories, Web pages and so on. You can set a program to run overnight to do this stuff for you, so it's not hard for a small business to set up a system that will give you literally millions of e-mail addresses very cheaply. Then you can mail to these lists for next to nothing.

To mail to a million people in the real world might cost you half a million dollars or more. To mail to a million people in cyberspace might cost nothing above the fixed costs of your computer and Internet connection, or it might cost $1,000 through a bulk-mailing service—perhaps only $2,000 to mail to three million people (these are actual costs I've seen advertised). You can even send three- or four-line ads as part of larger e-mail messages for as little as $50 or $60 a million.

That's the temptation: it's so cheap, it doesn't matter if you get a tiny response. In the real world, a 1 percent response to a direct-mail campaign is not unusual. If it costs you $500,000 to mail to a million people and you get 10,000 responses, each response cost $50. On the Internet, if you get only a tenth of one percent, each response costs a fraction of a real-world response, perhaps only $1, or even much less.

So much for the temptation. Now for the flip side of the coin. There's a significant problem with spam: people don't like it. In fact, some people dislike it so much that they'll come after you one way or another. They might sue you. They might get a court order banning you from sending e-mail to CompuServe or America Online (yes, it's been done). They might mail-bomb you—that's when they set up a system to send so much mail to your e-mail account that it effectively closes down your e-mail system. They might persuade the company hosting your e-mail account to dump you, or they might try to hack into your Web page and damage it (yes, it can be done). They might sign you up for thousands of magazine subscriptions, or call you in the middle of the night and scream at you. If you have a discussion group or chat group at your Web site, they might make a nuisance of themselves there, or they could set up a program to submit huge amounts of data through your Web forms. If you use an 800 number in your message, you'll get hit with hundreds of spurious calls. You could have a special category set up at Yahoo! listing Web pages related to your business—all complaining about your business, that is—or perhaps be added to the Blacklist of Internet Advertisers pages. You might even be subject to criminal prosecution. You wouldn't be the first.

If you want to learn more about spam—and what might happen to you if you try it—view some of these pages:

Blacklist of Internet Advertisers
   http://math-www.uni-paderborn.de/~axel/BL/

Fight Spam on the Internet!
   http://www.vix.com/spam/

Monty Python Spam Sketch (not much use for learning about spam, but you will learn the Monty Python Spam sketch)
   http://bau2.uibk.ac.at/sg/python/Scripts/TheSpamSketch

The Net Abuse FAQ
   http://www.cybernothing.org/faqs/net-abuse-faq.html

Spam Haters (a Windows program designed to hit back at spammers)
   http://www.cix.co.uk/~net-services/spam/spam_hater.htm

Yahoo!—Junk Email Registration
http://dir.yahoo.com/Computers_and_Internet/Communications_and_
Networking/Electronic_Mail/Junk_Email/Registration_Services/

I'm sure spam does provide a way to make money. But it can also make it very difficult for reputable companies to do business. Most companies using spam do all they can to hide their cyber-identities. Look at the next piece of spam you get carefully; you'll probably find no URL, and the From: and Reply To: addresses may not work. They use fake return e-mail addresses, for instance, to avoid being mail-bombed. If you're reading this book, though, you're probably trying to create a very visible presence on the Internet, not looking for a way to hide.

... But You Can Send E-mail Unrequested
I've heard it said that you should never send e-mail to someone without explicit permission first. I think this is quite absurd. I'm not saying you should carry out spam campaigns; apart from the fact that spam is very irritating to the recipients and even a significant expense to some companies, it can backfire and really hurt you. But surely there are reasons to send e-mail to people who haven't yet given you permission to do so. Aren't there reasons, now and then, to call people you've never spoken with on the phone?

I believe that it's possible to earn the right to mail a message to a list of people. For instance, I include my e-mail address in all my books these days (feedback@ PoorRichard.com), so I get a lot of e-mail from readers. Believe me, I plan to use this list now and then to let these people know about my new books—so be warned. Is that unreasonable? People often send me questions, and I do my best to respond to them all. Surely I've earned the right to mail a message now and again to people who've mailed to me.

If you collect e-mail addresses from people at your Web site, they have, in effect, given you permission to use their addresses. What do they think you want the addresses for, after all? Of course you should not abuse this privilege; you should never pass on those e-mail addresses to other companies, and you shouldn't think that you now have the right to flood those people's e-mail accounts with huge e-mail ads every day. But a discreet and reasonable message now and then, informing the recipients of a product or service that they are probably interested in, a product or service related to the Web site they were visiting when they provided their e-mail addresses ... that seems quite reasonable to me, and I believe to most Internet users.

Note also that some companies specialize in selling lists of e-mail addresses that have been provided voluntarily; some people actually sign up to get information about certain things. These are often small lists, though a few are very large. All of the sites below have lists that are supposedly voluntary "opt-in" lists, though I have no way to know for sure if that's true. Some of these companies also sell advertising space in electronic newsletters. Oh, and make sure you negotiate, because many—perhaps most—of these companies will give you a lower price than the one advertised. Ask if you can test the list—perhaps mail to 1,000 names, for instance—and see what sort of response you get.

BulletMail
http://www.bulletmail.com/

BusinessLink (650,000 business e-mail addresses at a very low cost)
http://www.businesslink.net/

DEMC.com
http://www.demc.com/

The Direct E-Mail List Source (a very useful site)
http://www.copywriter.com/lists/

MyPoints.com
http://www.mypoints.com/

PostMasterDirect.com (from $100 per thousand addresses)
http://www.PostMasterDirect.com/

Targ-it (ten cents a name, as little as five cents a name in quantity)
http://www.targ-it.com/

WebPromote
http://www.webpromote.com/

Yahoo!—Direct E-Mail
http://www.yahoo.com/Business_and_Economy/Companies/Marketing/
Direct_Marketing/Direct_Email/

But before you try advertising in an opt-in list, read an article I wrote in *Poor Richard's Web Site News* on this subject. Mailing to an opt-in list is often so incredibly expensive that there's a good chance you'll never get your money back. See Opt-In Email Advertising - A Warning http://PoorRichard.com/newsltr/017. htm#email. Of course you should be subscribing to *Poor R ichard's Web Site News*. It's free information, after all, literally books' worth. So visit http://Poor Richard.com/newsltr/, read the archived newsletters, and sign up.

PART III

PROMOTION

## Chapter Fifteen

Mapping the Internet—
Your Essential Research

Before you can effectively promote your Web site, you have to understand a little geography. You're going to have to find out where your prospective clients are, and what Web sites (and discussion groups and newsletters) are already serving them. In order to find these people and places, you need to understand the Internet—not just the World Wide Web—from a specific perspective. The Internet is huge, of course, spanning all the world's continents, most of its countries, millions of people, tens of millions of Web pages, tens of thousands of electronic newsletters and magazines, and well over 100,000 discussion groups. You are not interested in all this, though; it's simply too big to manage. Instead you need to look at the Internet from a different viewpoint. You need to create a "map" of the Web that shows the salient points that are of interest to you, a map that discards the unimportant pieces and shows the important ones. Do this, and the Internet immediately shrinks down to a manageable size.

For instance, if you are a technical writer promoting your business on the Web, you need to have a good feel for the Web sites that are of use to technical writers and to their clients. If you are selling teddy bears, you need to know where the people interested in teddy bears hang out. If you are promoting a book or magazine, you must think about where all your potential readers are likely to be.

In order to do this, you need to do a little research. Once you know where to find the people you are trying to attract to your Web site, you can use a variety of techniques to bring them to your site.

Planning the Survey

You've got to survey the Internet, create your map, then use that map for your promotion campaigns. Think of an Internet campaign as a military campaign; you wouldn't launch an invasion without knowing the lay of the land, would you?

The following, then, are the areas you must survey:

- Web sites
- Newsgroups
- Mailing lists
- Newsletters and other publications
- Web forums
- Online "communities"
- Online services.

You're looking for places where people meet on the Internet, places where you can do several things: learn more about the way the Internet is being used by the people you want to contact, find out what your competition is doing, and make contact with your potential clients.

Searching the Web

You should begin by finding out which other sites related to your business have been placed on the Web. You want to find the following types of sites:

- Link directories—Web pages that contain lots of links to other Web sites; that is, directories of Web sites related to a particular subject. You'll want to ask the owners of these sites to add your site to their lists—we'll talk more about that in Chapter 17.
- Your competitors' sites—You can see what they're up to and learn what they're doing right and what they're doing wrong.
- Sites that don't compete with you—but which in fact might want to work with you in some kind of complementary promotional campaign.
- Sites that might want to swap links with you—you link to them, they link to you.
- Sites that might want to swap banner ads with you—like the previous item, but this time you're using pictures rather than text links.
- Sites containing information that will help you keep up with goings-on in your business on the Internet.

Where are you going to search, though? Well, you can work with the Web search engines you've probably used before: Yahoo!, Infoseek, HotBot, and so on. Go to these sites and spend a little while searching on different words and phrases.

If you are promoting your bicycle-equipment store online, for instance, search on words such as *bike*, *bicycle*, and *biking*. If you want to be able to sell equipment overseas, you might also search for words such as *bicicleta*, *Fahrrad*, and *bicyclette*. Then spend some time just digging around, following links, and seeing what you come up with.

Keep an eye on the banner ads that appear when you search. Many search engines display banner ads that are selected according to the keywords you entered, so these often provide useful leads, too.

Look at the search sites' Help pages. You'll often find a number of useful little commands, such as the following AltaVista commands (read the Help page carefully; for some reason AltaVista hides these things away, and there are several other keywords that you may find useful):

title:"search words"	Searches for the search words in the titles of Web pages.
anchor:"search words"	Searches for the search words used as link text in Web pages.
domain:domain	Searches only pages with the specified domain: for instance, domain:org searches only .org domains.
host:host	Searches only pages held by a particular host computer: for instance, host:poorrichard.com.

Each search site gives very different results, because of the different ways in which they collect and catalog their data, so you'll probably need to use multiple search engines. You can go to each site individually, but you can greatly speed things up by using a meta-search site—a site that allows you to search multiple search engines at once. These sites vary greatly in convenience and utility. Some, I've found, actually present you with far fewer finds than if you search at the individual sites directly. Some allow you to fill in one form that is sent to multiple search engines; others simply provide forms that allow you to use each search engine one at a time. As an example, you can see theBigHub.com site in Figure 15.1. This site lets you search nine search engines at once, then displays a page containing all the links it found at those engines. But perhaps more importantly, it also has all sorts of other ways to search, including searching through specialty search engines (which we'll discuss next).

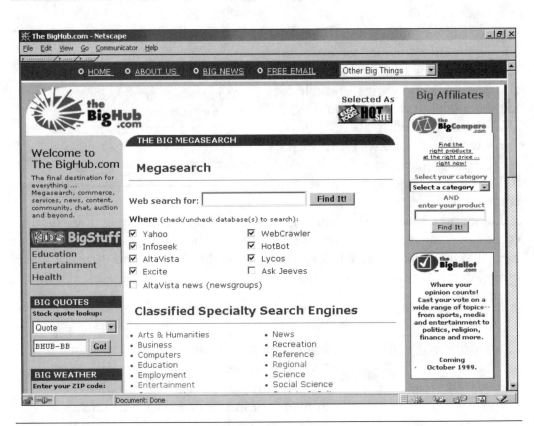

Figure 15.1: theBigHub.com provides lots of different ways to search.

You can find meta-search sites at the following addresses:

AccuFind
http://www.accufind.com/

Acroplex Metasearcher (12 sites)
http://acroplex.com/

All-4-One (AltaVista, Lycos, Yahoo!, WebCrawler)
http://www.all4one.com/

All-in-One-Search (500 search engines in 11 subject categories)
http://www.allonesearch.com/

byteSearch
http://www.bytesearch.com/

CUSI
http://cusi.emnet.co.uk/

Dogpile
http://www.dogpile.com/

FinderSeeker
http://www.hamrad.com/search.html

Inference Find
http://www.infind.com/

Mamma (10 search engines)
http://www.mamma.com/

MetaCrawler
http://www.metacrawler.com/

MetaFind (6 search engines)
http://www.metafind.com/

ProFusion
http://www.profusion.com/

SavvySearch (can search groupings of specialty search engines)
http://www.savvysearch.com/

Search.com from C|net (Web searches are through just one engine, but they have 100 different specialty searches)
http://www.search.com/

SuperSearch III
http://www.robtex.com/search.htm

SuperSeek (12 search engines, plus 1300 specialty search engines)
http://www.super-seek.com/

theBigHub.com (A smallish meta-search, but you can also search many specialty search engines individually)
http://www.thebighub.com/

TOSS—The Tribune Online Super Search (120 search engines sorted into classifications)
http://www.serv.net/~net_usa/toss/

Yahoo!—Searching the Net (more links to search-related sites)
http://www.yahoo.com/Computers_and_Internet/Internet/Searching_the_Net/

Specialty Search Sites and Link Directories

There are many "specialty" sites that are dedicated to helping people find information about particular subjects, sites such as **Aerolink** (over 11,000 links to aviation-related sites: http://www.aerolink.com/), **Yeh hai India!** (Indian and Hindu Web sites: http://huizen2.dds.nl/~bhulai/India.html), and **AJR Newslink** (American Journalism Review links to media-related sites: http://ajr.newslink.org/ news.html). Some of these sites are simply lists of links—link directories—while others actually have search engines. Both types provide a great way to find the information you need, and are good places to be listed, too.

You can find many of these sites at some of the meta-indexes noted above; as you saw, I noted that some of them have specialty searches, and in most cases you can both search the specialty sites and link through to the sites themselves and dig around. There are also a couple of sites dedicated to helping you find these specialty search sites:

Argus Clearinghouse
http://www.clearinghouse.net/

Beaucoup
http://www.beaucoup.com/

The problem with searching "by hand" is that it can be very slow, especially if you have a dial-up connection to the Internet. So there are a couple of ways to automate the process. You can use a search program, and you can use an offline browser.

Search Programs

There are a number of programs available that will automate a search for you. You enter a search term, click a button, and off goes the program, searching the Web for whatever you've specified. It searches a set of search engines—you'll probably be able to add new ones to the list—and retrieves a list of hits. Then the magic begins.

Up to this point, you see, you've simply searched the engines and gotten a list of links back in return. You can do that for yourself—not as quickly as the search program, but reasonably quickly nonetheless. What really takes a long time, though, is checking all of those links; if you find 10,000 links that might refer to something interesting, how do you check them all? There's no way you can, it's just too big of a job. But you can let the search program run overnight and do it for you.

Come back in the morning and what do you find? Something like the window shown in Figure 15.2. This is a screenshot from Quarterdeck's WebCompass, reputedly one of the best of these programs ... but Quarterdeck was recently sold to Symantec, and this product no longer seems to be available. Still, it's one I've used, so I'm using it again here as an example. In the illustration the search is

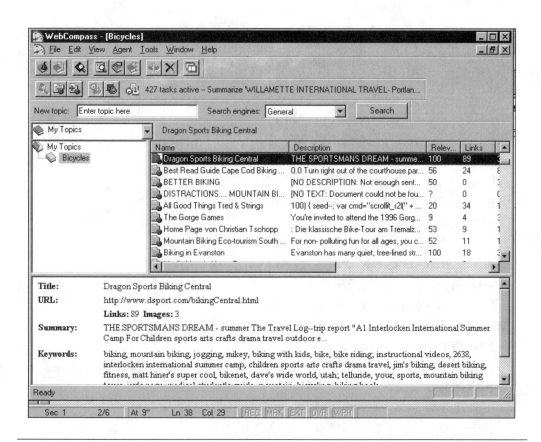

Figure 15.2: Quarterdeck's WebCompass, one of a breed of search engines that can prove invaluable.

actually in progress, but you can still see the sort of information that's presented. If you click on a link in the top-left pane, you see information about the Web page in the lower pane. In many cases this provides enough information for you to decide whether or not this will prove useful to you. If it is, or if you're not sure but want to see more to check it out, you can double-click on the entry. Up pops your browser, and the page loads.

Another nice feature of these programs is that you can use them to repeat searches periodically to find new things that have appeared. Search

> *There's less choice now in Internet software than there was a couple of years ago. Most categories of Internet software are shrinking, as companies realize there's too much competition, and that it's hard to sell these sorts of power-user tools.*

once or twice a month, and you'll be able to keep up with what's going on on the Web. A good program should be able to show you *new* matches, without bothering you with the old stuff you've seen before. Where can you find these programs? Try the following:

Arf (Windows 3.1/95/98/2000/NT)
    http://www.dwave.net/~bitsafe/arf/

BullsEye Pro (This is reportedly a very good one.)
    http://www.intelliseek.com/

Copernic 98 (Windows 95/98/2000/NT)
    http://www.copernic.com/

EchoSearch (Windows 95/98/2000/NT)
    http://www.iconovex.com/

Hurricane WebSearch (Windows)
    http://www.gatecomm.com/websearch/

Mata Hari (Windows 95/98/2000/NT)
    http://thewebtools.com/

QuickSeek (Macintosh and Windows—provides a fast way to search at Infoseek.)
    http://www.infoseek.com/iseek?pg=quickseek/Download.html

Trawler (Windows 3.1/95/98/2000/NT)
    http://www.dwave.net/~bitsafe/trawler/

WebBandit (Windows 95/98/2000/NT)
    http://www.jwsg.com/

WebFerret (Another very good one.)
    http://www.ferretsoft.com/

WebInfoFinder (Their search engine doesn't seem to find it, but if you look at all the Parsons Technology products you should find it.)
    http://www.shoptlc.com/

WebSeek (Windows 3.1/95/98/2000/NT)
    http://www-personal.umich.edu/~jeffhu/webseek/

WebSeeker (Windows 95/98/2000/NT)
    http://www.bluesquirrel.com/

WebSnake (Windows 95/98/2000/NT)
    http://www.intermk.com/products.html

By the way, a few products will grab e-mail addresses from pages you find. You could use this to get the addresses of people to whom you want to offer cooperative marketing promotions, for instance—the people running Web sites that your prospects are visiting. WebSnake and WebBandit, listed above, can both grab e-mail addresses.

Offline Browsers

Another tool that can be very handy is the offline browser. This is a program that grabs Web pages that you specify. For instance, you tell it to go to a particular Web page, look at all the links on that page and grab the referenced pages. You can even tell it to grab pages referenced by links on those pages, and even grab the pages referenced by links on that set of pages … I'm sure you get the picture. Most of these products allow you to state how many levels down you want to go. One's usually enough—if you do too many, it can take forever and end up filling your hard disk.

This is the sort of thing you set up to work overnight. Once it's finished, it stores the Web pages that it's downloaded in a special directory on your hard disk, so your browser can view them very quickly. You can then decide which are useful and which are not.

The following are some ways to use these programs:

- If you find a Web page with a lot of links to pages associated with your business—a link directory, for example—you can use the program to download the pages linked to this site and view them to see if they can be useful to you.

- If you use a search engine, you may want to save the results page on your hard disk, remove links that are clearly of no use—links pointing back to other areas of the search site, for instance, and links that clearly point to sites that are of no use to you—then use the program to grab the pages referenced by the links you're interested in learning more about. Some offline browsers make it difficult, if not impossible, to work on pages stored on your hard disk, though, so you may have to store the page at your Web site and then continue the operation.

- Do a number of searches, save the results pages on your hard disk, then merge them, keeping just the links that look as though they might be useful. Then use the program to get the referenced pages.

- Use the program to check links on your own site. There are programs that will check links to make sure they work, but they're "dumb." They can tell you if there's a page at the URL in the link, but not if that page has the information you think it has. So you can use an offline browser to make sure the links on your site really do reference the information you say they do—run the offline browser on your links page, then you can quickly view each page one by one.

These programs vary in price from free to around $70. Unfortunately, most are not worth anything. I've had all sorts of problems with these programs; I think offline browsers as a category are pretty shoddy, so it's hard to find a good one; even the ones highly rated by the computer press are often pretty awful. [I wrote that preceding sentence two years ago; I believe the situation remains the same!]

At one point WebWhacker seemed to be the most highly rated. However, I've had problems with WebWhacker—the demo version was buggy, though perhaps the bugs have now been fixed. ("Oh, yes," someone at ForeFront told me, "we've heard from a few people who've had problems with the download.")

Most of these programs that I've looked at seem to have problems. I've used quite a few, and think most could do with serious redesign work. I found that FlashSite seemed to work pretty well, with the exception that it will pull pages from only a single domain—it won't follow links across to other Web sites, which reduces its utility somewhat. At one point I found NetAttaché to be the best of the lot, but last time I tried it I was completely unable to get it to work—I'd upgraded to Windows 98 since I'd first used the product. I've found Teleport to be pretty good. Right now that's the one I would recommend. But even Teleport can lock up in the middle of big projects, so you may be limited to working with relatively small ones.

I wrote in the first edition that "undoubtedly [these programs] will improve over time." Now I'm not so sure. In fact what seems to have happened is that most of the programs have been frozen in time, as the publishers have decided that there is no real market for offline browsers and are no longer updating them. For instance, at the NetAttaché site you'll see that the publisher is still publishing recent favorable reviews, but that the software, at least at the time of writing, is two years old. Indeed there are fewer offline browsers available now than two years ago. That's a shame, because they can be very useful tools, but they're very much "power-user" tools, and power-user tools are hard to market.

Try a few and see which you prefer. I think it's worth spending a little time finding one that works for you, because these systems can really save you a lot of thumb-twiddling time. Don't sit in front of your computer waiting for things to transfer—let the computer do it for you while you're doing something else. Here's where you'll find a few offline browsers.

FlashSite (Windows 95/98/2000/NT)
http://www.incontext.com/

NetAttaché (Windows 95/98/2000/NT, Windows 3.1)
http://www.tympani.com/

Teleport Pro (Windows 95/98/
2000/NT)
http://wwwtenmax.com/

Web Buddy (Windows
95/98/2000, Macintosh)
http://www.dataviz.com/

WebFetcher (Windows 95/98/
2000/NT, Macintosh, UNIX)
http://ontv.com/webfetcher/

WebSnake (Windows)
http://www.anawave.com/
websnake/

WebWhacker (Windows 3.1/95/
98/2000/NT, Macintosh)
http://www.bluesquirrel.com/

Leaving a process to run overnight is often a problem, thanks to the unreliability of Internet connections. There's a good chance your connection will drop five minutes after you walk out the door. A better solution may be to let the program run while you're doing something else—filing, talking on the phone, or working on a different computer, for instance. Some of these programs can restart the process if the connection drops—an essential feature.

Track Down Company Directories

There are specialized company directories you may want to list with. You can find lots of these at **Yahoo!'s Company Directory** page (http://dir.yahoo.com/Business_and_Economy/Companies/Directories/). This page links to hundreds of directories in categories such as audio, biomedical, cleaning, home and garden, office furniture, packaging, trade, and travel. Find the ones related to your business so you can register with them.

Grabbing E-mail Addresses

While you are surveying the Internet, you'll come across a lot of useful e-mail addresses: newsletter editors, owners of Web pages containing link directories that you want to be listed in, owners of Web pages who are probably interested in your products, and so on. You'll want to collect these e-mail addresses for use later.

I'm trying to find a nice little program that will quickly grab e-mail addresses from a Web page. I want to be able to point at a mailto: link in a Web page, press a keyboard combination—Ctrl+G, for instance—and have the program grab the e-mail address from the link. So far I haven't found anything like this—let me know if you run across one.

The best I've figured out so far is this: if I'm out researching something, wandering around the Web grabbing e-mail addresses, I can start a text editor such as Windows Notepad, and copy mailto: addresses into there quite quickly. I have a programmable keyboard. These are wonderful devices that can save you many hours work in many different ways; you can record keystrokes and attach the recording to a particular key. Then, to repeat the keystrokes, just press that key once.

So, for instance, here's what I can do: I can right-click with my mouse on a mailto: link, and up pops the menu. I quickly press the key that's associated with the recording, and the recording plays; it selects the Copy Shortcut command on that pop-up menu, then presses Alt+Tab to switch from the browser to the text editor. It presses Ctrl+End to move the cursor to the end of all the text in the text editor, then presses Enter to move down a line, then presses Ctrl+V to paste the mailto: line into the text editor. Then it presses Alt+Tab to go back to the browser.

That's it, the address is quickly copied with a single mouse click and a single keystroke. You can do the same sort of thing with programmable mice, too. All the e-mail addresses captured this way now have the mailto: prefix, but they can be quickly removed using Search & Replace in a word-processing program.

I suggest you build address books while you're doing your research; one could be a list of addresses of people maintaining link directories, another a list of Web-site owners who might be interested in a cooperative promotion of some kind, and so on. Later you'll be able to mail to everyone in an address book very quickly.

If you're going to be doing much of this kind of work online—in fact, if you're going to be doing much of any kind of computer work, I believe—you really need a programmable keyboard. I buy mine from **Gateway** (http://www.gateway. com/), which used to provide one with every computer it sold. You can buy them separately, but I think you have to have bought a Gateway computer at some time (and note that they say the keyboard won't work with some types of computers for some reason). Here are a few other places to find programmable keyboards:

Avant Stellar Keyboard, Creative Vision Technologies, Inc.
(Recommended by Jerry Pournelle in *BYTE* magazine.)
http://www.cvtinc.com/

Datadesk (various keyboards, for Macs and PCs)
http://www.datadesk1.com/

Floating Arms Keyboard, Workplace Designs
http://www.wpdesigns.com/

InterFatron-BBc, Ltd. (This company designs keyboards, but doesn't sell them ... they link to sites where you can buy them, though.)
http://www.ifbbc.com/

Maxim Keyboard, Kinesis Corporation
http://www.kinesis-ergo.com/

MCK-142 Pro, Kbtek America (Their Web sites are awful—at the first you can view product information but not order ... at the second you can order but not view product information.)
http://www.ortek.com/
http://www.eagle-touch.com/
626-855-0325

Searching for Newsgroups

Next, let's find the newsgroups. How many newsgroups are there? Tens of thousands, though many are not distributed internationally. Many are local groups available only at a single news server. Still, you've got plenty of choice; more than 30,000 are internationally distributed.

Now, the quickest way to begin looking for newsgroups is by cranking up your newsreader and downloading the full list of newsgroups from your news server. Newsreaders all have a command somewhere for getting that list—the command is often well hidden for some obscure reason understood only by designers of newsgroup software—so find the command and retrieve the latest list. Most newsreaders also have a command for searching the list, so search using a few keywords related to your business, and see what you come up with.

The problem with this method is that your news server may not have all the newsgroups you want. Not all news servers subscribe to all groups, and you'll probably want to see a complete or more-or-less complete list. The following sites not only list newsgroups, but in some cases allow you to read the messages (sometimes free, sometimes for a fee):

AirNews (32,000)
http://www.airnews.net/

Deja.com (free service, with access to 80,000 discussion groups, including 30,000 newsgroups)
http://www.deja.com/

Liszt Newsgroup Directory (30,000)
http://www.liszt.com/news/

Master List of Newsgroup Hierarchies
http://www.magmacom.com/~leisen/master_list.html

Newsguy (22,000 newsgroups for $10 a month)
http://co-op.newsguy.com/

Randori (31,000 newsgroups for under $10 a month)
http://www.randori.com/

RemarQ (free access to 30,000 newsgroups through their Web site, or $12 a month to use your newsreader)
http://www.remarq.com/

The Robot Wisdom Newsgroup-Finder (search newsgroups by geographical location or historical period)
http://www.robotwisdom.com/finder/index.html

Supernews
http://www.supernews.com/

Tile.Net
http://www.tile.net/

Yahoo!—Newsgroup Listings
http://www.yahoo.com/Computers_and_Internet/Internet/Usenet/
Newsgroup_Listings/

Yahoo!—Public Access Usenet Sites
http://dir.yahoo.com/Computers_and_Internet/Internet/Usenet/
Public_Access_Usenet_Sites/

Searching for Mailing Lists

Mailing lists are a bit harder to track down. There are probably hundreds of thousands of mailing lists, but because there's no central distribution method, unlike newsgroups, there's no real way to track them all. However, you can track many down, and you really should try, because these days they're more important than newsgroups. Many newsgroups have degenerated into garbage, inundated with spammed messages for get-rich-quick schemes and porn sites. Mailing lists are much easier to control than newsgroups, and they're very easy to set up, so much of the "action" in the discussion world is in the mailing lists.

E-Mail Discussion Groups/Lists—Resources
http://www.webcom.com/impulse/list.html

Finding Newsgroups and Mailing Lists
http://www.synapse.net/~radio/finding.htm

Inter-Link E-Mail Discussion Group List
http://alabanza.com/kabacoff/Inter-Links/listserv.html

Liszt (probably the best mailing-list directory—more than 70,000 listed)
http://www.liszt.com/

Publicly Accessible Mailing Lists
http://www.neosoft.com/internet/paml/subjects/

Vivian Neou's List of Lists (allows you to search the SRI List of Lists)
http://catalog.com/vivian/interest-group-search.html

Also, don't forget the mailing-list services we talked about in Chapter 14, services such as eGroups, OneList, and Topica. You can search them to find mailing lists. You'll also run across relevant mailing lists during your other research; for instance, you may find information about mailing lists at the directory Web sites—the sites owned by fans and enthusiasts, who we'll learn about later in this chapter.

Searching for Newsletters and Other Publications

In Chapter 14 I discussed why you might want to send out e-mail newsletters as a promotional tool. Well, there are already thousands of newsletters being distributed via e-mail, and some of them may be of use to you. I just did a search on the word *newsletter*, and came up with things like the following:

- Pro-Wrestling Newsletter
- Carol Hurst's Children's Literature Newsletter
- Solar News
- SI Alumni Newsletter
- Internet for Christians Newsletter
- Shade's Landing Online Newsletter
- The AAMES Daily Email Newsletter
- Career Consulting Corner.

You need to find the electronic newsletters and other publications related to your business, subscribe to them, see how information about your product or service can fit in, and then contact the editors. How are you going to find these publications? You may have already run across some; many magazines are distributed via Web sites, and many newsletters have associated Web pages, so when you searched the Web you might have found them. You may also have found them in the link directories you've run across.

You can also search on the word newsletter at various search engines, and you'll come up with lots of hits. Yahoo!, for instance, has a newsletter subcategory in many areas, such as the following:

- Society and Culture: Religion: Christianity: Publications: Newsletters
- Government: Law: Newsletters
- Science: Earth Sciences: Meteorology: Newsletters
- Science: Psychology: Publications: Newsletters
- Regional: Countries: United Kingdom: Business: Electronic Commerce: Newsletters
- Entertainment: Science Fiction, Fantasy, and Horror: Star Trek
- Science: Earth Sciences: Meteorology: Newsletters.

… and much, much more. Some of these subcategories contain just one or two newsletters; others contain dozens. I looked in Society and Culture: Religion: Christianity: Publications: Newsletters, for instance, and found 38 newsletters. If you've got a subject, somebody's got a newsletter.

There are also some sites set up to help you find newsletters and other electronic publications. I'd suggest that you start at my *Places to R egister Your E-mail Newsletter* report, that you can find at http://PoorRichard.com/freeinfo/ezine.htm. It's a little out of date, so some of the links are dead, but it lists many places that contain directories of newsletters.

ETEXT Archives (A huge repository of zine and newsletter information; if you need a place to archive your newsletter, check this out.)
http://www.etext.org/Zines/

E-Zine Ad Source (If you plan to sell advertising, make sure you're listed here. It's free, but they ask that you run a small ad for their service twice a year.)
http://www.ezineadsource.com/

E-ZineZ (a search engine and searchable subject index just for e-zines)
http://www.e-zinez.com/

InfoBot.net (a zine subject index)
http://www.infobot.net/

John Labovitz's E-Zine List (This should be one of your first stops to register your newsletter. It's one of the best-known zine sites on the Web, with over 3,000 zines.)
http://www.meer.net/~johnl/e-zine-list/

Liszt (lists over 90,000 discussion groups and newsletters)
http://www.liszt.com/

Low Bandwidth
http://www.disobey.com/low/

NewJour (an e-mail publication carrying announcements about online publications)
http://gort.ucsd.edu/newjour/

NEW-LIST (another publication dedicated to announcing new newsletters)
http://scout.cs.wisc.edu/scout/new-list/

Newsletter Access (Paper and electronic newsletters. You can add a little information for free or a full listing for $19.95 a year.)
http://www.newsletteraccess.com/

Newsletter Library (Currently lists over 11,000 newsletters. Free samples of any are available. Cost to be listed in this resource is $50.)
http://pub.savvy.com/

Searching for Communities

It's now pretty easy to set up online "communities," with discussion groups, chat rooms, calendars of events, photo albums, and more. This is becoming a big thing, with clubs, professional associations, groups of friends, families, and businesses setting up these online communities. They're worth checking into. For instance, if you're selling model rockets, you might want to visit the **RocketLaunch community** (http://clubs.yahoo.com/clubs/rocketlaunch). Here are a few places to find community sites:

Cybersites
http://www.cybersites.com/

Deja.com
http://www.deja.com/

Delphi
http://www.delphi.com/

eCircles.com
   http://www.ecircles.com/
EdGateway
   http://edgateway.net/
eVine
   http://www.evine.com/
Excite Communities
   http://www.excite.com/communities/
FriendFactory
   http://www.friendfactory.com/
interClubs
   http://interclubs.com/
JointPlanning
   http://www.jointplanning.com/
Lycos Clubs
   http://clubs.lycos.com/
Network54
   http://network54.com/
Yahoo! Clubs
   http://clubs.yahoo.com/

If possible, find out how many people are in a "community" before bothering with it. Many of these communities have just two or three people; others have thousands. Incidentally, we think this community thing is both important and growing. We're publishing a book on the subject in 2000, *Poor Richard's Building Online Communities*, to help people understand the best way to create such a community, the dynamics involved, the mistakes to avoid, and so on. For more information, visit http://TopFloor.com/.

Finding Web Forums and Chat Sites

Web forums are discussion groups that operate at a Web site—we discussed how you could set up one of these at your own site in Chapter 12. There are over 300,000 Web forums, so some may be of interest to you. I know of only one Web-forum directory, though, **Forum One** (http://www.forumone.com/), which currently lists more than 310,000 forums. There used to be another, **Reference. com** (http://www.reference.com/), but I think they're probably out of business now.

By the way, be careful with Web forums, mailing-list discussion groups, and newsgroups. There are so many, they can easily turn into a big distraction. I suggest you find just a handful of the largest and most active groups to work with, rather than trying to cover everything that seems even tangentially related to your area of interest.

Don't Forget the Online Services

You may want to spend a little time taking at look at the major online services. There are millions of online-service users frequenting discussion groups that are not accessible to outsiders. That doesn't mean they're of no interest to you; outsiders may not be able to get in, but the members of these online services can definitely get out onto the Internet. All the major services now have good Web access, so when their members hear about a Web site that sounds interesting, they can start up the browser and go straight to the site.

These online services often have discussion groups that are every bit as busy and useful as Internet newsgroups and mailing lists, and sometimes they're even better. Some of these groups have been in existence for years, and so, partly through inertia, they remain important. For instance, fantasy and science fiction writers used to hang out in GEnie, while Windows Help and multimedia creators used to hang out on CompuServe.

A really comprehensive campaign shouldn't ignore the online services. Which ones? These at least: CompuServe, America Online, and Microsoft Network; perhaps, if you've really got time to spare, or if there's a particular discussion group you want to reach, also GEnie and Prodigy. In a few rare cases you may hear about other online services that have particular areas that many of your prospective clients frequent.

All these services provide free trials. You can install the software, then go online and search the directories. See what's useful. Use it for a month—or whatever the free trial period is—then cancel it if you've found it of no use. You'll promote your Web site in these services' discussion groups in the same way you promote it in the mailing lists and newsgroups, as we'll discuss in Chapter 17.

Look for Fans and Enthusiasts

You may have noticed that there are people on the Internet who get so involved with a particular product that they feel the need to set up a Web page related to that product. They're so enthusiastic about the subject that they just have to tell other people. They set up Web sites that explain everything they know about the subject, and list links to places where you can find out about everything they don't know. There are people with Web pages related to the Pegasus and Eudora e-mail programs, to Microsoft Word, to various sports teams and television programs, to just about anything you can imagine.

You should keep on the lookout for people like this, people who seem really to appreciate your products and services and who may host a Web site related to those products and services or who may want to do so. These people are well worth cultivating; they're the best salespeople you could ever want—disciples, almost. You should keep these people happy; listen to them, send them free samples, get to know them and keep them informed, carry out drawings for free products at their sites, and so on. Such people are very valuable to your promotional campaign, and shouldn't be ignored or allowed to lose interest.

Remember Your E-mail Filters

If you carry out a detailed survey of the Internet—the portion of the Internet of use to you, that is—you'll be receiving a lot of e-mail in the form of mailing-list messages, newsletters, and messages from people you've contacted. In fact, your e-mail account could be flooded with scores, even hundreds of messages every day. You may not necessarily maintain this level, but during your survey it's quite possible.

How are you going to manage all these messages? Get to know your e-mail program's filtering system and set up filters. Filter mailing lists into their own folders and each newsletter into its own folder. You may even want to use a special e-mail address while contacting people on the Web. Some mail programs allow you to use various From: addresses. Eudora Pro 4 and AK-Mail, for instance, let you set up separate "accounts," each account with a different e-mail address. So you could use one account just for sending e-mail to people you are contacting during your survey, then filter any incoming messages into a special survey folder.

What Are They Saying About You?

Before we leave, there's another important search technique. You can use research to discover not only what other people are doing and saying on the Internet, but what they are doing and saying related directly to you and your Web site.

In other words, you are going to search for you. For instance, let's say I'm Mr. Coca-Cola, and I want to know how my little soft-drink company is doing on the Internet—what people are saying about it. I can do a series of searches that will find out which Web pages link to my Web pages and what people are saying in newsgroups and mailing lists.

For instance, go to **AltaVista** (http://www.altavista.com/) and search for your domain name. I searched for cocacola.com here, and found 5,000 documents containing the cocacola.com domain name. The nice thing about AltaVista is that it doesn't simply catalog Web sites, it indexes every Web page it can

If you change your domain name or an important URL, you can search AltaVista to find everyone linking to you and let them know about the change.

find. So if the text cocacola.com is somewhere in the page—including in a link—it will find it for me.

What were all these Web sites saying about cocacola.com? One was a cybermall which seemed to claim that Coca-Cola was a client. There was a column called "Ramblings," which had the Coca-Cola link among a big group of recommended links. There was a list of Fortune 500 companies with Web sites, various people recommending the Coca-Cola site, and 4,996 other Web pages with lots more stuff.

You'll want to search for a variety of things: your domain name, your product names, your name and the names of your company's executives, and so on. You can also do a preliminary search for product names you might be considering, to see if anyone else out there is using them.

Searching Newsgroups

So you can search Web pages quite easily. What about newsgroups? That's easy, too—there are a number of services that allow you to search newsgroup messages.

This is a great way to find out what people are saying. Search for your company name, domain name, and product names, and see if people like your products. If people are criticizing your products, contact those people and find out why, and go to the newsgroups and try to defend your company.

These places allow you to search newsgroups:

When you defend yourself against criticism in discussion groups, you must do so very carefully. Don't get angry, and don't get into a fight. Simply put your side of the story as eloquently and logically as you can, and you'll find that people really will listen. If you get into a fight, you'll lose credibility.

AltaVista
   http://www.altavista.com/

Deja.com
http://www.deja.com/

Excite
http://www.excite.com/

HotBot
http://www.hotbot.com/

Infoseek
http://www.infoseek.com/

NewsFerret
http://www.vironix.com/netferret/

NewsMonger
http://www.techsmith.com/

Yahoo! (it actually searches the Deja database)
http://www.yahoo.com/

Yahoo!—Usenet Searching and Filtering Page
http://dir.yahoo.com/Computers_and_Internet/Internet/Usenet/
Searching_and_Filtering/

Searching Mailing Lists

There used to be a useful service called Reference.com, but it seems to have gone. I really don't know of a good place to search through a large number of mailing-list discussion groups at the same time.

## Chapter Sixteen

Registering Your Web Site

It's time to register your Web site, but where? Well, the obvious answer to that question—and the shortsighted one, as well—is: "The search engines, of course!" But the real answer is a little more complicated.

Certainly it's important to register information about your Web site at the search sites, and we'll be discussing how to do that a little later in this chapter. But there are more important sites to inform about your new Web site—places that are often overlooked by new Web marketers.

Link Directories—A Cure for Search Confusion

You'll remember that in Chapter 15 I discussed the link directories—Web sites that contain directories of links to related Web sites. There are link directories for just about any subject that's covered on the Web, from AIDS to zoos, from teddy bears to golf. These sites are often run by individuals, sometimes even by families; Mom and Dad think it's a good project for the kids, so they all get together and build a link directory.

You must find the link directories related to your business. Why? Well, let me give you an example. Let's say your Web site is related to model rockets. Your company sells or manufactures them, perhaps, or maybe you publish a magazine or newsletter related to the subject, or you sell accessories. Now, how are people interested in your product going to find you? They could go to a search engine and search for a variety of things: rockets, model rockets, rocketry, and so on. I just did that at a few search engines, and the following is what I found (this shows the number of matches at each site):

Search Word	Yahoo!	AltaVista	Infoseek
rocket	579	5,738,303	158,670
model rocket	102	over 5,876	3,864,181
rocketry	89	56,410	6,573

Wow, I'm lost already! Where do I start? The best I could manage was to narrow this down to 89 pages, and it'll take me forever to check each one. And as for some finds in the millions, what on earth am I supposed to do with them? Now, I did fairly simple searches, I didn't use any fancy Boolean search strings—but then, very few people on the Internet do; most simply type a word or two and click.

By the way, you've probably noticed by now that I like Yahoo!, and the above table shows why; Yahoo!'s a great site to start with, as it categorizes and sorts millions of pages on the Web, distilling an almost impossible range down to something you can work with. That's not to say the other search sites don't have their uses—they most certainly do. When you want to do a really in-depth search, for instance, a search engine such as AltaVista is very useful.

Now, it's important to note that most of these finds clearly have nothing to do with model rockets. I doubt whether this find from AltaVista will help us much:

```
ROCKET FROM THE CRYPT
ON WARPED TOUR! MEN | MUSIC | TATTOOS | SPEEDO'S ARMY
```

And even when the finds are associated with model rockets, they're often not very useful, especially from search engines such as AltaVista—they're individual pages that mention model rockets, rather than the main pages of rocket sites. That's rather like trying to buy a book by comparing single pages taken from the middle of each one.

But the person searching for information about model rockets will notice one thing. Assuming he doesn't get turned off immediately, he'll eventually stumble across entries like the following, found at Yahoo!:

- Recreation: Hobbies and Crafts: Models: Model Airplanes: Radio Controlled: Clubs
- Business and Economy: Companies: Hobbies: Rockets
- Recreation: Hobbies and Crafts: Rockets
- John Kallend's Rocket Page—Information on model and high-powered rockets
- Rocket Works—Model and high power rocketry photos, launch reports, and launch announcements in the central U.S.
- Ninfinger Productions: Model Rockets—Launch reports, launch and Astrocam photos, tips and reference materials with links to other model rocketry sites

- Irving Family—Model and high power rocketry
- Model Rocketry for Educators—provides teachers and students with information and lessons in the use of model rocketry as a learning tool
- Tad's Model & High Power Rocketry Page—pulls together rocketry-related info from all over the Net
- Mick's Rocketry Page—model and high-power rockets; also links to rocket sites
- Kilgore, Brandon M.—Model Rocketry Page—This is a home page designed for information about model rocketry
- Thimm, Dan—Electronic Experimentation Emporium—projects and tips for robotics hobbyists and model rocket builders
- Business and Economy: Companies: Hobbies: Models: RC Models.

This is just a small selection—there were plenty more. But notice a couple of things: some of these are general rocketry sites; they purport to provide an overview of the subject or an area of the subject. They're not just selling or discussing a single product—they have more of a general tone. And, more importantly for you, they also often have links to other rocketry sites. Notice that some site descriptions include: "with links to other model rocketry sites," "Pulls together rocketry-related info from all over the Net," and "also links to rocket sites." Notice also that some of these sites are created by hobbyists: Tad, Mick, John Kallend, The Irving Family—these are probably individuals and families who love rocketry. Such sites often maintain lists of useful links. I'll bet other sites in this list also maintain lists of links.

Now, back to our hobbyist, out searching for information about rocketry. He could be searching for a store where he can buy something, in which case he may bypass all these general sites and go straight to a store site—which is why you must be listed in the search engines. But he may feel overwhelmed by so many options and try to find a site that filters things for him. Sure, he may not think of it in that way, but nonetheless he's quite likely to go to a site that discusses rocketry or a site that "pulls together rocketry-related info from all over the Net." And that's where you need to be listed.

These Web sites contain lists of links to other Web sites. Some of these are simply link directories—lists of links to various pages of interest. Some are meta-indexes—indexes of index sites. That is, they contain links to other sites that contain link directories, providing a wonderful way to track down yet more important sources. So it's essential that you get listed in these link directories.

Discussion Groups, Too

Here's another reason to find these link directories. People learn about them in the Internet's discussion groups—the mailing lists and newsgroups. There are Internet discussion groups on just about any subject you can imagine, and yes, that includes model rocketry. For instance, I've tracked down these mailing lists:

amrocnet	Amateur Rocketry Network
hprConsumer	High-Power Rocketry
rocketsSEDS	Rocket Discussion List
scan-15-02	Sounding Rockets
scan-20-01	Rocket Engines, Nozzles and Thrust Chambers

I also found these newsgroups:

rec.models.rockets	Model rockets for hobbyists
rec.pyrotechnics	Fireworks, rocketry, safety and other topics
z-netz.alt.modellbau	Modellbauer unter sich (Model builders under themselves, or something like that—my German's not very good. Maybe model builders themselves …)

To be honest, I'm not absolutely sure what all these are about; is scan-20-01 really of interest to the hobbyist? I don't know, but if I were in this business, I'd definitely find out. Anyway, at least some of these discussion groups have as their members many people interested in model rocketry. Perhaps hundreds, maybe thousands. And it's not just the Internet discussion groups, either. There are probably discussion groups related to rocketry on AOL, GEnie, Prodigy, and CompuServe—in CompuServe, for instance, there's the Rocketry forum.

The link directories get mentioned in these groups. It doesn't take long for good link directories to become well known by a particular group of people, and these people pass on their knowledge of Internet "geography" to newcomers to cyberspace, too. Periodically, the link-directory URLs reappear in discussion-group messages, in response to someone's request for information.

Where else do the link pages get mentioned? In the press—I've seen articles and newspaper columns mentioning link directories as good places to start— and in private e-mail, as well. One friend sends a message to another, saying: "Check out this site, it's really useful." Even on the playing field, when rocketeers get together to launch their rockets, you can be sure that now and again a couple of hobbyists with Internet access will chat, and one will say to another: "You know, I found this site that's really useful …"

List at the Directories

How do you get a link to your Web site added to these link directories? Ask to be included. After all, the people running these sites want your links—what good is a link directory without links? I suggest you send a message to everyone in your link-directory address book (in Chapter 15 I suggested that you add the e-mail addresses you find during your research to various address books according to the use to which you plan to put them). Ask if they'll add you to their list. Provide a short description of your site, and the URL you want listed. If the site has several distinct areas of interest—a discussion group, a chat group, a classified-ad area, and so on—make this quite clear and provide several links; you may get listed several times.

Why not give the people running the site something? These are important people, after all. If you're a publisher, you probably send out hundreds of review copies of your books. If you publish software, you send out hundreds of free copies of your software. Well, these are people who can benefit you in several ways. They may well mention on their Web sites the free gift they received—I'll bet very few companies give gifts to the link-directory owners, and some of these owners will be so surprised and delighted that they'll mention you.

You might also suggest that they do reviews of the free product you're sending them—many of these people discuss the products they use at their sites or even have review areas at their Web sites. And finally, the mere fact that you have sent them a gift will help them remember you, which may be useful later. So when you send your message, ask for their mailing addresses.

Product Giveaways

You might also ask if they'd be interested in some kind of cooperative promotional campaign. Perhaps they'd like to give away some of your products at their sites; you can provide them with a Web form that sends e-mail to you, or saves the submissions in a text file, and you can hold a drawing at the end of the month. It's a nice little promotion for both you and them—and very low-cost. If you manufacture rockets, what's it going to cost you to give five away to each list directory—almost nothing compared to your other advertising costs. If you have a rocket magazine, what are a few subscriptions going to cost? Next to nothing, right?

The great thing about this sort of promotion is that you are, in effect, recruiting salespeople—and you don't have to pay them! Here's an example. When promoting a book about technical writing (***Making Money in Technical Writing***: http://TopFloor.com/techwr/), quite early on I found two Web sites that were willing to give away five free copies of the book each. I found more later that were prepared to host a free drawing once the book had been published. I set up a form, and they linked to the form. So what did visitors to their site see? Well, at one site the owner had added a block of text, taking up about 40 percent of the first screen of information that his visitors saw, talking all about my book. Of course, there was a big *Enter the Contest* link to the form, too.

But what was really great was that the owners of these sites used the giveaway as a promotional tool for their own Web sites. They went into various mailing lists and newsgroups and announced that they were giving away free books. Those two Web sites together garnered over 800 submissions to the free drawings, and although there were some duplications—people entering the drawing twice—most were unique, too. Each entrant received several announcements concerning the book—not bad for the price of 10 books. Furthermore, my book was getting an implied endorsement from people respected in the community of technical writers active on the Internet, which was a great form of advertising.

A Few More Ideas

How about a banner ad? Ask Web-site owners if they'll put a little banner somewhere at their sites. This might be done in conjunction with the free-product drawing or perhaps in return for some other goods or services—a free subscription to your magazine if you're a publisher, discounts for your products, and so on.

Finally, don't forget to register with the company directories I mentioned in Chapter 15, too—the ones you found at **Yahoo!'s Company Directory** page (http://dir.yahoo.com/Business_and_Economy/Companies/Directories/). Although less popular than list directories created by enthusiasts, they're free listings, so you might as well use them.

When you send the message to the list directories, remember to put one e-mail address in the To: line, and the rest in the Bcc: line, as we discussed in Chapter 14. That way the message will appear to be an original, not a copy.

Preparing for the Search Engines

The next place to register is with the search engines. But before that, you must configure your Web page properly. Many Web sites take the information you submit, then send out a "robot" to take a look at your site. Not all do this, but a significant number of the more important ones do. The robot will examine certain aspects of the site, then use the information it's gathered to describe or categorize your Web site. So before these robots visit, you need to ensure that you're ready.

The Page Title

Make sure that your page titles make sense, even to someone who hasn't yet visited your site. I'm talking about the text between the <TITLE> and </TITLE> tags. Some search engines, such as AltaVista, put the title right at the top of the listing; many use the title as the link to your page. The search engines usually also index the words included in the title, but don't put a list of keywords there—I'll show you how to add keywords in a moment.

If you've searched AltaVista, you've probably noticed a lot of really ambiguous links; I just searched for Albania and what do you know … there are an awful lot of links that just say Albania—not particularly helpful! This is not AltaVista's fault, it's the fault of the Web-page authors who put imprecise titles into their pages. In some cases you'll see *No Title* rather than a title; that's because there's no title at all.

The Content of the Page

Some search engines also look at the first few lines of the page and collect them as a short abstract of the page. So make sure the headings at the top of the page and the first few lines of text are really descriptive of what you want the search engines to index. Try to use lots of words that your prospective clients are likely to be searching for in that first important paragraph.

Even after the first paragraph, some search engines continue looking. AltaVista indexes everything, so the rest of the text on the page is important, too. Some people try to fool such search engines by including large lists of keywords at the bottom. This is sometimes known as spamdexing. I've seen pages in which the authors have tried to camouflage a list of hundreds of keywords by changing the color of the words to match the page background, for instance. Other authors put hundreds of keywords in the comment tags within the page, so they're not visible. Does this work? Almost always no. Most of the search engines in action these days are clever enough to figure out what's going on, and they ignore repetition. And many no longer index any text within HTML comment tags. Some will actually punish obvious spamdexing. They won't simply ignore the spamdexing, they'll actually dump the site from the directory and perhaps even blacklist you from the site so you can't get back in.

META Tags

One way in which Web pages are indexed is by referring to the META tags. Here's an example of a META tag:

```
<meta name="keywords" content="HTML Writers Guild,
HTML, WWW, World Wide Web, HWG">
```

As you can see, the META tag comprises three parts: the identifier (meta), the name= attribute, and the content= attribute. This example is the keywords META tag, and as you can see, the keywords are HTML Writers Guild, HTML, WWW, World Wide Web, and HWG. (There's another form of META tag, one that looks more like this: <meta http-equiv="" content="">, but this is generally not used by search engines.)

How exactly are these tags used? AltaVista and Infoseek, for example, include the description you provide in your description META tag along with the listing in the directory. So you can say something like this:

```
<META  name="description" content="The world's best Web
site for gerbil owners!">
```

… and your listing in these search engines will include the words *The world's best Web site for gerbil owners!*

Some search engines also look at the keywords entered into the keywords META tag, and use them to index the page. If someone searches for a word that appears in either your description or keywords tag, the search engine will find it.

Again, some authors have tried spamdexing by adding huge descriptions and keyword lists in the META tags. This no longer works. Some search engines look at only a specific number of characters—AltaVista ignores everything after 1,024 characters in these two tags—others will ignore repetitions over a certain number—I've heard some search engines will penalize for more than seven repetitions—or even strike you off their directories. As Infoseek says: "Repeating words frequently is not helpful and may in fact result in your page being removed from the index." Infoseek allows only up to 200 characters in the description and 1,000 in the keywords.

> If you have pages that you don't want indexed, use this tag: <META name="ROBOTS" content="NOINDEX">. *Also, add a* robots.txt *file at your site to tell robots which pages not to index; you can find more information at* **WebCrawler** (http://info.web crawler.com/mak/projects/robots/ norobots.html).

Not all search engines use META tags. Excite, for instance, ignores them. The people running this system believe that META tags are often used dishonestly to bring people to a site by misrepresenting the site: "If the user can't see or use it [the words], we don't bother to index it or search on it," Excite says. And some search engines don't index anything on your page; rather, your entry is based on the information you provide when you register, and, perhaps, also on what the search-engine staff think of the site when they take a look (Yahoo! works in this manner).

ALT Text in Images

Some search engines index the IMG tags so that people can search for graphics. Infoseek does this, for example. And even sites that are not creating image indexes may still read and index the text to get an idea of what the page is about. So it's a good idea to include a description of the images on your pages in the ALT attribute.

If You're Using Frames

If you are using frames at your site, search engines may have trouble figuring out how to index pages. When they arrive at the site, all they get is the frame-definition document, a document that tells a browser how to set up the frames— how many frames, their sizes, their positions, and which document is displayed within each frame. But most search engines don't bother examining the documents referenced by the frame-definition document—the documents that will actually appear in the browser window.

If your site has frames, you can provide information for the search engines in two ways. You can add META tags to the top of the frame-definition document, and you can use the NOFRAMES tags (<NOFRAMES> and </NOFRAMES>), which enclose information that is not displayed inside the browser window unless the document is loaded by a browser that can't work with frames. So it's a good idea to copy the information from the main frame into the NOFRAMES area of the frame-definition document. Then not only will nonframes browsers be able to see something, but so will the search engines.

If You Want More...

This is a complicated subject, and constantly changing. To learn more about how the search engines index pages, see the following sites:

AltaVista
http://www.altavista.digital.com/av/content/addurl.htm

Excite
   http://www.excite.com/Info/listing.html

Infoseek
   http://www.infoseek.com/AddUrl?pg=DCaddurl.html

WebCrawler
   http://webcrawler.com/Help/GetListed/HelpAddURL.html

Yahoo!
   http://www.yahoo.com/docs/info/addfaq.html

Do-It-Yourself Site Registration

Now that you've got your site ready, it's time to register. Although I've been using the term search engine, there are actually three different types of sites you need to register with, as follows:

- **Directories**—These categorize sites and allow people to browse through categories to look for what they want, and often allow users to perform searches, too.
- **Search engines**—These index pages. Generally you can search for certain keywords, but the pages are not categorized, so you cannot find them by working your way through a directory system.
- **Guides and review sites**—These pick a relatively small selection of sites and review them, telling their visitors what's good and what's not.

There's some overlap, of course. For instance, Yahoo! is a search directory that also uses a search engine to help you search through the directory.

The cheapest way to register a site—if you don't regard time as money, that is—is to do it "manually," by going to all the search sites and entering the required information. Is it worth it? If you're completely broke, perhaps, but you can get a registration service to register you with, for instance, 200 sites for as little as $39; it'll take you many hours, perhaps several days, to do it yourself, so figure out how much your time is worth.

On the other hand, it may be a good idea to add your site to a few of the major search engines by hand, to make sure it gets added exactly where you want it—the registration services and software generally don't allow you full control. (In particular you'll find that few automatic-registration services include Yahoo!, yet Yahoo! is probably the single most important search site.) Then use a registration service or registration software to do the rest. The ones you'll definitely want to do by hand are the following:

Excite
   http://www.excite.com/

Yahoo!
   http://www.yahoo.com/

It's less important to register these by hand:

AltaVista
   http://altavista.digital.com/

HotBot
   http://www.hotbot.com/

Infoseek
   http://www.infoseek.com/

Lycos
   http://www.lycos.com/

Magellan
   http://www.mckinley.com/

WebCrawler
   http://www.webcrawler.com/

You can register with these sites quite effectively through a service or program, as all they really care about is the URL of the site.

The search sites that I've mentioned here are the most important search engines to register with, the ones that are used the most by most Web users. Most searches, probably well over 95 percent, are done through these sites. In other words, registration with the top search engines is worth far more than with the hundreds of other small search engines put together. Of all search engines, Yahoo! is the most important. It's by far the most popular and most used search engine of all—some estimates of the proportion of all Web searches carried out through Yahoo! are as high as 70 percent. So it's worth taking some time with Yahoo!. For instance, you should probably submit several of your Web pages to Yahoo!, to increase the chance that you will be included and that people searching at Yahoo! will find you.

Note, by the way, that some search engines may find you eventually anyway. AltaVista, for instance, digs around in Web sites, following all the links it can find. If your page is linked to from a page that AltaVista has already found, it will find your site by following the link. However, registering your site speeds up the process. It may take a long time for the search engine to find your site, so telling it where your page is helps it to find it sooner. Once it knows where your page is, it goes there to take a look at the page and index it.

To register by hand, begin by creating a text file with basic information about your Web site: the name, URL, a short description, and so on. Then go to the search engines and look for a link labeled something like Add Link or Add URL. These are often tucked away near the bottom of the page somewhere. Click on the link, then follow the instructions; copy the text from the text file into the fields in the submission form. If you want to register by hand at more search engines, try the following sites for listings of search engines:

Eureka
http://www.best.com/~mentorms/eureka.htm

VirtualPromote (Small list)
http://www.virtualpromote.com/promoteb.html

VirtualPromote Top 500
http://jimworld.com/the500/

WebStep 100
http://www.mmgco.com/top100.html

Yahoo!—Searching the Web, Indices
http://dir.yahoo.com/Computers_and_Internet/Internet/World_Wide_Web/
Searching_the_Web/Indices/

Yahoo!—Web Directories
http://dir.yahoo.com/Computers_and_Internet/Internet/World_Wide_Web/
Searching_the_Web/Web_Directories/

Yahoo!—Web Search Engines
http://www.yahoo.com/Computers_and_Internet/Internet/World_Wide_Web/
Searching_the_Web/Search_Engines/

Note, however, that registering by hand provides diminishing marginal returns; that is, most search sites are not used a great deal, so the cost in terms of your time to register with the hundreds that are out there may simply not be worth it. To register with sites other than the few most important ones, you'll probably want to use a registration service or program.

You should be on the lookout for search sites associated with your area of interest, the specialized search engines we discussed in Chapter 15. It may be worth registering in these by hand, to make sure it's done correctly and you get placed. For example, there's **CampSearch** for summer camps (http://www.camp search.com/), **MathSearch** for mathematics-related related Web pages (http://

www.maths.usyd.edu.au:8000/MathSearch.html), **Totavia Aviation Search Engine** for aviation and aerospace sites (http://search.totavia.com/), and many others.

How about the guides and review sites? Places like NetGuide, Project Cool, Yahoo!'s What's New, and so on. There are many of these sites, and some can do you a lot of good—get listed as the USA Today Hot Site, and see how much traffic you'll get! (**Poor Richard's Web Site**—http://PoorRichard.com/—got listed at USA Today, and we saw *a lot* of traffic over a few days.)

NetGuide's Internet Sites of the Day
   http://www.netguide.com/

Project Cool
   http://www.projectcool.com/sightings/

USA Today Hot Sites
   http://www.usatoday.com/life/cyber/ch.htm

Yahoo!—Best of the Web Awards
   http://dir.yahoo.com/Computers_and_Internet/Internet/World_Wide_Web/
   Best_of_the_Web/

Yahoo!—What's New
   http://www.yahoo.com/picks/

Submit your site to these places. Even if you are modest about your achievements in the design area—maybe you don't have the best-looking site on the Web! Submit anyway. There are so many of these sites, many of which have to find 365 sites to discuss each year, that you may have a better chance than you realize. Many sites will list your site if you provide useful services—even if it's not a particularly pretty site.

By the way, it may take a few weeks to get registered with the search sites. With some, your site will be placed in their database almost immediately, but others won't add you until they've sent a robot to your site, or even checked the information you submitted with the services of a genuine human being. In such cases, it could be quite a while before you can find your listing at the site.

Registration Services

I really don't believe it's worthwhile manually registering your Web site with all the search sites. There are simply too many—hundreds. It will take you days, weeks maybe, to work through all of them. Many are little used, anyway.

It's cheaper to pay a service to register for you. You'll will save many hours, but the registration process will be completed within a matter of minutes or hours, so people will be able to find your site at these search engines much sooner.

There are many registration services available, and some actually provide free services. Following are a few services you can try—prices are for comparison only; they may—they will—change:

@Submit! (register with 30+ sites free)
http://www.uswebsites.com/submit/

!Register-It!
http://www.register-it.com/

1 2 3 Register Me (100 sites for $45)
http://www.123registerme.com/

A1 WebSite Promotions (50 sites for $89.95, 100 for $159.95, or 200 for $299.95)
http://www.a1co.com/

AAA Internet Promotions (50 sites for $99, 100 for $199; Also options to submit once a month for a year)
http://www.websitepromote.com/dls/

did-it.com (10 sites for $99)
http://www.did-it.com/

JimTool Free Site Submitter (12 sites for free)
http://www.virtualpromote.com/submitter/

PostMaster (350 sites for $249)
http://www.netcreations.com/postmaster/

QwikLaunch (7 sites for free, 400 sites for $9.95)
http://www.qwiklaunch.com/

Shotgun
http://www.peachmedia.com/shotgun/

SiteLaunch
http://www.sitelaunch.net/

SmartAge Submit
http://www.smartage.com/submit/

Submit It!
http://www.submitit.com/

TrafficBoost.Com (530 sites for $49, or 4 submissions for $99)
ehttp://www.contactdata.net/

WebStep
http://www.mmgco.com/top100.html

Yahoo!—List of Services
http://dir.yahoo.com/Business_and_Economy/Companies/Internet_Services/
Web_Services/Promotion/

Registration Software

There are also programs that automate the process of registering your site. You load the program on your computer, then fill in the information and let the program register for you. The advantage? Cost and convenience. It may be cheaper to buy a program than to pay a submission service. It may be particularly economical if you plan to register a number of URLs—with a service you'll have to pay for each Web page you register; with a program you'll get either unlimited use or a license to use the program for a certain period of time. In fact, Submission Wizard has a lower cost per submission even if you use it only once (you can submit to 500 search sites for $25). Also it's probably easier to enter information into a program once, then save that information for use later, rather than fill in a form at a service every time you want to register a site. (And, as one user told me, "The registration services seem to have a tendency to crash after you hit the Enter button mid-registration, so you have no idea whether a registration has been made or not … and all the information you so carefully entered is lost.")

These programs have versions that allow you to submit to some places free, though the number is limited and you may not be given much choice, either.

007 Submitter
http://www.007software.com/

AddSoft
http://www.cyberspacehq.com/

AddWeb
http://www.cyberspacehq.com/

GlobalSpider
http://www.globalspider.net/

Hired Hits
http://www.hiredhits.com/

Hurricane WebPromo
http://www.theoffice.net/webpromo/

HyperHits
http://webmastertools.com/

Net Submitter Pro
http://softwaresolutions.net/

Register Pro
http://www.registerpro.com/

SoftSpider
http://www.designmaker.com/

Submission Wizard (Windows 95, 500 search sites—the program will run for one month for $25, six months is $80)
http://www.exploit.com/
http://www.exploit.net/
http://www.submissions.com/

Submit Blaster (Windows 95; 120 sites for $100)
http://www.rtlsoft.com/

SubmitWolf
http://www.msw.com.au/wolfhq.htm

Web Promotion Spider ($50 to $100, 250 to 300+ search sites)
http://beherenow.com/

WebPosition
http://www.webposition.com/

www.SitePromoter (Windows and the Mac)
http://www.sitepromoter.com/

Check Your Search-Engine Position

Whatever method you use to register your site, it's a good idea to check how well your site is listed. You should probably wait a few days, possibly a week or two for some of the bigger search engines, then search for your Web site. You'll find that a lot of the search engines won't have you listed. I've found that Yahoo! in particular is very bad at adding listings; perhaps as many as 50 percent of all submissions are rejected. All I can recommend is that you check your META tags to make sure they're good, and try to register again, perhaps using different categories and keywords.

Some programs and services will help you check your position at the search engines—Web Promotion Spider and Did-It Detective, mentioned in the lists above, for instance. There are also programs designed purely for checking search-engine position, such as **WebPosition** (http://www.webposition.com/). Check the following Web sites for more information.

MetaMedic (free online meta-tag checker)
http://www.northernwebs.com/set/setsimjr.html

MyRank (free search-site rankings delivered by e-mail)
http://www.myrank.com/

Position Agent (free trial for a commercial rank-checking service)
http://www.positionagent.com/

Rank This! (free rank check with 10 different search sites)
http://www.rankthis.com/

ScoreCheck (a free trial of a commercial rank-checking service)
http://www.scorecheck.com/

SmartAge SiteRank (a free trial of a commercial rank-checking service)
http://www.smartage.com/rank/

WebPosition (rank-checking software; download version available)
http://www.webposition.com/

Yahoo!—Listings
http://dir.yahoo.com/Computers_and_Internet/Internet/World_Wide_Web/
Information_and_Documentation/Site_Announcement_and_Promotion/
Search_Engine_Placement_Improvement/

More Advice

Positioning a Web page at a search site seems to be a real science these days, and there's no lack of advice available. If you'd like more information about the best ways to work with search engines, check these Web sites and newsgroups and their associated reports and newsletters:

comp.infosystems.search (a newsgroup related to search-engine issues)

MarketPosition Newsletter
http://www.webposition.com/newsletter.htm

META Tagging for Search Engines
http://www.stars.com/Search/Meta/Tag.html

PlanetOcean—Search Engine Secrets ($97 for a book)
http://www.hitmasters.com/

Search Engine and Web Site Secrets Monthly
http://yellowpage.com/ses.htm

Search Engine Optimization Promotion Tools
http://www.bruceclay.com/web_rank.htm

Search Engine Tips—Submit It!
http://www.submit-it.com/subopt.htm

Search Engine Watch (a very useful site, lots of information)
http://searchenginewatch.com/

Search Engines—Submission Tips, Help and Use
http://www.sofer.com/research/

Yahoo!—Site Announcement and Promotion Placement Improvement
http://dir.yahoo.com/Computers_and_Internet/Internet/World_Wide_Web/
Information_and_Documentation/Site_Announcement_and_Promotion/
Search_Engine_Placement_Improvement/

Free-Link Pages

A variety of sites on the Internet provide free-link pages, also known as Free For All pages, that let you add a link from their pages to your site for free. Are these effective? I've tried them, and found that while they can send traffic to your site, it's not worth registering by hand. There are services that will register with hundreds for you. But it still may not be worthwhile.

I wrote an article on this subject in ***Poor R ichard's Web Site News*** Before you use these free-link pages, I suggest you read that and decide if they're worthwhile: http://PoorRichard.com/newsltr/016.htm#link.

If you *are* going to use the free-link pages, spend a few minutes thinking about what link text you'll use. Don't just create a link that says *Acme Gerbils*. Think of the link as an advert—use *The Best Gerbil Site on the Web!*, or *Free Gerbils!*, or *Everything You Ever Wanted to Know About Gerbils but Were Afraid to Ask!*

There's another form of free link: banner exchanges. With these you agree to carry a banner, and someone else agrees to carry yours. Such exchanges are carried out using services such as Link Exchange. The Banner Exchange and Christian Banner eXchange. In effect, you are swapping advertising. I'll deal with this subject in Chapter 20.

Chapter Seventeen

Bringing People to Your Site

In Chapter 16 you learned how to register your Web site with the list directories and the search sites. Now you can just sit back and wait for people to arrive.

Well, you could do that, but don't expect too much activity. Yes, people probably will find you, and you will get visits, but merely listing your site is not a terribly effective way to promote your business. Do you know any businesses that rely solely on the Yellow Pages, for instance, to bring people into their stores? Not many, probably. Yes, you need to be listed, and yes, listing will bring you some visitors, but it's not enough.

One reason that it's not enough is that there's so much choice on the Web these days. For instance, go to a major search engine and search for just about anything: bicycles, model rockets, chocolate, lingerie, astronomy, hardware, paragliding … I searched for *paraglid* at Yahoo! and found 12 categories and 227 sites. So how do you know that someone searching on the keywords you've used to list at a search engine—which are almost certainly the same keywords used by many other people—will choose your Web page over the hundreds of other options? How do you even know that people will even get to your listing before selecting a different one? You don't, and although some people claim to know the secrets to getting you listed at the top of every search engine, in practice there's not much you can do to make sure you get listed first, over and above the things we discussed in Chapter 16. (Well, okay, there might be, but it's almost a full-time job figuring out how to beat the search engines. If you want to play that game, look at the resources near the end of Chapter 16.)

Forget the billboard nonsense—as I've mentioned before, a Web site's not a billboard. Forget what you may have heard about how "the Internet changes everything!" It doesn't. Just like businesses in the real world, businesses in cyberspace need to go and find their clients and bring them to their Web sites. Where will you find people? One good place is in the Internet's discussion groups—mailing lists and newsgroups. And that's just what we'll be discussing in this chapter. (Remember, I told you how to find relevant newsgroups and mailing lists in Chapter 15.)

Before You Start, Visit

Before you begin posting messages to newsgroups and mailings lists, you should "visit." Take a look at the newsgroups and subscribe to the mailing lists. You could just post messages blind, but the problem is that you may be posting messages in a manner that's going to irritate other people who are members of those discussion groups. Unless you take a look, you don't know for sure the slant of the discussion group. You won't know what types of messages you can post without upsetting people. And for the moderated groups this is especially important, because if you send an inappropriate message, the moderator simply won't post it to the group. Many newsgroups and mailing lists have FAQs (Frequently Asked Question documents) and charters that explain the purpose of the group and what sorts of messages are acceptable. In the case of newsgroups, you'll sometimes find an FAQ posted to the newsgroup once or twice a week so it's always available. In moderated groups, you may find that the moderator puts his signature at the bottom of every message, with information about where to find the FAQ or charter. In the case of mailing lists, when you subscribe you'll generally be sent a document describing the group and explaining what is acceptable.

I suggest that you find all the discussion groups that might possibly be of interest to you, then visit them and narrow them down to the ones that will be useful. For instance, if you are promoting a model-rocket Web site, you can search for the word *space* and you'll find more than 60 related newsgroups. Some of these are clearly of no use: alt.alien.visitors (Space Aliens on Earth! Abduction! Gov't Coverup!) and alt.cyberspace (Cyberspace and how it should work), for instance. But how about can.schoolnet.space.jr (SchoolNet Space Sciences for elementary students), can.schoolnet.space.sr (SchoolNet Space Sciences for high school students), and york.club.seds (Students for Exploration & Development of Space)? Although they're not directly related to model rocketry, there's a good chance that some of the people subscribed to these groups are involved in the hobby, and it may be possible to post a message to these sites—as long as it's written properly, as you'll see.

Create a Signature

Before you start posting to newsgroups and mailing lists, design a good *signature*. A signature is a little block of text at the end of a message that says something about the person who sent the message—or something the person wants other people to know. These are great forms of advertising, especially if your message is intelligent and useful to other people in the discussion group. If people read a message and find something useful or interesting, they may want to know about the person writing the message, and they may spend a few moments visiting the person's Web site to learn more. Signatures are often used to carry little promotional ads, and this seems to be more or less accepted these days, as long as the signature isn't too large.

So think about what you want to tell people and how you can fit it into a few lines at the bottom of every message you send. You'll want to design several signatures and use the most appropriate for each discussion group. How many lines? It used to be said that four or five were about the maximum, but these days I notice people using nine or ten without too many complaints. Don't be too pushy in the signature, though. Try to give the person a reason to visit your site. For instance, which is likely to be the more appealing of the following two signatures?

```
Buy from us! The best prices and the best rocket
products on the Web! http://www.podunkrocket.com/
```

Or ...

```
Meet Buzz Aldrin in our discussion group next week!
(March 3-7, 2000) Also, free classified ads, great link
pages, fantastic selection of model rockets and
accessories. http://www.podunkrocket.com/
```

Think about what you can offer people to come to your site. Certainly the first signature may bring some people in, but the second is likely to be stronger because it's not selling, at least not until the last few words. Rather, it's talking about how your site gives something to its visitors.

If you post many messages in discussion groups, each message can contain a little signature ad, even if you don't mention your Web site in the message itself. We'll come back to this idea a little later in this chapter.

What sort of things should you remember to include in your signature? The following:

- The URL to the particular page at your Web site that you want people from this group to arrive at—which may not be the same page for each group; you may want to present different information first, depending on who's arriving at your site. (We'll discuss this a little later in this chapter.)

- The e-mail address of an autoresponder—many people still have slow Internet connections or minimal Web access, so they may prefer to obtain more information from an autoresponder.

- The e-mail address of a real person to which questions can be directed.

- Reasons for people to visit your site. Don't list reasons why you want them to visit, but give them reasons why they should want to visit— these are two very different things.

How to Write Messages

Let's say you want to promote your model-rocket site to various newsgroups. You could, if you were really reckless, write a message like this:

```
CHECK THIS OUT!
THE BEST MODEL-ROCKET SITE ON THE WEB!!!!!!
COOL STUFF, REAL CHEAP, SAVE $$$$$!!!
COME VISIT US AT HTTP://WWW.ROCKETFOOL.COM/!!!
```

You could even post this message to 20,000 newsgroups at once, though you might run into serious problems if you try—remember our discussion of spam in Chapter 14?

These types of message are obnoxious, and people generally hate them; you'll probably make more enemies than friends posting messages like this. It's clearly an ad, and it sounds like a poorly written ad, too. But it's similar to thousands of messages being posted to newsgroups every day, and people are getting sick of them.

Think of newsgroup messages in a different way. Don't think of them as advertisements but as informational messages. Don't "scream" your message at people—talk to them. Try a message like this:

```
Hi, I've just started checking out the model-rocket
discussion groups on the Internet. This one seems like
quite an active group. I run a mail-order model-rocket
business in Podunk, Texas, so I wanted to find out a
little about how other model-rocketeers are using the
Internet. We just set up a Web site (come visit us
sometime: http://www.podunkrocket.com/ ). We figured
we'd try to provide some services to other people who
```

```
love rockets, so we've got links to all the rocket
sites we can find (not just model rockets, but the real
things, too--lots of cool NASA links). We've got a
discussion group running, too--we're starting celebrity
discussions, soon, as well, so you'll be able to post
messages to the rocket designers at Estes, some top
prizewinners, and so on. Let us know if you've got any
suggestions for people you'd like to talk with. And my
partner says I'm crazy to do this--Why risk losing
business? he says--but we set up a free classified
area. If you have any rockets or accessories you want
to sell, you can post a classified ad (that's right, no
charge!).


If anyone else has any ideas for services we could
provide at a Web site, please let us know. Oh, and if
we're missing a link you know about that we really
should have, you can fill in a form at our site to add
it to the list.
```

Which message is more annoying? Which is more of an ad? They're really both ads, but the first is nothing but an ad, while the second has some character. You can "hear" a person's voice in that message—there's a real person there, not just a bulk-mail program. Notice, by the way, that when I wrote the URL in that message, I made sure it began and ended with a space, so that I can be sure it will work if people click on the link to start their browsers and display the Web site. I discussed this issue in Chapter 14.

Notice also that this message isn't directly selling something; it's actually giving something away—three things, really: free classifieds, a rocket discussion group, and a useful link page. It's also asking questions: Have you any ideas for people we could invite to answer questions in our discussion group? Are there any services you'd like to see us provide? Any links we've missed? Nowhere in the message do we ask people to spend money; we just suggest that they might like to visit our site, and give good reasons why.

Now, it's quite possible that a message like this one could get complaints. But because it's clearly from a real person and because it's chatty, any complaints are more likely to be similar to this: "Fred, we try to avoid ads in this group; could you be more careful in future?" Not so much a flame as a gentle rebuke.

So remember these basic principles about advertising in discussion groups:

Pure ads (Buy, Buy, Buy!) irritate people.

"Ads" in which you give people something are usually acceptable.

Look at your message carefully. Are you providing something useful to the members of that list? Is your message something that a significant proportion of the list is likely to find useful or interesting? Or is it purely an ad?

Not Sure About a Group?

What about groups that probably attract people who are interested in your products, but which are not directly related? Groups about rockets, though not specifically about model rockets, perhaps? I'd be very careful about what I posted in these groups, and I'd keep it short. And I'd try to think about the services that my Web site provides that are more directly related to this newsgroup. For instance, you might try something like this:

```
Anyone out there want to swap or sell rocket-related
products--books, videos, magazines, NASA souvenirs? I
run a Web site with loads of links to rocket sites, and
we've got a free classified-ad section too. You can
post messages to sell your stuff, for no charge. And
we're going to be having question-and-answer sessions
in our rocket discussion group soon; we're trying to
track down an astronaut or two to take part. If anyone
knows someone knowledgeable who might be interested,
please let us know.
```

In this message I've mentioned the things that might be useful to people on this list. It's a rocket discussion group, though not a model-rocket group, so I've mentioned the rocket-links page and the discussion group. I've mentioned the free classified ads, as well; after all, it's likely that there's a lot of overlap, that many people who are interested in rockets are also interested in model rockets, and so may be interested in the classifieds. I also kept it low-key and chatty; again—it's not a *Buy, Buy, Buy!* posting.

But That's Not an Effective Ad

Now, I know that some people, particularly people who are used to the world of direct mail, feel that this sort of discreet advertising in discussion groups is not real advertising—it's not direct enough. And indeed, you'll see many ads in discussion groups, in particular in newsgroups (because it's so easy to post messages in newsgroups), that look something like this:

```
* * * * * * * * * * * * * * * * * * * * * * * * * * * * * * * * * * *
MAKE MONEY WITHOUT PRINTING MONEY
* * * * * * * * * * * * * * * * * * * * * * * * * * * * * * * * * * *
SIXTY THOUSAND DOLLARS IN ONE YEAR
* * * * * * * * * * * * * * * * * * * * * * * * * * * * * * * * * * *
```

and this:

```
Register for a free internet downline and receive
absolutely free, your own internet web site. Sign up
now and get a massive internet downline and a web page
absolutely free. Its FREE! Its Easy and it can be your
answer to financial security. Visit my web site at ...
```

(What's *downline*? It's a bit of multilevel marketing—MLM—jargon, referring to income from people who you recruit; unfortunately, MLM discovered the Internet some time ago.)

Am I saying that ads like this can't work? No, they probably can. As we discussed in Chapter 14, spamming is very tempting because it's so cheap, and you need only a tiny response to make it pay. There are programs that will send your message to 20,000 newsgroups at once very quickly and cheaply. Of course you may not like the reaction you get—everything from insulting e-mail to eventually, perhaps, prosecution. And there are systems out there designed to look for this sort of cross-posting and destroy cross-posted messages.

But even if this type of advertising can pay, this is a book about setting up a Web site, not hiding in cyberspace, which you'll have to do if you do too much of this sort of thing. You're trying to build a very visible presence, and that will be difficult to do if you make a habit of this kind of advertising.

How Often Can You Post?

Don't post the same message over and over to the same places. If you do so, your chatty announcement turns into a blatant ad, the very thing you're trying to avoid. That doesn't mean you can't remind people about your Web site, of course. You can announce new services now and again. In fact you may not want to mention everything in your first post; keep something back for later.

If you have an active chat or discussion group, you can announce activities such as celebrity chats or extended question-and-answer sessions in your discussion group. And, as I'll discuss next, you can provide information and become an advisor as another way to keep a regular presence in the discussion groups. Your signature will still act as a reminder and an ad, and if you've set up a truly useful Web site, you'll find that other people will start to talk about your site.

Provide Information at Your Web Site

Another technique many people use is to provide information and post it at their Web sites. Then they can post messages in newsgroups and mailing lists that are directly related to the subject of that information. For instance, a lawyer who works in employment law might write an article about a particular issue in employment law, then post messages to the discussion groups related to employment law mentioning that the article is available.

Also, if you see someone asking for information—something that requires more than just a few lines in reply—and if you have the answer, why not post it at your Web site and then send a message saying where the information is available. This is very commonly done, and isn't regarded as a "teaser." It's not a matter of: "I've got the information, you can have it, but only if you come to my site"; it's more a matter of: "I have an entire article on this subject, but it's way too big to post to the mailing list because most people probably aren't interested, so why not view it at my Web site?" You're not only providing a service but doing it in such a way that you don't annoy people by posting a huge message to the discussion group.

Note, by the way, that you need to remember to set up your Web site so that people coming to your site for the information will see other things at your site. Some people doing this provide the main URL of their Web site, so the user must look for the information—don't make it too difficult to find, though—and at the same time is bound to notice other things at your site. Alternatively, you can give a URL to take people directly to the information while ensuring that there are obvious links to other information at your site.

Become an Advisor

Most discussion groups have a small core of regulars and a large number of lurkers—people who read the messages but never post responses or new messages. For instance, one group of which I used to be a member has about 650 members, but only around 30 or 40 regulars who seem to post messages frequently.

Among the regulars there's often a smaller group—maybe only five or ten—who are what I think of as *advisors*. When people send messages posing questions, members of this group are the first to answer, and they provide the best and most useful answers.

Get involved in a few of the active groups. Get known to the members as someone who understands the subject being discussed and can answer questions and provide leads to useful information.

There's a drawback to getting too involved in discussion groups—it can soak up a great deal of time. Try to discipline yourself and learn to use the Delete key. Immediately delete messages that are of little interest—the very chatty messages or messages about subjects that don't particularly interest you. You can't be expected to answer every question; just answer a few now and again with helpful information. Occasionally point people to your Web site, and make sure you have a good signature on all your messages.

Get to Know the Advisors

In Chapter 15 I suggested that you get to know the enthusiasts and cultivate them. Well, the advisors in newsgroups and mailing lists are just these people. (Group moderators are, of course, also advisors.) They spend a lot of time in these discussion groups, so they must be interested. They may be your competitors, but they may simply be people who are very interested in a subject.

Get to know these people; send them free goods, in the same way you would with people who run Web sites associated with your area of business. Send them e-mail and chat with them a little. They'll remember you and may well check out your Web site. If you've got something of value, they'll remember that and mention it to other people. And their status as advisors gives their comments and opinions great weight with many group members.

These people are often useful product reviewers, too. Sometimes they write in real-world magazines and sometimes they have Web sites that review products. So keep a watch for people who can leverage your marketing campaign by talking about your products for you. Remember, the very best advertising you can get is product endorsements from people who are not directly affiliated with, or paid by, you or your company.

Here's an example. I wrote *The Technical Writer's Freelancing Guide* in the early 1990s; this book was reviewed in four periodicals that I know of. In 1997 I revised this book, and it was republished as **Making Money in Technical Writing** (http://TopFloor.com/techwr/). This time I actively recruited reviewers. Many came to me after I announced the book in mailing lists and newsgroups and asked for reviewers. Others read other messages I'd written, visited my Web site, saw the invitation to reviewers, and contacted me. By the time *Making Money in Technical Writing* was published I had 90 reviewers lined up, some claiming to be planning multiple reviews. To this day this book continues to sell well.

Bear in mind, however, that the easier you make it to get a review copy, the more likely you are to be ripped off. Some of these 90 people may be asking for a free book without any intention of ever publishing a review. But even if only half of them publish reviews, it's still well worth the cost. And I believe the rip-off rate to be much lower than 50 percent—probably less than 5 percent. I ask reviewers to provide me with the names of the publications for which they're writing the reviews and when they think it'll be published; some have even provided information on how to contact the publication's editor. So I'm pretty sure that most of these review requests are genuine. The Internet provides a really easy and convenient way to contact reviewers—a way to leverage your promotional efforts tremendously.

Announcement Newsgroups

There are a number of newsgroups designed specifically for announcements, where you can post blatant ads and nobody cares. Some of these are general—comp.infosystems.www.announce, for instance, accepts announcements about new noncommercial Web sites. Others are more specific—comp.security.pgp. announce, for instance, contains announcements related to the PGP encryption program.

In your newsgroup program, search for these words: announce, forsale, market. Or better still, search one of the newsgroup directories mentioned in Chapter 15—if you search in your newsreader, the program will find only those groups in which the word you are searching for is within the group name; at some of the directories a group description is also searched.

You'll find groups like the following:

- alt.fandom.cons—Announcements of conventions (SciFi and others)
- chi.places—Announcements of Chicago-area events
- alt.aquaria.marketplace—Fish and aquariums
- alt.art.marketplace—Art for sale
- biz.marketplace.computers—Computers and computer equipment
- ithaca.marketplace—Stuff for sale in Ithaca, New York
- alt.autographs.transactions—Ads related to autographs for sale
- edm.forsale—Stuff for sale in Edmonton, Canada.

There's a flip side, too. There are also groups that take wanted ads, and though you're not supposed to post messages selling things, you can look in these groups for people who may be searching for the products or services you provide. And if you search for the word *wanted* in the directories, you'll often find groups that accept both for-sale and wanted ads, such as the following:

- alt.auto.parts.wanted—Described as "alt.american.automobile. breakdown.breakdown.breakdown"
- aus.ads.wanted—Goods for sale or wanted in Australia
- comp.binaries.ibm.pc.wanted—People seeking software
- nj.market.autos—Vehicles wanted and for sale in New Jersey.

Note, by the way, that some groups are really intended for classified-ad-type ads rather than for businesses. Also, many of the announcements are not necessarily about goods for sale—announcements about upcoming events, for instance. Another form of newsgroup that takes announcements of various kinds are the net-happenings groups, such as comp.internet.net-happenings. There are also a few newprod groups for announcements of new products, such as the following:

- biz.next.newprod—New product announcements for the NeXT computer
- can.newprod—New products/services of interest to Canadian readers
- comp.newprod—Announcements of new products
- eunet.newprod—New products of interest to Europeans.

Also take a look at the biz newsgroups, many of which contain announcements about commercial products. And there are also the Clarinet releases newsgroups, though you can't post messages directly to these groups. Rather, you must send a press release through one of several press-release services, which we'll discuss in Chapter 18.

Finally, there are scores of mailing lists and newsgroups that review products —books, software, music, theater, restaurants, bicycles, cigars, and so on. Search for the word review, and you'll find these groups. Then visit the appropriate ones and see if you can find someone to review your product. With luck, you may be able to contact a review writer who also sells reviews to magazines and newspapers. Some of these review groups—such as alt.books.reviews—allow redistribution of reviews, so a review of your product may end up going further than just the newsgroups—into newsletters and on Web sites, for instance.

Remember the Online Services

As I mentioned in Chapter 15, CompuServe, AOL, GEnie, Prodigy, and Microsoft Network are all great ways to find potential customers. These online services have a total membership of tens of millions of people, so somewhere on those services are thousands of people discussing subjects related to your business. (Perhaps one U.S. Internet user in seven is an AOL member.)

The discussion groups in these online services are similar in many ways to Internet discussion groups, though they're generally not as convenient. On the online services, you have to visit each group individually, changing to a completely different area of the service each time, whereas with Internet newsgroups, you can set up your newsreader so that just the groups you want to work with are displayed in the program, then click on one to read its messages, and with mailing lists, you can read all the messages in your e-mail program. Still, the online services are well worth checking into and can bring you into contact with many people you won't find on the Internet proper.

Many More Promotions

There are far more ways to promote a Web site than we have time for—enough for the next book! (Speaking of which, see the note at the end of this chapter.) Exercise a little imagination and think up new ways to do things. Perhaps the most important thing to consider is this:

Go to where the people you want are hanging out.

There are many Web sites being visited by people you are interested in, many newsgroups and mailing lists being read by these people, electronic newsletters being delivered to them, and so on.

Here's one example of a good promotion: search for the sorts of keywords people are likely to use when searching for your site, then use those keywords in a search engine, go to the first 10 or 20 sites that appear, and try to get links from those sites back to your site. Consider some kind of cooperative promotion, if possible, to encourage the site owners to link to you.

Track the Source of Visits

There's a simple technique used in direct mail that you can employ at your Web site. You've probably noticed all the department numbers on direct-mail order forms, or the department numbers you're sometimes told to ask for when calling an 800 number. These are usually not genuine department numbers, they're simply advertising codes used by the company to track where their clients are coming from. Each number refers to a particular magazine, newspaper, or television ad. The company can keep track of how many sales each ad generates, calculate the financial returns from advertising in different places, and calculate where it will be most effective to advertise in the future.

You can do the same by using different URLs each time you mention your Web site. Use a different URL for each newsgroup and mailing list in which you announce the Web site, for instance, and a different URL for each special promotion you announce. You'll have to create different Web pages for each URL, of course, but each page can be the same. For instance, let's say you find five newsgroups closely related to your business. You can create five Welcome pages: 1.htm, 2.htm, 3.htm, and so on. Each can be identical, or you could customize each page, welcoming people from the different newsgroups.

Here's another example. Let's say you're doing radio talk-show appearances and want to give out this URL on the show: www.acmesewercover.com/radio— it's nice and short, and you don't have to say "dot h t m l" at the end. All you need to do is to create a new directory named radio, then copy the main page (probably named index.html) from the main directory into the radio directory. You'll have to change the links in this new page, so they point to the correct pages in the other directory.

Now, as you'll learn in Chapter 21, it's possible to track hits on your site. So each time someone uses a URL to read your 1.htm page, that hit will be recorded. Each time someone uses 2.htm, or the index.html file in the radio directory, that hit is recorded. You can look at the logs periodically and see how many hits you are getting at each page, which will give you a good idea of how much activity your promotions in each newsgroup are generating.

There's something important to remember with this technique, though: it's not a good idea simply to put up a Web page for a while, then remove it after people seem to have stopped coming to the site. First, people may bookmark that page, and if it's gone a few months later, when they try to get to your site they may not find their way back. Also, some people may not see the message in which you've mentioned the Web site until months or even years later. So it's a good idea to keep these pages around for a long time, long after they appear to have served their purposes.

You might also want to set up a special Welcome page with a little introductory text rather than an actual duplicate of your home or main page. You can set up this page to move the visitor automatically onto the next page. You can also have a link from that page to your main page, with a message suggesting that your visitors bookmark the next page when they get to it.

There are several ways to forward people's browsers automatically from one page to another. You can use a piece of JavaScript in your Web page, such as the following:

```
<SCRIPT LANGUAGE="JAVASCRIPT">
<!--
alert("Welcome to our Web site; please bookmark our
site so you can find your way back later.")
//-->
</SCRIPT>
</HEAD>
<BODY onload="location='next.htm'">
```

Type this exact statement into your Web source document at the top of the file, immediately below the <HEAD> tag (open a Web page and you'll see that tag near the top; simply move the text down a line and insert the JavaScript). When a browser loads your page, a message box will be displayed, showing the message in the alert statement. When the user clicks on OK, the browser automatically loads the page (in this case next.htm) specified in the last line. This technique will work with the browsers used by the vast majority of users, probably over 90 percent of users—everyone working with Netscape 2 or later, or Internet Explorer 3 or later. Users not working with a JavaScript browser will not see the message box, so for that 5 or 10 percent, you need to include a link to the next page.

Here's a way to forward someone directly to another page without displaying an alert box or allowing the user time to see much at all; in fact if the visitor looks away for a moment, he may not even notice that he's landed at one page and then moved to another. Simply add this tag, above the <BODY> tag:

```
<META HTTP-EQUIV="REFRESH" CONTENT="0; URL=next.htm">
```

The number immediately after CONTENT=" (in this case 0) indicates how long the browser should wait until moving to the next document, which is specified after URL=; in this case the 0 means that the browser should continue to the next document immediately. Again, this won't work on some browsers, but it will work on the vast majority, and certainly it'll work for more than the JavaScript will; the above is not JavaScript but a piece of HTML.

There's a problem with both of the above methods, though. If the user clicks the Back button and goes back to this page, the page again instructs the browser to load next.htm; so the user may try to return the way he came, and keep getting "pushed" forward again. To get around this, you can use this slightly more sophisticated JavaScript:

```
<SCRIPT LANGUAGE="JavaScript">
<!--
function redirect() {
    if (confirm ("Welcome to our Web site; please
bookmark our site so you can find your way back later.
Click OK to continue."))
    {
        location='2-12A.htm'
    }
}
//-->
</SCRIPT>
<BODY onload="redirect()">
```

This script displays a confirmation box; it moves the visitor to the next page only if he clicks the OK button. So if he uses the Back button he won't be automatically pushed forward again.

Which of these methods do I prefer? I use the <META> tag method, as it's quick and simple, requiring no action on the part of the user, and will work in almost all browsers—though it still has the Back-command problem.

Using a special entrance page like this isn't perfect. Some of the search engines will eventually find the page, so you may get some people arriving at the page who have not seen your messages in the discussion groups. Still, though slightly imprecise, the method is close enough to give you an idea of how people are finding out about your site.

Less than one third of this book is about promoting your Web site. I could write an entire book on the subject. In fact I did, with Tara Calishain, *Poor R ichard's Internet Marketing and Promotions* It contains many more ideas and resources to help you bring people to your site, so check out the Table of Contents and sample chapters at http://PoorRichard.com/promo/.

Chapter Eighteen

Electronic Press Releases

There's yet another pernicious myth about the Internet—that it somehow replaces the real world, at least as far as business goes: everything that can be done in the real world can be done online. This is just another bit of twaddle, and the successful online businesses know it, which is why you see them mentioned in the real-world press. (In fact here's an interesting little factoid for you: most large Web businesses spend more money in real-world advertising than in Web advertising. Yahoo!, for instance, one of the companies making the most money in banner-advertising sales ... doesn't advertise on the Web at all.)

To successfully promote your Web site, you must promote it off the Web. You must get it mentioned in magazines, newspapers, newsletters, and radio and TV shows. Somehow you must reach the writers who produce the articles and shows, and convince them to talk about your Web site.

The press release is a time-honored method for getting the word out. Many businesses, small and large, have used press releases for years, but there's a new twist to the press release; you can now distribute press releases online. There are many services that will send out your press release to a closely guarded list of media contacts. You can also get these services to write the release for you for around $100 to $150. Or you can build your own media list and distribute the press release in the same way you would distribute an e-mail newsletter (see Chapter 14).

Writing a Press Release

When you write a press release, try to look at the product or service you are promoting from a client's perspective. Don't write a press release saying what a wonderful product you have—write a press release saying how much the product can do for the people who use it. These may seem to be the same thing, but they're not. There's a subtle but important difference, one that you can often

331

see by comparing press releases. If you've read many press releases promoting products and services, you'll find that most seem to be written by people who are very proud of their products. They seem to be saying: "This is wonderful—we are wonderful, everybody should want this product." But the better ones take a completely different slant, and although they explain what a great product it is, they do so from the perspective of the user of the product. Instead of including a dull list of features, for instance, they talk about the way people can use the product. If you'd like to see some example press releases to get a feel for what works and what doesn't, simply go to any major search engine and search for *press release*.

Look for a slant or angle—or spin, if you want to use the rather blunt jargon of the PR business—that sets your product apart. Look for something special to say about your product, such as the following:

- It's by far the lowest in cost of its kind, yet it's still high quality.
- You've just won an award. (Hopefully a well-known and important award, but whatever you can manage will do.)
- A celebrity uses your product and has said how great it is.
- A president has been seen using your product. (That's how Tom Clancy's writing career went into overdrive—Ronald Reagan was photographed with a copy of a Clancy book on his desk.)
- You've launched a product that does something unusual that people are sure to want to hear about.

Here's an example, explained to me by a friend, Mike Ceranski, onetime CEO of Dvorak Development. Dvorak had a product called WebSprite; you would install the program on your computer, select the Web sites with information that interests you, then WebSprite would periodically retrieve the information for you and display it on your computer's desktop—news, weather, updates to a shareware software archive, the location of your FedEx package, or whatever else you selected.

One morning while taking a shower, Mike had an idea—he'd make WebSprite talk. When he got to work, he searched around on the Internet for a text-to-speech program. He found one, paid $40 to download the program, then made some slight modifications to WebSprite so that it could interact with text-to-speech programs. By that afternoon, WebSprite was talking; as news headlines were transferred, for instance, WebSprite would read them out loud.

Mike put together a press release based on the premise that WebSprite was the world's first "intelligent offline radio." Thanks to that press release, WebSprite was mentioned in *PC Week, InfoWorld, WebWeek, Inter@ctive Week, Marketing News,* and *NewsLinx.* I need to show you an example press release, so you might as well see a successful one. Here's the release Mike sent out:

```
Broomfield, Colo.  FOR IMMEDIATE RELEASE

Offline Radio for the Web: highly targeted information
and low bandwidth combined with Text-to-Speech
capability makes WebSprite v1.0 a winner in the "push"
data market.

What do you get when you combine an Internet micro-
browser, otherwise called a "web scrubber," with text-
to-speech capability? The world's first intelligent
offline radio.

Here's how it works: WebSprite connects to the Web and
goes to a variety of Web sites, fetching specific
information from each. WebSprite fetches news
headlines, weather forecasts, stock prices, movie
reviews, and similar types of dynamic information. Once
the info has been fetched, WebSprite disconnects, then
scrolls the headlines it fetched in a small ticker-type
window on your computer's screen.

If you like, WebSprite can even read the headlines to
you at the same time it displays them in the ticker
window. This allows you to do other things while
listening to your own customized news radio broadcast.
Because WebSprite only gets the specific information
you've told it to fetch, you only hear what's
interesting to you.

It's called an "offline" radio because you do not have
to be constantly connected to the Internet to use it.
Unlike RealAudio and other streaming services,
WebSprite connects for only a short period, usually two
to five minutes, a couple of times throughout the day.
This ensures fresh, up-to-the-minute news, but without
tying up a phone line, modem, or internal LAN
constantly. WebSprite works in conjunction with popular
```

Text-To-Speech software to convert its customized text into your personalized radio broadcast.

Why listen to your computer when you can just as easily read it? "Of course, visually impaired users will find the WebSprite's Offline Radio capability to be very handy, but unimpaired users will find it useful too. For instance, I often turn it on and let it read headlines while I'm doing paperwork. Occasionally something catches my ear, and I can stop whatever I'm doing and read a quick summary of the headline from WebSprite. I get the news I want, but do it passively, in the background. It's sort of like having CNN on, but better, because when I hear something interesting, I can go back and get more info instantly ... I don't miss a thing," said Mike Ceranski, President of Dvorak Internet Development. "And when I don't want to listen to it, I can turn off the speech yet continue to scan the headlines as they scroll by," added Ceranski.

WebSprite offers a wide variety of information that you can both read or hear: stocks prices, news headlines, incoming e-mail, weather reports, science news, commodities, market indicators and indexes, soap opera summaries, business press announcements, movie reviews, sports news, Internet news, daily horoscopes, and much more. "The user chooses what he or she wants fetched from the Internet. A user can further refine the scope of the "fetch" so it is of the greatest possible relevance to their tastes and interests. This sort of "narrow-casting" makes WebSprite a wonderful way to keep up without being deluged with unwanted information," says Ceranski.

WebSprite is a very low-bandwidth solution, perfect for modem users or for corporate LAN users who don't want to tie up precious corporate bandwidth.

It works with Windows 95 and Windows NT 4.0. This newest version of WebSprite, version 1.0, will be available for free from Dvorak's Web site

```
(www.websprite.com) on Friday the 14th, Valentine's
Day.

For more information, or to download a copy of
WebSprite, visit www.websprite.com or e-mail
info@dvorak.com.

Dvorak Internet Development
PO Box 1524
Broomfield, CO  80038
```

Notice that this press release explains the product's features, but it's more than a simple list of specifications. It talks in a direct and personal manner: "If you like, WebSprite can even read the headlines to you …"; "Because WebSprite only gets the specific information you've told it to fetch …"; "… convert its customized text into your personalized radio broadcast." It also has a great hook: "The world's first intelligent offline radio."

This is a successful press release; it did its job and got the product into several important magazines. It's not quite a formal press release, though. You may hear all sorts of rules about formatting press releases, and this previous press release just proves that it's possible to break a few of the rules and still be successful. It's far more important to create an interesting, well-written press release than to follow the rules. Here, however, is one version of those rules:

- The very first line should be FOR IMMEDIATE RELEASE all in caps.
- Leave a blank line and then include the company name and address.
- Leave a blank line and then have the word CONTACT:, followed on the next few lines by the title and name of someone the reader can contact for more information, along with that person's phone number and e-mail address.
- Leave a couple of blank lines, then place the headline, typically five to ten words—don't make the headline too unwieldy. Type the headline all in caps.
- Start the press release with the city name and date, like this: Denver, Colorado—March 15, 2000. The date is important because it allows a journalist to quickly see if the release is "fresh" or not.
- Begin the body of the press release on the same line, immediately after the date.

- Finish the body of the press release by repeating the contact information; "For more information, please contact ..."
- End the press release with -30- in the middle of a line a couple of lines below the end of the body of the release. (-30- is simply a journalistic convention commonly used in press releases to signify the end of the text.)

As I said, though, this is just one version of the rules, and press releases vary greatly. You may also want to create more chatty and personal messages that can be sent directly to particular journalists. If you've read an article in a magazine and think that the writer might be interested in an idea you had for an article— an article about your Web site, of course—then why not write a more informal "release" and send it directly to that writer, a release in the form of a "John, I had an idea I thought you might like to hear about" letter.

Here are a few more quick pointers about creating press releases:

- Use quotes, even if you are quoting yourself. Mike Ceranski wrote the press release himself, but as you can see, he refers to himself in the third person: "'I can go back and get more info instantly ... I don't miss a thing,' said Mike Ceranski, President of Dvorak Internet Development." What's so important about quotes? Every journalist knows that quotes can be used to liven up an article, so feed them a few good quotes and they'll be more likely to use the press release.
- If possible, get quotes from celebrities or other well-known or important people, or from satisfied customers.
- You can provide a little background information about your company, but don't overdo it. Keep focused on why people are going to want to hear about your product. I've seen corporate press releases that are about as interesting as an annual report; half the report is dull corporate background.
- Make sure you include all the relevant contact information: phone number, street address, e-mail address, Web page (remember to ensure that the URL is preceded and followed by a space, so a journalist can click on the URL in his e-mail program to open the page). Include direct contact information—not the number of the company switchboard, but the direct line to the contact person.
- Consider including several autoresponder e-mail addresses. You shouldn't make a press release too long—releases are typically, in the paper world, one to three pages long—but you could include several

autoresponder addresses so that people who are particularly interested can get all the information they need; one address could retrieve an in-depth corporate background paper, another could retrieve detailed product specifications, another, a list of customer testimonials, and so on.

Formatting Problems

There's a very important formatting issue to consider when creating electronic press releases, and that's the width of the text. To be safe, you should make sure that all your lines of text are about 65 characters wide with carriage returns at the end of each line—that is, at the end of the line you press Enter rather than letting the text wrap to the next line. Some e-mail programs don't wrap text very well, so forcing a break will keep the news release looking "clean."

Here's another thing to consider. Make sure you write the release in a text editor, not a word processor, and then test it by sending it to yourself. If you use a word processor—or if you copy a block of text from another document and drop it into your release—you may unknowingly introduce non-ASCII characters—curly quotation marks, special typesetting characters for ellipsis (…) and em dash (—), symbols such as ®, ©, and ™, and so on. These characters can confuse some e-mail systems (notably AOL's, which accounts for 15 percent of all U.S. users). You may have seen e-mail messages like this:

```
WebSprite is a very low-
bandwidth solution,
perfect=20
for modem users, or for
corporate LAN users who
don't=20 want to tie up
precious corporate
bandwidth.=20
It works with Windows 95
and Windows NT 4.0.
This=20
newest version=20
```

Notice the =20 pieces at the ends of the lines? This is due to a message containing non-ASCII characters passing through an e-mail system that doesn't like them.

=20 is the hexadecimal code for a space. For some reason some mail servers, when they receive an 8-bit message, get a little confused and display the hexadecimal code for a space if there are no other characters to the right of the space except another space or a carriage return. (If a space is followed by a word, it's okay, but if followed by another space and then a carriage return (that is, a break to a new line), or immediately by a carriage return, it becomes =20.)

The only way to completely avoid the problem is by being absolutely sure that none of the characters creep into your newsletter. Before you send out your newsletter, it's a good idea to send it to yourself, and then look at the message header (most e-mail programs hide much of the message header, so you may have to use some kind of "Show Header" command to view the entire header). Look for lines like these:

```
Content-Type: text/plain; charset=iso-8859-1
Content-Transfer-Encoding: 8bit
```

You may also see something like this:

```
X-MIME-Autoconverted: from quoted-printable to 8bit by
bigbiz.com id UAA26184
```

The charset=iso-8859-1 piece, and the 8bit on the second line, and the Autoconverted line, all indicate that the message has been converted, because it contains these weird non-ASCII characters. Rather than charset=iso-8859-1, you want to see charset="us-ascii". And rather than the Content-Transfer-Encoding: 8bit line, you want to either not see the line at all, or see something indicating that it's 7-bit.

Also, as I've mentioned before, be very careful not to mail out press releases to lists of recipients using the To: and Cc: lines in your mail program; use Bcc: so everyone receives a message addressed to a single person and doesn't receive a huge list of e-mail addresses.

Make It Personal

It's a good idea to write personal notes to media contacts, rather than impersonal press releases. They're much more likely to be read than press releases that look like spam. For instance, look at the following two e-mail messages to the media:

```
Dear Sir/Madam
Your readers need "Under a Sewer Cover: The Life and
Loves of New York's Sewer Workers"...


Joe,
I was wondering if you might like to take a quick look
at a book I wrote about sewer workers; I think it may
be of interest to your readers. It's called "Under a
Sewer Cover: The Life and Loves of New York's Sewer
Workers"...
```

Which is likely to get the best response? The one that's mailed directly to a named recipient rather than Sir/Madam, To Whom It May Concern, or nobody at all. The first looks like a generic press release, and the e-mail inboxes of the world's media contacts are full of those. The second is more personal; the mere fact that you use the contact's name can make a big difference—it appears that you've written an individual note … though perhaps you haven't. It's possible to use e-mail merge software for this. (I listed a few programs back in Chapter 14.) These allow you to take a list of media contacts, write a single message, and personalize the message using merge fields so that it doesn't look like a form letter.

Build Your Own Contact List

You can build your own media contact list if you have the time. This may be laborious, but if you work smart, you can dramatically cut the time it takes to build a list. For instance, there are directories of links to newspapers on the Internet. If you use an offline browser (see Chapter 15), you can use the directories as a starting point to download pages at each newspaper, then find the newspaper's contact information. Many papers will have a Press Release link that contains the e-mail address the paper wants press releases sent to.

Also, you will already have done some of the research required to build a press-release list. In Chapter 15 I discussed the research you should do and explained how to track down online publications related to your business. These should be added to your list, of course, and receive your press releases.

The following are some useful directories of media contacts:

Editor & Publisher's Newspaper List (links to thousands of papers, magazines, radio shows, syndication services, and so on)
http://www.mediainfo.com/emedia/

Gebbie Press (a great site; includes a free downloadable directory of almost 8,000 papers and TV stations)
http://www.gebbieinc.com/

John Hewitt's Media Links
http://www.poewar.com/links.htm

MediaUK
http://www.mediauk.com/

Queer Resources Media Directory
http://qrd.tcp.com/qrd/

Yahoo!—News and Media
http://dir.yahoo.com/news/

Yahoo!—News and Media Directories
http://dir.yahoo.com/News_and_Media/Web_Directories/

After building your list, it's probably a good idea to check to see if you've got the right addresses; you might want to send a simple message explaining that you've tracked down the e-mail address on the Internet and wanted to check to see if it is acceptable to send press releases to that address.

By the way, don't forget your library. Here's another annoying Internet myth: you can find any information—or its equivalent—on the Internet. You can't. The vast majority of printed information, more than 99 percent of the world's printed matter, is not available on the Internet. (How do I know that it's 99 percent? I don't—I just made that figure up, but I'll bet it's very close to the actual number ... perhaps the actual number is a little higher.)

Your library is a great source of useful information. Look for the following guides:

- Bacon's Newspaper-Magazine Directory
- Bacon's Radio-TV-Cable Directory
- Newsletters in Print
- Writer's Market.

Consider, however, the law of diminishing returns. You can get a huge amount of media-contact information online. You can get contact information for most U.S. papers online, for instance, so trying to fill in the gaps by going to Bacon's directories may not be worthwhile. You'll spend a lot of time—that is, money—for just a few more contacts. On the other hand, you'll be able to find much more detailed information, such as the names of individual editors and writers. And some directories may provide information that's difficult to find online, such as real-world—that is, paper—newsletter addresses.

Note also that you'll run across publications that you want to contact but that don't have e-mail addresses. That's okay; you'll probably want to do a real—snail—mailing also, as we'll discuss in Chapter 18.

Spend a Day in a Bookstore
Another way to track down useful contacts is to spend a few hours in a large bookstore. Look at all the magazines your clients are likely to be reading, and note as much contact information as possible: the feature writers' and reviewers'

names, telephone numbers, e-mail addresses (and snail-mail addresses, too, if you're likely to do a snail-mail campaign). Some magazines these days list their writers' e-mail addresses or sometimes explain how you can figure out a writer's e-mail address—firstname_lastname@thismagazine.com, for instance.

Ideally you should be contacting the writers, the people writing about your area; you could send releases to the editors in chief and the managing editors, but it's probably more productive to contact the writers themselves. Get these people interested in your product, and you have a good chance of getting a story.

Unfortunately writers are, as one marketer pointed out to me recently, notorious for not responding to e-mail. So after sending a press release to a writer, you may want to follow up with a call. Call the publication's switchboard and ask to be put through to the writer. You'll often find that the writers don't work at the magazine—they're quite likely freelancers—but if you schmooze the secretary, you may be able to get a direct number.

You may also want to contact book authors—in particular, computer-book authors. Invite these writers to visit your site and explain why their readers may be interested in the site. Some are quite likely to visit, perhaps take a screen "snapshot" of your site for their books, and mention your URL. You could even send a short and humorous description of your Web site to the Yellow Pages directories. Take a look at the sort of descriptions they contain, then try to write something in the same vein and send it off—make sure you reword the description for each directory you submit to.

Buy a List

If you want to handle your own press releases but don't want to build a list, you can buy one. The most affordable I've found are the *U.S. All Media E-Mail Directory* from Direct Contact Publishing, the *PRProfitCenter* from Open Horizons, and the *All-in-One Media Directory* from Gebbie Press.

I'm sad to say that the *U.S. All Media E-Mail Directory* is no longer sold. **Direct Contact Publishing** (http://www.owt.com/dircon/) will send out e-mails for you, but they will no longer sell you the list. (Unfortunately it's going to cost *much* more to use their service than buying the list used to cost.) Their site is full of interesting information about online PR, so it's well worth a visit.

Bradley Communication's **Publicity Blitz** database is another huge contact list. For $295 you'll get a database with around 19,600 entries. For $445 you can get a one-year subscription that provides four quarterly updates. You can buy this directly from **Bradley Communications** (http://www.rtir.com/products.htm, 800-989-1400 or 610-259-1070).

Gebbie Press (http://www.gebbieinc.com/) publishes the *All-in-One Media Directory*. For $270 you can get its TV/Radio, Dailies/Weekly Newspapers, and Magazines directories, with a total of around 21,000 entries. Gebbie Press told us that virtually all of the entries have e-mail addresses (in the electronic version of the database—not in the printed version).

For a really massive list, see **MediaFinder** (http://www.mediafinder.com/), which sells a CD containing seven major media directories, including *Samir Husni's Guide To New Consumer Magazines*, *The National Directory of Magazines*, and the *Oxbridge Directory of Newsletters*, over 100,000 publications, for $1,095 (North American edition) or $1,500 (World edition). The CD has a lot of detailed information and allows you to build mailing lists by specifying the criteria. There's also a subscription that allows you to use the database online, pulling the data from their Web site, starting at $395 for three months. This may seem to be an expensive database, but when you look at it as a price per entry, it's around the same as the others I've mentioned here.

There are other companies selling databases, but generally they're more expensive (if you know of any low-cost PR databases, let me know and I'll add links to them from the Web site associated with this book). They're probably very good—regularly updated, tightly targeted, and full of useful, detailed information. But they can be too expensive for many small businesses, running in the thousands of dollars; one service, for instance, is about $6,000 a year, another is around $1,000 for a list of 1,000 television stations. However, the following are some of the "big boys," in case you're interested in getting the very best:

MediaMap
> http://www.mediamap.com/

Parrot Media Network
> http://www.parrotmedia.com/

PressAccess
> http://www.pressaccess.com/

There have been companies selling mailing lists for years, but e-mail addresses are only now being gathered and sold by mailing-list companies. Many of the traditional mailing-list companies do not sell e-mail lists. Some probably will soon, but there's a big debate in the business about how to sell e-mail lists without encouraging spamming. So before you buy a database, make sure it includes e-mail addresses. (On the other hand, as we'll discuss in Chapter 19, you may want to do snail-mailings, too, so you may need street-address mailing lists.)

Use a Service

If you don't have time to build a list right now or simply don't want to expend the time and energy it takes to do so, try the following sites for press-release services. I've included some example prices, but prices change, and a cheaper price doesn't always mean a better service, as the quality of the list the service is using is very important. Note also that you won't necessarily send press releases to the full list; rather, it will be narrowed to the most appropriate contacts.

Bacon's Info (Bacon's offers a wide variety of publicity tools and services; press-release distribution is just one of them)
http://www.baconsinfo.com/

BookFlash (promotes books)
http://www.bookflash.com/

BusinessWire
http://www.businesswire.com/

Collegiate Presswire (distributes to college newspapers)
http://www.cpwire.com/

eworldwire (can customize by several factors, including category, state, and area code)
http://www.eworldwire.com/

Internet Media Fax
http://www.imediafax.com/

Internet News Bureau ($225 for 1,200 contacts)
http://www.newsbureau.com/

Internet Wire (Distribution to over 6,300 media for $225. Includes archiving for 90 days. Plain-text releases only)
http://www.gina.com/

M2 PressWIRE
http://www.presswire.net/

NetPOST
http://www.netpost.com/

News Bureau (offers targeted releases in a variety of categories, including food and drink, travel, and sports)
http://www.newsbureau.com/

News Target (Several Internet categories and several vertical-market categories like beverages, farming, and power and energy. They recommend using their service in conjunction with a major wire service).
http://www.newstarget.com/

PR Newswire
http://www.prnewswire.com/

Press Flash
http://www.pressflash.com/

The Press Release Network (Dubai, United Arab Emirates. Strengths include distribution to global, India, and Middle East media)
http://www.pressreleasenetwork.com/

PRESSline Database for Press Releases (free inclusion of press releases in their database)
http://www.us.pressline.com/

PRWeb (free posting of news releases in dozens of different categories)
http://www.prweb.com/

TechWire (promotes technology information)
http://www.ezwire.com/

URLWire
http://www.urlwire.com/

Web Promoters (information about working with press releases)
http://www.wprc.com/pr/wprcpr.html

WebWire
http://www.webwire.com/

WPRC Press Release Resources (a large directory of press-release and other resources)
http://www.wprc.com/pr/wprcpr.html

Xpress Press
http://www.xpresspress.com/

Yahoo!—Communications and Media Services
http://dir.yahoo.com/Business_and_Economy/Companies/Communications_and_Media_Services/

Yahoo!—Press Release Page
http://dir.yahoo.com/Business_and_Economy/Companies/News_and_Media/News_Services/Press_Releases/

Yahoo!—Public Relations

http://www.yahoo.com/Business_and_Economy/Companies/
Corporate_Services/Public_Relations/

One of these services, PR Newswire, feeds news releases to Clarinet, the news newsgroup service. These news releases appear in Clarinet's releases newsgroups. There are around 90 releases groups, such as clari.biz.industry.agriculture. releases and clari.biz.mergers.releases. You can't send news releases directly to Clarinet—they have to go through one of these two services or through another premiere wire source, such as Reuters, United Press International, Newsbytes, BizWire, The Christian Science Monitor, and several others.

Do electronic press releases work? They definitely can work, if targeted to the right people and written well. My publishing business has done well with them about 50 to 75 percent of the time. But they can also turn into near-spam. Some recipients of electronic press releases simply trash the lot, partly because so many of the releases they receive are totally inappropriate for the business they are working in. Because it's so easy to e-mail press releases, some people send them out indiscriminately to any e-mail address they can find. You might test a press-release service, but don't be disappointed if it doesn't work well.

Even if you use one of these services, you should still be building a press-contact list of your own. At the very least, you should be keeping a record of which publications and writers mention your products; if they mention them once, there's a good chance they may mention them again when you launch a new product or modify an existing one.

When to Send a Press Release

You may send a press release when you have the information to put into it or simply when you manage to get around to it, but you should understand a little about lead times—the delay between a media outlet receiving information and using it. Sometimes your press releases will simply arrive too late to be included in the magazine or paper you hoped would use it.

For instance, newspapers typically require information for major feature articles to arrive two to four weeks before the publication date, though some articles—stories related to a seasonal event, for instance—often require even longer lead times. To get information into a magazine, you may need to submit it three to six months or more before publication.

Don't get discouraged, though. Some press releases will lead to stories fairly quickly, especially if your release is announcing something newsworthy or if the information will fit somewhere other than in the major feature stories. In some cases you can actually see responses—in the form of e-mail queries, for instance—within hours or even minutes of the release going out.

What day should releases go out, though? We send ours out on Tuesday through Thursday, based on the idea that if it goes out on Friday it may not get seen until Monday, at which point journalists have a big pile of releases to go through.

## Chapter Nineteen

Don't Forget Real-World PR

In Chapter 18 you learned about sending press releases across the Internet, using the Internet's e-mail system to carry them. But don't think it ends there. You already know my attitude about the Internet—it's another tool, not a complete replacement for real-world business. So you should also consider doing real-world promotions: sending out press releases through the mail or fax, chatting with journalists, getting on radio shows, and so on.

Mail Press Releases

You'll find that there are many journalists who still don't have e-mail addresses—or, at least, who have addresses that you won't be able to track down—but that doesn't mean they won't want to mention your Web site. And some journalists still prefer to receive things in the mail and may not pay attention to incoming e-mail. So for these reasons, mailing out press releases, or even faxing them, can be a good idea. Also, as all good marketers know, hitting someone with your story from multiple directions can often help push your story to the front.

The Gebbie Press directories (http://www.gebbieinc.com/) and **Bradley Communication's Publicity Blitz** (http://www.rtir.com/products.htm, 800-989-1400 or 610-259-1070) are especially good values if you want to try some real-world promotions. The **MediaFinder CD** (https://www.mediafinder.com/) is good, too, if you want a really huge and correspondingly more expensive directory. **Para Publishing** (http://www.parapublishing.com/) sells mailing-label-formatted lists of media contacts: seven trucking magazines, 67 travel writers, 1,857 newspapers, and so on.

We've had some good luck with fax, too. There's a great system called **ImediaFax** (http://www.imediafax.com/). You can "drill down" through a database of media contacts, picking exactly the ones you want to fax to—you "hand pick them," as they put it—then send ImediaFax the press release you want to fax. They'll send it out for 25¢ per fax. For another 5 cents per name they'll give you the contact information so you can follow up.

This company is the same one that used to sell the *U.S. All Media E-Mail Directory*, **Direct Contact Publishing** (http://www.owt.com/dircon/). They'll put together custom media programs for you. It's more expensive than working with one of the media lists I've mentioned and putting the whole program together yourself. But Paul Krupin, the owner, knows what he's doing, and can build a really effective program.

Talk to Journalists

E-mailing news releases is a good way to start, but it's not perfect. Ideally you should be calling journalists. "I'll call a writer and suggest a story," Mike Ceranski of Dvorak Development told me. "I'll have a press release ready to go in three formats: e-mail, fax, and a printed press kit. I'll ask which format the writer prefers, and if necessary I'll FedEx the press kit to them." This sort of personal contact, and the willingness to provide the information in whatever format the journalists require, can pay off. Mike will also ask if it's okay for him to call in a few days to make sure the writer received the information and to answer any additional questions. That's a great way to keep your story in the writer's mind and to make sure that the writer has all the information necessary to write the story.

You should understand two points: first, that writers get scads of press releases; and second, that they actually *need* press releases. A writer's job is to write—he continually has to find new story ideas. If you can provide an interesting story and ensure that the writer has all the information he needs, there's a good chance he'll write the story.

You might even hire someone to call writers for you. One entrepreneur I know does this, and he discovered a secret worth sharing: "Hire a girl with a sexy voice to do follow-up calls. Ninety percent of writers are men—in the computer business, anyway—and it really does make a difference." What a shame it is that the males of this species are so shallow, eh? This entrepreneur discovered that when his wife made 200 follow-up calls, and another 200 follow-up calls were made by a professional—yet male—PR person, his wife outdid the PR man almost three to one. Out of 200 follow-ups she got 28 articles published, while the PR man got only 10. On the other hand, PR guru Marcia Yudkin believes that follow-up calls are not necessary, that it's quite possible to market your products without follow-up calls, though "if you're especially effective on the phone and have the time, follow-up calls might be worth a try." The problem for many small businesses is finding the time, and you may find it a more effective use of your time and money—which, you'll remember, are much the same thing—to send out a follow-up press release, or the same press release to another couple of thousand contacts, than to call and talk with people. You should probably limit calls to just high-profile publications, the sort of places that will give you a large payback if they do run your story.

You should also create relationships with writers whenever you can. Keep a list of writers you've worked with in the past and those you've chatted with. A writer who's already done a story on one of your products or Web services may do another. Remember, writers need stories, which means they need information, so if you can help them find that information, you're doing them a real service—and helping yourself at the same time.

Don't Forget Your Print Ads

I have in front of me a printed flyer from a small publishing company. This company sells books—some published by the company itself, some by other companies—and software. This little flyer explains how to place orders; it provides the full street address, a telephone number and, even a toll-free phone number. But it includes neither an e-mail address nor a Web URL. Yet I know for a fact that the company has both a Web site and an e-mail address. So why isn't that information on the flyer?

One reason might be that the company has a lousy Web site. It's a billboard-style Web site—it just sits there in cyberspace, a couple of pages of vague description about the company and its products; it gives no way to order online, no way even to find much information online. Why isn't the information in the flyer online, I wonder? Perhaps the Web site isn't mentioned because the company doesn't see how to get any value out of it, and it's only there to catch people who pass by in cyberspace—which it won't, unless people already know where it is. But that doesn't explain why the flyer doesn't at least list the e-mail address.

However, this sort of thing is common; less common than it was a couple of years ago, but still, many companies with Web sites and e-mail addresses hide them away, either not mentioning them at all or mentioning them in small print so it's almost invisible. It's a simple step to include your cyberspace addresses in everything you print—on business cards, in newspaper ads, Yellow Page ads, brochures, flyers, and everything else. If you put your phone number on these things, why not your e-mail address and URL? If your Web site provides value to your customers and prospective clients—if it provides information and customer support, a way to order online, and various services that they might find useful—then don't hide all this, let people know about it.

Don't just put URLs in your print ads, though—explain why people should visit your site. Mention the services you offer, and give them a reason to come to your site. If you plan to use your Web site as an extension of your business—as a way to reduce order-taking and customer-service costs, for instance—herd your customers in the right direction. Mention, for instance, that your customers can get the latest product information at your site. (They can, can't they?) That's important to many people in this instant-gratification world. People want information right away, and the Web site is a way to provide it.

Here's an example. Many companies selling products in bookstores, toy stores, whatever stores, have Web sites. Some put their URLs on the product packaging, but it's almost an afterthought. Do they really want people to visit the site? If so, invite them, and give them a reason. Tell your buyers that if they visit your site, they can enter a drawing to win something—you'll give away 10 products (or 100, or a 1,000, depending on your company size and the type of product) every month. A lot of companies that spend tens of millions of dollars a year in advertising, don't use this cheap and easy promotional tool *that really works!*

I recently noticed a very simple promotional technique by Mile High Comics, a comic store in Denver, CO. This company distributed flyers at a science fiction conference. All people needed to do was fill in their e-mail addresses and drop the forms in a box; Mile High Comics then adds these people to its mailing list—very simple, but very effective, and something that can be combined with other forms of print advertising, too. For instance, your ads can have a line at the bottom saying: "Sign up for our free e-mail newsletter! E-mail us at signup@ acmesewercover.com."

Give Stuff Away

In most businesses, you must give stuff away to the right people. I've run into plenty of people doing business—or rather, trying to do business—on the Internet who don't understand that concept, so let me elaborate.

Let's say you create and sell software, and let's say I'm a writer (I am, of course) who works for the computer press (I actually do) and who's contacting you about your product (there's a good chance I will be) via e-mail. I've heard about your product, I think it may be of interest to my readers, so I want to review it. Which of these statements do you use to respond to me?

1. Oh, yeah? You can download a demo from the Web site—it does almost everything the full version does.

2. I don't like to hand out registration keys; this is shareware, you know.

3. I'll send a copy out right now, or you can download it from our Web site, and I'll e-mail you a key to unlock it.

4. I'll ship a press kit out right away, too.

5. How else can I help you?

6. Can I call you in a few days to see if you have any questions?

Here's the answer, in case you haven't figured it out. You use statements 3, 4, 5, and 6. You do not treat a member of the press with the level of disinterest shown by the statement in 1, and you never, *never*, use 2.

You need people like me. You need people who write about products in books, newsletters, newspapers, magazines, and Web sites, or who talk about them on the radio and TV. Let me explain how much you need us.

You may have heard of Paul Mace. He designed a set of programs for the PC that could help you recover your valuable data from hardware and software problems. Mace became a very wealthy man through promoting and selling these programs, and he eventually sold off his company to a large rival. Why was he so successful? Reportedly, he believes that much of his success was due to a single box of software he sent to computer columnist John Dvorak.

One day Dvorak was having problems with his computer and had lost some files. He just happened to notice Paul Mace's box of software—it had arrived a few days before—so he installed it and recovered his files. Dvorak was so pleased that he wrote about the program in his next column, brought it to the attention of millions of PC users ... and the rest is history.

Here's another example, a little more modest and a little closer to home. I ran across a program recently that I really liked. In a discussion in a private Internet-writer's mailing list I mentioned the program, and another writer e-mailed me to ask about it—he was doing a series of reviews in *Windows Magazine*, and was interested in reviewing the program I'd mentioned. Writers talk to writers. They hang out with writers, they pass on information to other writers. Even if they don't write about your product, one of their buddies might.

You need people to talk about your products, and that often means you must give samples away. If you are selling chocolates, send out press kits about your chocolate Web site—and include a box of your best. If you're selling flowers, send flowers to certain key reviewers. If you're promoting a book or music, send review copies.

This should all be so obvious that it goes without saying. But it appears that many people see the Internet as a cheap way to get into business, so there are now many people promoting products on the Internet who might not otherwise be doing so, and who evidently don't understand this very basic concept. An example: I recently asked a company if I could review one of its products—a product I might have mentioned in this book. The software was shareware, but in order to use all the features, you have to register the program and get a key. The author of this program refused to give me a key … so the software went unreviewed and unmentioned.

Another Form of Cyberspace—Radio

I've always believed that cyberspace really began around 150 years ago with Samuel Morse's first telegraph transmission in 1844. After all, that was the beginning of electronic communications, crude as it may have been. Since then we've seen the development of a variety of electronic forms of communication—systems that create "an imaginary space where electronic communications take place," as one dictionary describes the term cyberspace: telephones, television, radio, computer bulletin board systems, the online services, the Internet.

Right now, of course, people are scrambling around trying to sell products on the Internet, and as I discussed in Chapter 1, there's an awful lot of hype about how many people there are on the Internet. But there's one area of cyberspace with a truly enormous number of "users," an area that's very cheap and easy to use for the marketing of products, and that's radio. There are almost 12,000 radio stations in the U.S., and hundreds of different talk shows playing on these stations or syndicated to multiple stations.

*See **The Victorian Internet: The Remarkable Story of the Telegraph and the Nineteenth Century's On-Line Pioneers**, by Tom Standage (Walker & Co.), for a fascinating comparison of telegraph and the Internet.*

One way to promote your site is to promote yourself as a talk-show guest. If you've got something worth saying, you can easily get onto a radio talk show. (That's not hype, it really is easy; I went on perhaps 60 shows while promoting the first edition of this book.) As Joe Sabah, author of *How to Get on Radio Talk Shows All Across America*, points out, radio talk shows need guests. As an example, his book discusses a radio station in Pittsburgh, PA, which has five hosts, each with an average of about 65 guests a month—or almost 4,000 guests a year.

People buy products they hear mentioned on talk radio; Joe Sabah has been on well over 600 talk shows and has sold more than $330,000 worth of the books he promotes on those shows. TV shows are even more productive; popular TV talk shows can launch best-sellers and celebrity careers.

Radio is a relatively efficient way to get the word out about your Web site. You generally don't have to go anywhere; you do the show at home or your office using the telephone. And you can track down the talk shows through a variety of radio-show databases. You may be able to build your own using the Web sites I mentioned earlier, or you can buy one. Joe Sabah (http://members.aol.com/talkshows/, talkshows@aol.com, 303-722-8288) sells a database of 700 talk shows, along with his book *How to Get on R adio Talk Shows All Across America*, for around $99. Gebbie Press' directories contain more than 2,100 radio stations with Web sites and include many of those stations' e-mail addresses, and Bradley Communication's Publicity Blitz also includes thousands of stations.

Another way to reach radio stations is to advertise in **Radio-TV Interview Report**, also published by Bradley Communications (http://www.rtir.com/). This publication is a large directory of people available for talk shows. If you don't have the time to contact the stations directly, advertising may be a good way to do it, though it may be expensive. For instance, ads in Radio-TV Interview Report range from $744 to $2,574, though the owners of this publication claim that, as a "rule of thumb," for $2,574 you can expect 50 calls from talk-show producers. (I've used the $744 ad, and it did indeed bring me quite a few interviews.)

*Here's another service that may help you: **GuestFinder** (http://www.guestfinder.com/). This service "is a Web-based service designed to make it easy for people who work in the TV, radio, newspaper and magazine industries to find guests and interview sources." You buy space at the site ($149 a year), and people in the media use the site to find interesting interview subjects.*

*A similar service is **HotTopics** (http://www.bookpromotions.com/hottopic.htm), which has a Web site and a paper newsletter that goes to 6,000 media contacts; prices begin at $175 for a half-page ad. And there's **Radio Tour** (http://www.radiotour.com/), which also promotes people both online and off.*

Look For the Unusual

Unusual real-world promotions can bring people to your site by the millions. Consider, for instance, mass suicide. It's a rather drastic form of promotion, admittedly, but it certainly works—it's been done before by the **Heaven's Gate cult**; their Web site's daily hits went from pretty much nothing to around 3 million in the 24 hours after their mass suicide hit the news. The server handling the site got so busy that it couldn't handle the volume and had to close down the site, but so many mirror sites—copies of the Web site held at other Web servers to help share the load—were set up that Yahoo! established a category to list them all (http://www.yahoo.com/Society_and_Culture/Religion/Faiths_and_Practices/New_Age/Organizations/Heaven_s_Gate/). Yahoo! categories come and go, but this one's *still* there a couple of years after the event, so as a promotional method it clearly worked.

If suicide strikes you as going a bit too far just to promote a Web site, you could always try something dramatic but with less finality. For instance, why not attack a party hosted by an important diplomatic figure and hold scores of important people hostage for a few months? When **Tupac Amaru** did just that in Lima, Peru, the world discovered that they had a Web site: http://burn.ucsd.edu/~ats/mrta.htm. (Well, okay, it turned into suicide, but perhaps you can arrange a different result.)

Maybe that's going a little too far, too. Then there was the "first birth on the Internet," that got a lot of press, and the "teenage couple" who claimed they were going to lose their virginity online (of course it turned out to be a stunt by a porn site, but it certainly got a lot of press). And how about the first "Internet Public Offering," in which a brewing company, **Spring Street Brewing** (http://plaza.interport.net/witbeer/) looked for investors online (they wanted $5M, and ended up with $2M).

These examples show how events in the real world that get extensive real-world media coverage—newspapers, news magazines, television, and radio—can also drive people to Web sites. But consider also that being first works better than being second or third. The second online birth won't get near the attention, and companies that have tried to go public online since Spring Street Brewing have generally failed.

The Internet Is No Different …

Finally, a quick suggestion: read a few good marketing books. Go to your bookstore and pick two or three books about marketing. The Internet is really no different from the real world. It's a new tool, and certainly there are ways in which communications between people on the Internet are different from off the Internet, but basic human nature remains the same. Read a few good marketing books, then consider how to use the ideas online.

Here are a few books to get you started:

1001 Ways To Market Your Books, by John Kremer, Open Horizons (http://www.bookmarket.com/). You may not be publishing books, but nonetheless this is a great primer on marketing. Kremer comes up with many different ideas that can be applied to all sorts of products. Flick through this book at a bookstore and see if you can apply any suggestions to your situation … then buy the book.

Guerrilla Marketing, by Jay Conrad Levinson, who has written about a zillion Guerrilla Marketing books: *Guerrilla Marketing, Guerrilla Marketing Attack, Guerrilla Marketing Excellence, Guerrilla Marketing Online*, and so on. They're well known and well respected.

Six Steps to Free Publicity, by Marcia Yudkin, Plume/Penguin. From a well-known publicity guru.

Chapter Twenty

Advertising—Buying and Selling

There are two aspects to advertising, and the unusual thing about running a Web site is that the site owner can be involved in both: the owner can both buy and, perhaps, sell advertising. You can most certainly buy advertising, of course. And if you get enough traffic at your Web site, you may be able to sell advertising, too. There's one more aspect of advertising you can get involved with right away and at no cost—you can swap advertising. But let's not get carried away here. The chance of making money—real money—from advertising is pretty slim. And even the chance of making money by advertising your products is slim, too. (Not that it can't be done, but don't get carried away by the hype you may have read about how everyone should be using banner advertising.)

In this chapter we'll discuss advertising, and I've structured the chapter in the order of the most probable. I'll talk about swapping, I'll talk about buying, and I'll talk about selling. But first, I'll talk about whether you really want ads scattered around your Web site.

Ads—A Double-Edged Sword

If you sell or swap ads, you have a problem in the form of something designed to take your visitors away from your Web site. Think about this—the Web is probably the only form of advertising in which the purchaser can instantly follow the ad with a mere flick of the wrist. That's what's so appealing about advertising on the Internet, but it's also what's so dangerous about it.

Consider an ad in a newspaper. You begin by buying the newspaper. Right there and then you've satisfied the main purpose of the newspaper company. In much of the world, that means the owner has made money from your purchase, plus a little from the fact that you're now a statistic that can be used to justify or boost advertising rates. In the U.S., it's the other way around; you've become an essential statistic, plus the paper's made just a little money from the purchase price you paid.

What you do with the paper next doesn't really matter to the newspaper owner, except that the owner would like you to find the paper useful so that you buy it again tomorrow. You can burn it, wrap fish in it, or even read it—it doesn't really matter. So if you see an ad and put the newspaper down to pick up the phone, that's fine.

A Web site is very different. You may have brought people to your site to sell something to them. The last thing you want them to do is to leave your site. Yet many, many sites provide attractive links designed to encourage visitors to do just that. We've discussed this issue before in relation to links (see Chapter 10). You must be careful with the way you use links, because you usually don't want to encourage people to leave your site, and the same applies to carrying ads.

Of course some sites, just like many newspapers, are designed as advertising vehicles and little more—they get paid for getting you to pay attention to the ads they carry. Some search sites, such as Yahoo!, for instance, really don't care if you search or not … except that when you search they get a chance to show you a few more ads. The search engine's there to bring you to the site, but all they really want you to do is look at the ads. Why? Because they get paid each time you do so. They provide a good search engine to make sure you'll come back again, and, they hope, look at another ad. You'll notice that when you search for something at Yahoo! (and various other search engines), an ad that is eerily related to the search term you used pops up at the top of the results page.

Are you sure you really want ads at your site? How many people are going to find the ad more interesting than your site and leave you before they've had a chance to see what you can offer? As you'll see in this chapter, the purpose of carrying someone else's ad is often not fulfilled unless your visitors do leave your Web site, because you may be paid according to the number of people who click on the ad; that is, according to the number of people who leave your site because of the ad. (This is known as a *click-through*.) So before you put ads on your Web site, decide which business you are in. Are you using your Web site to promote or sell a product or service, or as a vehicle to carry ads?

You Scratch My Back, I'll Scratch Yours

The easiest way to get into the advertising business is by swapping ads. Don't worry—this won't take a lot of time; it's remarkably easy to do using a number of automated swap systems. Here's how it works. You go to one of the banner-swap sites (I'll list a few below) and sign up for the service. You then take a little bit of HTML and insert it into one or more of your Web pages. This HTML uses the <IMG> tag to insert an image—the banner—into your Web page, and pulls the image from the banner-exchange site. The banner-exchange site sends a different banner each time, and has a program that keeps track of how many times your site pulls in a banner. This record is used to keep track of your credits and to assign your banner to other sites according to how many credits you accrue. Some services provide free credits when you sign up, so your ad starts displaying on other sites right away.

You have to have a banner, of course. This is generally a standard size—often 468 pixels wide by 60 pixels high—which is why you're seeing so many banners the same size on the Web these days. They have to be a particular size in bytes or smaller, generally under 10k.

Some of these banner-swap systems sell advertising; that's how they make their money. In other words, you get your ad shown for free but you don't get equal time. Generally, your ad will be shown once for every two times that someone visiting your site sees an ad from the banner exchange. The banner displays that aren't given away either are used by the exchange itself to advertise its services, or are sold.

Some of the services allow you to specify where your banner will be shown, so you can target your advertising. Others accept only certain types of banner ads to make sure you don't get inappropriate advertising at your site. Some even allow you to pick who you will swap with; rather than an automatic banner exchange, they provide a way for people wanting to swap to meet and arrange to swap.

Another service provided by these banner-swap sites—and a very important one—is statistic reports. Some of these systems will provide statistics showing you how often you displayed an ad and how often your ad was displayed. This information is important because it can help you decide how effective the service is. You can see an example in Figure 20.1 of the type of statistics available (in this case these are from BannerSwap).

The following are a few banner-swap systems you can try:

1-2-Free Banner Exchange
   http://www.1-2-free.com/
BannerSwap
   http://www.bannerswap.com/
Cyber Link Exchange 2000
   http://cyberlinkexchange.usww.com/
Do the Wave
   http://DoTheWave.com/

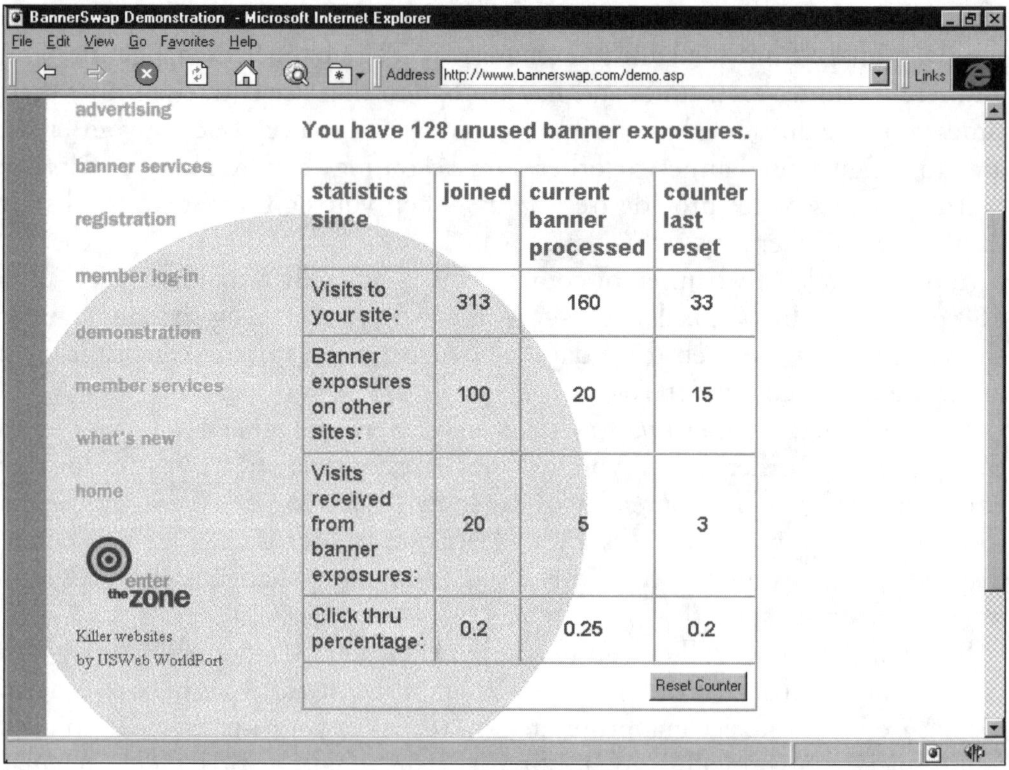

Figure 20.1: Example statistics, showing how often a banner was displayed at your site, how often your banner was displayed, and how many people visited your site.

Internet BannerExchange
> http://www.bannerexchange.com/

Link Exchange
> http://www.linkexchange.com/

NarrowCast Media
> http://www.narrowcastmedia.com/

NetAdNet
> http://www.netadnet.com/

NetOn's Banner Exchange
> http://www.net-on.se:81/banner/

PostMaster Banner Network
> http://www.PostMasterBannerNet.com/

Web Site Banner Advertising (a large list of banner-swap programs, including a number of European programs)
http://www.markwelch.com/bannerad/

W PRC Banner Exchanges (a list of banner-swap systems)
http://www.wprc.com/pldb/wrcpldb.shtml

Yahoo!—Banner Exchanges
http://dir.yahoo.com/Computers_and_Internet/Internet/World_Wide_Web/
Announcement_Services/Banner_Exchanges/

Finding Banners

You don't have the artistic skills to create a banner, you say? That's okay. There are low-cost and even free services that provide banners. With the free services there are likely to be conditions, such as that you must post a banner linking back to the company that created your banner. Makes you dizzy, doesn't it? Try some of the following:

The Banner Generator (free automatic banner creation)
http://www.coder.com/creations/banner/

Ezart Graphics
http://www.ezart.com/

GW WebDesign (free and low-cost)
http://www.gwwebdesign.com/

LinkExchange Banner Creators List
http://adnetwork.linkexchange.com/help/bannermakers.html

LinkExchange Banner Generators List
http://adnetwork.linkexchange.com/help/bangen.html

W PRC Banner Design
http://www.wprc.com/pldb/bdesign.shtml

Also take a close look at the banner-exchange sites; they often contain links to free and low-cost design sites.

Another Form of Ad Swap—Web Rings

There's another cooperative system that is used to bring visitors to Web sites: Web rings. They are not quite the same as banner swaps, but they are a form of free reciprocal link. Web rings are really a game; I can't take them too seriously. On the other hand, if you find a Web ring associated with a subject related to your business, maybe it makes sense to be part of it. Here's how they work: you create a link from your Web site to someone else's, who has a link to someone else's, who has a link to someone else's, and so on. You can generally travel through the ring in a variety of ways. Each site in the ring has several links: Previous, Random, Next, Skip Next, and Next 5, for instance.

There are other names for Web rings. I've seen the Line Around the World and The Rail. They vary slightly, perhaps, but the concept is the same—sites linked to other sites. A true ring, however, is a truly continuous circle; you can continue along the ring until you get back to where you started. If you want to see a few rings at work, try the following sites:

Heartland Ring
http://www.geocities.com/Heartland/3126/heartlandring.html

Looplink (a system that helps you create a Web ring)
http://www.looplink.com/

People Chase
http://www.rainfrog.com/pc/

The Rail
http://www.therail.com/

Sadiq's Webring Directory
http://www.users.dircon.co.uk/~majaffer/webrings/

Texas Webring
http://www.txdirect.net/~crazi/texasring.html

WebRing (An organization that sponsors 40,000 Web rings!)
http://www.webring.org/

Webring Index (a large index of Web rings—more than 6,000 of them)
http://www.webring.org/rings.html

Yahoo!—Web Rings Page
http://dir.yahoo.com/Computers_and_Internet/Internet/World_Wide_Web/Searching_the_Web/Indices_to_Web_Documents/Rings/

Buying Advertising

Is buying advertising such a good idea? There's a general principle in the PR business that money spent on PR is more effective than money spent on advertising, so you may want to forget about advertising, return to Chapters 17 through 19, and think a little more about the public-relations methods that you can use to promote your site.

Obviously public-relations people are biased toward PR, but I think there's a good chance that they're quite correct; remember, the most effective promotional claims are those that appear to come from people not directly affiliated with your company. Everyone knows advertising is biased toward the person paying for the advertising, whereas reviews and feature stories in the press are generally trusted.

Still, if your company budget can bear the burden, you might want to experiment with a little banner advertising. How much of a burden? Let's look at that subject now.

How Much Does It Cost?

Banner advertising varies in price greatly. You'll generally see costs stated in terms of *cpm—cost per thousand impressions* (the *m* coming for the Roman numeral for 1,000); that is, the cost charged for 1,000 people to see your ad. Costs may be as low as $8 a thousand, or perhaps as much as $80 a thousand for a particularly specialized and valuable audience. I've heard of rates as high as $150 a thousand, though that's probably quite rare and may come from the early days of Web advertising when people didn't know any better. I recently read that the average banner ad is sold at a cpm of $34.

Yahoo!, for instance, charges $1,000 for a one-week placement on its Web Launch page. This page contains just six ads in total, and each ad also appears in a banner that appears on the various Yahoo! category pages. Yahoo! guarantees that each ad will be seen by at least 120,000 people during the week, so that's a cpm of just $8.33, perhaps less. However, the Web Launch banners are not targeted—they appear in all areas of Yahoo!—and each ad gets one third of a banner, hence the low cpm.

If you want to put a banner ad of your own at Yahoo! and even have it appear in targeted categories, you'll be charged for each impression—each time someone sees the page. Rates vary from 1.5¢ per impression ($15 cpm) to 6¢ per impression ($60 cpm) depending on the type of service. You can provide keywords for some of the service levels so that when someone searches for a particular word, your ad will appear. You can also target regions, through Yahoo!'s regional pages, and demographic groups—kids or women, for instance. Other major search engines are comparable; for example, Excite's rates range from $24 cpm to $60 cpm, and Infoseek ranges from $13 cpm to $60 cpm.

Published rates are not always set in stone. There are often quantity discounts and even "smart negotiators' discounts." It's rumored in the press that very few sites actually charge the full published rates for their advertising, and that rates may be considerably lower in some cases. A site that advertises a rate of $30 cpm may be willing to sell for as little as $15 cpm. "The listed price is rarely final," says one advertising firm. "Discounts [go] as high as 60 percent."

Can advertising in this manner be effective? Well, maybe, if you have a good banner, a good location, a good rate, and you're selling the right kind of product. But there's a good chance you'll lose money on banner advertising. Be careful about some of the advice you hear on the Internet; a number of Internet publications have suggested, over the last year or so, that banner advertising is good, easy, and effective, and that every business should be involved. This is simply untrue, and generally the conclusion of journalists who have investigated banner advertising but never actually paid for a banner-advertising campaign.

The truth is, there's a good chance that banner advertising won't work for you. I've heard that banner ads are often quite effective for Web-hosting companies. If you're charging, say, a $50 initial setup fee and $30 a month, and you expect someone who signs up for an account to stay with you for perhaps 18 months, then each sale is worth $590. If you sell ancillary products and services, too—design services, upgrade hosting services, and so on—then your income per sale may be much more. In such a case banner advertising may be very effective.

What if you're selling a $20 or $30 product, though? Ah, well, it depends what game you're playing. A number of large businesses, companies such as Amazon.com and CDnow, are playing a "grab as much cyberspace real estate as quickly as possible" game. Advertising doesn't have to lead to profits right away for them—as long as it leads to regular customers who, perhaps, will be profitable over the long term. You can play this game only if you have a lot of money to play it with, and are prepared to lose money for several years. (As Jim Bezos, the President of Amazon.com, has said, if Amazon.com turns a profit any time soon, it'll be a miracle.) But what about the average small business? A business that has to turn a profit, and can't afford to lose money this month, let alone for several years? In that case, banner advertising is probably not a good way to sell a low-cost item.

Before you jump into an expensive banner-ad program, run all the numbers—see what sort of click-through you'll need into order to break even, and if possible do a small test. And don't believe a salesperson who tells you that in order to test properly you need to spend a minimum of $5,000, as one once told me. This ignores basic rules of statistics; you can get a damn good idea of your possibility of success with a *much* smaller sample than 100,000 impressions!

Here's a quick rule of thumb. Assume that one impression in five or ten thousand leads to a sale, and then figure out how much those impressions will cost you. One in five to ten thousand is a pretty common range for this sort of thing. Yahoo! claims an average click-through rate of 2 percent, while ZDNet claims click-through rates as high as 5 percent at its site. The **Web Site Promoter's Resource Center** (http://www.wprc.com/) claims an industry average of 3 percent. Not too long ago I/PRO Research and DoubleClick stated that an industry average click-through rate is 2.11 percent.

So let's say one or two people in 100 who see your ad will click on it to visit your site, and one in 100 visiting your site will buy something; that's one impression in five or ten thousand leading to a sale. (Your numbers may be better; but then, they may be worse.) Can't make money with one in five or ten thousand at the cpm you've just been quoted for a banner ad? Then there's a good chance the banner-ad campaign won't work for you, unless you've got good reason to believe you can get significantly more people clicking on the banner, and convert more of them to sales.

If you want to be a little more certain of the payback on your advertising budget, you can sometimes negotiate rates based on clicks rather than impressions. That is, instead of paying for someone to see the ad, you pay for someone to click on the ad. I've seen rates as low as 40¢ to 45¢ per click, which may sound good, but consider that if just one person in 100 who visits your site buys something, then you'll spend $40 to $45 to get that sale. (Again, that's fine if you're selling Web-hosting services, not so good if you're selling a book.)

Oh, one more thing about click-through rates. You'll often hear people selling advertising claiming that click-through rates are comparable to direct-mail response rates. They're not. True, actual direct-mail response rates are in the same sort of range; 1 or 2 percent is typical, up to 10 percent is possible with some very good promotions. But a direct-mail response rate refers to the number of people actually buying something. In fact, a click-through rate is more comparable to a direct-mail "envelope-opening" rate.

Pick a Good Location

Where is a good place to put a banner ad? Where the people you want are hanging out, of course. But there's more to it than that. You need a location in which most of the people hanging out are your potential customers or audience. If you are paying for the number of impressions—the number of times someone sees your ad—you don't want to pay to show your ad to people who have absolutely no interest in your Web site.

So you need to target the viewers, and that can be done in two ways. You can use some kind of system that displays the ad just to people who are likely to be interested. That's what the search engines do with the keyword schemes; they display ads according to what the searcher is looking for. And you can pick a

Web site that is designed to attract the people you are interested in. For instance, if you are a publisher of fiction or a bookstore, you might want to advertise on a Web site that contains short stories. A model-rocket manufacturer might want to advertise at Yahooligans!. the kid's version of Yahoo!. And a Web site that sells computer games might want to advertise at a gaming site.

Another point to consider is not just which Web site you should advertise with, but where at the Web site. An ad placed near the front of the site may work several times better than the same ad placed a few pages down the hierarchy, inside the Web site.

It's easy enough finding information about advertising at the most popular Web sites: at the search engines, at Netscape, at HotWired, and so on. Simply go to the site and look around for a link to information about advertising. You may find a rate card, though you'll more likely find an e-mail address or phone number to call for more information.

If you find a small site you think might be a good place to advertise, simply contact the site owner and see if you can negotiate a good rate. Or see if the owner will swap advertising. If the other Web site is not a direct competitor but attracts the same people you want to attract, then the owner may well be interested in such an arrangement.

You may also want to consider using an advertising agency. Agencies often charge their clients nothing

Keyword banners at search sites may be a good deal, and can have fairly high click-through rates. If someone enters a keyword, and then almost immediately sees your banner, there's a good chance he'll click it. Jim Daniels, writing in an article that ran in my newsletter, Poor Richard's Web Site News, says that he got an 8 percent click-through rate using the keywords "home business," "business opportunities," and "online marketing."

Some small sites charge for time, rather than impressions or click-throughs. This is not necessarily a problem. If you know a site is popular among people you are interested in, and can pay to have your banner displayed for a week or a month, for instance, you might consider this as a "branding" tool, getting your name out in front of people. A friend, who works for an exhibits company, has used this sort of branding, and it's worked well. But then, he's selling products that cost tens of thousands of dollars.

directly, except perhaps a deposit which is used to pay for the ads, but make a commission taken from the advertising fee—typically 15 percent. An agency can save you a lot of research time by putting you in touch with the right people, and can also help you negotiate a fair rate. Yes, I realize there's a conflict of interest here; the agency is supposed to negotiate a good rate for you, but gets paid a percentage of the cost. That's the way it generally works, though.

If you want to look into banner advertising, try some of these places:

24/7 Media
   http://www.247media.com/

ADSmart
   http://www.adsmart.net/

Ad.Up
   http://www.ad-up.com/

BannerMedia
   http://www.bannermedia.com/

BURST! Media
   http://www.burstmedia.com/

DoubleClick
   http://www.doubleclick.net/

eAds
   http://www.eads.com/

Flycast
   http://www.flycast.com/

Public-Service Announcement Banner Ads for Nonprofits
   http://www.markwelch.com/bannerad/baf_psa_bann.htm

ValueClick
   http://www.valueclick.com/

WAB Directory
   http://www.wab.co.uk/

Web Site Banner Advertising (a great list of advertising resources)
   http://www.markwelch.com/bannerad/

WPRC Banner Consulting
   http://www.wprc.com/pldb/bmanage.shtml

WPRC's NarrowCast Program
   http://www.wprc.com/pldb/narrow.shtml

Yahoo!—Advertising on the Web
http://dir.yahoo.com/Computers_and_Internet/Internet/Business_and_
Economics/Advertising_on_Web_and_Internet/

Designing a Banner Ad

The basic theory behind banner design is very simple: boring banners don't work; exciting banners do. Before you begin designing a banner, I suggest that you take a quick look at the **Bannertips/Four Corners Effective Banners** site (http://www.bannertips.com/). You can see examples of banners that work and banners that don't—banners with click-through rates of less than 1 percent and those with rates of over 8 percent.

Take a look, and I think a few things become obvious. Some of the ineffective banners are really horrible, even illegible. They scream out: "This is a low-cost amateurish banner, and my Web site's probably the same!" Some of the ineffective banners are what I think of as "here I am, come and get me" ads. They simply show the company names. Why would I want to click on a banner that contains nothing but a company name? What are they selling? What are they promising me? How will I benefit? I don't know the answer to any of these questions, nor does anyone else, and few people bother to click and find the answers.

Other banners may be well designed, but they're simply of little interest to most people who are likely to see them: THE FIRST GREEK CIVILIZATION 2 SITE banner comes to mind. Luckily these banners are free banners (they're from the Internet Link Exchange), but if a company with a site that isn't likely to be interesting to a large proportion of Web surfers plans to pay for advertising, it had better target very carefully.

On the other hand, it's obvious why some of the really effective banners work. Take a look at Figure 20.2, and you'll get the idea right away.

Actually some of these banners are a long way from being works of art. But they all have one thing in common: they aim to get you to click somehow. In some cases they actually say the word *click*, a very simple technique that many advertisers claim is an effective way to get people to do just that. Others are so obvious that they need no invitation. Free Stuff? Sure, I want free stuff, I'll click on that. Supermodels? Hey we're getting back to the old sex-sells maxim, and it really does. Money and Power? Who doesn't want them. I'm not sure about the Melanie Lynskey banner, though perhaps it's the flesh that subtly alludes to sex. However, click-throughs are not everything. Some studies show that some of the advertising campaigns that garner the highest click-throughs ... get the lowest conversion rates (that is, the lowest conversion of click-throughs to sales). And

Figure 20.2: These banner ads work well; you can probably figure out why.

why not? If you trick someone to visit your site, there's a good chance they're not really interested in what they find when they get there.

The following are a few simple guidelines to help you design banner ads:

- Animated banners often work better than static banners—perhaps as much as 25 percent better, according to a survey carried out by I/PRO Research and DoubleClick.
- Banners that are not immediately understandable often do well—they make people want to click to find out what it's all about. For instance, see the "Find what you are looking for" banner in Figure 20.2.
- Posing a question really helps.
- Use the old marketing rule: tell people to do something. Tell them to click or "visit us right now."
- Bright colors are generally more effective than dark colors.
- Don't expect a mere product name or company name to do you any good. Remember to look at an ad from the viewers' point of view, not yours, and give them a reason to click.

- Change your banners frequently. Yahoo!'s Eastern Sales Manager, Jeremy Ring, claims that banners "burn out" in two weeks.

- Ring also suggests putting a blue border around banners—to make quite clear that the banner can be clicked, and adding a text link below the banner.

- Jeremy Ring claims that limited-time offers can help. However, I/PRO Research claims the opposite: that trying to rush people actually hurts click-through rates, perhaps because people see it as hype.

- See the **Bannertips/Four Corners Effective Banners** site for useful links to articles about designing and locating banners (http://www. bannertips.com/).

Verify the Effectiveness

You must try to figure out how effective your ads are. Most advertising locations will provide impression and click-through figures—statistics showing how often the banner is seen and how many people click on it. Remember, though, that clicking on a banner and coming to your site are two very different things. Have you ever clicked on a banner, then changed your mind and clicked the Stop button? If so, you're definitely not alone. Or perhaps you've clicked a banner and been unable to get to the page due to network problems. You can make sure your site is at a good Web server, but you can't ensure that the user is working with a good ISP.

So clicks are not visits, an important thing to consider. Ten clicks may represent as few as seven-and-a-half visits, according to some researchers. You really need to check the visits at your end (I discussed a simple way to do this in Chapter 17). You can set up a page that will be seen only by visitors sent to your site from a particular ad. Then you can use your hit logs (see Chapter 21) to find out how often people visit this page. You'll end up with a solid figure, one created yourself so you don't have to rely on other people's possibly biased numbers. When talking with a potential advertising site, make quite sure you understand what the site regards as a click-through. Many mean a single click on a picture. Others actually count visits to your sites, and some count only a single click from a single IP address each day, so if one person clicks on the ad twice during the same dial-up session, it's still regarded as a single click.

Not Just Banners

The banner, a picture in a block just sitting on a page, is getting a bad name. It may work a little, but it doesn't seem to work anywhere near as well as it did a year or two ago. It appears that as people become accustomed to wandering around on the Web and as they see more and more banner ads, the novelty wears off, and they don't bother clicking on them any more. Whereas in the "old days" they'd click on just about anything, these days they'll click only if they are really interested in what the banner ad says.

Although the banner ad is by far the most common form of Web advertising, other forms are appearing. For instance, one method is to create a full-page ad. A Web magazine might have links to its articles, but when the reader clicks on the link to that article he doesn't see the article itself; rather, the reader sees a "sponsored by" page with a large banner linking back to the advertiser, and a smaller link to the article itself.

I've written a lot about advertising, using real-life examples of banner and e-mail newsletter advertising campaigns, in my newsletter **Poor Richard's Web Site News.** *You can read these articles in the archives, at* http://PoorRichard.com/newsltr/.

You might also run into what have been termed blipverts—full-screen ads that appear for a moment after a visitor clicks on a link, then disappear a few moments later as the visitor is shown the page referenced by that link. A lot of sites are also using secondary windows, which drive me nuts. When you arrive at a site another small window opens, with an ad inside it. It's a real nuisance in some cases, at sites that have lots of links to articles or other information you want to see. Each time you leave an article to return to the main site another stupid window opens!

Other Forms of Advertising

Keep your eyes open for other forms of advertising that are not Web-based and that may be more direct and effective than Web advertising. Here's an example. There's a mailing list called **Studiob** (you can find out about this list at http://www.studiob.com/). This list is owned by a computer-book agency, though it's open to the public. At present there are around 650 computer-book writers, editors, and publishers taking part in this list.

Now, you may recall from Chapter 14 that I said some mailing lists are used for advertising; once a day a message containing a few ads is sent to all the members of Studiob. Each ad costs $50 and is sent out five times. I've heard few complaints about this message—for several reasons. The fact that a single ad message is sent each day is made clear to new subscribers, and the messages are sent from a special e-mail address so if people really object to them they can easily delete the messages automatically using their e-mail program's filtering system. And in any case, many of the people on the list want to see the ads because they are useful, containing job offers, for instance.

This advertising medium can be very effective, and why not? It's a tightly targeted advert; if you are advertising a position at a publishing company or looking for authors to write a book, what better place to send an ad? Of course, this is also a perfect place to advertise your Web site—no, I'm not getting paid by Studiob, though I am a member of the mailing list—as there are hundreds of computer-book people on this list. Whatever you do, don't use this to send an "I've got a Web site, why not visit" advert. Rather, you'd better provide a good reason for people to visit your Web site.

Studiob isn't the only mailing list that sells ads; keep on the lookout for other lists associated with your business that carry these ads; they can be a very effective way to reach people.

Don't forget electronic newsletters. There are thousands of these, on a wide range of subjects, and many of these lists accept advertising. Some studies indicate that ads in e-mail newsletters have a much higher response rate than banner ads. You can find a list of a few that accept advertising at the **Direct E-Mail List Source** (http://www.copywriter.com/lists/ezines.htm), and some of the e-mail advertising companies listed in Chapter 14 sell space in electronic newsletters, too. If you find a newsletter that's targeted at the people you want to reach, ask the owner if you can advertise. What should you pay? Prices vary a lot, but typically range from around one to four cents per subscriber for a small ad (five to ten lines).

If you'd like to advertise in *Poor Richard's Web Site News*, to over 40,000 subscribers interested in setting up and promoting Web sites (probably a lot more subscribers by the time you read this), e-mail us at prwebads@TopFloor.com.

Selling Advertising

If you listen to the industry analysts, it sounds as though there's a lot of money to be made selling advertising on the Internet. It also sounds as though there will be huge sums of money to be made selling advertising just a year or two from now. I take both claims with a grain of salt. First, most of the money being made today is being made by companies such as Netscape and Yahoo!, companies with very high visibility on the Internet. That doesn't mean they're actually making a profit from their advertising, just that they are getting the lion's share of the advertising dollar. Secondly, technology prophets are notoriously optimistic, so just because some group predicts some vast sum is going to be spent on advertising within a year or two, it doesn't necessarily mean it really will.

Furthermore, there are problems in the world of Internet advertising—its dirty little secret is that it may not work particularly well. Okay, it's not so much of a secret any more. An article a couple of years ago in Britain's *Daily Telegraph*, for instance, was titled *Death to the Banner*, and stated that: "Advertising on the Web has proved so ineffectual that many sites are losing cash." This is not an isolated case of banner-bashing, either. The difficulty of making money through banner advertising, and of making money by selling advertising at Web sites, has been a much-discussed subject in the Internet press over the last two years.

I'll give you the same advice I gave a friend recently, who asked me if I thought she could make money selling advertising on her, as yet unknown, Web site. My answer? Probably not. I hate to be dogmatic about this … perhaps she'll figure out a way to bring vast numbers of people to her site, and she'll make money. Chances are she won't, and very few people have. Because it really does require vast numbers of visitors to make any money. With an average cpm of $34 or so, and small sites, in general, getting lower rates, just do the numbers and figure out how many people you'll need to pay your costs and make a decent profit!

Still, if you'd really like to try, I suggest you contact advertising agencies and the directories of Web sites selling and swapping advertising that I mention above. Register your site and see if you get anyone offering to pay you something—you never know, you might be lucky. Also note that there are companies that have set up to sell advertising for small Web sites. A number of small companies promise you that if you carry ads that they provide, you'll be paid for each time someone sees the ad, or perhaps each time that someone clicks on the ad. However, note that some of these services are apparently unreliable, and many Web-site owners have been unhappy with the performance of such systems. If you decide to try one, I suggest that you talk with some of the Web sites carrying the ads first.

Why not set up your own click-through program? You can contact other sites with the sort of audience you are looking for, and offer to pay for click-throughs. One thing you need to consider if getting into the advertising business is the tools you'll use to manage the ads. You need to be able to report the click-throughs and related statistics to the buyers. You may also need to rotate and select ads on the fly. The whole process can be complicated and a lot of work, though you can get software to help you. This software ranges from free to around $50,000. As one banner ad I've seen said: "Professional banner-ad management tools don't need to cost $40k!" No, apparently they cost, in the case of the advertised product, only $50k.

Try the following places for banner-ad management programs:

AdBot
  http://www.adbot.com/

Banner Ad Server Software (a huge list of advertising software, including the expensive stuff)
  http://www.markwelch.com/bannerad/baf_ad_sw.htm

Banner Generator ($49.95)
  http://www.vedia.com/banner/

BannerMatic (Free)
  http://www.GetCruising.com/crypt/

Central Ad ($30 to $159)
  http://www.CentralAd.com/

NYISP Banner-Ad Software ($45)
  http://www.nyisp.com/software/BannerAd/

WebMeister Banner Ad System ($50)
  http://www.counsel.net/banner/

The low-cost programs are generally Perl CGI scripts (discussed in Chapter 12 and 13). Remember that you can often get these installed for a small fee, perhaps only $50 to $100 if you can find a programmer who's run out of cola and donuts.

Affiliate and Associate Programs

Here's another form of advertising you may want to look into: advertising products that pay sales commission. Here's how it works: You have an ad at your site for a particular product. When a visitor clicks on a link or a banner to the other site, his entrance to the site is logged with your ID number. If that person then makes a purchase during the same visit, you get a commission. Such programs are known as *affiliate* or *associate* programs.

These systems are, in most cases, definitely not a way to get rich. One problem is that visitors often leave the site they're visiting, then come back to buy later. If they bookmark a page at the site, and go directly back to the bookmark, you probably won't get a commission because they won't be logged as your customers (some systems will be able to recognize the visitor on a second visit, and credit you as long as the visit is within a certain time). Also, a variety of rules can limit your potential profit. For instance, for a long time Amazon.com, *the* online bookstore, paid a commission if someone coming from your site bought a book—unless the book was a special order, or the buyer browsed around the site and then bought the book (the system only worked if the buyer purchased right away), or if the buyer purchased a book other than the one linked to from your site. In those days it was possible for you to send literally thousands of visitors to their Web site, and be paid enough for a beer (as **Phillip Greenspun** explained in an article at http://www-swiss.ai.mit.edu/wtr/dead-trees/53002.htm). Amazon.com has changed its rules considerably, and is far more generous with its commissions, but these are the sorts of things that are worth watching for when you sign up with a commission program. And the bottom line with commission systems is that unless your Web site gets a *lot* of traffic, you're not likely to make much money.

If you want to check into commission advertising, there are a number of directories available:

Affiliate Trade Links Network
  http://www.atlnetwork.com/

AffiliatesDirectory.com
  http://www.affiliatesdirectory.com/

AssociateCash
  http://www.associatecash.com/

AssociatePrograms.com (perhaps the largest directory of such programs)
  http://www.AssociatePrograms.com/

Associates Online
  http://www.associatesonline.com/

CashPile
  http://www.cashpile.com/

ClickQuick
  http://www.clickquick.com/

ClicksLink
  http://www.clickslink.com/

LinkShare
  http://linkshare.com/

Mark Welch's Affiliate Programs List
  http://www.markwelch.com/bannerad/ba_commission.htm

NetAffiliate
  http://www.netaffiliate.com/

Partnerprogramme.com
http://www.partnerprogramme.com/ (in German)
http://www.partnerprogramme.com/english.htm (in English)

Refer-It.com
http://www.refer-it.com/

SiteCash.com
http://www.sitecash.com/

Yahoo!—Business Opportunity Directories
http://dir.yahoo.com/Business_and_Economy/Business_Opportunities/
Directories/

Many sites offer such deals, and you might want to set up your own commission-based system or even suggest such a plan to another Web-site owner—someone you trust, of course. However, setting up affiliate software can be expensive and complicated. I recently ran across a product that looks pretty good and reasonably affordable, though, **The Affiliate Tracking Network**: http://www.affiliatetracking.com/.

It's a Tough Business

Selling Web advertising is a very difficult business, so I wouldn't expect to get rich if I were you. While Yahoo! can charge a cpm of $60, smaller sites are more likely to be getting 30¢ per click-through. Think about those statistics for a moment. If Yahoo! really gets its claimed 2 percent average click-through, a $60 cpm rate would be the equivalent of $3 per click-through, 10 times the rate you're likely to make selling ads (2 percent of 1,000 impressions is 20 click-throughs).

If you have a click-through rate of 2 percent, and if you're making only 30¢ a click (you may actually be making less), you'll need 50 impressions for every 30¢ you make. You're going to need an awful lot of visitors to make any reasonable amount of money. Want to gross $5,000 a month? You'll have to display an ad 833,333 times a month.

So where are all those advertising dollars going on the Internet? Well, there probably aren't as many dollars being spent as some in the press are claiming (because some estimates are based on rate cards rather than the actual discounted rates). And in any case, most of the money is currently going to a handful of large Web sites: Netscape, Yahoo!, Excite, and so on. It's very difficult for the little site to compete. Don't feel bad, though; it's quite likely that even some of the big sites are not making great money from advertising either, because their costs are so high.

Chapter Twenty-One

Tracking Site Use—
Hits and Access Logs

I've explained several ways in which Web sites are not billboards, and in this chapter we're going to look at yet another way in which they differ from billboards on the side of a freeway. With a billboard, you can never be sure that people see or pay attention to the billboard. Sure, you can get traffic figures so that you know how many people are driving by, but how many really look at the billboard?

Well, with a Web site you can make a variety of measurements to figure out how many people are coming to your Web site, and what they do when they get there. There are a number of ways to do this, and we'll begin by talking about *hits*—though as you'll learn at the end of this chapter, there are more important ways to measure site activity—and access logs.

First, what's a *hit*, and why do we care? There's a lot of nonsense spoken about hits. You'll often see huge hit claims pertaining to particular sites, for instance: *10,000 hits a day!*, *50,000 hits a day!*, *1,000,000 hits a day!*, and so on. And some Web-site owners are clearly trying to imply that they are getting this number of *visitors* each day. I'm suspicious when people use the term hits, and even when they use the term *visits*, you can never really be sure if they mean individual visits, or they're just using the term as a synonym for hit. But what really is a hit? It's a transfer from the server to a browser. So here's a quick way to double or triple the hits at your site: add more graphics. Each time a browser transfers a text page that has no graphics, that's one hit. But if the page has a graphic inside it, that's two hits. If it has five graphics, that's six hits. Each transfer is a single hit. Or simply add a lot of errors—links to nonexistent graphics. That's a great way to increase your hit count, because each error will be counted as a hit, yet you won't be transferring much data.

This means, of course, that a site designed to carry lots of small graphics on every page, or a site with lots of broken links, can generate very large hit rates. One major cybermall claims 11 million hits a month. And at least some of that mall's clients believe that the mall means 11 million visitors a month: "Hits are classified as people that actually came to my Web site," one client told me. (Think again, buddy!)

A single visit to your Web site might generate a single hit—or ten hits, perhaps, or several hundred, as the visitor makes his way through a variety of graphic- and error-laden pages. Each page viewed, and each graphic within those pages, is a single hit. Here's an example, from a couple of years ago. I found a Netscape press release which began with this statement:

```
"2.9 MILLION VISITORS PROPEL NETSCAPE INTERNET SITE TO
OVER 100 MILLION HITS A DAY."
```

It also included this:

```
Nielsen I/PRO undertook an independent audit of the
Netscape site, which found that an average of more than
2.9 million visitors accessed the site daily, with an
average visit length of 9 minutes. On the average
business day, visitors to the site view a total of
close to 10 million pages.
```

Let's consider this: 2.9 million visits, 10 million pages, 100 million hits. In other words, for every 100 hits, Netscape was getting only 2.9 visits, and the average visitor was viewing only 3.5 pages, so an awful lot of those hits were images and error messages.

There are other terms you might hear in addition to hit. There's *request* or *access*, for instance, defined by some as a page that is transferred; it doesn't include the in-line graphics or errors. And a *visit* should mean that a single browser comes to your site and requests single or multiple pages. You'll also hear the term *page view*, a much less ambiguous term (again, assuming that the person you're talking with isn't using the term as a synonym for hit). It should mean the number of times that a page is displayed.

What Can You Learn?

It is possible to measure visits to your site, though you don't hear these figures as often because they're so much lower than hits or even requests. But Web-server access logs list the host names of the computers reaching your site, so it's possible for a log program to show you how many visitors you get each day.

An access log is a record of activity at your Web site. The Web server records information in the log each time someone requests something from your Web site. What sort of information is saved in the log? It varies, depending on the system being used to create the log, but typically it's information such as the following:

- **Weekly Report**—the number of requests for data and amount of data transferred each week
- **Daily Report**—the number of requests and amount of data transferred each day
- **Hourly Report and Hourly Summary**—the number of requests and amount of data transferred each hour of each day, and the amount transferred each hour of an average day
- **Domain Report**—the number of requests and amount of data transferred to different domains … that is, a report showing you the domains of your visitors
- **Host Report**—a list showing the domain names of the top 100 host computers visiting your site (the people who spent most time at your site)
- **Directory Report**—the number of requests and amount of data transferred from each directory in your Web site
- **File Type Report**—the number of requests and amount of data transferred, broken down by file types (.htm, .gif, .zip, and so on)
- **Request Report**—the number of requests and amount of data transferred, broken down by specific file names
- **Referrer Report**—the number of requests that originated from the top 100 referrers; that is, it shows you who is linking to you
- **Browser Report**—the number of requests broken down by the type of browser sending the request
- **Status Code Report**—the status codes sent to the browser, such as error codes for missing pages.

Not all systems provide all this information, and some provide more. The reports listed above come from a program called Analog, from the University of Cambridge Statistical Laboratory, whose programmers claim that it is the most popular log-file program in the world. Nonetheless, there are many others; Analog may have around 20 percent of the "market" (it's actually a free program). So there's a good chance you'll have these or similar reports available.

You can use this information in a variety of ways. You can see, for instance, which areas of your site visitors find most interesting. Perhaps you should find out why they're so important to people, and perhaps even highlight these areas of your site in promotional efforts.

You can correlate visits with your promotional and advertising efforts and use the correlation to figure out how well you are turning visitors into customers. If you see a lot of visits after a magazine article appears, for instance, then the article has probably helped send visitors to you. But if you notice only a small rise in sales of your products, then you're not taking advantage of those visitors.

You can also get a good feel for the hit-to-visit ratio—that is, how many hits the average visit generates—which indicates how busy each visitor is at your site. Do they mostly come, look around for a moment, and leave? Or do they give your site a thorough viewing? You can also experiment with your content and see how changes cause people to move through your site in different directions. You can see which areas people are interested in; if you've created an area of your site that nobody spends any time in, for instance, perhaps you should dump it and focus on the more popular areas.

You can also go to the owners of sites that are sending people to you—some logs include *referrer* reports, showing the links used to get to your site—thank the owner of that site, and perhaps invite the owner to join in some kind of cooperative advertising or promotion.

Getting to Your Access Logs

Most Web-hosting companies provide logs. Some companies even e-mail you a log regularly; with others, you have to go to a specific Web page to view your logs. You can see an example of a log page in Figure 21.1. This particular log shows information about the browsers that requested data from a Web site; each line represents requests from Web browsers in a particular domain. In the right column you can see the host name. In other words, this information won't point back to an actual browser, but rather to the domain in which that browser is operating. You may in some cases find that visitors are coming from a particular small domain—one of your competitors' domains, for instance, or a customer's domain—but more often it will be a domain owned by an ISP or online service. For instance, if you found, say, ad19-039.compuserve.com in the report, this would be a domain owned by the online service CompuServe.

However, in some cases you may be able to follow a visitor through your site using this domain name; it will remain the same throughout the session. For instance, look at this information extracted from a report provided by a different log program:

Figure 21.1: A log file from Analog, a very popular log program.

```
dialup-06-38.netcomuk.co.uk "GET /ipn/techwr/
dialup-06-38.netcomuk.co.uk "GET
/ipn/techwr/guideline.htm HTTP/
dialup-06-38.netcomuk.co.uk "GET /ipn/images/redarrw.gif
HTTP/
dialup-06-38.netcomuk.co.uk "GET
/ipn/techwr/testimon.htm HTTP/
dialup-06-38.netcomuk.co.uk "GET
/ipn/techwr/$100k_frm.htm HTTP/
```

This program provides specific information about particular data transfers. In this case, a single visitor started by requesting /ipn/techwr/; in other words, the server sent the default file (index.html) from this directory. But then he clicked on a link to the guideline.htm file. You can also see that the redarrw.gif file was transferred, but this doesn't mean much, as that's probably an embedded file inside guideline.htm. (See, that's another hit!) We can see that he then went to testimon.htm, and finally to $100k_frm.htm.

Some Web-hosting companies also provide simple log summaries showing the hosts that accessed your site, the files that were requested, when all this took place, the total amount of traffic, and so on. These may be daily, weekly, or monthly reports, so you can get a quick overview of what's happening at your site. You can see a sample in Figure 21.2.

Manipulating Access Reports

If you want more statistics than your Web-hosting company provides, you can add your own log programs, from simple single-page counters to sophisticated $10,000 programs. You can also use services provided by other companies, which may be necessary if you want to sell advertising; the third party keeps track of your traffic and provides the report to you and any advertisers you authorize.

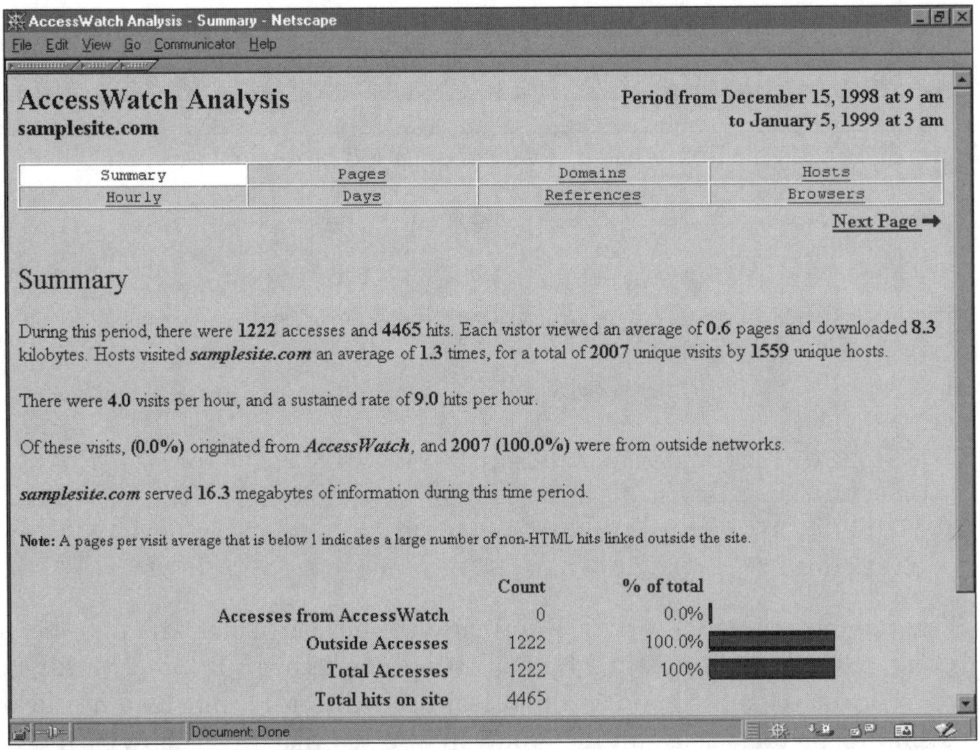

Figure 21.2: "A summary report from a program called AccessWatch"--Access Watch Anaylsis Summary. I'll fax it to the fax box.

What sort of statistics might you expect if you use a good service or logging program? The following list is an example taken from the NetIntellect Web page:

- General Summary
- Visitor Profile by Origin
- Visitors by Continent
- Top Visitor Organizations
- Top Visitor Countries/Zones
- Top Requested Files
- Top Referring URLs/Sites
- Top Requested File Types
- Top Referred Files
- Activity by Hour of the Day
- Top Visitor Browsers
- Activity by Day of the Week

- Technical Summary
- Peak Day of the Week
- Server Errors
- Client Errors
- Daily Statistics
- Weekly Statistics
- Monthly Statistics
- Executive Summary Report
- Complete Summary Report
- Marketing Summary Report
- Technical Summary Report
- BPA Standard Report.

Some of these programs don't run on the server at all. Rather, they take the log files created by the server and manipulate them to put the information into a useful form. So while the server may be a UNIX server, the analysis program may be running in Windows NT. Following are some programs to check out:

AccessWatch ($18 per year)
http://accesswatch.com/

net.Analysis (from $7,900 and up)
http://www.netgen.com/

NetIntellect and NetIntellect Express ($49 and up)
http://www.webmanage.com/

Web Page Access Counters and Trackers
http://www.markwelch.com/bannerad/baf_counter.htm

WebTracker ($495)
http://www.cqminc.com/webtrack/

WebTrends ($299 and up)
http://www.webtrends.com/

Yahoo!—Log Analysis Tools
http://dir.yahoo.com/Business_and_Economy/Companies/Computers/
Software/Internet/World_Wide_Web/Log_Analysis_Tools/

There are also a number of services that provide free site statistics for small sites, sometimes in exchange for your carrying a banner at your site. Most provide very simple statistics, though. The following are low-cost and not-quite-so-low-cost services:

Accrue Insight ($17,000 and up)
   http://www.acrue.com/

Audit Bureau of Circulations (Charges big bucks!)
   http://www.accessabc.com/

HitWatchers
   http://www.hitwatchers.com/

InternetCount (free)
   http://www.icount.com/

NetCount and AdCount (Price Waterhouse—starts at $98 per month)
   http://www.netcount.com/

PageCount (in exchange for a banner)
   http://www.pagecount.com/

Siteflow ($950 and up)
   http://www.siteflow.com/

StatTrax ($5 per month to 10,000 hits)
   http://www.stattrax.com/

WebSideStory's HitBox (free)
   http://wss5.websidestory.com/wc/world.html

I'm not suggesting that you run out and find a program or service, by the way. Most small businesses have more important things to do than track this sort of stuff, as we'll discuss in a moment (see "Not Just Hits" below).

You Want E-mail Addresses, Right?

Many new Web-site owners want to be able to grab the e-mail addresses of their visitors from the log files. After all, they've heard people talk about these wonderful log files, and heard that you can track "who" visits your site. Unfortunately—or fortunately from the visitor's point of view—the term "who" has been used very loosely in the Web-tracking business. You cannot grab an e-mail address from a browser unless the user chooses to give it to you. (We discussed that subject back in Chapters 11 and 12.)

I know a lot of people won't believe this. After all, they've read in the press that it's possible for Web sites to grab e-mail addresses that have been entered into the browser's mail program settings. This is completely incorrect. While there is a system called identd that works on UNIX servers, this is rarely used. For identd to work, the Web server and the computer the browser is working on must both be running UNIX and both be using identd, a situation that is quite rare these days—how many users are working with UNIX, for instance? Most are using some form of Windows or MacOS.

There's another trick I've heard of, in which the Web page includes an <IMG> tag that uses FTP to grab the embedded image. If the browser is one that can send the user's e-mail address as a login name to FTP sites, and if the user has told the browser to do so (it's an option in Netscape Navigator), that address is sent to the FTP site and included in the log. In Netscape Navigator this option is turned off by default; that is, the browser won't use the e-mail address unless told to. Apparently some older browsers—very old browsers that are hardly in use anymore—may launch an FTP program, but then the user can see what's going on. All in all, this method is, to quote one Web administrator who's tried it, "pretty useless."

There is currently no reliable way to grab e-mail addresses from Web browsers visiting your site; the only way to grab addresses is by using one of these unusual exceptions or by exploiting a software bug in some browsers. And as the vast majority of browsers in use don't have any such bugs—at least, bugs that have been discovered—and won't work with identd or the FTP trick, you can forget about grabbing e-mail addresses. Such bugs existed in some earlier browsers, such as Netscape Navigator 2. But the browser companies fix these bugs as soon as they find them, and so the bugs are removed from the Web as people upgrade their browsers. No browser company with the slightest bit of sense would knowingly create a browser from which a Web site could take an e-mail address without the user realizing.

In any case, it would be a trifle rude to steal e-mail addresses even if there were a reliable way to do it, so even if such a system existed—and I'd tell you if it did—I wouldn't explain how to use it.

Not Just Hits

I think people have got a little too wrapped up with hits. Hits don't often mean much. Let me tell you something that Edward Tufte has said about hits (we heard from him way back in Chapter 9—remember, the "visionary"). "Look at the phoniness of the statistics," he said, talking of "overproduced" Web sites, "their hit numbers, 'One million hits to our site!' All those hits are to the home page, and most people never make it to the next screens. The numbers drop almost exponentially; 90 percent never make it to the second page, and 90 percent of those people never make it to the third page."

What does a hit to your site really mean? It means that something was transferred from the Web server to a Web browser. It doesn't mean that the data actually arrived, nor that the person receiving it wanted it or paid any attention to it. It doesn't prove that the person receiving it took action as a result, or plans to return, or will act in any manner that is beneficial to you or your company.

Surely, there has to be a better way! Of course there is. Far more important than a measure of hits is genuine activity at, or related to, your site, such as the following:

- How many people are filling in a form to give you their e-mail address, so you can tell them when the Web site is modified or when you release your next product?
- How many people are signing up for your electronic newsletter?
- How much activity is there in your discussion group or chat group?
- How many hits to your autoresponder are you getting—that is, how many people are looking for more information?
- How many people are adding links to your link pages (if you have an automatic link-adding CGI), or sending you links via e-mail?
- How often is your Web site mentioned in the newsgroups and mailing lists?
- How often is your Web site mentioned in the real-world media— magazines, newspapers, TV, and so on?
- How many sites have links to your site?
- How many people are e-mailing you directly with questions?
- How many orders are you taking?

These are all really strong indications of how your Web site is doing, of how useful it is to other Internet users—and to you. So hits can be useful, but don't concentrate on them to the exclusion of more important measures. You can spend an awful lot of time analyzing hits and requests and visits, time that, in many cases, can be better spent in some other way—by setting up some kind of promotion to bring people to your site, for instance.

PART IV

APPENDIXES

Appendix A

Choosing a Web Host— The Checklist

This appendix will help you when looking for a Web-hosting company. There are a lot of things to keep straight, so use the table below to mark down the information you gather from the Web-hosting companies you contact. You can photocopy these pages, if you wish, or—what the heck, it's your book—write on them if you really want to. (It is your book, isn't it?)

Starting the Search

The following Web sites provide good starting points for tracking down Web sites. (Remember, all URLs in this book are available at our Web site in a links page, at http://PoorRichard.com/.)

budgetweb.com—(a great place to find a low-cost Web host)
http://www.budgetweb.com/budgetweb/

Budget Web Hosts List
http://www.callihan.com/budget/

C|Net Web Services
http://webhostlist.internetlist.com/

The Directory
http://www.thedirectory.org/

FindaHost.com
http://www.findahost.com/

Host Find
http://www.hostfind.com/

HostFinders.com
http://www.hostfinders.com/

HostIndex
http://www.hostindex.com/

Host Investigator
http://www.hostinvestigator.com/

HostReview.com
http://hostreview.com/

HostSearch
http://www.hostsearch.com/

ISPcheck
http://www.ispcheck.com/

Leasing a Server list at budgetweb.com
http://budgetweb.com/hndocs/list.shtml

Microsoft FrontPage Web-Presence Providers
http://www.microsoftwpp.com/wppsearch/
http://www.microsoft.com/frontpage/

NerdWorld—Internet Servers Resources
http://www.nerdworld.com/nw1642.html

Top Hosts
http://www.tophosts.com/

WebHosters.com
http://www.webhosters.com/

webhostseek!
http://www.webhostseek.com/

Web-Quote Central
http://www.centeroftheweb.com/webquote/

Web-Hosting Company Comparison Table

The table on the following pages will help you compare Web-hosting companies. You might want to make copies of this table so you'll have a clean version available next time. For more information about the questions in this table, see Chapter 4. The index numbers in the left column on this table refer to the index numbers in Chapter 4.

Note also that many of the questions will not be important to you; read through Chapter 4 first and decide which ones are important, then cross out the ones you don't care about, and fill in the rest.

Many of the answers you need will be displayed at the Web-hosting company's Web site, so start there. I suggest you review that information to get a general feel for whether or not the company has the services you need; if it appears to have most of what you need, fill in a column in the form. Then call the company and get answers to the questions that aren't answered at the Web site. You'll probably want to leave the more complicated things, such as checking references, until the very end, when you are sure that the company can provide everything you need. It may be difficult to get through to the company; if no one calls you back, you're better off skipping that company.

Hosting-Company Name ➡				
URL ➡				
Phone Number ➡				
Contact Name ➡				
#1	**Required account type available?** (Virtual, fake virtual, nonvirtual, subdomain, dedicated server)			
#2	Microsoft FrontPage?			
	Version?			
	Setup fee? Monthly fee?			
#3	Account setup fee, $			
	Monthly fee, $			
#4	Minimum contract? Guarantee?			
#5	How much disk space?			
	Cost for MB upgrades?			

#	Item				
#6	**Hit and data transfer charges?**				
	Cost for hit and data transfer upgrades?				
#7	**Commercial use allowed?**				
#8	**Discounts for nonprofits?**				
#9	**Fee for domain registration?**				
#10	**How many domains** can point to the same Web site for one fee? **(Parked domains)**				
	Price for extra domains? (Each domain points to different directory).				
	Price for extra domains? (All domains point to same directory).				
E-mail and Mailing Lists					
#11	**POP E-mail account** included?				
	Extra for POP account?				
	Number of individual accounts?				

Unlimited e-mail addresses through the POP account (i.e., unlimited aliases)?				
#12	**Mail forwarding** available?			
	How many forwarding accounts?			
	Additional fee for forwarding?			
	How is mail forwarding set up? (Web form? procmail? Other funky system?)			
#13	**Mail responders** available?			
	How many?			
	Additional fee for responders?			
	How are responders set up? (Web form? procmail? Other funky system?)			
#14	**Mailing-list software** available?			
	Additional charge to use mailing-list software?			

	How many lists allowed?			
	How many members per list?			
FTP and Telnet				
#15	Shell account available? (Telnet access)			
#16	FTP access available?			
	Can I change file permissions using FTP?			
#17	Anonymous FTP site available?			
	Can the FTP site resume interrupted downloads?			
Taking Orders Online				
#18	Secure server available?			
	Additional charge to use secure server?			
#19	Shopping-cart software available?			
	Additional charge to use shopping-cart software?			

#20	**Online credit-card and check processing** available?								
	What are the charges?								
Running Programs on the Server									
#21	Server-side image maps allowed?								
#22	CGI scripts allowed?								
	Is there a library of CGI scripts?								
	Can I use my own?								
	How do I **change permissions** on CGI scripts? (FTP? Telnet? Or company changes permissions?)								
#23	Server side includes allowed?								
#24	Database linking to Web pages provided?								
#25	Java applets allowed?								
#26	RealAudio server available?								
	Additional charge to use it?								

Various										
#27	**Access reports** provided?									
	By e-mail, or Web page?									
#28	**Password-protected pages** available?									
	Additional charge to set up password-protected pages?									
#29	**Reselling Web space** allowed?									
#30	**Promotional and design services** available?									
	What are the charges?									
#31	**Technical support by phone?**									
	Toll-free?									
	Additional charge?									
	What hours?									
#32	**Does the company own the server?**									
#33	**How many computers?**									

#34	Number of staff and other issues?										
#35	What's the connection speed?										
#36	How many jumps to the backbone?										
Final Site Check											
#37	Check traceroute										
#38	Get references										
#39	Look and feel										
#40	Real-world check										
Other Features											

Promoting Your Web Site— The Checklist

This Appendix provides a quick checklist of ideas you can use to promote your Web site, and references to the chapters in which these things were discussed:

Working With List Directories	(Chapter 16)

☐ Have you registered with the link directories?

☐ Have you listed several of your pages at the list directories?

☐ Have you given free samples to the list-directory owners?

☐ Have you asked the list-directory owners to review your products?

☐ Have you asked the list-directory owners to do a promotion with you?

☐ Have you asked the list-directory owners to carry a banner?

Preparing for Search Robots   (Chapter 16)

- ❒ Have you made sure all your Web pages have good page titles?

- ❒ Have you used keywords in your page content?

- ❒ Have you set the META keywords tag?

- ❒ Have you set the META description tag?

- ❒ Have you used ALT text in your images?

- ❒ Have you used the NOFRAMES tag?

Registering Your Site With Search Sites   (Chapter 16)

- ❒ Have you registered by hand with the most important search sites?

- ❒ Have you registered by hand with search sites associated with your business?

- ❒ Have you registered with the guides and review sites?

- ❒ Have you used a registration service or software to register with hundreds more sites?

- ❒ Have you registered with free-link sites associated with your business?

Discussion Groups   (Chapter 17)

- ❒ Have you found all the newsgroups and mailing lists possibly related to your business?

- ❒ Have you viewed these discussion groups to see if they're appropriate for your messages?

- ❒ Have you created suitable signatures for your messages?

- ❒ Have you sent messages promoting your Web site to the discussion groups?

- ❒ Do you provide information at your Web site and announce that it's available in the discussion groups?

- ❒ Have you become an advisor in important and active discussion groups?

- ❒ Have you cultivated the other advisors?

❏ Have you sent freebies to the other advisors?

❏ Have you asked other advisors to review your products?

❏ Have you posted messages in various announcement newsgroups (announce, forsale, wanted, net-happenings, and newprod)?

❏ Have you visited the online service discussion groups?

❏ Have you set up Web pages to track the source of visits to your site?

Electronic Press Releases   (Chapter 18)

❏ Have you written a press release?

❏ Have you checked to make sure the release contains all the necessary information, including contact information?

❏ Have you visited the Web sites containing media directories?

❏ Have you visited the library and bookstore?

❏ Have you bought one of the low-cost media directories mentioned?

❏ Have you examined the press-release services?

Real-World PR   (Chapter 19)

❏ Have you snail-mailed press releases?

❏ Have you spoken with journalists?

❏ Do all your print materials contain your e-mail address and URL? (business cards, newspaper ads, Yellow Page ads, flyers, etc.)

❏ Are you actively giving potential reviewers and other media contacts free products?

❏ Have you tried getting on radio talk shows?

❏ Have you read any real-world marketing books?

❏ Have you tried faxing press releases?

Advertising Your Site (Chapter 10)

☐ Have you considered whether you should carry ads on your site or not?

☐ Have you considered using banner-swap programs?

☐ Have you found a banner-design service?

☐ Have you found a Web-ring program associated with your area of business?

☐ Have you looked for useful sites selling advertising at the advertising registries?

☐ Have you contacted any of the advertising brokers and agencies?

☐ Have you set up pages to track visitors arriving from your ads?

☐ Have you found any other, perhaps non-Web, advertising mediums—such as mailing-list ads—that might be useful to you?

Index

About the Poor Richard's Series

The *Poor Richard's* series provides geek-free, commonsense advice on a number of computer-related subjects. Written by authors who really know what they're talking about (most computer books are written by professional writers hired to research and write about a subject), the books are packed with good advice based on real-world experience. Rather than focusing on "point-and-click" computer subjects, these books examine real-world *tasks*, and explain how to use computer software and hardware to accomplish those tasks.

The first *Poor Richard's* book, *Poor Richard's Web Site: Geek-Free, Commonsense Advice on Building a Low-Cost Web Site*, was published early in 1998. Thanks to the down-to-earth, commonsense advice it provided, *Poor Richard's Web Site* was widely reviewed and praised—in *USA Today online*, the *Philadelphia Inquirer*, *Windows Magazine*, *BYTE*, *Library Journal*, and *Fortune.com*. In fact, *Poor Richard's Web Site* is probably the most widely reviewed and praised computer book ever.

There are currently three *Poor Richard's* books in print. As well as *Poor Richard's Web Site*, there's *Poor Richard's Internet Marketing and Promotions*, and the best-selling *Poor Richard's Email Publishing*. Two more are on the way: *Poor Richard's Affiliate Marketing* (May 2000) and *Poor Richard's Building Online Communities* (July 2000). These books will help you succeed in your online endeavors—don't learn the hard way. Let the experts guide you.

Poor Richard's Web Site: Geek-Free, Commonsense Advice on Building a Low-Cost Web Site, 2nd Edition

By Peter Kent
ISBN: 0-9661032-0-3
http://PoorRichard.com/

Poor Richard's Internet Marketing and Promotions: How to Promote Yourself, Your Business, Your Ideas Online

By Peter Kent and Tara Calishain
ISBN: 0-9661032-7-0
http://PoorRichard.com/promo/

Poor Richard's E-mail Publishing: Creating Newsletters, Bulletins, Discussion Groups and Other Powerful Communication Tools

By Chris Pirillo
ISBN: 0-9661032-5-4
http://PoorRichard.com/email/

Poor Richard's Affiliate Marketing: Using Internet Affiliate and Associate Programs to Make Money and Sell Products (June 2000)

By Glenn Sobel
ISBN: 0-9661032-3-8
http://PoorRichard.com/pram/

Poor Richard's Building Online Communities: Create a Web Community for Your Business, Club, Association, or Family (July 2000)

By Margy Levine Young and John Levine
ISBN: 0-9661032-9-7
http://PoorRichard.com/prboc/

Table of Contents:
Poor Richard's Internet Marketing and Promotions: How to Promote
Yourself, Your Business, Your Ideas Online

Table of Contents:
Poor Richard's Email Publishing: Creating Newsletters, Bulletins, Discussion Groups and Other Powerful Communication Tools

Publishers' Stories
The Importance of the End-User Experience
>   by John Funk

This is True
>   by Randy Cassingham

I-Advertising
>   by Adam Boettiger

The Accidental Publisher
>   by Fred Langa

Poor Richard's Web Site News
>   by Peter Kent

The Naked PC Newsletter
>   by T. J. Lee

In the Trenches with The Kleinman Report
>   by Geoffrey Kleinman

Appendices

POOR RICHARD'S INTERNET MARKETING AND PROMOTIONS:

How to Promote Yourself, Your Business, Your Ideas Online

Much of what you've read about marketing on the Internet is wrong: registering a Web site with the search engines *won't* create a flood of orders; banner advertising *doesn't* work for most companies; online malls *do not* push large amounts of traffic to their client Web sites …

What you really need is some geek-free, commonsense advice on marketing and promoting on the Internet, by somebody's who's actually done it! Most books and articles are written by freelance writers assigned to investigate a particular subject. *Poor Richard's Internet Marketing and Promotions* is written by a small-business person who's been successfully marketing online for a decade.

Poor Richard's Internet Marketing and Promotions uses the same down-to-earth style so highly praised in *Poor Richard's Web Site*. You'll learn how to plan an Internet marketing campaign, find your target audience, use giveaways to bring people to your site, integrate an e-mail newsletter into your promotions campaign, buy advertising that works, use real-world PR, and more.

You'll also learn to track results by seeing who is linking to your site, by hearing who is talking about you, and by measuring visits to your site.

If you are planning to promote an idea, product, or service on the Internet … you need *Poor Richard's Internet Marketing and Promotions!*

Available in bookstores both online and offline, and at
http://PoorRichard.com/promo

Poor Richard's Internet Marketing and Promotions:
How to Promote Yourself, Your Business, Your Ideas Online
by Peter Kent and Tara Calishain
ISBN: 0-9661032-7-0, $29.95

POOR RICHARD'S EMAIL PUBLISHING

Creating Newsletters, Bulletins, Discussion Groups and Other Powerful Communications Tools

E-mail publishing is booming—it's growing faster than the World Wide Web. Publishing newsletters, bulletins, and announcements, and running mailing-list discussion groups is a powerful way to promote a product or service … it's also a cheap and relatively low-tech tool.

E-mail publishing can also be a simple one-person business. Newsletters such as *This is True* and *Joke of the Day* have subscription lists well over 100,000 people, in over a hundred countries around the world, yet are run by individuals working on their own or even part time. These entrepreneurs are using their e-mail newsletters to generate a comfortable income in advertising sales and ancillary product sales.

You can learn everything you need to know about e-mail publishing the way these people did: the hard way, by trial and error. Or you can read *Poor Richard's Email Publishing* for geek-free commonsense advice on how to publish using e-mail. Written by a successful e-mail newsletter publisher, *Poor Richard's Email Publishing* will explain how to host a simple newsletter or mailing list using a free or low-cost e-mail program; how to find people to sign up for your service; how to write an e-mail message so that it won't get messed up en route to the subscribers;

how to find articles and information; how to find an e-mail publishing service when your list grows too large; and plenty more.

You'll even find out how to sell advertising, in both newsletters and discussion groups. You'll also learn how to host a mailing list discussion group. Hundreds of thousands of discussion groups are run through the Internet's e-mail system. You'll find out how to moderate a list; how to encourage people to join; how to use the list to promote a product without alienating members of discussion groups; how to find advertisers; how to price your ads, the different types of ads; etc.

If you want to get in on the fastest growing area of Internet communications … you need *Poor Richard's Email Publishing!*

Poor Richard's Email Publishing
is available in bookstores, both online and offline, and at http://PoorRichard.com/pr/email
by Chris Pirillo
ISBN: 0-9661032-5-4, $29.95

MP3 AND THE DIGITAL MUSIC REVOLUTION:

Turn Your PC into a CD-Quality Digital Jukebox!

Hundreds of thousands of computer users around the world are discovering new ways to play and manage music—through their computers. Music is software, and computers are being used to play and manipulate it. Using the new MP3 format, computers can store CD-quality music in 1MB per minute files. Along with the music, the computer files can also store album art, recording-artist bios, notes, and even the songs' lyrics.

With the tools on the included disk, PC users can play music on their computers—if they have good sound cards and speakers, it will sound as good as a CD. They can copy music from their CDs—or tapes and vinyl—and save it on their computers. With a low-cost cable they can connect their computers to their audio systems, integrating the two systems. They can create playlists, selecting tracks from different CDs. Having a party? Create an 8-hour playlist, start playing at the beginning of the party, and the computer will handle the rest.

Digital music is portable, too. Users will learn how to create customized tapes—cassettes and DAT—from their music collection, and even how to cut their own music CDs. And they'll hear about the new MP3 players, products with no moving parts that allow you to carry your music with you wherever you go. This book explains the entire process, from installing the enclosed software to cutting CDs. Readers will learn how to shift their music from one medium to another with ease, and even how to find public domain and "freeware" music on the Internet. Band members will learn how to use the new music formats to promote their bands by releasing music on the Internet.

MP3 and the Digital Music Revolution

is available in bookstores, both online and offline, and at http://TopFloor.com/mp3

MP3 and the Digital Music Revolution:
Turn Your PC into a CD-Quality Digital Jukebox!
by John Hedtke   ISBN: 0-9661032-4-6 $27.95
Includes a CD with software and hundreds of minutes of CD-quality music.

THE CDNOW STORY: RAGS TO RICHES ON THE INTERNET

How Twin Brothers in a Basement Built an Internet Success

Early in 1994 twin brothers Jason and Matthew Olim began creating CDnow, an Internet music store. Working in their parent's basement, on a shoe-string budget, they competed against Fortune 500 companies with tens of millions of dollars to spend … and won. In 1997 CDnow earned almost three times as much as its nearest rival, and owned one third of the online music business. From first-month revenues of $387 in August of 1994, the company grew to sales of $16.4 million in 1997, and industry analysts predict 1998 revenues of $60 million.

How did two kids barely out of college, with no business or retail experience, build one of the world's largest Internet stores? By focusing on a single purpose—building a better music store. *The CDnow Story* explains how they did it: what they did right and what they did wrong. Jason Olim describes how he and his brother began by creating a store that had no shelves and no stock—customers buy CDs online and the Olims pass the orders on to a distributor. He explains how they brought people to their Web site and compares their strategies with their competitors, explaining why they came out on top.

With Internet commerce growing at a tremendous pace, many companies are floundering in cyberspace. Millions of dollars have been lost on ill-conceived and poorly executed online projects. Unlimited budgets are no guarantee of success, but CDnow has shown that shoe-string operations *can* succeed. Let the Olims, founders of one of the most successful companies in cyberspace, teach you how to compete online.

Twin brothers Jason and Matthew Olim are the founders of CDnow, the world's largest online music store. Peter Kent is the author of 36 computer and business books, including *Poor Richard's Web Site* (also from Top Floor Publishing), and the best selling *Complete Idiot's Guide to the Internet* (Que).

**The CDnow Story:
Rags to Riches on the Internet**
is available in bookstores, both online and offline, and at http://TopFloor.com/cdnow
by Jason Olim, with Matthew Olim and Peter Kent
ISBN: 0-9661032-6-2 $19.95

☞ *(con tin ued from the back cover)* ...

Much of the advice found in the computer press is just plain wrong. Make your Web site "cool" they say, and people will come. But cool is expensive, and in any case, it doesn't work. Peter Kent, author of *Poor Richard's Web Site*, has another idea: "Forget Cool, Remember Useful!" He describes low-cost methods for creating Web sites that really work.

Poor Richard's Web Site will show you how to set up your Web site without blowing the budget; and you don't have to learn all the geek stuff. Peter Kent explains the answers to all the important questions, questions such as these:

- How can you add forms that grab people's e-mail addresses?
- How do you add free chat and discussion groups? (See Chapter 13— someone else will set up your chat group, and you won't pay a dime!)
- How do you take orders online? (Checks, credit cards, 900 numbers, and more—without buying expensive software)
- How do you bring people to the Web site? (Registering with the search engines is not enough.)
- How do you read your Web logs? (And why you may not want to spend much time doing so.)
- How do you buy and sell advertising?

There are thousands of books about setting up Web sites, and all but *Poor Richard's Web Site* take the geek view. They explain HTML (which you don't have to know). Or they explain how to set up a Web server (for an explanation of why you mustn't set up a Web server, see Chapter 3).

Poor Richard's Web Site was written for the rest of us, people who want a Web site but don't want to learn programming or Web-server management ... and can't afford to waste thousands of dollars or thousands of hours. Setting up a Web site can be a simple—and cheap—procedure, once you know how. So *Poor Richard's Web Site* describes all you need to know, step by step, in three main sections: Preparation, Creation and Promotion.

You'll find out ...

- How to avoid the most common mistakes in Web-site design
- How to make it easy for visitors to your site to find their way around ... and how to lead them where you want them to go
- How to find free programs that make your Web site "come alive"
- How to make your Web pages load quickly
- How to add discussion groups, chat groups, guest books, and much more

- How to create a simple system for collecting e-mail addresses—so you can mail newsletters or product announcements
- How to take credit-card orders, even if you don't have a credit-card merchant account
- How to create a "map" of the Internet, so you know just where the people you want to reach are hanging out

There's a lot more to a successful Web site than just setting it up. Contrary to much that you've heard over the last couple of years, a Web site is not a billboard on the information superhighway. You have to bring people to the site. So in the Promotion section of the book you'll find out ...

- How to use newsgroups and mailing lists to bring people to your site—and get praised, not criticized
- How to send electronic press releases
- Where to find huge directories of newspaper columnists, TV and radio shows, magazines, and more (and some of these directories are free)
- The most effective ways to register your Web site with the search engines
- Why registering the search engines is not enough—and where else you should be registering
- How to use special promotions at other people's Web sites to get Internet users to visit yours
- How to use real-world promotions to bring in visitors
- How to know where your visitors found out about your Web site

The World Wide Web provides a fantastic new tool for promoting your products, your services, your ideas ... if you know how to use it. Millions of people are fumbling around on the Web, spending too much money for their Web sites, spending too much time creating them, and getting little in return. You don't have to join them; find out how to build a low-cost Web site, how to build it efficiently and quickly, and how to make your Web site truly successful!